THE CAMBRIDGE COMPANION TO
MEDIEVAL PHILOSOPHY

The Cambridge Companion to Medieval Philosophy takes its readers into one of the most exciting periods in the history of philosophy. It spans a millennium of thought extending from Augustine to Thomas Aquinas and beyond. It includes not only the thinkers of the Latin West but also the profound contributions of Islamic and Jewish thinkers such as Avicenna and Maimonides. Leading specialists examine what it was like to do philosophy in the cultures and institutions of the Middle Ages and engage all the areas in which medieval philosophy flourished, including language and logic, the study of God and being, natural philosophy, human nature, morality, and politics. The text is supplemented with chronological charts, biographies of the major thinkers, and a guide to the transmission and translation of medieval texts. The volume will be invaluable for all who are interested in the philosophical thought of this period.

The Cambridge Companion to

MEDIEVAL PHILOSOPHY

Edited by
A. S. McGrade

CAMBRIDGE
UNIVERSITY PRESS

PUBLISHED BY THE PRESS SYNDICATE OF THE UNIVERSITY OF CAMBRIDGE
The Pitt Building, Trumpington Street, Cambridge CB2 1RP, United Kingdom

CAMBRIDGE UNIVERSITY PRESS
The Edinburgh Building, Cambridge, CB2 2RU, UK
40 West 20th Street, New York, NY 10011–4211, USA
477 Williamstown Road, Port Melbourne, VIC 3207, Australia
Ruiz de Alarcón 13, 28014 Madrid, Spain
Dock House, The Waterfront, Cape Town 8001, South Africa

http://www.cambridge.org

First published 2003

Printed in the United Kingdom at the University Press, Cambridge

Typeface Trump Medieval 10/13 pt.   *System* LaTeX 2$_\varepsilon$ [TB]

A catalogue record for this book is available from the British Library

ISBN 0 521 80603 8 hardback
ISBN 0 521 00063 7 paperback

CONTENTS

vii

NOTES ON CONTRIBUTORS

E. J. ASHWORTH is Professor of Philosophy at the University of Waterloo, Canada. She is the author of *Language and Logic in the Post-Medieval Period* and of numerous articles on medieval and early modern language and logic. She has edited the *Tractatus de obligationibus* of Paul of Venice's *Logica magna*. She was editor of the Renaissance section of the *Routledge Encyclopedia of Philosophy* and continues as editor of the on-line version.

ANNABEL S. BRETT is Lecturer in History at the University of Cambridge and a Fellow of Gonville and Caius College. Her work in medieval and early modern political thought includes *Liberty, Right and Nature: Individual Rights in Later Scholastic Thought* and an edition of Ockham's *On the Power of Emperors and Princes*. She is now preparing a translation of Marsilius of Padua's *Defender of Peace*.

IDIT DOBBS-WEINSTEIN is Associate Professor of Philosophy at Vanderbilt University. She is the author of *Maimonides and St. Thomas on the Limits of Reason* and an audio book, *Moses Maimonides and Medieval Jewish Philosophy*, as well as many articles on medieval Jewish philosophy, with a special interest in its relations to medieval Islamic and Christian thought and to the philosophy of Spinoza.

THÉRÈSE-ANNE DRUART is Professor of Philosophy and Director of the Center for Medieval and Byzantine Studies at the Catholic University of America. Her recent publications include "The Human Soul's Individuation and its Survival After the Body's Death: Avicenna on the Causal Relation Between Body and Soul." She is preparing a section on metaphysics for *The Cambridge Companion to Arabic Philosophy* and will be directing a continuing bibliography in medieval Islamic philosophy, theology, and the sciences for the Société Internationale des Sciences et de la Philosophie Arabe et Islamique.

P. J. FITZPATRICK is Emeritus Reader in Philosophy at the University of Durham. His writings include *Birth Regulation and Catholic Belief*, *Apologia pro Charles Kingsley*, and *In Breaking of Bread: The Eucharist and Ritual*.

JOHN HALDANE is Professor of Philosophy at the University of St. Andrews, where he is also Senior Fellow of the Centre for Ethics, Philosophy and Public Affairs. He is a Fellow of the Royal Society of Edinburgh and the Royal Society of Arts. Besides editing and coediting several collections of essays, he has written numerous articles on the history of philosophy, philosophy of mind, metaphysics, and moral philosophy, and is coauthor of *Atheism and Theism* in the Blackwell Great Debates in Philosophy series. He will be Gifford Lecturer in Natural Theology at the University of Aberdeen in 2003/4.

BONNIE KENT is Associate Professor of Philosophy at the University of California, Irvine. Since publishing *Virtues of the Will* she has worked especially on issues of motivation in medieval moral psychology. Her recent essays include "Habits and Virtues," in S. Pope, ed., *The Ethics of Aquinas*, and "Rethinking Moral Dispositions," in T. Williams, ed., *The Cambridge Companion to Scotus*.

GYULA KLIMA is Associate Professor of Philosophy at Fordham University. He is the author of *Ars artium: Essays in Philosophical Semantics Medieval and Modern* and numerous articles on medieval logic and metaphysics. He has translated John Buridan's *Summulae de dialectica* and is currently working on a monograph on Buridan's logic and metaphysics.

D. E. LUSCOMBE is a Fellow of the British Academy and Research Professor of Medieval History at the University of Sheffield. He is the author of *The School of Peter Abelard*, *Peter Abelard's Ethics*, *Medieval Thought*, and many articles on Abelard and on medieval conceptions of hierarchy. He is joint editor, with J. Riley-Smith, of parts 1 and 2 of volume IV of *The New Cambridge Medieval History* (forthcoming) and is currently completing an edition of the *Letters of Peter Abelard and Heloise*.

JAMES MCEVOY is Dean of the Faculty of Philosophy at the National University of Ireland at Maynooth. His special interests in medieval philosophy include Scottus Eriugena, Thomas Gallan, Robert Grosseteste, and the theme of friendship. He is the author of *Robert Grosseteste* (2002) and of two volumes on theories of friendship in antiquity and in the Christian era, *Sagesses de l'amitié* (1997 and 2002). He is a contributor to the edition of Grosseteste's unedited works and is preparing a book on friendship and associated concepts in the history of philosophy.

A. S. MCGRADE is Professor Emeritus of Philosophy, the University of Connecticut, and the author of *The Political Thought of William of Ockham*. He has edited, with John Kilcullen, two volumes of Ockham's political writings and, with John Kilcullen and Matthew Kempshall, volume II of *Cambridge Translations of Medieval Philosophical Texts* (on ethics and political philosophy).

JOHN MARENBON is Fellow and Director of Studies in the History of Philosophy, Trinity College, University of Cambridge. He is the author of a two-volume history of medieval philosophy; *The Philosophy of Peter Abelard; Aristotelian Logic, Platonism, and the Context of Early Medieval Philosophy in the West*; and *Boethius*. He is now at work on a new introduction to medieval philosophy (to replace his earlier history) and a study of medieval views of pagans (especially ancient ones).

STEVEN P. MARRONE is Professor of History at Tufts University. His studies of thirteenth-century epistemology include many articles and three monographs, *William of Auvergne and Robert Grosseteste: New Ideas of Truth in the Early Thirteenth Century, Truth and Scientific Knowledge in the Thought of Henry of Ghent*, and *The Light of Thy Countenance: Science and Knowledge of God in the Thirteenth Century*.

STEPHEN P. MENN is Associate Professor of Philosophy at McGill University and works on ancient and medieval philosophy and the history of mathematics. He is the author of *Plato on God as Nous* and *Descartes and Augustine*. He is completing a book manuscript on *The Aim and the Argument of Aristotle's* Metaphysics and is working with Calvin Normore on a book about nominalism and realism.

ROBERT PASNAU is Associate Professor of Philosophy at the University of Colorado and the author of *Theories of Cognition in the Later Middle Ages* and *Thomas Aquinas on Human Nature. A Philosophical Study of* Summa Theologiae *1a 75–89*, as well as numerous articles and reviews on topics in late medieval epistemology. He has edited Aquinas's commentary on Aristotle's *De anima* and volume III of *Cambridge Translations of Medieval Philosophical Texts*, on mind and knowledge. He is general editor of the Hackett Aquinas Project, a series of translations, with commentary, of Aquinas's central philosophical texts, and has contributed to that series a volume on Aquinas's treatise on human nature.

EDITH DUDLEY SYLLA is Professor of History at North Carolina State University. She has written extensively on fourteenth-century natural philosophy, especially the work of the Oxford Calculators. She is currently working on Walter Burley's physics and on the origins of mathematical probability, particularly in the work of Jacob Bernouli. Her forthcoming publications include "Business Ethics, Commercial Mathematics, and the Origins of Mathematical Probability" and, with A. Maierù, a short biography of Anneliese Maier.

THOMAS WILLIAMS is Assistant Professor of Philosophy at the University of Iowa. He has translated works by Augustine and Anselm and is now preparing volume v of *Cambridge Translations of Medieval Philosophical Texts*, on philosophical theology. His work on Duns Scotus includes "A Most Methodical Lover? On Scotus's Arbitrary Creator" and the editing of *The Cambridge Companion to Duns Scotus*.

PREFACE

This book presents one of the most exciting periods in the history of philosophy, a millennium of thought extending from Augustine to Wyclif in the Latin West, from al-Kindi to Ibn Rushd in Islam, and in medieval Jewish communities from Ibn Gabirol to Gersonides. As a Companion, the volume seeks to do more than present authoritative information *about* its subject. The contributors aim to take their readers as far as possible *into* medieval philosophy. I explain in the introduction how we hope to achieve this. For now it will be enough to say that we do not assume any prior knowledge of medieval philosophy or the languages in which it was written. We expect that most readers will have had some exposure to contemporary philosophy, but we welcome and hope to assist interested nonphilosophers as well. The volume is meant to be useful in medieval philosophy courses at all levels, but we also have very much in mind those who are approaching medieval philosophy on their own, without access to specialists in the field. We will be delighted if our efforts incite a degree of student agitation for more medieval courses in mainly modernist philosophy departments and if we encourage teachers who skipped or were deprived of the Middle Ages in their own training to offer such courses. It could be a liberating experience for all concerned.

The contributors to this volume have shown great public spirit and enthusiasm for medieval philosophy in setting aside more specialized research in order to make the whole subject accessible to others – not an easy assignment, but, they have found, a rewarding one. I am grateful for their counsel regarding my part in the volume and for their patience and good humor in adjusting their work to suit the common good (most often by cutting out fine material for which there simply is not room). I am happy to thank the reviewers of an early prospectus for this Companion for highly effective criticism and the following for advice and information given along the way: Donald Baxter, Stephen Lahey, Miri Rubin, Paul V. Spade, Eleonore Stump, John Wippel, and Jack Zupko. My debts to Professor B. J. McGrade are easily borne but boundless. Individual contributors wish to acknowledge the advice or inspiration of Julie Allen, Paul Freedman, Ester Macedo, Mrs C. M. L. Smith, and Katherine Tachau. Final thanks are due to the editorial and production staff of Cambridge University Press, and especially to Hilary Gaskin, who has supported and judiciously overseen the volume from start to finish.

A. S. McGrade

ABBREVIATIONS AND FORMS OF REFERENCE

For works cited with a number in square brackets (e.g., Kretzmann [41]), a full reference is given in the bibliography.

a.   article
ad   reply to (ad 1: reply to first objection)
CCAq   *The Cambridge Companion to Thomas Aquinas*, ed. N. Kretzmann and E. Stump (Cambridge, 1993)
CCAug   *The Cambridge Companion to Augustine*, ed. E. Stump and N. Kretzmann (Cambridge, 2001)
CCOck   *The Cambridge Companion to Ockham*, ed. P. V. Spade (Cambridge, 1999)
CCScot *The Cambridge Companion to Duns Scotus*, ed. T. Williams (Cambridge, 2003)
CH12   *A History of Twelfth-Century Western Philosophy*, ed. P. Dronke (Cambridge, 1988)
CHLMP *The Cambridge History of Later Medieval Philosophy*, ed. N. Kretzmann *et al.* (Cambridge, 1982)
CT I–III *The Cambridge Translations of Medieval Philosophical Texts*
          I *Logic and the Philosophy of Language*, ed. N. Kretzmann and E. Stump (Cambridge, 1988)
          II *Ethics and Political Philosophy*, ed. A. S. McGrade, J. Kilcullen, and M. Kempshall (Cambridge, 2001)
          III *Mind and Knowledge*, ed. R. Pasnau (Cambridge, 2002)

d.	distinction (in textual references)
obj.	objection
Ordinatio	The text of some or all of a *Sentences* commentary put in order for publication by the author, in contrast with a *reportatio*
PG	*Patrologia graeca*, ed. J. P. Migne, 162 vols. (Paris, 1857–66) (Greek text with Latin translation)
PL	*Patrologia latina*, ed. J. P. Migne, 221 vols. (Paris, 1844–64)
q.	question
q. disp.	disputed question
quodl.	quodlibet
Reportatio	The "reported" form of some or all of a *Sentences* commentary (see p. 330)
ScG	Thomas Aquinas, *Summa contra Gentiles*
Sent.	Peter Lombard, *Sententiae in IV libris distinctae* (Four Books of Sentences), 2 vols. (Grottaferrata, 1971–81) or commentary thereon (see p. 28)
ST	Thomas Aquinas, *Summa theologiae*: references are to the four parts – I, IaIIae (first part of the second part), IIaIIae (second part of the second part), and III
un.	unique (e.g., where a question has only one article)

A. S. McGRADE

Introduction

The study of medieval philosophy is flourishing, as witness the selective bibliography for this book. And yet, from some philosophical viewpoints – analytic, continental, or science-oriented – the subject of this volume can still seem remote. Where ontology recapitulates philology, or *Dasein* replaces being and essence, or naturalism needs no arguing, the immersion of medieval thinkers in questions about eternity, God, and the immateriality of intellect can seem incomprehensible, if occasionally intriguing. This Companion seeks to enhance fascination while diminishing incomprehension. The contributors hope to bring readers into medieval discussions as directly as possible, enabling them to appreciate for themselves the philosophical motives instigating these discussions and the boldness, subtlety, and analytic rigor with which they were carried on. The aim is to exhibit the variety and freshness of medieval approaches to problems rather than to evaluate solutions. This is not to deny that timeless truth can be found in the material presented. Many students of medieval metaphysics would hold that the discipline had entered on "the sure path of a science," in Kant's phrase, several centuries before Kant restricted its scope to laying bare the conditions of possible experience (and would attribute Kant's dismissal of earlier efforts as "random groping" to typical Enlightenment ignorance of medieval thought). We are convinced, however, that the insights of medieval philosophy appear most clearly in the midst of the discussions in which the medievals themselves sought them. Medieval treatments of philosophical problems are not as a rule easy to get *through*. If that were so, there would be no need for this volume. We hope to demonstrate that the medieval discussions are well worth getting *into*.

I

ENTRY POINTS

The strangeness of medieval philosophy should not be exaggerated.
A great deal of what is presented here can readily be engaged with
by readers in a philosophically current frame of mind. This is due
in good measure to the fact that recent philosophy has caught up
with some characteristic medieval interests. Here are some examples. The high esteem now enjoyed by medieval logic rests partly on
the brilliance of scholastic semantics in treating paradoxes of self-
reference and the problems posed by intentional contexts, "modern"
topics touched on in Jennifer Ashworth's chapter on medieval language and logic. Increased sophistication in the disciplines of history
and philosophy of science lets us appreciate the sophistication to be
found in medieval natural philosophy. Even the physics of angels,
as Edith Sylla shows, has points of interest for the philosophically
scientific mind. Thanks largely to the work of David Armstrong,
the medieval problem of universals no longer seems "merely" medieval. Indeed, as Gyula Klima's discussion in this volume makes
clear, the philosophical and theological stakes in this problem are
very high, involving the possibility of science and the intelligibility
of discourse about God. The rise of interdisciplinary programs in cognitive science and recent critiques of the Cartesian epistemological
tradition make certain aspects of medieval philosophical psychology
more accessible now than formerly. On the other hand, Descartes's
newly affirmed relation to Augustine means that there are medieval
sources for Cartesian as well as non-Cartesian ideas of mind and self.
Robert Pasnau's chapter on human nature takes advantage of both of
these medieval–modern connections.

There are similar points for engagement in moral philosophy. In
the last fifty years philosophers have displayed substantial interest
in moral psychology and virtue ethics, central concerns in Bonnie
Kent's chapter on the moral life. Medieval political thought has become both more intelligible and more relevant to current concerns
for a number of reasons. Recent scholarship has led to greater awareness of the role of medieval thinkers in providing foundations for
modern political thought. Conversely, widespread current criticism
of modern secularism and a recognition that the assumptions of
modernity are by no means inevitable are clarified by reflection on
contrasting assumptions in medieval thought. It is not only medieval

political thought proper, as presented here by Annabel Brett, that has gained significance. Our debates today about "modern" or "western" values are given sharper point by the claims now urged for Islamic tradition and, in a critical part of our world, for traditional Judaism. The tensions between philosophy and religious faith in medieval Islamic and Jewish culture, treated among other topics by Thérèse Druart and Idit Dobbs-Weinstein in their chapters on philosophy in Islam and Jewish philosophy, thus provide additional ways into medieval thought from where we stand today.[1]

OTHERNESS

In spite of such promising points of entry as the preceding, much of medieval philosophy is apt to seem inaccessible, even for those who are prepared to approach it sympathetically. In its otherworldliness it may seem to have been written in another world, and one may suspect that even the parts that seem assimilable are not entirely what they seem. There is a distinctively medieval conception of *eternity*, for example, as John Marenbon's discussion in chapter 2 makes clear, and it is taken very seriously. Again, the idea of *hierarchy* presented in the same chapter by D. E. Luscombe is ubiquitous in medieval thought, ordering social classes, the powers of the soul, and the angels of heaven. In devoting a chapter to these two ideas, we resist the temptation to fold what is "other" in medieval thought into what appears familiar.

Even the apparently familiar has aspects of otherness, however. Once more, some examples. The scholastic development of Aristotelian and Stoic virtue ethics places the classical virtues in a scheme crowned by the "theological" virtues of faith, hope, and Christian love of God and neighbor. Medieval discussions of friendship, civic happiness, and the philosophical life, as presented in James McEvoy's chapter on ultimate goods, are of great interest, yet the ultimate interest of most of the authors considered is in beatitude – not earthly happiness but eternal bliss. The Aristotelian inspiration for medieval metaphysics is clear, but in the medieval period there is a huge expansion of often very confident discussion of a divine reality dealt with by Aristotle briefly and tentatively. Accordingly, Stephen Menn's chapter on metaphysics in this volume is predominantly concerned with the being of God. Similar observations of the unfamiliar in the midst of the familiar could be made regarding each of the topics mentioned in preceding paragraphs. How is this mixture of sameness and difference to be understood?

History helps. Steven Marrone's presentation of medieval philosophy in context (chapter 1) shows when and how the more remote and the more modern-seeming strands of medieval thought arose and came to be woven together. There were important changes in attitudes toward philosophy and in the very character of philosophy in its millennial medieval career. Virtually all medieval thinkers carried with them something of the classical Greek and Roman conception of philosophy as a way of life, but the styles of the philosophical life varied markedly over centuries and milieux. (This opening historical narrative provides food for thought, incidentally, on the topic of a – possible? imminent? – "death of philosophy." The moral suggested by the medieval experience is that philosophy indeed can die, but that it has a tendency to rise from the dead.) The final section of chapter 1, on the sources and genres of medieval philosophical writing, provides further reference points. In this section, the place of authority in medieval thought is briefly discussed, the availability of classical philosophical texts in different places and times in the medieval world is charted, and an account is given of the forms in which philosophy was published, forms often unfamiliar to the modern reader: *Sentence* commentaries, summas, quodlibeta, disputed questions, sophismata, and the like.

WHAT IS MEDIEVAL PHILOSOPHY?

To speak of historical changes in the character of philosophy prompts some nonhistorical questions, however. Given such changes, we may well ask: is medieval philosophy in any sense the same as philosophy as we know it? If not, what is it, and should we really call it philosophy at all? An answer (preliminary to the one this Companion as a whole provides) can be given by way of an idea just referred to, the classical idea of philosophy as a way of life. If virtually all medieval thinkers carried something of this idea with them, few regarded themselves as "philosophers" in what we might think of, without defining it precisely, as the classical or modern sense of the term. It will be useful to elicit the difference between medieval philosophical ways of life and philosophy in this other sense by stages. Augustine, the most influential thinker in the West in our period and a case study in tensions also felt in Islamic and Jewish thought, will serve as a leading example.

The course of Augustine's life was set by his reading of Cicero's lost dialogue *Hortensius*. He says that this text inflamed him with a desire for "wisdom." What he thought himself to be doing in his better moments for more than twenty years after reading Cicero was pursuing wisdom. So far so good. The quest for wisdom in some sense identifies the philosopher even now, and this quest must shape the philosopher's life in at least some respects, if only in the choice of conversations to join. Augustine's quest carried him through a number of intellectual positions, including Manichaean dualism, skepticism, and Neoplatonism, to what he sometimes called "our philosophy," a genuine "understanding," as he saw it, of reality, truth, and the good, a share of the wisdom he had been after and which philosophers had been seeking over the centuries. Again, so far so good. If we think of philosophy as the quest for wisdom, a philosopher as someone engaged in such a quest, and a philosophy as what such a seeker arrives at, Augustine must be regarded as a philosopher, and the understanding he achieved must be regarded as a philosophy.

In setting out "our philosophy," however, Augustine sometimes characterizes "the philosophers" as antagonists or, at best, necessarily unsuccessful aspirants to the wisdom he had found. For what Augustine means by "our philosophy" is a specifically Christian understanding of things, an understanding possible only through faith. "Unless you believe you shall not understand" (Isaiah 7:9) became the motto for a whole tradition of "faith seeking understanding" which defined the quest for wisdom in the Latin West from Augustine through Anselm and beyond. "The philosophers" Augustine characterized as adversaries lacked faith. Thus, for him, philosophy as engaged in by philosophers was necessarily abortive and hence not the best example of what philosophy ought to be.[2]

Here is where we run up against a more familiar conception of philosophy. Far from thinking that success in philosophy is impossible without religious faith, a modern reader may assume the contrary: that philosophy is defined by *not* proceeding on the basis of faith. Philosophy, it is commonly thought, proceeds within the limits, or on the basis, or by the light, of "reason alone." This does not preclude the same person's having faith and doing philosophy, but it does entail that philosophizing and believing are distinct activities. From this point of view, the fact that Augustine makes no such distinction renders him a suspicious character. He is apt to seem rhetorically proselytizing where a true philosopher ought to be disinterestedly rational.

The difficulty should not be exaggerated. One can always gather from thinkers in Augustine's tradition anything that seems interesting from a different perspective. Augustine's conception of the mind as a trinity of memory, understanding, and will, each in its own way "comprehending" the others, might stimulate useful thought quite apart from Augustine's own use of this analysis to gain understanding of Christian belief in God as triune. The same could be said of other trinities in medieval thought. Likewise, Augustine's theory of language as involving an inner, mental word was for him a way to tie the understanding of spoken and written signs to divine illumination. Even in the Middle Ages, however, this theory was developed in ways free of specific theological import. It should also be remembered that Augustine's project was faith seeking *understanding*. This means that the results of his quest for wisdom can often be formulated in systematically related propositions that can be examined for the virtue of consistency and might have other "purely philosophical" virtues as well.

Accommodation of medieval philosophy to a "reason alone" view of the discipline is still easier for the latter part of our period. This is because the purely reasonable view is not in fact distinctively classical or modern. It is actually a medieval conception, enshrined most famously in the first *quaestio* of Thomas Aquinas's *Summa theologiae*. There Thomas seeks to determine the relation of theology (*sacra doctrina*) to "the philosophical disciplines." The line of demarcation he proposes is set precisely at what can be discovered by "reason" ("human reason" or "natural reason"). This is philosophy (including the natural sciences). Sacred doctrine may use the methods and results of philosophy, but its own foundations are truths disclosed by God in "supernatural" revelation. For Aquinas, then, and for the majority of late medieval thinkers in the Latin West, there is a clear distinction between philosophy and theology that usually allows us to mark off philosophical ideas from the rest of their thought on a basis they themselves have provided, one that seems to square, furthermore, with modern views of the subject.

In this Companion we will take advantage of both paths of accommodation just sketched. That is, we will often attempt to extract material of independent philosophical interest from Augustinian faith-based thought, and in presenting the ideas of thinkers who distinguished between philosophy as reason and theology as revelation we will focus primarily on what the authors would themselves take to be philosophical. It would, however, be a disservice to philosophy in any sense of the term to follow such policies too rigidly. The relationship of philosophy to biblical or qur'anic religion is too pervasive a theme in medieval thought and too fruitful a stimulus to self-awareness in its contrast with typical modern assumptions to be muted in the interest of quick access from the direction of current philosophy. Accordingly, instead of attempting to deal with the interactions of religion and philosophy in a single chapter ("Faith and Reason," say), we will consider them in different chapters as they occur in different contexts. For example, medieval understanding of God's creation of the universe *ex nihilo* will be discussed along with medieval understanding of natural processes. Central concepts in moral philosophy, such as virtue and vice, will be discussed along with related theological concepts, such as merit and sin. More generally, when we extract elements of independent philosophical interest from texts inspired by faith seeking understanding (or by an interest in using philosophy to provide "preambles to faith," as in Aquinas), we do so without prejudice to the religious projects in which the medieval authors of our texts were engaged. In this volume, Augustine counts as a philosopher not only for what he says that may seem reasonable apart from faith, but also for his pursuit of intelligibility in Christian believing. The same inclusive principle applies to Islamic and Jewish thinkers as well as to Augustine's western successors.

GOING FURTHER

I have been arguing that medieval philosophy is worth studying both for what is or seems familiar in it and for what there is in it or about it that differs from philosophy as usually practiced today. If the succeeding chapters confirm this double claim, readers will wish to pursue the subject further. The concluding parts of the volume will help them do so. For purposes of orientation, P. J. FitzPatrick and John Haldane show in chapter 13, on the presence of medieval philosophy in later thought, how medieval philosophy itself has gone further, indicating some of the medieval elements in Renaissance and early modern philosophy and sketching the present state of scholarly interest in our subject. Thomas Williams then discusses the problems of transmission and translation that must be taken into account in any ongoing engagement with the epoch of philosophy introduced here. A further aid to going further is the bibliography. References to major texts and studies in the body of the volume and in the section of brief biographies of major thinkers are keyed to works listed in the bibliography, which also includes other resources.

A FINAL IMAGE: MEDIEVAL PHILOSOPHY AND FREEDOM

Perhaps the best single representation of medieval philosophy as a whole is Boethius's image of philosophy as a beautiful woman offering freedom of intellect and spirit in even the most miserable of circumstances. The picture is drawn, in five books of superb prose and poetry, in *The Consolation of Philosophy*. Imprisoned in the early sixth century on charges of treason against a king in whose administration he had held the highest posts, Boethius was sick with grief, when, as he tells us, philosophy appeared to him, chided him for placing his happiness in things subject to the vicissitudes of fortune, and showed him that true happiness is to be found in God, the supreme Good and providential ruler of the universe. The religious vision animating this and much other medieval philosophy did not preclude – in some cases it even demanded – rigorously secular treatment of secular subjects. Furthermore, there was not universal agreement on the capacity of philosophy to produce the liberating results we find in Boethius, and there are even medieval materials for the critique of religion as myth and the rejection of religious institutions as corrupt. The serious consideration of more hopeful views in the Middle Ages was itself a kind of liberation, however, and this mindset arguably heightened the quality of thought in every area of philosophy. This framework for the medieval pursuit of wisdom is one important reason among others why medieval philosophy can be presented in this volume as a potentially liberating resource for the reader's own pursuit of wisdom, wherever that pursuit may lead.

NOTES

1. A few chapters elsewhere in the volume are concerned exclusively with
    the Latin West, but references to Muslim and Jewish philosophy in other
    chapters, especially in chapter 6, give some impression of the intercul-
    tural scope of medieval philosophy. Further comparative work is needed.
2. For a more nuanced account of faith seeking understanding as
    Augustine's charter for Christian philosophy than I have given, see
    N. Kretzmann [71]. Also see E. Gilson [68] 25–111 and C. N. Cochrane
    [398] 399–455.

1 Medieval philosophy in context

What was it like to do philosophy in the Middle Ages? In this chapter I will try to answer that question by looking at relevant sociopolitical and economic circumstances, specific institutional settings for practicing philosophy, and several competing or cooperating intellectual currents. At the end of the chapter, I will say something about the place of authority in medieval thought, the philosophical sources available to medieval thinkers at different points in the period, and the literary genres into which they put their own ideas.

Briefly, the story runs as follows. What we know as medieval philosophy emerged in the late Roman Empire from a surprisingly complete mutual accommodation of Christian belief and classical thought. It then passed through centuries of dormancy in the West, while at the same time it began afresh in the Islamic world. In the eleventh and twelfth centuries philosophy reemerged in a new Europe, in altered form and against resistance. Then, both augmented and challenged by the work of Islamic and Jewish thinkers, it enjoyed in the thirteenth century a golden age of systematic analysis and speculation corresponding to a new degree of rationalization in politics and society. And finally? The significance of fourteenth-century thought remains contested, despite substantial recent scholarship demonstrating its brilliance. As my narrative ends, therefore, readers will need to move from context to content, acquainting themselves in succeeding chapters with the ideas and arguments on which their own assessment of medieval philosophy, not just the fourteenth century, must depend.

Before beginning, we should notice an obvious but important fact. Medieval thinkers did not know that they were medieval. The expression "Middle Age" (Latin *medium aevum*; thence *medievalis*, "medieval") was first used to designate the period between the "ancient" and "modern" worlds in the seventeenth century. In later historical writing and popular consciousness a radical opposition is often posited between the Middle Ages (or "Dark Ages") and the initial phase of the modern era called, since the nineteenth century, the Renaissance. As we shall see, even the least philosophical of medieval centuries were not wholly benighted, and the relations between medieval and Renaissance thought are a good deal more complex than is suggested by depictions of the latter as a revolutionary enlightenment.

EMERGENCE OF MEDIEVAL PHILOSOPHY IN THE LATE ROMAN EMPIRE

The emergence of medieval philosophy looks surprising not only from a "reason alone" view of philosophy but also in light of a polemic of opposition between Christianity and philosophy dating back to St. Paul's disparagement of "the wisdom of the world" (specifically, the wisdom sought by Greeks) and his warning against "philosophy and empty deceit" (1 Corinthians 1:20–24, Colossians 2:8). It was an incompatibility that the early north African apologist Tertullian (c. 160–c. 230) celebrated as absolute. His taunting question "What has Athens to do with Jerusalem?" was a challenge to the cognitive commitments of his philosophically minded contemporaries (On Prescription Against Heretics 7 [428] 8–10). If today we think of philosophy as requiring complete insulation from the engagements of religious belief, we can imagine ourselves as displaying the same attitude in reverse.

But historically speaking, Tertullian's conception of a dividing line between religion and philosophy was odd man out. Indeed, when Paul himself was actually confronted with philosophers at the hill of the Areopagus in Athens, he took a conciliatory line, noting agreement between his own preaching and the verses of a Stoic poet (Acts 17:28). In the ancient Mediterranean world, philosophy did not consist of arcane reflection on the nature of what can be known or the value of what must be done, abstracted from the day-to-day business of living in society. It called instead for the engagement of the whole person in striving to know truth and to do good. For philosophers themselves it amounted to an all-absorbing way of life.[1] Indeed, by the second and third centuries CE, philosophy, as practiced by Stoics, Platonists, and Epicureans, and Christianity, as professed among educated Greek and Roman converts, were beginning to look very much alike. Philosophy had come, in E. R. Dodds's words, "increasingly to *mean* the quest for God."[2] In such a world, it was easy for a person like Justin (d. 163/67), searching among the philosophers for an answer to the riddle of life, to end up a Christian, and ultimately a martyr. As an apologist for his faith he continued to wear the philosopher's distinctive garb and advertised Christianity as philosophy in the fullest sense of the word (*Dialogue with Trypho* 8 [411] 198b). There was, to be sure, a literature of controversy pitting Christian against pagan thinker, but the sometimes bitter tone of this writing was partly due to the fact that the antagonists were fighting over common intellectual ground. The third-century Christian writers and teachers Clement of Alexandria and his pupil, Origen, and their pagan counterparts Plotinus and his disciple, Porphyry, spoke the same philosophical language, drew from the single conceptual reservoir of emergent Neoplatonism, and even traveled in the same circles.[3]

Medieval philosophy was born in precisely this intellectual setting. Not by coincidence, these were also the circumstances under which Christianity came to be the official religion of the Roman Empire. It is indeed only a slight exaggeration to characterize the legal conversion initiated in the early fourth century by the emperor Constantine as an epiphenomenon arising out of this more general cultural milieu. The way had already been prepared by the spread of Jewish communities and their religion throughout the Mediterranean, with a corresponding Hellenization of Jewish thought from acquaintance with Greek philosophical ideas. By the third century a common currency of learned discourse flourished among the elite – pagan, Jewish, and Christian. Constantine's contribution was simply to make the Christian variant of this discourse the dominant one, eventually oppressively so, from the fourth century on. But the conceptual apparatus, intellectual inclinations, and interpretative tools that were used in the course of this process were neither specifically Christian nor very new. In other words, the conversion simply ensured that the philosophizing of Christian thinking previously underway should continue apace and come to typify the culture of learning in late Rome. It likewise inaugurated the first of three phases in the career of medieval philosophy.

The style of thinking characteristic of this phase is exemplified in Augustine, the Latin rhetorician turned Christian philosopher and later bishop of Hippo in north Africa until his death in 430. Persuaded, as he later explained in his *Confessions*, by Cicero's "exhortation to philosophy" that he must forsake his life of vanity and promiscuity and devote himself to the internal quest demanded by the love of wisdom, he set out on a path leading by way of knowledge "upwards [away] from earthly delights" to God (*Confessions* III 4 [59]). Here, a crucial direction-setting role fell to "some books of the Platonists translated from Greek into Latin," almost certainly works of the Neoplatonists Plotinus and possibly Porphyry. These writings led Augustine to the conviction that the universe emerged from and inevitably tended back toward a unique principle of good that is itself God, a reality shining above, yet still within, each of us as the eternal light of truth (VII 9–10).[4] In Augustine's eyes, the further step from Neoplatonism to Christianity was natural, almost inevitable. "Now that I had read the books of the Platonists and had been set by them toward the search for a truth that is incorporeal... I seized greedily upon the adorable writing of Your Spirit, and especially upon the apostle Paul" (VII 20–21). From this point of view, Paul's words to the Athenians at the Areopagus were plainly an exhortation to continue in their chosen way of life to the perfection of truth and right behavior laid bare in Christianity (VII 9, referring to Acts 17:28). The philosopher's pursuit of wisdom was therefore not just compatible with Christian teaching. It was received, raised sublime, and rendered fully realizable through God's revelation and grace in Christ.

Christian intellectuals of Augustine's day thus had no doubt that they were following the philosopher's way. Accordingly, they incorporated as much as they could of the classical philosophical heritage, both habits of mind and conceptual content, into their patterns of discourse and way of life. Stoicism and Neoplatonism, the Antique schools that appeared most supportive of previous Christian intellectual and practical commitments, were taken over virtually intact into Christian speculative and moral schemes. For example, Augustine's mentor, the learned and socially eminent bishop Ambrose of Milan, followed Cicero's *On Duties* in writing his guide to the considerable secular as well as religious duties of a bishop. Augustine himself explored the psychological and theological implications of Neoplatonic theories of emanation in his treatise *The Trinity*. And in one of the most prominent indicators of Christian aspiration to inherit the mantle of Graeco-Roman higher studies, he labored during the last fifteen years of his life to produce in his masterpiece, *The City of God*, proof that Christianity could compete on equal terms with the best that pagan erudition had to offer.[5]

The immediate stimulus for Augustine's historical and transhistorical account of the human condition in *The City of God* was the accusation that abandonment of the old gods of paganism was responsible for the sack of Rome by the Visigoths in 410. When Augustine died, the Vandals were at the gates of Hippo. From the early fifth century the western parts of the empire – modern Italy and Libya to the Atlantic – were increasingly brought under military control of barbarian, largely Germanic, armies, those groups of soldiers and their families referred to in textbooks as tribes. Such Teutonic interlopers established their political preeminence in what Romans taught them to call kingdoms. Their overlordship did not, however, drastically reduce the influence of Roman elites or diminish the importance of Latin culture and Latin learning among the ruling classes. In the early sixth-century Ostrogothic kingdom of Italy, for example, Latin high culture shone as brilliantly as at any point since Cicero.

In this setting, official patronage of philosophical studies led to an emphasis on the purely speculative or theoretical that went beyond Augustine and Ambrose. The prominent senator Boethius, Roman consul and adviser to the Ostrogothic king Theodoric, undertook a complete translation of and commentary on the works of Plato and Aristotle, in the hope of bringing Latin philosophical discourse to a level of sophistication hitherto found only in Greek. His execution in 525 on charges of treason prevented him from advancing beyond the logical works making up Aristotle's Organon. Besides these exegetical writings, however, Boethius also left behind a brilliant epitome of Greek wisdom, *The Consolation of Philosophy*, and a few short treatises in which he applied philosophical analysis to questions of theology. This body of work established a lexicon of Latin equivalents for Greek terms and concepts upon which medieval philosophy would draw for another thousand years. Cassiodorus, a Roman of even higher social standing and similarly adviser at the Ostrogothic court, managed a less technically prodigious but perhaps equally influential feat. His *Institutes of Divine and Secular Letters* offers a syllabus for Christian education in which the canon of rhetorical and philosophical classics continued to play a major role.

In the Greek-speaking orbit of the eastern Roman Empire, it was the otherworldly character of late Antique philosophy which came to the fore in the late fifth and sixth centuries. The *Elements of Theology*, written by the Neoplatonist Proclus, head of the Academy founded by Plato in Athens, is an important example. Among Christians, the same mystical tendency, perhaps intensified by contact with the angelology of Hellenized Jewish literature on contemplating the divine, appears in a series of short treatises on subjects such as the divine names and the celestial hierarchy written in Syria or Palestine. Authored by someone plainly beguiled by Proclus's ideas, these works circulated under the name of Dionysius, mentioned in Acts 17:34 as one of those ancient pagans Paul confronted at the Areopagus who was converted by the apostle's words. Under so august an imprimatur, the works of Pseudo-Dionysius rose to a position of great prominence in subsequent Christian traditions of Neoplatonizing mystical theory and practice.[6]

The early centuries following the conversion of the Roman Empire thus witnessed the maturation of a current of Christian speculation in great part continuous with late Antique patterns of thought that either preceded the conversion or were evident after it outside Christian circles. Consequently, this first phase of medieval philosophy responded to some of the concerns of philosophy as practiced today. We can plot it along a historical trajectory connecting the philosophy of classical Greece with that of the modern world.

The situation changed dramatically from the late sixth century on. After Boethius and Cassiodorus, educated discourse in the western part of the empire became less hospitable to the kind of reflection involved in Augustine's vision of Christian life as the successful completion of the philosopher's quest for wisdom. Glimpses of the earlier tradition are found in Spain, politically subject at the time to kingdoms of the Germanic Visigoths. Work continued there in the Latin encyclopedic tradition, into which much of Greek speculation had been poured in the centuries of Rome's greatness. Most renowned in our period are the *Etymologies* of Isidore, bishop of Seville. Elsewhere in the West, attention was devoted increasingly only to narrative, affective, and practical ends. Even writing on solely religious subjects became less theological, in the sense of being less engaged in the systematic examination and exploration of doctrines, and more devotional and inspirational. In the eastern part of the empire, the Emperor Justinian is commonly assumed to have closed the schools of philosophy in Athens in 529. If there actually was such a closure (the argument has been made that pagan philosophers continued to attract students in Athens after Justinian), it should not be thought of as delivering the deathblow to Graeco-Roman philosophical thought.[7] Already here, too, "philosophy" even in Christian form, as promoted from Justin to Boethius, was hardly at the center of learned attention any longer.

MONASTIC DISCIPLINE AND SCHOLARSHIP

This brings us to the second part of our story, which runs to the middle of the eleventh century and focuses on the West. From the end of the sixth century the western half of the Mediterranean world suffered a series of profound economic and demographic shocks, which drew it further and further away, commercially, politically and, finally, culturally, from the still vital centers of Roman empire and economy in the Greek-speaking East.[8] What followed was not the extinction of the classical Latin learning that had nourished the first phase of medieval philosophy, but a narrowing of focus and a redirecting of interest. Already since the fifth century in Gaul, the sixth in Italy, public schools of Latinity and literature had disappeared. Prominent Romans, and Germans who aspired to eminence, learned their letters in the home, perhaps with a private tutor. These were the individuals who carried on what was to remain of literate discourse, as the politics and economy of empire withered away. It was among Christian bishops and in the households or *familiae* of dependents and advisers gathered around them where such learning occasionally rose above an elementary level. Increasingly, however, the tools did not include what previous generations had called philosophy, nor even, among the three fundamental linguistic arts known as the trivium, logic or *dialectica*. What was learned at home was simply grammar, which included familiarity with the classics of Latin prose and poetry, and the rudiments of rhetoric or style. The products composed in the episcopal foyers of higher culture were primarily sermons, accounts of miracles, and history.[9]

Thus began what I have called a period of dormancy for medieval philosophy. With one startling exception, there is little in these centuries we today would identify as "philosophical," and perhaps more importantly, not much that Augustine or Boethius would have called philosophy either. Instead, the inspiration and vehicle for learning and literacy lay with a new culture of Latin monasticism. When abstract speculative and analytic thought emerged again in the late eleventh century, however, it emerged in the monastic milieu, which therefore deserves our attention.

By tradition, the origins of Christian monasticism are traced to the heroic founders Antony and Pachomius in early fourth-century Egypt. Some of the desert communities of ascetics that sprang up from these beginnings interacted significantly with the center of Hellenistic learning in Alexandria. Guided by the ideal of Christian philosophy epitomized by Origen, they situated the monk's quest for holiness along the path of the philosopher's pursuit of wisdom.[10] But those currents most influential for early western developments followed another course. Here Antony's search for inner peace and in-difference to the world through passionate combat with the demons of temptation and despair provided the model for ascetic discipline. It was a mission at once more practical than speculative and more routinizing than developmental.

In the early fifth century this way of life was introduced into the western Mediterranean on the islands of Lérins, off what is now southern France, and in Marseilles. These areas rapidly became train-ing grounds for monastic discipline in the Latinate West, schools of monastic practice and springboards for proselytism into Roman ter-ritory to the north and west. They were not, however, schools for letters. As with the contemporary episcopal centers of late Antique erudition, entry into these communities required a minimal founda-tion in grammar and rhetoric, but the goal here was not to advance Christian scholarship or shape learned Christian sensibilities. Their program thus mirrored even less Augustine's idea of the search for wisdom. The aim was to acquire the habits of the monastic heroes and beat down the desires of the flesh. Besides the Bible, the litera-ture most relevant to the monastic curriculum consisted of saints' lives and homely accounts of monastic virtue, the most famous of which were circulated in various collections as the *Apophthegmata patrum* or *Sayings of the Desert Fathers*.[11]

It is in this light that we must view the invocation of Psalm 34:12 in the *Rule* of Benedict, written in mid-sixth-century Italy and normative within western monasticism from the ninth century on. There God calls out to his human handiwork: "Who is the man that

will have life, and desires to see good days?" The expected response is
to "[lay] aside [one's] own will [so as to] take up the all-powerful and
righteous arms of obedience to fight under the true King, the Lord
Jesus Christ" ([362] 43). The quest for goodness, already for several
centuries defined as the Christian equivalent of the philosopher's
way of life, is now interpreted to mean withdrawal behind claustral
walls in assumption of a discipline of communal prayer and personal
submission to one's abbot. For those willing to follow a directive of
this sort, classical figures like Socrates and Plato, or, still closer to
home, Augustine and Boethius, no longer provide appropriate exemplars. Ruder, more heroic models step forth, greatest of all the fourth-
century Gallo-Roman hermit, Martin of Tours. Tellingly, his lessons
for living were transmitted not by means of dialogue, confession, or
meditation, but rather in the life of a saint.[12]

Not that the Latin monastic milieu was entirely hostile to more
speculative sorts of learning. A tradition of active scholarship originated in Ireland, which had been converted to Christianity in the
fifth century, just as Roman military authority was being displaced
in the rest of western Europe by Germanic warbands. Here, where
the Graeco-Roman social order had never taken root, there arose a
Christian learning that depended on the grammatical and rhetorical
minimum of the Antique syllabus but which, unlike on the continent, where letters survived in the homes of the elite, was generated
entirely within the monastic milieu in which it was applied. By the
mid-seventh century this Latin-Irish hybrid of personal mortifica-
tion and the discipline of Roman letters had been transplanted via
missionary activity to northern England. There a cluster of monastic
foundations nurtured an efflorescence of literacy in which some of
Augustine's intellectual vision reappears. The double monastery of
Wearmouth and Jarrow yielded the finest fruit of this culture in the
prolific writer and virtual type of central medieval monastic scholar,
Bede (d. 735). Besides composing biblical commentaries, Bede was,
so to speak, an expert on time: he wrote both a history of the
English church and a treatise on the esoteric calculations involved
in determining the date of Easter.

On the basis of eighth-century English monastic learning, along
with a likely infusion from the apparently still uninterrupted cultivation of late Latin higher studies in northern Spain, a remarkable if relatively brief cultural phenomenon arose on the European continent

in the protective shadow of a dynasty of expansionist Frankish kings, Charlemagne and his immediate successors.[13] In the writings of Carolingian scholars during the late eighth and first three-quarters of the ninth century there breaks to the surface a taste for speculation and inquiry, and an application of the nearly forgotten art of logic. For the first time in the West since the fifth century, theological controversy about specific doctrines engaged the curiosity of intellectuals eager to reason about their faith. The philosophical giant among them, and a sometimes alarming figure for later thinkers to deal with, was John Scottus Eriugena (d. c. 877). Born in Ireland (hence "Eriugena"), he knew Greek and read and translated Pseudo-Dionysius. John's access to the Platonizing mystical tradition provided some of the elements for his *Periphyseon*, a daring speculative vision of "natures" coming from and returning to God.

Yet the exceptional erudition of the Carolingian period was just that, an exception – in Eriugena's case a stunning one. Western monastic culture of the central Middle Ages fostered a learning inclined toward *ascesis*, capable of producing marvelous choreographies of chant, prayer, and liturgy but hardly works of speculative import.[14] We must wait another two centuries for significant philosophizing in the West. Elsewhere the situation was very different.

ISLAM

In 622 the Arab prophet Muhammed fled from his native city of Mecca to the more welcoming Medina, where he began in earnest his ultimately successful mission of bringing to the whole of the Arabian peninsula what he presented as God's final revelation to humankind. Here, at the opposite extremity of the Roman world from Ireland, so important about the same time for the medieval West, there arose in a whirlwind a movement, both religious and profoundly social, that within a century would sweep up much of what remained of the politically integrated parts of the Roman Empire, along with its even more ancient imperial rival, Persia. By the 720s the military and political domain of Islam stretched from Spain in the west through northern Africa, Palestine, Syria, and Arabia, to the Tigris and Euphrates valley, Persia, and the frontiers of India in the east. A core of the eastern Roman Empire was preserved in Greece, the Balkans, and Asia Minor. This was what nowadays is called the Byzantine

Empire, centered on Constantinople. However, the bulk of the lands in which the Christian version of Hellenized learning still retained some vitality fell under a new dispensation.

It is important to note that despite its expansionism and its insistence on absolute submission among believers to the new rule of faith embodied in the Qur'an, the conquering Muslim political elite was not intolerant of either the peoples or the cultures over which it established hegemony. In Syria, for example, late Antique philosophy, as exemplified in the Hellenized Jews of Alexandria, Origen, Porphyry, and even the more mystical Proclus and Pseudo-Dionysius, continued to be promoted among a learned stratum at the top of the dominated society. By the late ninth century this type of literate discourse had established a beachhead within Arabic intellectual circles. Al-Kindi, a sometime resident of the city of the caliphs at Baghdad, is commonly venerated as the father of Arab philosophy, both for his own writings and for the work he encouraged in others. For the next two hundred years, the central period of monasticism in the West, it was preeminently in the Islamic world that the intellectual quest for wisdom persisted and advanced. Here we may place a beginning of the third major phase in the history of medieval philosophy.

Already, with al-Kindi, Muslim interest in Greek philosophy displayed a particular fascination with the works of Aristotle. In this it paralleled a direction Boethius had taken three centuries before, which undoubtedly facilitated the reception of Arabic thought in the West when Boethius's work itself was revived around the end of the eleventh century. But the rapidity with which the Islamic world developed a mastery of the whole Greek heritage and began to chart a path of its own is astounding. The great Persian polymath Ibn Sina (Avicenna, d. 1037) produced the most impressive speculative synthesis since the early Neoplatonists. In its influence on critics and defenders alike, both in Islam and in the West, Ibn Sina's thought easily bears comparison with that of Kant or Hegel in modern times.

In Spain, site of an emirate opposed to Baghdad since the mid-eighth century and then home of the caliphate of Córdoba from 929, a separate flowering of the same extraordinary culture began only slightly later. Here the dynamism of Jewish communities ensured that learned Jews would play a prominent role. The strongly Neoplatonizing *Fountain of Life*, written in Arabic by the eleventh-century

Jewish poet Solomon Ibn Gabirol (Avicebron), was influential among Muslims and also, in Latin translation, in later Christian circles to the north. By the twelfth century the focus had narrowed even more sharply on Aristotle than before, and the interpretative sophistication applied to his works by Spanish intellectuals had taken a qualitative step beyond all earlier treatments. Moses Maimonides, a Jew born and educated in Córdoba but active for many years as a physician in Cairo, pointed the way with his *Guide for the Perplexed*, written, like Gabirol's work, in Arabic. In Ibn Rushd (Averroes), a contemporary Córdovan physician and lawyer who ended his days in Marrakesh in 1198, Muslim scholarship produced a monumental series of commentaries on Aristotle's writings that provided a focus for some of the most important philosophical debates of the following centuries. Later Christian thinkers, for example, would find enunciated in Averroes the challenging ideal of a purely philosophical way of life superior to the way of religious faith.

Taken in its entirety, the evolution of speculative thought in the Muslim world marked a considerable enrichment of the philosophical heritage of late Antiquity. And Arabic achievements in mathematics and natural philosophy, especially astronomy, laid the foundations for later medieval science in the West and ultimately set the stage for the Scientific Revolution of the seventeenth century.

THE RISE OF THE WEST AND THE REEMERGENCE OF PHILOSOPHY

By the year 1050 the western European territories of the old Latin world had absorbed, Christianized, and politically acculturated Germanic lands all the way to Scandinavia, as well as Slavic regions in central Europe. The West now projected a more formidable presence on the global stage. Here, in the homeland of the monastic learning of Bede and the magnificent Benedictine abbeys of the central Middle Ages, philosophy reawakened. The first stirrings were independent of developments in Islam. We may thus speak of two separate beginnings of the third phase of our story, one in Islam with al-Kindi and his successors, another in Europe with Anselm and Abelard. In the sometimes turbulent confluence of these two currents of thought we shall find some of the major achievements of high-medieval philosophy.

The roots of the western social transformation reach back at least to the tenth century in what would become an economic revolution across medieval Europe. By a combination of technological innovations (including the wheeled plough, horseshoes, and the horse collar) and a reconfiguring of the social structure that was tied to the spread of feudalism and the increased power of feudal lordships, northeastern Europe evolved between 900 and 1100 from a sparsely populated rural landscape of virtually subsistence agriculture to a more complex topography of surplus production, rapidly rising population, emergent towns (or even small cities), and the beginnings of significant markets and commerce.[15]

It was this fundamental transformation, from a backward to a dynamic society, that explains the rise of the West in late medieval and early modern times. Internal signs of the new order can be seen in the reinvigoration of royal monarchies in France and England, the appearance of self-governing urban communes in Italy, and reform in the ecclesiastical hierarchy of the church, evidenced in a push toward clerical celibacy and greater independence from secular control. Externally, the change announced itself in a more aggressive posture toward Latin Europe's neighbors. The Reconquista – the military expansion of northern Christian principalities into the central and eventually southern heartlands of Muslim Spain – was well underway by mid-eleventh century. In 1054 an increasingly self-assured and uncompromising papacy in Rome excommunicated the patriarch of Constantinople. The schism with Eastern Orthodoxy remains to this day. Most famously, in 1095 there began the first of those massive, and for two hundred years periodic, invasions of western soldiers of fortune and salvation into the Mediterranean east, the Crusades.

The importance of all this for European, indeed for world history, can scarcely be exaggerated. Here lies the origin of what is seen today as western global hegemony, the desirability, inevitability, durability, or even reality of which is hotly debated but which nevertheless seems to haunt the collective consciousness as a sort of pan-ethnic nightmare or dream-come-true.

With regard to philosophy, these events meant the birth of a society in which the learned were free to turn their efforts to analysis and speculation for their own sake, and eventually to that use of pure reason on which philosophy prides itself today. Symptoms of the new habits of mind, and of a type of literate culture entirely different from any of those described before, first appeared within the very institutions of scholarly activity and literary production most characteristic of western Europe in the central Middle Ages: the monasteries. These had not only been at the vanguard of the preaching, religious devotions, and historical writing of our second medieval period, but had also provided the pedagogical foundation for it. As indicated above, that foundation included grammar and rhetoric but generally not the other linguistic art of Antiquity, logic. Beginning in the eleventh century, some of the most learned monks started to search among the logical texts of Aristotle and Boethius, which were conserved in their libraries, for something they felt was missing from their education.

A powerful voice promoting the fascination with logic was heard at one of the centers for ecclesiastical and spiritual reform, the abbey of Bec in the duchy of Normandy. There the Italian prior Lanfranc, who had previously composed a commentary on the epistles of St. Paul in which he analyzed their logical as well as rhetorical and grammatical structure,[16] took up the challenge to apply the tools of dialectic to matters of religious doctrine currently in dispute. In the controversy and exchange of treatises between Lanfranc and Berengar of Tours over the nature of the Eucharist, the art of logic assumed a place of prominence in the discourse of the literate elite for the first time in Latin western Europe since the Carolingian period. By the end of the eleventh century even more persuasive advocates had begun to be heard, such as the embattled early nominalist, Roscelin, and Anselm of Aosta, who was Lanfranc's successor as prior at Bec and eventually also as the second Norman archbishop of Canterbury.

Medieval speculation achieved a new clarity and rigor in Anselm's writings. The most famous of these among philosophers, the *Proslogion*, sets forth what can be read as a reason-based proof of God. It provided the historical foundation for what later became known as the "ontological argument." The *Proslogion* was originally entitled "Faith Seeking Understanding." Here, in a meditation fully grounded in the Benedictine monastic tradition, reappear the lineaments of Augustine's ideal of a Christian intellectual quest for wisdom. Describing himself as "one who strives to raise his mind to the contemplation of God and seeks to understand what he believes," Anselm insisted, not only that the use of reason did not undermine faith, but that it was in fact fully appropriate to it. "I am not," he said, "trying, O Lord, to penetrate thy loftiness...but I desire in some measure to understand thy truth." His celebrated characterization of the project he was engaged in is this: "I do not seek to understand in order to believe, but I believe in order to understand" (*Proslogion*, preface and ch. 1).[17]

This new model for intellectual endeavor revived a form of discourse long absent from the West. It also altered the character of that discourse. With its exceptional emphasis on logic, it infused the erudition of the high Middle Ages with a deeply analytic hue. In his dialogues on such subjects as truth, free will, and the fall of the Devil, even the devout contemplative Anselm can sound more like a late thirteenth-century university master than like the rhetorically molded Augustine. The bent for logic took hold in the late eleventh- and early twelfth-century West at a breathtaking pace. By 1100 it had found a champion at Paris in the person of Peter Abelard, whose brilliance outshone all contemporaries and pointed toward the first significant advances in logical theory since the late Antique Stoics. Twelfth-century thinkers were indeed so much aware of what they were adding to the heritage of Aristotle and Boethius, especially in propositional logic and the theory of terms, that they coined a phrase for the dialectic of their own day, the *logica modernorum* or "logic of the moderns."[18]

Such a desire to apply the tools of reason, honed by dialectic, extended to every area of learning. The first signs of the new habits of thought in Berengar and Lanfranc had appeared in discussion of an important but limited theological subject, the sacrament of the Eucharist. With Abelard in the early twelfth century the methodical study of religious belief took flight. Now the full panoply of rational speculation and logical analysis was turned toward understanding the whole range of Christian faith and practice. The result was a virtual reinvention of theology as systematic and in places highly abstract discourse, a marked departure from the memorative and associative meditative habits of the monastic past. Abelard spoke for a new sensibility when he defended his pathbreaking efforts in theology. He explained that he was responding to "students who were asking for human and logical reasons on this subject, and demand[ing] something intelligible rather than [the] mere words" they were fed in the traditional sacred learning of their day (Abelard, *Historia calami-tatum* [152] 78).

The same thirst for reasoned understanding was felt with regard to human conduct and the external world. Abelard's *Ethics* presents an intentions-based explication of moral accountability that commands respect to this day on its philosophical merits. And where previously a minimal natural philosophy centered on astronomy and the calendar had sufficed, along with the rich symbolic interpretations of biblical and literary exegesis, learned minds of the twelfth century began to demand causal explanations of processes and careful categorizing of the properties and types of things. Echoing Abelard on religious thought, Adelard of Bath, an Englishman who led the drive toward new methods of inquiry about externalities, insisted that God had endowed humankind with reason just so that we could ferret out the rules under which the created world operated. Far from undermining a fundamental confidence that God was ultimately responsible for all that was and all that happened, such an understanding revealed the extraordinary providence of a Divinity who chose to work through regular but mediating causation.[19] Indeed, the growing tendency among twelfth-century thinkers to view the cosmos as a rationally ordered structure, amenable to investigation and analysis by the rational mind, has prompted some historians to describe this period as a time of the "Discovery of Nature."[20] There can be no doubt that *"natura"* and its Greek equivalent, *"physis,"* were increasingly used by Latin scholars both to describe the external world and to indicate the regularities upon which its workings depended.

A convenient way to conceptualize this ordered harmony was readily available in Neoplatonic cosmological texts preserved in monastic libraries. Indeed, the prototype itself could be used: the single work of Plato that had been translated into Latin in the late Empire, his *Timaeus*. The popularity in France of treatises in natural philosophy built upon a Platonizing metaphysics and vision of the universe has encouraged historians to propose that there was a specific School of Chartres, an episcopally supervised center of learning where key writers of such works were to have studied and taught and from which their views were disseminated throughout the Latin West. Though it is no longer fashionable to think of Chartres as the physical location of a school of this sort, a Platonic worldview did shape most approaches to nature in western Europe in the twelfth century.[21]

A similar inclination also made Latin intellectuals receptive to the vigorous traditions in natural philosophy and mathematics in Islamic territories to the south and east: Spain, southern Italy, and Sicily. The cultivated medical and philosophical circles of Toledo, Córdoba, Valencia, and Seville, where Hebrew, Arabic, and Latin met in a truly multivalent scholarly environment, drew individuals like Adelard from England and Gerard of Cremona from Italy, who steeped themselves in Jewish and Muslim learning and began to translate texts into Latin: firstly the speculative riches from this part of the world and eventually works from the classical Greek and Hellenistic eastern Mediterranean. Southern Italy was also a locus of intense activity, particularly at the centers of medical learning in and around Salerno, where texts were composed that transmitted much of Greek and Islamic natural philosophy to the West.

So radical a shift in educated attitudes and interests, and so massive an infusion of learning from foreign sources, could hardly avoid provoking opposition. At stake was nothing less than the fate of two divergent if not necessarily opposing cultural forms. On the one hand stood the old liturgical, devotional, and meditative routine of the monasteries; on the other, the new thirst for speculation and analysis applied to everything in mind and the world. For some of those committed in spirit to the older rhythms of Latin monastic culture, the relation of Abelard's style of theology to genuine Christian faith was much like the relation of Athens to Jerusalem in the eyes of Tertullian. Prominent among such cultural conservatives was the influential religious reformer and preacher, Bernard of Clairvaux. Spurred on by traditional teachers of sacred studies, he managed the condemnation of some of Abelard's doctrines in 1140 at the ecclesiastical Council of Sens, the second to be called against the great logician become theologian. In a letter to Pope Innocent II, composed for the occasion, Bernard pilloried the pedagogical methods of such a man who, he said, would "[put] forward philosophers with great praise and so [affront] the teachers of the Church, and [prefer] their imaginations and novelties to the doctrine and faith of the Catholic Fathers." Making clear that it was Abelard's method as much as the substance of what he said that brought offense, Bernard alluded to

Abelard's own justification, sure that his antagonist's words would stand as their own condemnation: "I thought it unfitting that the grounds of the faith should be handed over to *human reasonings* for discussion, when, as is agreed, it rests on such a sure and firm foundation" (Letter 189 [23] 89; emphasis added).

Yet for all Bernard's prominence as an institutional reformer and spokesperson for a newly triumphant ecclesiastical hierarchy, his call for a united stand against the novel learning was doomed to failure.[22] The enthusiasm for speculative wisdom and an analytical approach to interpretation was too powerful to be suppressed. Already, before Bernard, institutions were developing which nurtured and disseminated the new ways among an ever-widening cohort of logicians and speculative thinkers – indeed, philosophers in both the late Antique and modern senses of the word. By the end of the eleventh century circles of erudition again gathered around prominent bishops, as in the latter centuries of the western Roman Empire, but in an original form. We now find what can legitimately be called cathedral schools, with masters paid by the bishop and students drawn from beyond the resident clergy. A scattering of these schools across France and England became known for intellectual specialties: religious teaching at Laon, grammar and dialectic at Paris, rhetoric at Orleans, Arabic and Greek natural philosophy at Hereford. It was to such educational hotspots that bright minds like Abelard were drawn, and, as in his case, it was in such places that they often began their own teaching careers. At times an individual with a reputation like Abelard's would even offer instruction without seeking formal ecclesiastical sanction, taking on students who paid for their lessons in a sort of private school.

In centers of higher education like these, from cathedral schools to monastic and *ad hoc* private gatherings of students, the whole Antique curriculum was revived, not just grammar and rhetoric, but also of course logic, third of the arts of the trivium, and now the four mathematical arts or quadrivium as well: arithmetic, geometry, astronomy, and music. Given the burgeoning interest in natural philosophy, indeed in philosophy of any sort, broadly conceived, it comes as no surprise that the educational program at a few of these locales expanded beyond anything offered in late Rome. We begin to see places where inquiry into nearly every area of thought or practice was formally promoted.

At the heart of it all stood logic, now the paradigm for investigation and summary in all fields. Starting with the reading and literal exposition in the classroom of the fundamental texts in a subject, a formal system of question and answer arose, whereby students could both exercise their logical skills in debate and put the words of the authorities under the lens of critical analysis, advancing toward greater comprehensiveness, increasing consistency of exposition, and enhanced clarity of understanding. This classroom method of analysis, debate, and resolution quickly became standard throughout the emerging schools. The major disciplines of high medieval learning started to take shape, crystallizing around the seed of newly composed and soon universally adopted textbooks that were structured as collections of debating points touching on all significant aspects of the subject field.[23] In theology there was the Parisian Peter Lombard's *Sentences* of the mid-twelfth century, in canon law the scarcely earlier *Decretum* of Master Gratian of Bologna, and in logic the numerous commentaries, summaries, and collections of questions associated with various academic factions, particularly at the metropolis of learning in Paris.

RATIONALIZATION IN SOCIETY: POLITICS, RELIGION, AND EDUCATIONAL INSTITUTIONS

From a broader perspective, the explosive advancement of reasoning – that is, the explicit application of logic as both analytic and synthetic tool – into the method of choice for learned discourse was linked to a more general phenomenon of the rationalization of society itself. Rationalization is meant here in the sense of a differentiation of social functions and regularization of the practices by which they were carried out, all accompanied necessarily by increased complexity of institutions – what we would associate today with "bureaucracy." The two sorts of rationalization, intellectual and social, went hand in hand, for each encouraged and was dependent on the progress of the other. I mentioned above that royal monarchies had risen by the late eleventh century to a position of eminence as instruments of political order in the increasingly prosperous and populous lands of western Europe. The twelfth century saw consolidation of these achievements, to the point where a few kingdoms became by far the dominant political structures, foundations for the nation-states that would emerge in early modern times. Evidence of the new political reality can be seen in the effective implementation of a "royal peace" over broad swaths of England, France, northern Spain, and southern Italy. In this case, "peace" meant not just a muting of the hostilities that had characterized the competition among feudal lordships during the central Middle Ages, but also the dynamic expansion of royal power to enforce compliance with kingly expectations of acceptable behavior.

The state of the ecclesiastical order was also changing. Controversies over the customary rights of lay rulers to control the appointment of bishops in their domains were increasingly resolved in favor of the church's independence. As archbishop of Canterbury, Anselm had played a part in this in the early twelfth century. A century later, the first article of Magna Carta declared that the king should leave inviolate "the rights and liberties of the English church." By this time, the papacy had become a recognized and effective monarchy in its own right, claiming unique and comprehensive authority as heir to the prince of the apostles, St. Peter. Papal dominion was exercised primarily over officers of the institutional church, first and foremost bishops and abbots, but in the thirteenth century there were also implicit claims to an authority in secular affairs vying with or perhaps even superseding that of kings and emperors.

For lay and ecclesiastical government in this period, the most concrete achievement was the elaboration of a dual system of royal and papal courts. These reached out into localities that had hitherto known only the customary justice of feudal law. They brought the possibility of appeal to monarchical, and thus from a local point of view less lordly and partisan, adjudication within reach of people farther down on the social scale than ever before. Such agency and intervention required funding. Taxation by both lay and ecclesiastical authorities developed rapidly over the course of the twelfth and thirteenth centuries, with some of the most ingenious innovations being made by the popes. Taxes brought with them the need for administration of collection and expenditure, and so the first real treasuries arose. The most famous of these was the English Exchequer, with written accounting procedures and permanent personnel: in short, a primitive bureaucracy.

Transformation was not limited to officialdom and the upper reaches of society. There was ferment at the popular level, too. From

the late eleventh century this took shape most noticeably in agitation for increased lay participation in religion and the development
of novel devotional forms. There was also widespread criticism of
the way of life and moral standards prevalent among the clergy. The
predictable strain between such grass-roots activism and official efforts at organization and control erupted in accusations of heresy,
marks of the first instances of anything that could be characterized as popular or broadly social heresy in western Europe since
late Rome.[24] By the last decades of the twelfth century parts of
southern France, northern Italy, and the Rhineland counted at least
two well-developed networks of popular religious communities,
the Cathars and the Waldensians, each opposed to the dominance
and challenging the authenticity of the established ecclesiastical
hierarchy, and each labeled heretical by most secular and clerical
officials.

The response from the higher authorities was to erect institutional
bulwarks against dispersion of power, either material or ideological.
On the ideological side, the popes began in the twelfth century to
call the first universal or "ecumenical" church councils since the
eighth century, the first ever in western Europe. Such gatherings,
which did not of course include representatives of the Orthodox eastern churches, lent support to papal claims to lead a church in which
lines of authority coalesced at the top. They also defined acceptable –
that is, orthodox – doctrine and constructed an apparatus of discipline. In 1215 at the Fourth Lateran Council in Rome, for instance,
Pope Innocent III presided over an assembly of officials from all over
Latin Christendom. The result was an authorized statement of the
faith that all Christians were required to accept, and a call for personal confession to a priest and reception of the Eucharist at least
once each year by all believers. After centuries of relative indiffer-
ence, these measures showed a serious intent to bring the laity into
the churches and in touch at minimum with the rudiments of belief.
But the council also issued an unmistakable threat of retribution
for dissent. This became explicit in the formal reaffirmation of an
injunction delivered by an earlier pope in 1184, which commanded
bishops to investigate their dioceses annually for evidence of non-
conformity. Here lie the origins of the medieval and early modern
Inquisition.[25]

Measures like these, and the often more brutal steps taken by
lay governments to suppress dissent and manufacture at least the

appearance of acquiescence and uniformity, have brought historian R. I. Moore to write of the "formation of a persecuting society" in western Europe in the twelfth and thirteenth centuries, a view increasingly adopted in recent scholarship on the late medieval and early modern periods.[26] In this light, one of the salient institutional accomplishments of ecclesiastical organization in the early thirteenth century, the founding of the first two orders of mendicant or begging friars, the Franciscans and the Dominicans, assumes a profoundly ambiguous character. Wandering among the populace as irreproachably unworldly and impoverished preachers of orthodoxy, the mendicants quickly became assimilated into official mechanisms of education and ecclesiastical discipline. On the educational side, the friars' preaching and teaching was greatly informed by instruction in their own houses of study and at the developing centers of higher learning. On the disciplinary side, Dominicans, followed soon by the Franciscans, assumed a conspicuous role in a centralizing papal inquisition, which was set up during the thirteenth century to circumvent the bishops' yearly inquisitorial forays. This was the broader social context of high medieval philosophy, one fraught with strategies for control and efforts to impose order in a disorderly and protesting world.

The immediate institutional context in which the new learning took place was itself also rationalized. There were a number of models: Italian communes, the new monastic orders, and particularly the growth of merchant and artisan guilds in commercial centers. With these as examples, hitherto unregimented clusters of schools at some of the most prominent sites of educational activity began to consolidate and organize themselves along corporate institutional lines. The impetus for such moves arose from the community of masters (or students!) at each site. The legal basis was the newly revived Roman law concept of a corporation, a group of individuals acting at law as one person. Though steps in this direction must have been taken at places like Paris and Bologna by mid-twelfth century, it is in the thirteenth century that the first documents appear attesting to the existence of these pedagogical monopolies. By then Paris, Bologna, and Oxford were universally accepted producers of higher learning, and at least five more such centers were founded by century's end: Cambridge, Padua, Naples, Toulouse, and Montpellier. By the fourteenth century these institutions were habitually named by one of the synonyms for corporations, "universities."

It was in the universities that the apparatus of advanced education associated with the European high Middle Ages took shape. Within each university, the groups of masters and scholars working in the emergent disciplines organized themselves into faculties, with their own sense of subcorporate identity and their own official seals to ratify documents. Foundational for all other higher studies were the arts, developed out of the traditional trivium and quadrivium but including a more varied selection from what would be thought of today as philosophy and natural science, and giving greatest attention to logic. The Faculty of Arts thus came together at the nucleus of each university and was the faculty from which the majority of matriculating students would receive instruction. Among more advanced studies, for which certification as a Bachelor in Arts would ordinarily be expected as precondition, a classic trio soon established itself: Law, divided into the two major subdisciplines of civil and ecclesiastical or canon law; Medicine; and by the mid-thirteenth century the queen of faculties and most prestigious, Theology. At the same time each faculty began to formalize its curriculum, with required texts and courses, examinations, teaching apprenticeships or bachelorhoods, time limits, and ceremonial certification of accomplishment, the bases for modern academic degrees. Thus grew up an elaborate system for obtaining credentials in fields tailored to complex societal demands. It was, of course, a society swiftly advancing in institutional specialization and hence requiring increasingly technical and differentiated skills of writing and reasoning in government, religion, and, in areas of commercial wealth, even services like medicine. We see here the early stages of professionalization for a growing number of the learned elite in western Europe.

This whole complex underlay the high and late medieval "scholasticism" that constitutes the discursive form for learning and speculation in the western heyday of our third phase of medieval philosophy.

ARISTOTLE AND THIRTEENTH-CENTURY SCHOLASTICISM

Perhaps the most significant single event associated with the ripening of this culture, and surely the one attracting most attention in histories of medieval thought, was the assimilation of nearly the complete corpus of Aristotle's surviving writings. On the material side, this amounted to the integration into the curriculum, primarily for the Faculty of Arts but also to a considerable degree for Theology, of Aristotle's works beyond the first books of the Organon. Driven by an assiduous program of translations, first from Arabic versions but increasingly from the original Greek and frequently subsidized by ecclesiastical or secular officials, late twelfth- and thirteenth-century academics familiarized themselves intimately with the rest of the Organon and then with Aristotle's contributions to the natural sciences, followed by his metaphysics almost simultaneously with his ethics, and lastly his politics.

On the formal side, the story has to do with a new paradigm for knowledge. Most critical here were the unpacking and ostensible adoption of Aristotle's prescriptions for cognition of the highest sort: "*epistèmè*" in Greek, "*scientia*" in Latin. For each field of investigation the goal became the identification of basic principles defining "evidently" the essential nature of the subject and then the rigorous deduction, from such principles, of a systematic body of truths concerning the subject's properties. The key to this schema of what high medieval thinkers regularly accepted as the ideal toward which "science" should aspire lay buried in Aristotle's *Posterior Analytics*. John of Salisbury, a paragon of twelfth-century erudition, had pointed to this treatise around 1160 as crucial for comprehending "the art of demonstration, which is the most demanding of all forms of reasoning." John complained that the material of the *Posterior Analytics* was "extremely subtle," confessing that in his day "but few mentalities [could] make much headway" in it (*Metalogicon* IV 6 [157] 212). Only toward the second quarter of the thirteenth century did the text receive written commentary and interpretation by Robert Grosseteste, eventual master of theology at Oxford and subsequently bishop of Lincoln.[27] Starting with Grosseteste, scholars in all disciplines sought to construe their work as scientific. Even theology was a candidate, at least until the mid-fourteenth century, despite the irksome problem that its first principles would seem to have been received from God by faith rather than grasped as evident in themselves in the present life. "Science" in scholastic eyes thus embraced much more than the natural and mathematical sciences recognized today.

To be sure, much of this Aristotelian content and form was received into a set of broader intellectual commitments that can only be described as Neoplatonic, including a hierarchical notion of being and a sense of the subordination of material things to, and eventual sublimation into, the immaterial and spiritual. Furthermore, there were able minds critical of many aspects of Aristotle even at the height of his influence, such as Bonaventure and Peter John Olivi. What is called "Aristotelianism" thus took many forms in the scholastic world, none of them pure. With all these qualifications, however, it was largely under Aristotle's tutelage that extraordinary efforts were made during the thirteenth century, even in theology faculties, to establish a body of knowledge to which all rational minds, Christian or not, could be expected to assent. One result was that a great deal of what would now be considered philosophy was done by theologians.

The finest and certainly the most celebrated examples of theological speculation in which extensive philosophizing took place present themselves in the writings of a number of latter thirteenth-century theologians, all of whom taught for at least part of their career at the University of Paris, the jewel in the high medieval theological crown. They range from the Dominican friars Albert the Great and Thomas Aquinas, through the Franciscans Bonaventure and John Duns Scotus, to the "secular" – that is, still clerical but neither mendicant nor monastic – masters Henry of Ghent and Godfrey of Fontaines. Professional religious thinkers like these, all trained extensively in arts faculties and expert in logic, regarded what they, too, called philosophy – reasoning applied to evidence naturally obtained – as distinctively different from understanding based on truths supernaturally revealed by God. Yet they considered the former sort of thinking to be an important concomitant of the latter. If religion was to attain its full intellectual dignity, theologians had to be conversant with all that the mind could know, no matter what the source. They should never bypass a natural or logical argument when one was available, even for truths that were vouchsafed by revelation. For such intellectuals, philosophy possessed value even within their ecclesiastically sanctioned discipline just because it was theology's handmaiden, *ancilla theologiae*. And since the assistance philosophy provided was more effective the more fully its integrity was preserved in all its natural, nontheological autonomy, the speculation and analysis in which they engaged in the name of philosophy can be read and appreciated by even the most nonreligious rationalist of today.

There were in fact some scholastics, mostly in arts faculties and especially at Paris, who held that philosophy by itself could lead to the heights of truth which the masters of theology considered attainable only in their professionally privileged discourse guided by faith and the teachings of the church. Among such thinkers, most notably the arts masters Siger of Brabant and Boethius of Dacia, the ideal of a philosophical way of life carried on independently of religious institutions reappeared in the West for the first time since the days when pagan philosophers competed with "philosophized" Christians. According to some historians, these philosophers were convinced that the use of "natural reason" by itself would bring the seeker after truth to the wisdom which Origen or Augustine had sought by sublimating the Platonic quest into a striving for Christian contemplation. Unlike Origen or Augustine, they thought that taking into account the unreasoned dictates of faith or the doctrinal prescriptions of orthodoxy would get in the way.[28] Here the high medieval scholastics' distinction between philosophical and religious thought subordinated the latter to the former, perhaps even eradicating it altogether.

Not surprisingly, there was a reaction to this often-called Averroism even in the enlightened precincts of the "scientifically" oriented universities. Already in 1210 and 1215 ecclesiastics at Paris had banned public lectures on Aristotle's books of natural philosophy and well-known Arabic works, probably Ibn Sina's above all. These restrictions fell away with the virtual absorption of Aristotle into the academic curriculum by the 1240s. But the radical association of "wisdom" with "pure reason" by arts masters at Paris in the late 1260s and early 1270s, and even the respect such theologians as Albert and Thomas paid to philosophy as self-contained source of truth, led to renewed fears. In 1270, and again more extensively in 1277, the bishop of Paris officially condemned the teaching of a host of propositions, most of which we would consider purely philosophical, that conservative masters of theology viewed as detrimental to Christian faith but circulating freely in the Parisian schools. Aquinas's writings themselves were at least indirectly implicated in the denunciations, a situation brought nearer to the surface in like-minded condemnations by archbishops of Canterbury in 1277, 1284, and 1286.[29] Scholars now debate even the short-term effectiveness of these prohibitions, and by the mid-fourteenth century many masters in arts and theology felt free to debate without regard to any of the lists of proscribed teachings. It was clear, however, that higher studies in religion and philosophy could not coexist without the risk of conflict.

By the end of the thirteenth century a similar but more ominous tug-of-war had started to emerge in circles less sequestered behind the walls of academe, more open to the laity at large. A number of theologians who maintained close ties with devotional communities of literate and semiliterate laity in the Rhineland saw the call to pursue wisdom through reason, not as an injunction to separate philosophy from theology, but as an invitation to see how, by following reason into the depths of the soul, one could come to discover the truth of revelation without recourse to ecclesiastical supervision. The Dominican friars Ulrich of Strassburg, Dietrich of Freiberg, and most famously Meister Eckhart (1260–1327) reached back to the Neoplatonic traditions of Pseudo-Dionysius and the pagans Proclus and Plotinus to reinstitute a program of personal mental enlightenment as the way to a near-beatific encounter with God. The fact that they all, again especially Eckhart, were deeply involved in ministry to the nonclerical populace lent their speculative efforts a resonance markedly different from that of earlier arts masters, such as Siger of Brabant and Boethius of Dacia. Among these first of the Rhineland mystics, we begin to see a startling cross-pollination of learned and popular discourse and the taking root of what can only be called a philosophizing attitude among the ranks of the common people.[30] Most intriguingly, it was communities of laywomen, popularly known since the early thirteenth century as "beguines," that proved most receptive to this kind of thinking and provided inspiration for much of the mystical philosophy of late medieval and early modern Europe.

THE CONTESTED FOURTEENTH CENTURY

In some histories, the culmination of medieval philosophy, or indeed, of all philosophy, is in the thirteenth century. Over the last fifty years, however, scholars attuned to contemporary logic and analytic philosophy have also found much to admire in fourteenth-century thought. The scholastics of this period took as their point of departure the propositional and terminist logic that had begun to be developed in the time of Abelard, and in the spirit of Abelard they put their results in logic to work in other fields. The new approach, the "*via moderna*," flourished in the universities throughout the late fourteenth and fifteenth centuries.

The inception of the *via moderna* is sometimes credited to the brilliant Oxford Franciscan, William of Ockham (d. 1347/48). Ockham is also celebrated – or attacked – for his nominalism, that is, for holding that universals, such as *man* and *red*, are names (*nomina*), not things (*res*). It has been argued that "conceptualism" would be a better label for Ockham's view, but in any case, neither Ockham nor his position on the problem of universals should be regarded as the whole of the *via moderna*. What is clear, however, is that fourteenth-century universities devoted enormous intellectual energy to the investigation of logical puzzles – puzzles involving self-reference, for example – and to games called "obligations," where the aim was to catch an opponent in contradiction as a result of accepting apparently quite consistent premises. Such activities bespeak a preoccupation with the philosophy of language and issues of logical form that makes scholastic discourse of the period seem curiously at home in the world of twentieth-century analytic philosophy. At the same time, there was a bent in the fourteenth century for intense analysis of the nature of quantity and for experimentation with modes of quantitative reasoning in the most disparate academic disciplines, from physics to theology. Leaders here were a group at Oxford called in their own day the "*calculatores*." In their work and in that of such thinkers as the Parisian masters John Buridan and Nicole Oresme, some scholars have discerned foundations for the Scientific Revolution.[31]

The logical acuteness that came to rule the universities in the first part of the fourteenth century gave rise to critical attitudes in metaphysics and theology, a degree of skepticism about the solidity of systems of thought such as those of the previous century. In some cases, it has been argued, psychological analysis of how we think and act replaced metaphysical insight into the intelligible reality of what there is to think about or act for.[32] Be that as it may, the status of academic theology as science or wisdom came into question. Faith served as the basis for religion without as much in the way of philosophical preamble as a Thomas Aquinas had thought to provide.

The fourteenth century also saw the bitter fruition, both in action and in theory, of political conflicts inherent in late medieval Christendom. As was mentioned above, by the end of the twelfth century the papacy had achieved monarchical authority over the ecclesiastical hierarchy. The popes were also in a position to exert considerable influence in secular affairs. Innocent III, convener of the Fourth Lateran Council, intervened decisively in such matters on a number of occasions, skillfully managing contests between king and king, as with France against England, or between emperors and imperial electors, as in Germany. In the 1240s, in a remarkable clash between Pope Innocent IV and the German king and Holy Roman Emperor Frederick II of Hohenstaufen, the pope called on all Catholic monarchs to join in a crusade against the emperor himself. This initiative proved unsuccessful, but papal diplomacy managed nonetheless to check Frederick's hopes for effective rule over all of Italy and lay the basis for the collapse of the Hohenstaufen dynasty in the early 1250s.

By century's end, however, some kings had amassed an effective power to enforce compliance with their commands that dwarfed the popes' power to withstand them. It took two confrontations between Pope Boniface VIII and the king of France, Philip IV, one involving taxes and the other royal jurisdiction over high ecclesiastical officials, to make the practical state of affairs plain for all to see. But after Boniface's arrest and humiliation at the hands of French mercenaries in 1303 and his subsequent speedy disappearance from the scene, no one in Europe could doubt that what is commonly thought of as "real" power belonged to the lay ruler. For nearly seventy-five years, in fact, the court of the popes was planted just outside the French kingdom, on the banks of the Rhône in Avignon, where it was widely suspected that the French made all the critical decisions in a period described by a scandalized contemporary as the "Babylonian captivity of the church."

On the side of political theory, papal and lay powers each had their defenders. There were also thinkers who attempted to maintain a more or less balanced dualism. Around the close of the thirteenth century, the Parisian theologians Giles of Rome and James of Viterbo composed treatises espousing a view of clerical authority throughout society that has been dubbed "hierocratic," because of the governmental power it ascribes to the priesthood, transcendently to the pope. In the early fourteenth century a more realistic prescription for the separation of powers between secular and ecclesiastical monarchs surfaced in the works of witnesses to the recent political events, such as the theologian John of Paris. A radically antihierocratic line was taken in Marsilius of Padua's *Defender of Peace*, completed in 1324, which depicted papal claims to "fullness of power" (*plenitudo potestatis*) in temporal as well as spiritual matters as an overwhelming threat to tranquillity and order. A final medieval contribution on the papalist side came in 1326, with the *Summa on Ecclesiastical Power* of Augustine of Ancona (called Augustinus Triumphus from the sixteenth century). However, the largest body of medieval "political" writing was produced by the same William of Ockham who is traditionally given so much credit or blame for nominalism and the *via moderna*. Ockham believed that the Avignonese pope John XXII had fallen into heresy by officially condemning assertions of the absolute poverty of Christ and the apostles that most Franciscans regarded as accepted Christian truth. He accordingly wrote a massive dialogue on heresy, "especially of the pope." In later works more broadly addressed to questions of ecclesiastical and lay power, Ockham defended the normal independence of each from the other while allowing that departures from the norm – in either direction – were sometimes necessary.

It is easy to exaggerate the radicalism of antihierocratic or anti-authoritarian themes in the thought of a Marsilius or an Ockham. Legal theory and moral philosophy in the preceding centuries contain much that is supportive of individual conscience and natural rights, including the rights of secular and religious communities to take action against their rulers in extreme cases. Students of Thomas Aquinas drew from his thought and from Aristotle's *Politics* a strong interest in a "mixed" constitution as the best form of government, one combining elements of monarchy, aristocracy, and democracy.[33] However, when all of these ideas are combined with those of Marsilius and Ockham, and with the theories of sovereignty elaborated by the hierocrats, we have the tumultuous beginnings of modern European political thought.

Before the turn of the century the attentive ear might also discern other signs of change. After decades of terminist logic and nominalist metaphysics, John Wyclif, master of theology at Oxford, brought the counterclaims of realism, never entirely extinguished at any point in the Middle Ages, resoundingly back to center stage. For him, the common and universal, far from being a matter of mere names, was a higher reality than the individual and particular. In politics, Wyclif drew upon traditional attacks on ecclesiastical wealth and worldliness to advocate the virtual disendowment of the church. This gained him a momentary hearing in royal circles of the 1370s in England. The Peasants' Revolt of 1381 soured aristocratic patrons on Wyclif's ideas, but more seeds for a reordering of society had been sown. Meanwhile, scholasticism itself, or at least the unquestioned dominance of the dialectical and disputatious methods of the high medieval universities, began to show signs of retreat. In England, it has been argued, law replaced theology as the paramount field of study. Men of affairs thus ousted inhabitants of the ivory tower as leaders in the literary culture of the social and ruling elite.[34] By then, a new air had been stirring for some time in Italy, a self-consciously antischolastic humanism, convinced that learning and thinking had to be totally reformed for anything of value to emerge.

Yet what did the leader of this movement, Francesco Petrarca, think fitting to carry with him on his ascent of Mount Ventoux, a venture frequently taken as emblematic of the beginning of the Renaissance? Nothing other than the *Confessions* of St. Augustine, the philosophical and spiritual autobiography of the thinker with whom our narrative of medieval philosophy began. Contrary to the image of the Renaissance as anti-Christian, Augustine and other church fathers continued to exert great influence on Petrarca's followers.[35] Scholasticism itself survived – the scholastics berated by Renaissance luminaries were more often their own contemporaries than the figures touched on in this chapter – and the tradition of Aquinas in particular had a rebirth in the sixteenth century at Paris and in the Spanish school of Salamanca. These and still later developments are touched on in chapter 13 of this Companion, on the presence of medieval philosophy in later thought. Between this chapter and that one, my colleagues will present the ideas for which I have attempted to provide a setting, the inside story, so to speak, of the philosophy created in the contexts described thus far.

THE PLACE OF AUTHORITY IN MEDIEVAL THOUGHT

Most medieval philosophizing was done in a framework of religious beliefs primarily grounded in acceptance of particular texts as divinely inspired. Jewish, Christian, and Muslim thinkers offered arguments for accepting the Bible or Qur'an as divine revelation,[36] but, once thus accepted, the sacred text acquired an authority transcending human reason. As the utterly reliable source of truth, especially truth about God's nature and purposes, Scripture henceforth served as data or pretheoretical commitment for further reasoning, not, as in much modern thought, as an object of critical – perhaps skeptical – scrutiny.

The difference between medieval and typical modern attitudes toward the authority of Scripture (and toward other authority as well) is real and cannot help but affect our reading of medieval philosophy. It is also a difference that should not be exaggerated. Two points may be made to gain a sensible perspective. The first is that authority, or something like it, plays a role in thinking at any time. No thinker, not even a Descartes, really starts from scratch or, in even the most scientific fields, attempts to provide proof for everything claimed as true. In our own day, reliance on experts is so universal as to be invisible. And the assumption that political or institutional sanction, when invoked, rests upon transparent criteria for consent is more often unexamined, maybe even unjustified, than not. The self-conscious medieval acquiescence in an authoritative voice is therefore not so blindly credulous in comparison with modern habits of thought as might be supposed.

The second point is that medieval reliance on Scripture (or respect for institutions claiming scriptural authorization) provoked thought as well as limiting it. As the word of God, Scripture could not be false, and anything contrary to Scripture could not be true. That said, however, it was no easy matter to decide in particular cases precisely what constituted the truth. Both Bible and Qur'an commonly spoke on several sides of an issue, requiring reconciliation to establish a definitive position. Did the gospel, for instance, require Christians to be pacifists (the common early view) or countenance just wars (as Augustine and others after him argued)? More importantly, most, if not all, of Scripture was subject to interpretation. The formulation by third- and fourth-century church councils of such fundamental dogmas of medieval Christian orthodoxy as the Trinity and Incarnation was the outcome of intense debate about the import of key scriptural passages (a debate, incidentally, in which Greek philosophical ideas made a significant contribution).

In a tradition with roots in classical Greek and Roman strategies for reading the canonic texts of myth and epic, Christian exegetes by the central Middle Ages recognized four interpretative levels. There was the literal meaning of the words (which could itself be metaphorical, as when physical qualities were ascribed to God), the figural signification where the Hebrew Bible foreshadowed the Christian New Testament, the moral lesson embedded in the letter, and finally the anagogical meaning, presaging wonders to come at the end of time.[37] Such a hermeneutics made for extraordinary flexibility in the employment of Scripture as a standard of truth.

A considerable step down from the Bible and the Qur'an, but still of eminent authority, were the writings of authors to whom tradition had granted special prestige. A number of Christian thinkers came to be especially respected as "doctors" or teachers of the church: in the East, Athanasius, Gregory of Nazianzus, Basil, and John Chrysostom; in the West, the four late Roman writers Ambrose, Jerome, Augustine, and Gregory the Great.

With the rise from the eleventh century of institutions of ecclesiastical discipline in western Europe, and the accompanying efforts to enforce dogmatic orthodoxy – a phenomenon anticipated by several centuries in East Rome and various power centers of Islam – it became common to cite pronouncements of the church hierarchy as evidence for truth and falsehood and perilous to gainsay them. There was unique respect for papal authority, especially as exercised in and with church councils but also as expressed in other declarations and mandates. To be sure, no precise theory of papal, episcopal, or conciliar authority gained universal acceptance in our period, even in the West. As dedicated a hierocrat as Augustine of Ancona acknowledged the possibility of papal heresy, a possibility which, as we have seen, Ockham regarded as actualized in John XXII. Nevertheless, about the time the twelfth-century schools start to coalesce, ecclesiastical oversight comes to assume a significant presence even in debates of completely secular import concerning, for example, natural philosophy.

By the time of the fully developed university system of the late thirteenth century, a few renowned "modern" theologians are also accorded almost authoritative status, especially within their own religious orders. Despite disputes over who counted as a veritable doctor, the presumption of truth increasingly clung to the statements of such thinkers as Thomas Aquinas, for Dominicans, and Bonaventure, for Franciscans.

In the late Antique philosophical schools, the texts of their founders were regarded with profound respect. This usually remained true in the face of subsequent developments in quite different directions. Early Christian thinkers inherited this sense of reverence, though not without a touch of the countervailing suspicion of pagan thought expressed by Tertullian. Augustine not surprisingly thought of Plato as divinely inspired, even if not illumined with the fullness of Christian truth.

When these philosophical traditions were resurrected in the West in the late eleventh century, old attitudes reemerged. Plato, or any teaching attributable to him, was practically unassailable for most of the twelfth century. In the thirteenth, the secular guide to truth *par excellence* was Aristotle, "the Philosopher." Again, interpretation insured flexibility.

To understand the use of classical philosophy by medieval thinkers (or the use of Islamic and Jewish thought by Latin scholastics), it is vital to know when earlier texts became available to later readers. For the availability of classical texts in Islam, see chapter 4 below. A summary of dates of accessibility in Latin for selected texts is provided in table 1.[38]

Few medieval thinkers fit the modern image of professional philosophers. Accordingly, the philosophically significant ideas of the period are to be found in literary genres unlike the journal articles or systematic treatises of today. Major forms include meditative works, theological treatises, commentaries, compendiums or summaries, and various types of "questions" (which are in some respects rather like journal articles!). I will say something about each of these and a few others.

Meditative or devotional works abound in the Middle Ages. Some are of considerable philosophical interest. Among the earliest is Augustine's *Confessions*, one of the greatest monuments to speculation of all time. Boethius's *Consolation of Philosophy* provides a classic example from the sixth century. With the return of interest in philosophical thinking in the West in the eleventh century, the

Table 1 *Earliest translations of Greek, Hebrew, and Arabic works into Latin*

Author	Work	Translator	Date
Plato	*Timaeus*	Calcidius	*c.* 400
Aristotle	*Categories*	Boethius	*c.* 510–22
	De interpretatione	Boethius	*c.* 510–22
	Prior Analytics	Boethius	*c.* 510–22
	Posterior Analytics	James of Venice	? 1125–50
	Topics	Boethius	*c.* 510–22
	Sophistical Refutations	Boethius	*c.* 510–22
	Physics	James of Venice	? 1125–50
	De anima	James of Venice	? 1125–50
	Metaphysics (nearly complete)	Michael Scot	*c.* 1220–24
	Nicomachean Ethics (complete)	Robert Grosseteste	? 1246–47
	Politics	William of Moerbeke	? 1260
Porphyry	*Introduction (Isagoge)*	Boethius	*c.* 510–22
Proclus	*Elements of Theology*	William of Moerbeke	1268
Anonymous	*Liber de causis* (drawn from Proclus)	Gerard of Cremona	before 1187
Ps.-Dionysius	*Mystical Treatises*	Scottus Eriugena	862
Ibn Sina	*Metaphysics* (*Book of Healing* IV)	Dominicus Gundisalvi	after 1150
	De anima (*Book of Healing* III.6)	Ibn Daoud and Dominicus Gundisalvi	after 1152
Ibn Gabirol	*Fountain of Life*	Iohannes Hispanus and Dominicus Gundisalvi	after 1152
Maimonides	*Guide for the Perplexed*	Anonymous	*c.* 1230
Ibn Rushd	*Great Commentary on Aristotle's Physics*	Michael Scot	*c.* 1220–35
	Great Commentary on Aristotle's De anima	Michael Scot	*c.* 1220–24
	Great Commentary on Aristotle's Metaphysics	Michael Scot	*c.* 1220–24
	Middle Commentary on Aristotle's Nicomachean Ethics	Herman the German	? 1240

mode revives, Anselm's *Proslogion* and *Monologion* leading the way and Bonaventure's *Mind's Road to God* continuing the tradition for high scholasticism of the thirteenth century.

Theological treatises investigating religious doctrine or combating perceived error were also numerous. They tended to rely heavily on scriptural or other religious authority, but the desire to understand what was believed or to express it clearly often yielded philosophical insights. Again, Augustine established the pattern with his *The Trinity*, and Boethius contributed with a cluster of short works highly influential in shaping the terminology of Latin philosophy for the later, scholastic period. The Carolingians produced writings of this sort, spectacularly in the case of Scottus Eriugena, as did scattered figures in Islam and Judaism. Maimonides' *Guide for the Perplexed*, for example, retains its prominence up to the present. The universities of the high medieval West proved especially fertile ground for this kind of composition, examples ranging from Grosseteste's thirteenth-century *Hexaëmeron*, a many-sided exploration of the six days of Creation, to the Englishman Thomas Bradwardine's *On God's Cause, Against Pelagius* in the fourteenth century. Despite their immediate focus on dogmatics, all these works turn constantly to philosophy for argument and elucidation.

The ancient tradition of commentaries, particularly on the classics of the philosophical legacy, was continued and further developed in the Middle Ages.[39] Boethius made a conspicuous start with his intention of commenting on all of Plato and Aristotle. The commentaries he did achieve, on much of Aristotle's Organon and on other logical texts, such as Porphyry's *Introduction*, like his theological treatises set the stage, after centuries of incubation, for the speculative renaissance of the eleventh and twelfth centuries. Commentaries on classical philosophical works, and not just in logic, proliferated in western Europe in the twelfth century. More important in the long run were the efforts of Muslim scholars. Ibn Sina's *Book of Healing* can be considered a vast commentary on all of Aristotle. Ibn Rushd took the commentary form to its height. Although he did not escape criticism (Aquinas, with rare bitterness, called him "the Depraver" of Aristotle, not "the Commentator"), his glosses on the Aristotelian corpus dominated the field for hundreds of years, in the Latin West most of all.

From these models sprang a virtual industry of commentary on the philosophical classics among university scholars, not only arts masters like John Buridan, who commented on Aristotle's natural science and ethics in the fourteenth century, but also theologians. Albert the Great introduced the West to the whole range of the Philosopher's thought, and his student Thomas Aquinas at the summit of his career as teacher of sacred doctrine produced detailed expositions of major Aristotelian treatises in logic, metaphysics, and natural and moral philosophy. Some scholastic commentaries, including most of Aquinas's, were "literal": phrase-by-phrase explications of the text. Others were in question form, posing and resolving objections to Aristotle's doctrine and sometimes taking the opportunity to put forward the commentator's own ideas at some length.[40]

By far the greatest number of medieval compositions with significant philosophical content were peculiar to the schools of western Europe in the high Middle Ages, first cathedral centers and then universities. Already in the twelfth century textbooks designed for classroom use were being produced in Italy, France, and England. A prominent type was the compendium (*summa* or *summula*) on logic. The all-time classic in this line was the *Summulae logicales* of the thirteenth-century Dominican, Peter of Spain. The fourteenth century saw many more, from William of Ockham's *Summa totius logicae* to Paul of Venice's numerous handbooks.

The question (*quaestio*), the genre most closely identified with high medieval scholasticism, arose from the classroom exercises that typified pedagogy in the West from the twelfth century on: debate or disputation.[41] Pitting student against student, sometimes master against master, these debates not only honed skills in logic but also served as the principal vehicle for investigating the issues. Abelard's *Sic et non*, a classroom text for theology, opened the way to the literary appropriation of this initially oral technique, and by the thirteenth century all disciplines, from arts to the higher professional studies, including theology, had accepted the disputational form as standard for the written dissemination of ideas. Collections of questions, sometimes drawn from the schoolroom, sometimes from formal debates between masters, sometimes composed privately in the author's study, dominated the Latin scholarly world.

A typical question began with a statement of a problem or thesis, followed by a list of arguments on one side of the issue and another list in opposition. The core consisted in the determination (*deter-minatio*). Here the master laid out his considered response. At the end usually came a series of shorter answers to arguments from the initial listings that remained unresolved. From the later thirteenth century onward, more complexly structured questions are not uncommon: the initial sets of arguments may include objections and responses (though not the final responses), and there may be an additional round of arguments at the end (*dubitationes additae*), after the initial or "principal" arguments have been dispatched. Great care is sometimes needed to track the author's position.

Gatherings of questions drawn from a master's classroom disputations on a particular topic, in theology most often in conjunction with the required course on Lombard's *Sentences*, were published – offered for public dissemination by university booksellers – as "ordinary questions" (*quaestiones ordinariae*).[42] Scotus's and Ockham's courses on the *Sentences* are major sources for their philosophical as well as theological ideas. The polished revisions of special magisterial debates where questions were posed from the audience about "anything at all" (*quaestiones quodlibetales*) are our chief source for the ideas of such important thinkers as Godfrey of Fontaines and James of Viterbo and are crucial also for our understanding of Henry of Ghent. In the thirteenth century masters would occasionally design their own compilations for a whole field, even one so vast as theology. They come down to us as *summas*, the most celebrated of which is Aquinas's *Summa theologiae*. The fourteenth century witnessed the evolution of several kinds of disputation of exceptional formal rigor, for example those associated with the logical puzzles and the "obligations" mentioned above. Each produced a literary subgenre of a specific type.

In all cases, for questions debated in an actual course or academic exercise, what circulated was not always a revision overseen by the master but sometimes a report (*reportatio*) assembled from the notes of someone in the audience. On this and related matters, see chapter 14 in this volume.

There remain three genres about which a few words are required. The Latin and Greek traditions from early on, and eventually the Arab as well, yielded works devoted simply to natural philosophy. They might be compendia, as Isidore's *Etymologies*, or dialogues, as Adelard's *Natural Questions*. Arab scholars excelled in astronomy and optics, and their works in these fields profoundly influenced science and philosophy of the late medieval and early modern West. Collected letters and sermons, the Christian and Jewish equivalent to the orations of the classical golden age, can be mined for nuggets of philosophical speculation from practically any century in our period. Finally, we must not forget polemics, especially those inspired by political strife.[43] The evolution of government in the high and late medieval West stimulated exceptional demand for such works, many of which implicate matters of moral and political theory still resonant in the modern world.

NOTES

1. See the compelling recent statement of the case by P. Hadot [406]. There is also his *Philosophy as a Way of Life* [407].
2. E. R. Dodds [402] 92.
3. See ibid. 105–8 and P. Brown [66] 90–93.
4. See P. Brown [66] 94–95 on these Platonists and how they influenced Augustine.
5. See ibid. 299–307.
6. Proclus, *Elements of Theology* [381]. Pseudo-Dionysius, *The Complete Works* [78].
7. See A. Cameron [395] and H. J. Blumenthal [393].
8. See recent work on culture in W. A. Goffart [404] and P. Amory [392], and on economy by way of archaeology, in R. Hodges and D. Whitehouse [409].
9. Still the best introduction to this culture of late-Roman, early medieval Europe is P. Riché [421] 139–210 and 266–90.
10. On this, see O. Chadwick [397].
11. On this culture of early western monasticism, see again P. Riché [421] 100–22 and 290–303.
12. See the perennial favorite among medieval Christian readers, *The Life of St. Martin* by the learned Roman stylist, Sulpicius Severus [427]. On Martin as paradigm for a type of Christian prominence, see P. Brown [394] 106–27.
13. W. Levison [414].
14. As R. W. Southern has observed, by the eleventh century the reality of the Benedictine life for monks at the most prestigious of monastic communities, Cluny, was almost entirely absorbed in the routine of common celebration of services in the choir ([425] 160–64). Still the best description of the intellectual and spiritual inclinations of this monastic

culture is by J. Leclercq [413]. For a more recent take on the same subject, see M. Carruthers [396]. See also J. Coleman [399]. All of the latter, however, draw heavily on developments after 1100.

15. For an introduction, see L. White Jr.'s classic *Medieval Technology and Social Change* [431].

16. R. W. Southern [146] 33–35, 40–41.

17. For Anselm's defense of the employment of reason in theological matters as a way of achieving an "understanding" that is "midway between faith and direct vision," see his letter to Pope Urban II at [138] I (II) 39–41, translated in part by G. Schufreider [144] 240–41.

18. See for a start, L. M. de Rijk [471] and G. Nuchelmans [468].

19. Adelard of Bath, *Quaestiones naturales* 1 and 4; trans. R. C. Dales [401] 39–40.

20. M.-D. Chenu [507] 4–18.

21. See R. W. Southern's definitive contribution to the debate in [426] 61–85.

22. Despite his opposition to the new rationalism, Bernard's own writings represent a considerable reorientation of monastic thought toward Augustinian aspirations to wisdom. The presence of these more "philosophical" rhythms in Latin monastic speculation from the twelfth century on is what makes modern studies of western monastic learning – for example, the three mentioned above at the end of note 14 – typically more reliable guides to high than to central medieval monastic sensibilities.

23. See B. Lawn [412] 10–13.

24. See R. I. Moore [420].

25. See selections from the canons of the council in E. Peters [23] 173–78.

26. R. I. Moore [419].

27. See S. P. Marrone [200].

28. A. de Libera [415].

29. For a start on the enormous literature on the condemnations, begin with R. Hissette [408].

30. See A. de Libera [416] as well as K. Ruh [423], R. Imbach [410], and in English, B. McGinn [364].

31. The historiographical story goes back to P. Duhem [510]. For an introduction, see J. Murdoch [528].

32. E. Gilson [403].

33. On rights, see B. Tierney [589] and A. S. Brett [572]. On the mixed constitution, see J. M. Blythe [571].

34. See W. Courtenay [400] 365–68.

35. C. Trinkaus [429].

36. See, for example, Augustine, *The Advantage of Believing* [55]; Aquinas, *ScG* I, cc. 3–6; *ST* IIaIIae, q. 2, a. 9, ad 3. The relationship of natural,

philosophical reasoning to revealed truth is a major theme in philosophy in Islam and in medieval Jewish philosophy, as discussed in chapters 4 and 5 below.

37. See H. de Lubac [417] and B. Smalley [424].

38. This table draws heavily upon the compendium in *CHLMP* 74–79. Attributions and dates for the translations of Ibn Sina and Ibn Gabirol rely on A. Rucquoi [422]. The complex and often uncertain history of translations of Greek philosophy in the Islamic world resists tabulation. See D. Gutas [490], C. d'Ancona Costa [476], G. Endress and J. A. Aertsen [168], F. Rosenthal [496], and J. Kraye *et al.* [18] for guidance.

39. See E. Jeauneau in [36] 117–31.

40. For examples of both literal commentary and commentary in question form, see *CT* II.

41. See C. Viola in [36] 11–30.

42. On the various types of scholastic *quaestio*, consult the chapters by B. C. Bazán, J.-G. Bougerol, J. F. Wippel, and J. E. Murdoch in [36] 31–100; B. C. Bazán *et al.* [37]; and O. Weijers [430].

43. For one subtype, see J. Miethke in [36] 193–211.

2 Two medieval ideas: eternity and hierarchy

Both of the ideas presented in this chapter have roots in late Antique Neoplatonism, but their development is distinctively medieval. Boethius framed a fresh definition of eternity, and if Pseudo-Dionysius the Areopagite did not invent the term *hierarchy*, he put a stamp on the term that was to carry it through many centuries in many contexts. Eternity and hierarchy can be regarded as something like the temporal and ontological coordinates of medieval thought, with eternity embracing all time and hierarchy vertically grading all beings. The two ideas are at any rate both presuppositions and problems for much of what follows in this volume.

ETERNITY (JOHN MARENBON)

What did medieval thinkers mean when they called God "eternal"? We now give two main senses to "eternity": perpetuity ("P-eternity") – when something lacks (Pi) a beginning or (Pii) end or (Piii) both; or ("O-eternity") being altogether outside and unmeasurable by time. Philosophers usually explain O-eternity as "timelessness." Something is timeless, they say, when it is without either extension or position in time, and so no sentences that contain time references of any sort are true of it. On this account, nothing can be both P-eternal and O-eternal, since a P-eternal thing exists at many times (all times in the case of Piii), whereas an O-eternal thing exists at no time.

Medieval philosophers and theologians also talked about eternity, sometimes in the sense of P-eternity and sometimes in the sense of O-eternity. But a number of them thought that God is eternal in both senses: indeed, some even considered that he is O-eternal *because* he is P-eternal. Clearly, then, many medieval philosophers did not understand O-eternity as timelessness – although most of their modern interpreters insist that they did. And there are at least two other surprising elements in the medieval discussion that will baffle unless they are clearly recognized.

First, there was an asymmetry between attitudes toward beginninglessness and those toward endlessness. Angels, human souls, and, indeed, the punishment of the damned were all thought to have beginnings but no ends. Many thinkers, however, took a quite different view about beginninglessness. They were not content merely to accept on authority that all of God's creatures in fact have a beginning: they argued that it was incompatible with being a creature to lack, not just an end, but also a beginning.[1] The view was spelled out by the twelfth-century thinker Richard of St. Victor and frequently cited in the thirteenth century;[2] at the end of the century, Henry of Ghent proposed a sophisticated argument for it.[3] From this point of view, then, Piii-eternity is a way of being metaphysically different from that of other things, and peculiar to God.

Second, time was generally considered to have been created. To medieval thinkers, then, if something began with time, it did not mean that the thing is without a beginning. Of course, it did not have a beginning *in time*. But there is a very strong tendency in the medieval discussions – sometimes made explicit – to think of time as just one species of duration; other species of duration, such as eternity and also aeviternity (the special endless duration of angels), were apparently considered by some as stretching out beyond time, and by others to stand in different and more complicated relationships to time.[4]

Boethius

The treatment of God's eternity by Boethius, a Christian thoroughly familiar with Greek pagan Neoplatonism, was the starting point for most medieval discussions. At first sight, Boethius's analysis seems to show none of the puzzling features mentioned above. Both in *On the Trinity* (§4) and in the *Consolation of Philosophy* (V, pr. 6.2–12),[5] he clearly differentiates the way in which the world, according to the philosophers, has no beginning or ending and "never begins nor ceases to be, and its life is extended along with the infinity of time," from God's eternity, which, in a definition that became classic, is "the whole, perfect and simultaneous possession of un-ending life." There can be no doubt that Boethius is making a clear distinction between P-eternity and the O-eternity that characterizes God's life. But what exactly does Boethius understand by O-eternity? Almost all modern commentators consider that he regards it as time-less eternity,[6] although some acknowledge that it is a richer idea than that of mere lack of temporal extension and position, because it involves life, and even grant that, although timeless, it involves duration.[7] Timeless duration, however, is a difficult concept; some would say an incoherent one.[8]

Boethius's discussion of O-eternity can be interpreted in a less problematic way. Boethius discusses eternity in order to explain God's way of knowing. His description of divine eternity need be taken as no more than an account of how God lives his life and car-ries out his life activity of knowing. To say he is eternal means that he has all his life at once. There is, therefore, no movement or change in his life.

It has been argued that Boethius must have considered divine eter-nity as timeless, because the topology of simultaneous temporal eter-nity is self-contradictory: it requires earlier and later temporal parts to be simultaneous.[9] But Boethius, on the reading proposed here, is describing, not the topology of a special sort of duration, eternity, but God's way of living. One passage does seem at first sight to be comparing the structures of time and eternity: Boethius says that the never-ending motion of temporal things is made up of moments that are each imitations, failed attempts to "fulfill and express" the "ever-present state of unchanging life" which is eternity. But, as this phrasing indicates, Boethius is not talking here about time but about the changing existence of temporal things.

So Boethius may be claiming no more than that everything which happens in God's life happens together, rather than in succession: God's life, then, is a single, indivisible, unchanging act, without end or beginning. On this reading, when Boethius contrasts God's eter-nity with the world's unending duration, he is not denying that di-vine eternity itself endures unendingly, but is pointing out that it has a special characteristic – that of being a life lived wholly simul-taneously – which is not shared by any other everlastingly enduring thing. Many sentences about God that are temporally qualified or tensed will be true, although they will be misleading if the temporal language is taken to mean that God can change in any way.[10]

Anselm

In his *Monologion* (1076), Anselm sets out the problem of God's eternity far more explicitly than Boethius.[11] First (§18), he establishes that God has no beginning or end: since it was always true that something will exist, and will always be true that something existed, truth is without beginning or end, and God is truth. Then Anselm goes on to draw out a paradox. On the one hand, he says (§20), God exists at every time, because everything, including time, depends on him in order to exist at all. Yet, from this position, its contrary can be shown to follow (§21). God has no parts, and so if he exists at all times, he must exist as a whole at all times. It will not be enough for him to exist, as humans do, in a certain sense as a whole but "separately and distinctly" at different times, for in that case he would be broken up into temporal parts – an impossibility for something absolutely simple. But how can he exist properly as a whole at all times, when times themselves are consecutive, not simultaneous (Anselm's version of the topological objection to simultaneous temporal eternity mentioned above)? The only way to preserve divine simplicity is to say that God exists at no time.

Anselm resolves the contradiction by arguing (§22) that God is able to exist properly as a whole at all times, because it is only those things bounded and measured by time that time breaks up into parts. God does indeed exist at every time, but it is better to say that he exists "with time," rather than "in time," because when the phrase "in time" is used of other things, it means that time contains them, whereas in God's case he is not contained by time, but is present at every time. Anselm believes, then, that God's Piii-eternity helps to explain how, though not timeless, he can be O-eternal.

Why does Anselm think that, by lacking temporal beginning and end, God is able to be eternal in this special, simultaneous way, especially since he has noticed the topological objection to such simultaneity without timelessness?[12] To say that God is not bounded by time means at least that no moment of time is God's first or last moment. Anselm considers that time measures things by bounding them. It cannot bound, and so cannot measure, something that has no first or last moment. Time's failure to act as a metric for eternity seems, in Anselm's view, to have topological consequences: divine eternity, he considers, will lack the topological structure of successive moments shared by all things that time bounds. God, then, is sufficiently different from temporal things to be able to live his life simultaneously, but without being timeless.[13]

The early thirteenth century

Two of the fullest discussions of eternity from the early thirteenth-century University of Paris are those in the *Summa Fratris Alexandri* (*SFA*), compiled in 1236–45 by the Franciscan pupils of Alexander of Hales,[14] and in the *Summa de bono* of Philip the Chancellor (d. 1236).[15]

SFA borrows a great deal from Anselm's *Monologion*, but it adds the idea (mem. 1, cap. 1, a. 2; §57) that there is a series of different sorts of durations, ranging from eternity to time. God's eternity has neither beginning nor end, nor is it changeable; the aeviternity of the angels has a beginning but no end, and it is not changeable; time has a beginning, it has no end from itself but it will be ended by another (God), and it is changeable. This series can be used to establish a degree of common meaning between "eternal" used of God and used of, for instance, the punishments of hell. Clearly, then, although *SFA* considers that there is more to God's eternity than just lacking beginning and end, it is working from the idea of it being some sort of P-eternity with extra conditions, in particular unchangingness. Like Anselm, *SFA* is both unwilling to give up God's omnitemporality (mem. 4, q. unic., §71), and yet does not think that omnitemporality tells the full, or even the most important, story.[16] At moments, *SFA* moves toward defining eternity as a duration of a different sort from time: lacking in succession (mem. 1, cap. 3, ad. 4; §59) and distinguishable from time, even were time infinite in both directions, because it is an unmoving state of ever-presentness.

Philip's rather briefer treatment is more definite in bringing out the idea of eternity as duration, like time, but of a quite different sort (yet not timeless). Philip considers that the two durations, time and eternity, are together (*simul*), although one is contained by the other. But on this view, time seems to be equal to a part of eternity, and so, by using time as a measure many – perhaps infinitely many – times, will it not be possible to measure out eternity? And, since stretches of time make up nothing other than time, time will be equal to (the whole of) eternity. Philip offers two different responses. On the first, which has similarities with Anselm's approach, he argues that even if time were stretched out infinitely (presumably by multiplying it), it would extend without limit only into the future, whereas eternity has no beginning. On the second, Philip allows that time might be infinite in both directions and so it might be *equal* to eternity, but it would still not be the *same* as eternity. Time is a succession and is divided into parts, whereas eternity is without parts and succession. Philip offers a further explanation of how the two sorts of duration are related. The now of the present moment, considered in itself, without the preceding and following nows, is "a part of eternity or eternity": "remaining in itself" it produces eternity, but with its preceding and following nows it makes time. Overall, Philip seems to view time and eternity as two concurrent durations, different in their topology. Although God exists in eternity, not time, Philip's view allows temporal statements to be true of God, so long as they do not imply any change in him.

Do such views make sense? The idea that there are different sorts of duration is not far distant (vocabulary apart) from the notion of dis-unified time entertained by some modern philosophers.[17] But there are further problems. The multiple time streams of modern philoso-phers are all timelike in their topology, by contrast with thirteenth-century thinkers' eternity. And it is hard to see how their concept of eternity does not entail that God is timeless, although they clearly do not think he is.

Aquinas and Albert the Great

In Aquinas's treatment of eternity – brought most fully together in q. 10 of the first part of his *Summa theologiae* – the tension is even greater than in the early thirteenth-century accounts. By changes in emphasis from these earlier accounts, he presents the topology of eternity in such a way that eternity might well be considered time-less duration;[18] yet some passages indicate that he does not consider it timeless.

Like *SFA* and Philip, Aquinas (a. 4) accepts that one difference be-tween time and eternity is that time has a beginning and end, whereas eternity has neither, but he goes on to explain that this difference is accidental. His views on the eternity of the world required him to make such a qualification. By the time of his maturity, Aquinas

held that God could have created a world that lacked temporal beginning (and that he could have created things that lacked beginning
and end – cf. a. 5). He could not, therefore, make lack of beginning
and end the distinctive feature of divine eternity. Rather, he looks to
the other characteristic brought forward by Philip, the lack of succession, to distinguish God's eternity from any sort of time, even
everlasting. Eternity is (as Boethius said) "all at once" (*tota simul*);
there is (a. 1; a. 5) no ordering of earlier to later in it. Although there
are passages where Aquinas, like the earlier writers, envisages eternity as stretching out beyond time, he places more emphasis on the
idea that eternity is "all entirely at once." The suggestion seems to
be that eternity is unextended, and it is reinforced by the famous passage in the *Summa contra Gentiles* (I 66), where Aquinas compares
eternity to a point at the center of a circle, and time to the circle's
circumference.

It would be tempting, therefore, to conclude that Aquinas thought
of eternity as timeless. But there are parts of this discussion that
make it hard to draw this conclusion. Consider, for example, how
he explains why the Bible refers to God using temporal language.
"Words referring to various different times are attributed to God,"
he explains (a. 2, ad 4), "insofar as his eternity includes all times,
not because he himself varies according to past, present and future."
The first part of this reply seems to make God exist at all times (not
at none), and the second shows why he thinks temporal language
misleads about God: *not* because he is timeless, but because he is
immutable and such language suggests that he changes from one
time to another.[19] In his late *Summa theologiae* (c. 1270),[20] Aquinas's
former teacher, Albert the Great, comes nearer to proposing divine
eternity as timeless. Considered in itself, eternity is just God's never-
beginning and never-ending existence. There is indeed another aspect
of it: infinite extension into the past and the future. But this aspect
is merely in the mind of those who think about God's eternity. As
Albert puts it:

Eternity is called a duration and a span not because the substance and the
what of eternity is extended, but because of the extension of the soul, which
extends itself unfailingly and excellingly above all duration that is beneath
it. And so eternity is not divided according to substance and parts that are
in eternity itself, but according to the substance and parts that are in the
things beneath it that have duration. (cap. 1, a. 1, ad 1)

Albert thus strips divine eternity itself of any temporal or quasitemporal characteristics, while providing through his psychological account the links to the world of time that every medieval author seems to have found necessary.[21]

Timelessness and the Problem of Prescience

Medieval discussion of God's eternity was often linked to the "Problem of Prescience." God is omniscient, and so he must know future events as well as past and present ones. But this knowledge seems to determine the future, so that there are no future contingent events. If God knows already now that I shall go to the opera tomorrow, then it seems that I will have no choice tomorrow over whether I do or do not go: for how could I, by spending the evening at home, make God's knowledge into a false belief?

The most obvious way of formulating this idea more strictly is to say that, since as a matter of definition what is known is true, then

(1) If God knows e will happen, then e will happen necessarily.

(1), however, is a logical blunder. All that we are entitled to assert is

(2) Necessarily: if God knows e will happen, then e will happen.

(2), however, is perfectly consistent with there being contingent future events. So, is the Problem of Prescience merely the result of a logical confusion? No: the intuition on which it is based is sound, but the logical form in which it is expressed needs to capture the point that God's knowledge *comes before* the event known. Suppose (2) is adjusted to read:

(3) Necessarily: if God knew e will happen, then e will happen.

Not only is the antecedent of (3) ("God knew e will happen") true for any event e, but since it is about a past event, it is *necessarily* true, in the sense (called "accidental necessity") that what has happened cannot be altered. We can, then, assert

(4) Necessarily, God knew e will happen.

Most modal logics hold that, from "Necessarily, if p then q," and "Necessarily p," there follows "Necessarily q." And so (3) and (4) do seem to entail

(5) *e* will happen necessarily.

The argument (3–5), the "accidental necessity argument," is the most cogent way of presenting the Problem of Prescience. God's timelessness provides a neat way to avoid it. If God is timeless (in the strict sense, according to which no temporal or tensed sentence is true of God), then God's knowing that *e* will happen is not a past event and so it is not accidentally necessary: (4) is false and so the accidental necessity argument fails. Modern philosophers of religion usually call this way of tackling the Problem of Prescience the "Boethian solution," and they regard Aquinas as one of its followers. If Boethius and Aquinas really did tackle the accidental necessity argument in this way, then – despite what was argued above – they must have considered God's eternity to be timeless.

In fact, although both thinkers use their view of divine eternity to resolve the problem of prescience, neither of them appeals to God's timelessness. Boethius's own formulation of the Problem of Prescience is along the lines of (1) and, although he has an intuitive idea that there is a deeper difficulty, arguably he never notices the logical error in (1).[22]

When Boethius looks to the idea of divine eternity, he is not answering the accidental necessity argument. Rather, he is trying to explain how future events can have the necessity needed in order to be known and yet be open in such a way that human agents can freely will to perform one course of action or another. Our knowledge of *present* events, he argues, is necessary in precisely this way. On the Aristotelian view of necessity, what is happening is necessary when it is happening, and so knowledge of the present has necessary events for its object. But no one believes that this knowledge constrains the events or limits their agents' freedom. Boethius then points out that, because God's way of knowing all events, in his eternal present, is like our way of knowing present events, his knowledge of events that, to us, are future will have the characteristics of our knowledge of present events: the events will be necessary in relation to God as their knower, but not in a way that constrains their outcome and removes human freedom.

Aquinas, by contrast, knew the accidental necessity argument and answered it explicitly.[23] Had he held that God is timeless, he would have had an easy way of responding to it. In fact, he chooses to answer it in quite a different way, far closer to Boethius's. Rather than rejecting (4), Aquinas concedes

(5) If God knew that *e* will happen, *e* will happen necessarily.

But then he claims that where "something about cognition is signified in the antecedent, it is necessary that the consequent is taken according to how the knower is, not according to how the thing known is." By this principle, he says, the necessity of *e* is just the type of nonconstraining necessity Boethius had in mind. Aquinas's argument for the principle is a convoluted and rather unconvincing one. It would have been extraordinary for Aquinas, had he held God to be timeless, to have appealed to this uncertain reasoning, when a simple way of rebutting the accidental necessity argument was open to him. Aquinas's treatment of the Problem of Prescience is, therefore, another strong piece of evidence that he did not consider divine eternity timeless.

HIERARCHY (D. E. LUSCOMBE)

The idea of hierarchy supported medieval visions of order in the universe by assuring some or even every form of being – transcendent, intelligible, and material – a particular position and an appropriate function. Although it was often used to support a broader conception, that of "the great chain of being," hierarchy is a distinct idea with its own particular range of references.[24] Its niche was determined by its principal source and authority, Pseudo-Dionysius the Areopagite (Denis the pseudo-Areopagite). Hierarchy offered a model derived from the ordering of the celestial world where purely spiritual beings were arranged in orders. It signified the graduated manifestation of God to the universe of spirits and their assimilation to God. Denis, writing around the year 500 and using a pseudonym to link him with St. Paul at Athens (Acts 17:34), defined the term in *Celestial Hierarchy* III 1: "Hierarchy, to me, is sacred order, knowledge, and activity assimilating itself, as far as it can, to the likeness of God, and raising itself to its utmost, by means of the illuminations granted by God, to the imitation of God."[25] He then set forth two hierarchies, one that is celestial or angelic and which provides the exemplar for the other, which is ecclesiastical and human.[26]

Denis portrayed the harmonious angelic hierarchy as a magnificent, vertical arrangement of nine orders divided into three superimposed triads according to their levels of knowledge and purity and of participation in God's secrets and goodness. Each triad and within it each order mediates purification, illumination, and perfection between the order above and the order below. The process is both a descending and an ascending one, a going out and a coming back, as spirits are brought closer to God through their purification, illumination, and perfecting by the higher orders. The measure of the resemblance of spirits to God – their deiformity – is the *order* they occupy in the hierarchy. For the division of the angels into groups of three, Denis claimed the authority of a certain Hierotheus (otherwise unknown),[27] but Proclus (d. *c.* 485) had already assimilated the pagan gods into triads communicating light and knowledge to each other; Denis adapted this in effect and presented three triads of orders of angels. He also presented two triads of orders of human beings, with bishops occupying the highest grade and communicating directly with the lowest order of angels above:

The celestial hierarchy[28]
Seraphim
Cherubim
Thrones

Dominations
Virtues
Powers

Principalities
Archangels
Angels

The ecclesiastical hierarchy[29]
Bishops
Priests
Ministers

Monks
Holy people
Purified orders

Each order communicates directly with the order above and with the order below. All the orders spring from God directly; higher orders do not produce subordinate orders. But within each triad, the *activity* of purifying, illuminating, and perfecting is the task, respectively, of the lowest, middle and highest order. All, save the lowest order of the ecclesiastical hierarchy, work to convert to God the orders below by helping them to conform as fully as possible to the order above, which is more deiform. Hierarchic activity is a process of mediation. Every divine intervention in history – such as the gift of the Law to Moses, the purifying of the lips of Isaiah, and the Annunciation of the birth of Christ – was mediated to people on earth through the angelic hierarchy. *Knowledge* of Thearchy (the rule of God) is likewise mediated through the orders, the function of hierarchy being to bring God out of his silence and to reveal what is obscure, thus leading the lower orders to union with God. Angels receive illumination instantly and intuitively. The ecclesiastical hierarchy shares in their intellectual contemplations but grasps divine knowledge in fragments and in stages, with the assistance of material, sacramental things. The ecclesiastical hierarchy was constructed by Denis in the light of the historical reality of the church in the fourth and fifth centuries. The first triad includes the initiators: the bishop, who is purified, illuminated, and perfected by angels and transmits purification, illumination, and perfection to the order of priests, who in turn communicate these to ministers (porters, lectors, acolytes, exorcists). Hence they come to the second triad of the initiates: first to monks, then to the holy people, and finally to the purified orders (penitents, energumens, and catechumens).

From Gregory the Great to William of Auvergne

Pope Gregory the Great (d. 604) presented the nine celestial choirs of angels in his *Moralia* on Job, and in Book II of his thirty-fourth *Homily on the Gospels* he makes reference to Denis the Areopagite. Unlike Denis, Gregory is lucid and uncomplicated in describing the mission of angels to God, the universe, and the human race. The human race, he wrote influentially, when it is raised to heaven in the next life, will form a tenth choir and thereby will remedy the losses that followed the revolt and fall of those angels who defected to Lucifer. Denis's writings circulated among the clergy and the religious in Byzantium,[30] and translations were made into Syriac, Armenian, and Arabic. Although his works were translated into Latin by 835,[31] they were cited in the West only rarely before the twelfth century. Gregory the Great's teaching on angels dominated. An exception, however, is provided by Hincmar, archbishop of Rheims from 845. Drawing upon the *Celestial Hierarchy* to emphasize his superiority to a bishop, Hincmar produced one of the most powerful of all medieval statements about authority and subjection. He portrayed the church as a single, divine institution consisting of both angels and human beings who are divided into different orders or, as he also called them, paternities. Inequality is as necessary a fact of life for human beings as it is for angels. Angels and human beings are each equal by nature but they are not equal in power or order. Just as in heaven angels both minister and assist, on earth too the ecclesiastical hierarchy acts in like manner: archbishops minister to bishops and bishops assist archbishops. Hincmar has adjusted the scheme of the ecclesiastical hierarchy set forth by Denis, but his argument gains in importance through being placed within a universal frame because, as Gregory the Great had written, "The universe could not subsist by any other reason than because a great order of difference conserves it."[32]

This particular way of reasoning reappeared but infrequently until the revival of interest in the thought of Eriugena evident in the writings of Honorius Augustodunensis (early twelfth century)[33] and of subsequent authors, including Hugh of St. Victor (d. 1142), who wrote an influential commentary on the *Celestial Hierarchy*.[34] Book I of this commentary sets forth Hugh's understanding of the difference between natural and divine theology. Created nature provides knowledge of God but by means of signs; grace alone, mediated to creatures by the angels, gives divine illuminations or theophanies, and the hierarchies lead human beings back to God: "By these hierarchies or sacred powers the whole world is governed."[35] Theophany, as Chenu observed,[36] is a mark of Latin Areopagitism in the twelfth century; the mysterious manifestations in this world of the unknowable, hidden God are achieved by the hierarchies. A small collection of definitions circulating in the late twelfth century helped to disseminate the notion, distinguishing three hierarchies – supercelestial, celestial, and subcelestial – and three angelic theophanies – epiphany, hyperphany, and hypophany.[37]

In the writings of Alan of Lille and of William of Auvergne detailed, luxurious descriptions of the hierarchies blossomed. Alan (d. 1203), in a work called *Hierarchia*, commented on the collection of definitions mentioned above. He defined hierarchy as lordship (*dominium*). Following Gregory the Great, Alan wrote that humankind had been created to fill the gap left by the fall from heaven of the bad angels. Alan watered down the elevated ideas of Denis by using imagery that was more popular and more readily understood. He described the specific functions of angels in relation to the different types of human beings who will, after receiving appropriate angelic tuition, join the angelic order that most suitably corresponds to their condition. To each of the nine orders of angels there corresponds an order of men and an antiorder of demons, nine in each. The orders of the human hierarchy are: (1) contemplatives, (2) students of Scripture, (3) judges, (4) and (5) rulers, (6) defenders against diabolic temptations, (7) miracle workers, (8) major preachers, and (9) lesser preachers and teachers. The somewhat vague imagery is taken from the contemporary world.[38]

With William of Auvergne, the university master who became bishop of Paris in 1228, the idea of hierarchy became politicized. William wrote a vast encyclopedia embracing knowledge of the Trinity, the universe of spirits and of humankind, of planets, stars, and the elements, as well as of the realms of faith, law, sacraments, virtues, and vices. William was an enthusiast and an optimist. He loved the beauty and magnificence of the universe. In the second of the seven treatises of which his encyclopedia – *Magisterium divinale sive sapientiale* – is composed (*De universo*) he described the "universe of creatures." He wrote of heaven as a kingdom that enjoys peace and which has many and varied orders of ministers who preside over the nations on earth. William tells us that when he was young he had the idea of comparing the ranks of angels with those of a well-ordered earthly kingdom. He was apparently much influenced by Alan's scheme of nine orders in heaven, nine on earth, and nine in hell. But he went further. William compared the nine orders of angels not only with the *clerus*, the ecclesiastical hierarchy, but also with the offices found in a secular kingdom. He portrayed the church, too, as a well-ordered kingdom following the model of a secular monarchy as well as of a celestial monarchy. Remarkably, William does not present the earthly, secular hierarchy as a reflection of the ecclesiastical hierarchy and subordinate to it. The holders of secular office directly reflect the tasks of the heavenly court and kingdom. William privileges the state: its offices are modeled upon the orders in the city of the angels. In addition, William reports that some philosophers have sought to assimilate the Avicennian doctrine of the Intelligences – eight of them moving the heavens, the ninth being the agent intellect – into Christian angelology; the divine ideas or the intelligible reasons of creatures are transmitted through the angelic theophanies.[39]

The later Middle Ages: criticism and change[40]

The way was now open to construct ecclesiastical and secular hierarchies to express personal views of how earthly hierarchies do or should reflect the celestial exemplar. William, for example, excluded friars from the ecclesiastical hierarchy; friars retaliated vigorously on clerics who denied them a due place and role in the ecclesiastical hierarchy. Vigorous quarrels occurred during the 1250s (and, indeed, for centuries to come).[41] One great champion of the friars was Bonaventure, from 1257 minister-general of the Franciscans. Like William of Auvergne, Bonaventure applied the conception of hierarchy to the whole universe – to the divine Trinity, the planets, the individual human soul, and much else, and, like William, he analyzed in fine detail the correspondences between each and every hierarchy.[42] Bonaventure grasped the idea that the divine Trinity – itself a hierarchy but of three equal persons in one God[43] – impresses its triune character upon the angelic hierarchy so as to assimilate it and to make it resemble God. Likewise, the angelic orders impress their hierarchic features upon the church militant, that is, the church in this world. This is the procession (*processus*) or descent from the Trinity through the angels to the world of humanity. In return there is what he calls a "reduction" or an ascent of creatures to God. Human beings are purified, enlightened, and perfected by the ecclesiastical hierarchy led by the prelates of the church. But within the church Bonaventure distinguished between an active, prelatical hierarchy and a higher, contemplative one – an outer and an inner hierarchy. He also sees hierarchy as evolving or unfolding in the course of history.[44] Above the prelates are those who have arrived at a higher state of contemplation. These are the members of the religious orders: Cistercian monks and Premonstratensian canons, then above them Franciscan and Dominican friars, and finally perfect contemplatives such as St. Francis of Assisi himself. Ultimately, the pope could use the members of this contemplative hierarchy to override the active hierarchy led by bishops.

One of the most contested documents in the entire history of the ideological relationship between clerical and lay power was the papal bull of Boniface VIII in 1302 – the bull known from its opening words in Latin as *Unam sanctam*. Boniface declared that every human being is subject to the pope as the chief intermediary with God. The role of intermediaries was of paramount importance: "For according to Saint Denis the law of divinity is to lead the lowest through the intermediate to the highest things. According to the law of the universe, therefore, all things are reduced to order, not equally and immediately, but the lowest through the intermediate, the intermediate through the higher."[45] This reflects the views of Giles of Rome who, in his *De ecclesiastica potestate* (1300–2), wrote about hierarchy and tripartite division as being the law of the universe.[46]

By the time that Giles wrote, however, the fashion for modeling the ecclesiastical upon the celestial hierarchy had received a severe knock from Thomas Aquinas. Thomas accepted that the universe consists of orders of unequal beings, the highest level of being in a lower genus being the participant in the lowest level of being in the immediately higher genus.[47] And he accepted that hierarchy was a universal fact: no multitude of beings will be well arranged if it is not divided into orders possessing different functions, nor will it be well arranged unless higher beings use intermediate beings to bring lower beings to union with God.[48] Lower than the angels as human beings are, Aquinas emphasized some essential differences between them: the latter are not simply miniature, incarnate versions of the former, each possessing the soul of an angel and the body of an animal. The orders of angels differ not only in the divine grace that they receive, but also in nature. Human beings, on the other hand, although they too differ in the divine grace that they receive, are all equal by nature. No angel-like hierarchy among human beings can be constructed on the basis of human nature (because of the fundamental equality of human nature) or upon the basis of divine grace (because to human beings such grace is invisible in its reception). In practice the hierarchy of the church militant is constituted not by levels of grace or of personal holiness (which are invisible) but by levels of public power, juridical as well as sacramental. Human hierarchy cannot imitate celestial hierarchy in all things.[49] As for a supercelestial hierarchy – that of the divine Trinity – Aquinas rejected it: no divine person possesses rule (*principatus*) over another, nor was this the doctrine of Denis.[50] Moreover, Aquinas challenged the Dionysian idea that angels are essential intermediaries between humankind and God. God can enlighten any created intellect directly. The principal mediator is Christ himself. Within angelic society angels can enlighten lower grades only by passing this enlightenment from one order to another according to a strict hierarchy; but within human society any enlightened person may transmit his enlightenment to anyone else.[51]

Aquinas's doubts made a great impression upon some later writers, who focused upon their implications for the role of spiritual authority as the intermediary between lay power and God and who denied that the ecclesiastical hierarchy possessed temporal authority, that secular society is modeled upon a celestial exemplar, and that laymen and kings are subject to the pope even in temporal matters. Insofar as men do resemble angels, the celestial hierarchy is their model, but angels are not physical beings, nor do they live in time, so the organization of their society does not provide a model for the organization of human society in physical space and time. John of Paris is a notable exponent of these lines of criticism: John saw laypeople occupying the lowest order in the church but, guided by Aristotle's *Politics*, he also wrote that the natural and civil order that they also create is separate from the spiritual order provided in the ecclesiastical hierarchy and is not, in civil matters, subject to it.[52]

Henceforth, there were growing disagreements about the implications of the conception of hierarchy. In general, popes insisted upon the role of mediators – be they priests or angels – in the work of bringing people back to God and in bringing God to people. But there also developed what one may call the "Lucifer problem" and which was put by John Wyclif. Wyclif broadly accepted traditional theories of hierarchy. But in his book on *The Church* (*De ecclesia*, 1378) he wrestled with the problem of corruption within the priestly hierarchy. He did not believe that the members of a hierarchy are unconditionally entitled to remain members of their order. Lucifer and the bad angels had conflicted with Michael and the good angels and had as a result been cast out from the angelic hierarchy, thereby losing their power to purify and enlighten others. Surely, therefore, clergy, if they lose the power to purify and to enlighten others, should be cast out from the ecclesiastical hierarchy and become subject to laymen. Wyclif was here taking further an argument in support of resistance in the name of hierarchy that had first been presented by Robert Grosseteste in 1253 on the occasion when he refused to admit the nephew of Pope Innocent IV to a canonry at Lincoln cathedral: "No faithful subject of the Holy See," wrote Grosseteste, "can submit to mandates, precepts, or any other demonstrations of this kind, no, not even if the author were the most high body of angels."[53]

It would be easy to multiply examples of debates in the later Middle Ages in which hierarchical schemes were adjusted to suit the objectives of their supporters. Most notably, in the quarrels between the mendicant friars and the secular clergy and between the supporters of conciliarism and those of papal monarchy, there were repeated, frequent appeals to Denis's treatises on hierarchy – but in opposing directions, depending on which ideology was being canvassed or criticized.[54] In the fifteenth and sixteenth centuries hostility to such discourse was expressed. Around 1455 Lorenzo Valla expressed reservations concerning the claim of Denis to be a contemporary and disciple of St. Paul; these gained the support of Erasmus and others in the following century. The doubters were heavily outnumbered both then and in centuries to come by the believers in Denis's claims. Renaissance Platonists such as Bessarion, Marsilio Ficino, and Pico della Mirandola showed enthusiasm for Denis's Platonism, and John Colet explored his two treatises on hierarchy. But Martin Luther objected to the dreamlike curiosities that he found: "To accord so much credit to this Dionysius, whoever he was, altogether displeases me, for there is virtually no sound learning in him."[55] Luther thought that he could construct a better scheme of ecclesiastical hierarchy than Denis had done simply by putting in the pope, the cardinals, and the archbishops above the bishops who occupied the top position in Denis's work. This is exactly what supporters of papal monarchy had done very frequently, and perhaps Luther had his tongue in his cheek as he wrote. Calvin also dismissed the *Celestial Hierarchy* as "for the most part nothing but talk" and denied that there was any basis "to philosophize subtly over a comparison of the heavenly and earthly hierarchies."[56]

On balance, in spite of all controversies, hierarchy enriched medieval visions of a stable, permanent, dynamic, articulated structure in the church and in society at large, visions that reflected and mirrored the eternal structure of the angelic society and of the angelic orders in Heaven. The conception of hierarchy *stricto sensu*, that is, as it is found in the treatises of Denis the pseudo-Areopagite, was widely and increasingly regarded as a necessary point of reference from the twelfth century. It had to be accommodated and brought round to the point where it supported a vision of why structures exist and of what structures should exist. The trouble, of course, was disagreements about the latter. So the conception of hierarchy was tugged in conflicting directions ingeniously, polemically, and flexibly in writings on evangelical poverty, on papal provisions to ecclesiastical benefices, on the exemption of monasteries from episcopal jurisdiction, on Angevin rule in the kingdom of Sicily, on the dispute between King Philip the Fair and Pope Boniface VIII, on the Great Schism of the papacy in the fourteenth century, on Lollardy, and on the Hussite movement in Bohemia. Arguments based on the celestial exemplar were found and, indeed, had to be found in the course of almost all debate among philosophers as well as theologians about the later medieval church.

NOTES

The first part of this chapter, on eternity, is by John Marenbon. The second part, on hierarchy, is by D. E. Luscombe.

1. The dispute centered on whether or not the world could have been created by God without a beginning. For a thorough survey, see R. Dales [433]; and for an analysis of the arguments, see R. Sorabji [438] 193–252. Most thinkers believed that there could be nothing that lacks a beginning but has an end.

2. See, e.g., *Summa Fratris Alexandri* I, Inq. 1, tract. 2, q. 4, mem. 1, cap. 4 [358] 89 (§60), quoting from Richard of St. Victor, *De Trinitate* 6, 8, 11; *PL* 196, 894ff.

3. No creature exists through itself. If something always exists, then (on an Aristotelian view of modality) it exists necessarily, and so exists of itself: Henry of Ghent, *Quodlibet* I [219] V, especially 39.4–42.67.

4. This important point is well made by R. Fox [434].

5. *De Trinitate*, in [84] 175.231–176.248, 155.5–156.51. The quotations that follow are from the passage in the *Consolation*.

6. See R. Sorabji [438] 115–16 and 119–20 for a good defense of the standard view.
7. E. Stump and N. Kretzmann [439]; and see their later [440]. Their views are defended (with modifications) in B. Leftow [435] 112–46.
8. But see below, on nontemporal duration in the thirteenth century.
9. B. Leftow [435] 115.
10. See J. Marenbon [88] 172–73.
11. Chapters 18–24. I omit in my account Anselm's treatment of God and place, which is alongside the discussion of God and time.
12. In the fullest and best investigation yet of Anselm's concept of eternity, B. Leftow ([435] 183–216, especially 203–09) answers this question by appealing to Anselm's view that God is better described as "justice" than "just," "truth" than "true," and so on. But this answer is not Anselm's, though it may well be Anselmian.
13. Anselm also discusses God's eternity in his *Proslogion* (chs. 18–22) and his *On the Harmony between God's foreknowledge, predestination and grace with free will* (I 5). Although in these accounts he emphasizes the senses in which God is *not* in time, they do not show a fundamentally different position from that in the *Monologion*.
14. I, Inq. 1, Tract. 2, q. 4 [358] 84–111 (§§56–71).
15. *Summa de bono* I, q. 4 [379] 52–54.
16. Writing a little later than the *SFA*, probably in the 1250s, Robert Kilwardby shows an even greater reliance on the *Monologion* and a wish to stress God's omnitemporality: see [372] §§133–43.
17. As R. Fox [434] points out; a good introduction to the modern debate is given in W. Newton-Smith [436] 79–95 and M. MacBeath [437].
18. Most modern commentators say that Aquinas thought eternity timeless (see, e.g., W. L. Craig [432], M. M. Adams [318], and C. Hughes [242]). Stump and Kretzmann apply their idea of timeless duration to Aquinas as well as Boethius, and it *does* help to explain much, though not all, in Aquinas's conception.
19. R. Fox [434] is one of the very few authors to argue through the case that for Aquinas divine eternity is not timeless. He points especially to Aquinas's need of God's presence to time in order to sustain all things, and to affirm the analogous relationship between time and eternity.
20. Tract. 5, q. 23 [203].
21. Space does not permit discussion of eternity and timelessness in the later Middle Ages. The standard scholarly view is that ideas about timeless eternity became less important and widely accepted, perhaps from the time of Duns Scotus (but see R. Cross [292]) and certainly from the time of Ockham: see W. L. Craig [432] 129–33 and M. M. Adams [318]

1137–38. But, if the view proposed here is correct, then the fourteenth-century thinkers will be exhibiting more continuity with their predecessors than has been believed.

22. See J. Marenbon [88] 162–64 and [87].

23. I *Sent.*, d. 38, q. 1, a. 5, ad 4; *ST* I, q. 14, a. 13, ad 2; *On Truth*, q. 2, a. 12, ad 7.

24. A. O. Lovejoy, in his classic work on the broader idea [447] has very little to say about medieval notions of hierarchy; see E. P. Mahoney [451]. On levels of being in Neoplatonism see D. J. O'Meara [453]. For the development by medieval Christian thinkers of the idea that the closer creatures are to the likeness of God the higher is their being, see especially E. P. Mahoney [452, 451, 80]. On degrees of being in Aquinas's "third way" of demonstrating the existence of God, see chapter 6 below.

25. *Celestial Hierarchy* [79] 87; *PG* 3, 164D.

26. In the New Testament angels and wicked spirits figure prominently as manifestations of God or of the Devil; different names were used of the former. See Colossians 1:16 and Ephesians 1:21; 9 (thrones, dominations, principalities, powers, virtues). Also Isaiah 6:2 (Seraphim) and Ezekiel 1:14–24; 10:4–22 (Cherubim). Denis was also deeply influenced by late Antique Neoplatonists such as Proclus and his precursors, Plotinus, Porphyry, and Iamblichus – although most of Denis's medieval readers were unaware of these sources. During the fourth century, Christian angelology and Neoplatonic philosophy had drawn closer together. Marius Victorinus situated four classes of angels in the intelligible, supercelestial world (archangels, angels, thrones, and glories) and also situated angels in the material world, along with gods and demons (P. Hadot [446]). Gregory of Nyssa identified the intelligible world as the city of the angels to which human souls, through contemplating supernatural goodness, may be admitted (J. Daniélou [444], part 2, ch. 2, "La cité des anges").

27. *Celestial Hierarchy* [79] 104; *PG* 3, 200D.

28. *Celestial Hierarchy* 7–9.

29. *Ecclesiastical Hierarchy* 5–6.

30. See A. Wenger [83] for modifications by Nicetas Stethatos in the eleventh century.

31. By Hilduin the abbot of Saint-Denis. His version was twice revised by Scottus Eriugena. G. Théry [82]. The medieval Latin translations of Denis's works are collected in *Dionysiaca* [77]. For the complete edition of Eriugena's commentary on the *Celestial Hierarchy* see J. Barbet, ed., *Iohannis Scoti Eriugenae Expositiones in Ierarchiam Coelestem* (Turnhout, 1975).

32. *Opusculum LV capitulorum*, *PL* 126, 282–494, especially chs. 11–15. Cf. W. Ullmann [454] 114–16.

33. M.-T. D'Alverny [441] and J. A. Endres [445] 64–69, 140–45.
34. *PL* 175, 923–1154. Cf. D. E. Luscombe [155].
35. I, 5, *PL* 175, 931CD; I, 2, *PL* 175, 927C–930B.
36. M.-D. Chenu, *La Théologie au douzième siècle* (Paris, 1957), 304–05; see also Chenu [507] 80–85.
37. H. F. Dondaine, *RTAM* 17 (1950), 303–11. M.-T. D'Alverny [357] 94–99 cautiously attributed these definitions to Alan of Lille.
38. *Hierarchia* [357] 223–35; *Expositio prosae de angelis*, 206–10; *Sermo in die sancti Michaelis*, 249–51.
39. *De universo*, II, ii, ch. 112 [391] 908. Cf. H. Corbin [122] 101–17.
40. Cf. D. E. Luscombe [448].
41. The classic study of these fights is Y. M.-J. Congar [443].
42. *Collationes in Hexäemeron*, in [211] V 327–454, [212]. Cf. J. G. Bougerol [216].
43. *Collationes in Hexäemeron* [212] *Visio IV, coll.* II (spoken version); [211] V 431–37 (enlarged reported version).
44. *Apologia pauperum*, XII 10 [211] VIII 319.
45. For the early development of the maxim *lex divinitatis est inferiora per media, et media per superiora reducere* in the writings of Bonaventure see J. G. Bougerol [217] 70. Also D. E. Luscombe [449].
46. *On Ecclesiastical Power*, especially II 13 [270].
47. *ScG* II 68.
48. *ST* I, q. 108, a. 2; q. 106, a. 3; *Contra impugnantes Dei cultum et religionem* 4 [224] XLIA.
49. II *Sent.*, d. 9, q. 1, a. 7.
50. II *Sent.*, d. 9, q. 1, a. 1.
51. *ST* I, q. 117, a. 2. Cf. D. E. Luscombe [248].
52. *On Royal and Papal Power*, written in 1302/03.
53. Grosseteste, *Epist.* 128 [194] 432–37. On Wyclif, see D. E. Luscombe [353].
54. The debates between supporters of conciliarism and of papal monarchy during the fourteenth and fifteenth centuries often revolved around interpretations of hierarchy. See especially A. Black [569]. Important contributions include the *Catholic Concordance* of Nicholas of Cusa [613].
55. Martin Luther, *The Babylonian Captivity of the Church*, 1520. *Ordinatio* [450] 109–10.
56. John Calvin, *Institutes of the Christian Religion* I 14, IV 6 [442] I 164–65, II IIII.

3   Language and logic

It is impossible to overestimate the importance of the study of language and logic for the understanding of medieval philosophers and theologians. Many of the subjects discussed by grammarians and logicians are of interest in themselves and have an obvious relevance to theological and scientific problems, but at a deeper level, all the writing and thinking of the period is permeated by a technical vocabulary, techniques of analysis, and inferential strategies drawn from the basic training in the liberal arts that every medieval student received. The nature of this training reveals two important features of medieval education. On the one hand, thinkers focused on authoritative texts – the Bible, the works of Aristotle and Augustine, Priscian's *Institutiones grammaticae*, Peter Lombard's *Sentences* – and the attempt to reconcile and reinterpret these authorities lies behind many developments. On the other hand, the method of teaching was largely oral, and this influenced written expression in many ways, from the philosophical dialogues of Augustine and Anselm to the highly structured disputational presentation of Aquinas's *Summa theologiae*.

One cannot capture the richness and complexity of medieval theories of language and logic in a short chapter.[1] In what follows I shall first give a brief overview and then focus on a few principal themes.

SOURCES AND DEVELOPMENTS

The shape of the basic arts faculty curriculum was given by the seven liberal arts: the three linguistic arts of grammar, logic, and rhetoric, and the four quadrivial arts of arithmetic, geometry, astronomy, and music. This structure had first been fully set out by Augustine in his *De ordine*, where the liberal arts are presented as preparing the soul for its orderly journey upward to the contemplation of intelligible things. The structure was taken up and handed on to later ages by Martianus Capella, in whose poem on the marriage of Mercury and Philology Mercury symbolized the double sense of the *Logos* as word and divine reason and Philology, the lover of *Logos*, personified the seven liberal arts.[2]

The chief text in grammar, Priscian's *Institutiones grammaticae*, was written in Constantinople during the first quarter of the sixth century. It was a lengthy systematic treatise particularly noteworthy for its semantic approach. That is, parts of speech were defined in terms of their meaning rather than by their function in a sentence. Another important text was the fourth-century *Ars maior* of Donatus, whose third book, the *Barbarismus*, was especially used for training in figures of speech, a topic ignored by Priscian. Once Priscian's work had entered the Carolingian curriculum, it became the subject of commentary, and in the twelfth century Peter Helias wrote his influential *Summa super Priscianum*, the first full *summa* on any subject. Helias's work signaled a change in the approach to grammar, since he classified parts of speech not so much in terms of their signification as in terms of the linguistic properties that constitute their *modi significandi* or modes of signification. At the same time, logicians took over the problems of reference and of different types of signification from the grammarians, and the training in grammar became less philosophical and more a training in general linguistics. The university curricula tended to pay most attention to *Priscianus minor*, the last two books of the *Institutiones*, which dealt with syntax, and Donatus was replaced by such newer teaching grammars in verse form as Alexander de Villa Dei's *Doctrinale* (c. 1199) and the *Graecismus* of Evrard de Béthune (c. 1210), both popular at European universities until the end of the Middle Ages.[3]

The second half of the thirteenth century saw a partial return to philosophical themes in grammar with the appearance of the speculative grammarians or *Modistae*.[4] They tried to present grammar on the model of an Aristotelian science, which meant that it had to deal with what is common to all languages. They found this commonality in the postulated parallelism between the modes of being of things (*modi essendi*), the modes of understanding in the mind (*modi intelligendi*), and the modes of signifying of words (*modi significandi*).

They were not, however, committed to the view that language mirrors the world, because once the intellect has formed modes of signifying, it can make various attributions. *Chimera* is a fictional term, but it is a substance word; *movement* signifies change and impermanence, but the word has the modes of signifying of any noun, namely, stability or permanence. Both the insistence on universality and the focus on modes of understanding led to a clear disassociation of speculative grammar from spoken language in the fourteenth century.

Logic is the linguistic art that underwent the most dramatic changes. In the early period the texts available were limited in number. They include Marius Victorinus on definitions, the *Categoriae decem*, a work wrongly attributed to Augustine, which was the most intensely studied logical work in the ninth and tenth centuries, and Augustine's own *De dialectica*, as well as discussions in such encyclopedists as Isidore of Seville. The works of Boethius are the most important. He seems to have been responsible for translating Aristotle's six works on logic into Latin, and all but the *Posterior Analytics* survive. He also translated Porphyry's *Isagoge*, an introduction to Aristotle's *Categories*. He wrote commentaries on some of Aristotle's logic, on Porphyry, and on the *Topics* of Cicero. In addition he composed monographs of his own on Division, on categorical syllogisms, on Topics, and on hypothetical syllogisms, that is, on conditional propositions and arguments built up from them. The work on Division was particularly influential.[5] By the end of the tenth century Gerbert of Aurillac was teaching Porphyry's *Isagoge*, Aristotle's *Categories* and *On Interpretation*, Cicero's *Topics*, and a good deal of Boethius in the cathedral school at Rheims. Twelfth-century masters used the same basic curriculum, which, with the addition of the *Liber sex principiorum* attributed to Gilbert of Poitiers, was soon to be known as the *logica vetus* or Old Logic.

From 1150 enormous changes took place. The rest of Aristotle's logical works, along with other texts, were recovered; and thinkers began to develop new areas of logic. Aristotle's *Topics* and *Sophistical Refutations* were known by the 1130s, and the entire *logica nova* or New Logic, including the *Prior* and *Posterior Analytics*, was known by 1159, when John of Salisbury referred to all four works in his *Metalogicon*. In the second half of the twelfth century people began to translate Arabic logic, including writings by Avicenna. In the

1230s several logic commentaries by Averroes were translated, though they were less successful than the Arabic works translated earlier. Some Greek commentators were also translated. These texts, given their number and advanced content, provided a full logic curriculum for an organized institution.

While the writings of Aristotle were always central to the logic curriculum and were the subject of numerous commentaries, there were matters that he did not discuss. This left room for a considerable number of new developments, all of which have their roots in the second half of the twelfth century. The most prominent is terminist logic, which includes supposition theory and its ramifications. Treatises on supposition theory deal with the reference of subject and predicate terms in propositions, and they have as a corollary the treatises on syncategoremata, which deal with all the other terms in propositions, including *every, not, and, except,* and so on. Three other important developments are found in treatises on insolubles or semantic paradoxes, on obligations or the rules one is obliged to follow in a certain kind of disputation, and on consequences or valid inferences. Another new form of writing is the comprehensive textbook. At least six survive from the thirteenth century, including those by William of Sherwood, Peter of Spain, and Roger Bacon. In the fourteenth century we find those by William of Ockham, John Buridan, and Albert of Saxony. Some universities, especially Oxford and Cambridge, preferred to use loose collections of brief treatises on various topics; a good example of such a collection is the *Logica parva* of Paul of Venice, who studied at Oxford.

All the new developments had ramifications beyond the treatises particularly devoted to them, but the new technique involving the analysis and solution of sophismata was particularly pervasive in medieval grammar and logic.[6] A sophisma sentence is a puzzle intended to introduce or illustrate a difficulty, a concept, or a general problem. Examples in logic include "Every phoenix exists," given that only one phoenix can exist at a time, and "Socrates is whiter than Plato begins to be white." Examples in grammar include "Love is a verb" and various sentences beginning with "proch dolor" (O the pain!). Here the problem concerns the mixture of an interjection and an ordinary noun, the one expressing pain in a natural way, the other referring to it in a conventional language. By the end of the twelfth century the sophisma was established in different genres of logical and grammatical writing, which included special treatises devoted to sophismata. Typically, these treatises would start with a sophisma, and, using disputational techniques, show that the very same reasoning which supported a plausible thesis could also establish something implausible. The problem would then either be solved by appealing to grammatical or logical distinctions, or dissolved by showing that different truth-values were possible according to different senses of the sophisma sentence. These disputational techniques were employed in the oral training of students.

Other new developments were never the subject of special treatises. In order to understand medieval reflection on the nature and function of language and logic in general, and on the differences between spoken language and the language of thought, we have to look at a variety of philosophical and theological sources. I shall take up these general topics in the next two sections, before turning to some more specialized topics.

THE PURPOSE AND NATURE OF LANGUAGE AND LOGIC

Both language and logic were seen as having a primarily cognitive orientation, language having been formed to state the truth and logic to lead us from one truth to another. This orientation gave rise to a number of tensions that are particularly obvious in both Augustine and Aquinas. Augustine was skeptical about the human ability to convey truths through speech. As a professional rhetorician, he had a keen appreciation of the multifarious uses of language, as well as its dangers;[7] but he also argued in *The Teacher* that we must turn away from ordinary speech altogether in order to learn from Christ, who is at once the Inner Teacher and the Divine Word.

Aquinas was more sanguine about the role of speech. He noted that the proper function of language is to make known the truth by means of making known our concepts (*ST* IIaIIae, q.110, a. 1).[8] Speech is needed to fulfill the ends of social life, to communicate notions of what is harmful and useful, just and unjust, and society is founded on truth-telling. His primary notion of language, like that of the later *Modistae*, seems to have been of a rational, rule-governed system that could be studied in isolation from context and speaker intention and which concentrates on propositions as linguistic units that convey the information necessary for organized knowledge (*scientia*).

This view implies that significant utterance requires sentences that are neither syntactically nor semantically deviant, whose components are neatly lined up with the speaker's concepts, and whose end is the statement of truth. Other uses of language, such as invoking or summoning, questioning, ordering, and requesting or begging, should be left to rhetoric and poetry. Nonetheless, Aquinas paid some attention to the expressive function of speech. For instance, we praise a man not merely to let him know our good opinion of him but also to provoke him to better things and to induce others to have a good opinion of him, to reverence and imitate him (*ST* IIaIIae, q. 91, a. 1). In his discussion of the sacraments, he also recognized the factive or performative nature of speech ("I baptize you," "I pronounce you man and wife"). Most important of all, he paid close attention to the role of human intentions in compensating for slips of the tongue and other linguistic errors.

So far as logic is concerned, thinkers agreed that logic has to do with truth. As Augustine remarked (*De dialectica* [60] 102), "the business of dialectic is to discern the truth," and later Avicenna insisted that the function of logic is to lead us from the known to the unknown. There was never any suggestion that the study of logic is the study of formal systems, and even though later medieval logicians used a semitechnical language in order to bring out distinctions, it was in order to bring out distinctions of meaning. This had an effect on the notion of formal inference. Since there are no systems, no system-relative definition of formality is possible, and so a formal inference is one that can be justified only as obviously truth-preserving. As Augustine remarked, the truth of valid inference (*ueritas conexionum*) is not invented by men but is "permanently and divinely instituted in the reasonable order of things [*in rerum ratione*]" (*De doctrina Christiana* II 32). Of course, this attitude was compatible with some disagreement about which inferences were acceptable, and also with the belief that some inferences could be justified by reference to others. Moreover, it was recognized both that even the best inference is only useful if its premises are true, and that mistakes are frequently made in inference as a result of confusing and ambiguous premises. The study of fallacies and how to avoid them was the focus of much logical discussion.

It is relevant to note at this point that there is a sense in which logic can aim at the truth without using the method of formal discursive inference at all. While the Stoic and Aristotelian approach to logic certainly focuses on formal inference, Neoplatonic dialectic was more a leading of the soul upwards to the place where it can see intelligible reality directly. This dialectical process is clearly exemplified by Augustine's proof for the existence of God in *On Free Choice of the Will* II. The same process is also found in Anselm, whose so-called ontological argument (which is more about greatness than being) seems to aim at putting the soul in a position where it can go beyond words to grasp intelligible reality itself. However, Anselm's argument, unlike those of Augustine, is formalizable as a valid argument, in this case a classic *reductio ad absurdum* argument. Similarly, his proofs in the *Monologion* are presented as fully-fledged arguments with premises and conclusions. Anselm was a careful logician as well as an Augustinian.

Leaving Neoplatonic dialectic aside, there is still much to be said about uses of the term *dialectica*. In the broad sense, dialectic just is logic, and this name was most prevalent until the thirteenth century, when *logica* gained the upper hand. The word also has three narrower senses: dialectic as the art of debate; dialectic as the art of finding material for arguments; and dialectic as a kind of reasoning that falls between demonstrative and sophistical reasoning. The first sense is found in Cicero, who calls dialectic the correct method of discussion (*disserendi diligens ratio*) and in Augustine, who wrote (*De Dialectica* [60] 82): "Dialectic is the science of disputing well." The second sense is associated with the discussion of Topics, the headings under which the material for arguments can be sorted.[9] Because the study of Topics also included maxims, or self-evidently true generalizations that could provide the warrant for different types of argument, there is a close link between Topics and argumentation. Hence, the third and most usual sense of dialectic had to do with topical or dialectical syllogisms as a subpart of logic. Medieval logicians treated Aristotle's distinction between dialectical and demonstrative syllogisms as an epistemological one concerning the status of their premises, so that while dialectical syllogisms had the same formally valid structure as demonstrative syllogisms, their conclusions lacked certainty.

Just as there were different senses of the word *dialectic*, so there were different senses of *logic*. Isidore of Seville noted that *logica* comes from the Greek word *logos*, which can mean *sermo* (word) or *ratio* (reason). As a result logic could be called either a *scientia sermocinalis* (linguistic science) or a *scientia rationalis* (rational science). There were considerations supporting both titles. On the one hand, the Stoics had divided philosophy into natural, moral, and rational, and the last was equated with logic, which could then, as Boethius pointed out, be seen as both an instrument and a part of philosophy. On the other hand, logic was one of the liberal arts and belonged to the trivium, along with rhetoric and grammar, which made it seem a linguistic science. This emphasis was intensified by the discovery of Arab logicians who included Aristotle's *Rhetoric* and *Poetics* in his logical works, a classification accepted by Albert the Great and Aquinas, among others. Some logicians, such as William of Sherwood, preferred to call logic just a linguistic science, but many others in the thirteenth century, including Robert Kilwardby and Bonaventure, called it both linguistic and rational.

In the late thirteenth and fourteenth centuries the notion of logic as purely a rational science became predominant. This move was partly associated with the rediscovery of the *Posterior Analytics* and the new emphasis on demonstrative science, and it raised certain problems about the nature of logic. If a science consists of universal necessary propositions, if it proceeds by demonstration, and if it deals with being (*ens*), how can the study of fallacies or of individual arguments count as science? Similar problems were raised about grammar, and as we saw above, the *Modistae* provided a solution in terms of universal principles underlying spoken languages. Similar principles were adopted by logicians who argued that logic did count as science, both because it dealt with the universal, necessary principles governing logical phenomena, including the apparently deviant phenomena of fallacious arguments, and because the notion of being included not only real beings but also beings of reason, which owe their existence to the mind's activity.

Beings of reason included fictional and impossible objects, such as chimeras and golden mountains, but here they can be identified with second intentions, those higher level concepts we use to classify our concepts of things in the world, and they include such notions as genus, species, subject, predicate, and syllogism. Nominalists and realists disagreed over whether second intentions pick out special common objects, including both universals and logical structures, or whether they just are mental constructs reached through reflection on individual things and on actual pieces of discourse or writing, but this did not prevent such nominalists as Ockham from following Avicenna in saying that logic deals with second intentions and that the syllogism the logician considers is neither a thing in the world nor a piece of writing or speaking. Some people preferred to say that logic was about things in the world as they fall under second intentions. Others preferred to pick out some special second intention, such as argumentation or the syllogism, as the subject of logic, but there was still a strong consensus that the objects of logic are rational objects.

SIGNIFICATION, CONVENTIONAL AND
MENTAL LANGUAGE

Signification

The central semantic notion was that of signification. However, we must not confuse signification as "a psychologico-causal property of terms"[10] with meaning. The meaning of a term is not an entity to which the term is related in some way, but one can say that an utterance signifies or makes known an entity, whether conceptual or real, universal or particular. Moreover, meaning is not transitive, but signification is. Lambert of Auxerre (or Lagny) wrote: "An utterance that is a sign of a sign – i.e., of a concept – will be a sign of the thing signified – i.e., of the thing; it is, however, a sign of the concept directly but a sign of the thing indirectly."[11] This is not to deny that medieval thinkers had a notion of meaning. They did talk about sense (sensus), about thought or meaning (sententia), and about the force of a word (vis verbi). Moreover, they often used significatio itself along with its cognates quite widely.

There were two not entirely compatible approaches to signification, each based on a sentence from Aristotle. According to the first approach, based on On Interpretation 16b9–21, to signify is to generate or establish an understanding. This definition places emphasis not on the speaker but on the hearer. Given this emphasis, it is possible to regard groans and perhaps also animal sounds as significant. So long as the hearer can acquire some understanding through hearing, the utterance is significant even if the speaker is incapable of rational, abstract thought, and even if the speaker has no intention of conveying a message. The second approach tied the significative power of an utterance to its making known a concept. The crucial text here is *On Interpretation* 16a3–4, read as saying "Spoken words are signs of concepts." This supports the view that it is the speaker's intellectual capacity and intentions that are crucial to significant utterance. Animal noises and groans reveal specific passions and sensory states, such as fear and pain, but they are not linked to concepts and are not properly part of language.

Aristotle, as interpreted by medieval commentators, had gone on to say that concepts were similitudes or signs of things, and this raised the question of what is meant by "thing." In other words, what is it that we understand when an utterance such as "man" or "animal" establishes an understanding? While the usual assumption from Boethius at least until the end of the thirteenth century was that the understanding is of some kind of universal, an essence or common nature, we must bear in mind the impact of different epistemologies.

For Augustine and Anselm, who accepted the doctrine of an intellectual acquaintance with eternal ideas and truths through divine illumination, the distinction between knowing words and knowing the things themselves was all-important (e.g., *The Teacher* 1.2). In *Monologion* 10 Anselm draws a distinction between speaking words, thinking the words spoken, and thinking the thing, the universal essence "rational mortal animal." He employs much the same distinction in *Proslogion* 4 when explaining how the fool said in his heart what cannot be thought, namely, "God does not exist." To grasp the essence "being greater than which none can be conceived" is to grasp a real intelligible, and in grasping it one cannot fail to see that it exists necessarily. The issue is quite other for Aquinas and those who accepted an Aristotelian epistemology which made concept formation dependent upon sense experience, and knowledge of intelligible realities subsequent to knowledge of sensible realities. For them there was no simple (albeit divinely aided) way to move from thinking the words to thinking the things themselves.

The interposition of concepts between words and intelligible things lies behind the late thirteenth-century debate over whether words signify concepts or things. For Lambert of Auxerre (or Lagny) in the 1260s, the intelligible species was the primary significate of words, and the essence or common nature the secondary significate,[12] but Aquinas's development of a distinction between the intelligible species, as an essential ingredient in the intellective process but not the intellect's object, and the inner word or concept, the thing as thought about, altered the terms of the debate. Does a word signify first the intelligible species, not as a mere accident of the mind but as a representation of the external thing, or does a word signify first the inner word? If the latter is the case, then what is the status of the inner word? Is the thing as thought about a purely mind-dependent construction? If so, concepts are primarily signified. Or is the thing as thought about to be identified with the external object taken as related to the mind in a certain way? If so, the thing as thought about is the same as the external essence, and it is things that are primarily signified. This was the position taken by Siger of Brabant and discussed by Duns Scotus.[13]

The terms of the debate were to change completely in the four-teenth century with the rise of nominalism, the doctrine that all that exists are individual things, and that only concepts can be common. The question now became one of priority: does a word signify an individual thing in the world directly, or does it signify first the gen-eral concept which is a necessary condition for signification? Buridan and Ockham differed on this issue. Buridan held that words first sig-nify concepts, because only then can we explain why terms such as *being* and *one* which have the same extension nonetheless differ in signification. Ockham preferred to say that words signified individ-ual things while being subordinated to concepts. Both thinkers are also noteworthy for their new insistence that the concept itself was a representative sign.[14]

Conventional and natural language

There was some discussion of whether language was conventional, as Aristotle and Boethius had clearly held, or in some sense natu-ral. The issue arose in relation to Adam's naming of the animals in Genesis 2:19: "Whatsoever Adam called every living creature, that was the name thereof." Was the language instituted by Adam, or by God through Adam, a natural language in the sense of one that enabled users to grasp essences by virtue of a natural relationship between spoken words and the things named? Here we find a ten-sion between biblical exegesis, which emphasized a natural relation-ship while recognizing that it could not involve onomatopoeia, and

Aristotelian logic, which emphasized conventionality.[15] In the twelfth century Thierry of Chartres had put forward the theory that the words God spoke when creating gave essence to things, and that through the inspiration of the Holy Spirit Adam used these same words to name created things. He clearly believed that this doctrine was compatible with Boethius's belief in the conventionality of spoken language. Later authors, including Pseudo-Kilwardby and Aquinas, insisted that imposition (the original endowment of words with conventional signification) should be a rational deliberate activity, but Aquinas suggested that this was by virtue of the inner word, which captured the essence of the thing named rather than any correspondence between arbitrary sound and essence.

Mental language

The corollary of conventionally significant spoken language is the natural inner language.[16] By the second century BCE the notion of inner discourse (*logos endiathetos*) had become common to Greek schools of philosophy, and the data suggest that the notion was not that of a silent conventional language but rather that of a genuine inner discourse, albeit not yet one endowed with a compositional structure. Inner discourse played a particularly important role in discussions of how human beings differ from other animals, including those (such as parrots) capable of uttering words. In the early Christian era, there is a bifurcation. On the one hand, the notion of inner discourse is used in Neoplatonic commentaries on Aristotle and, through Boethius, is passed on to Latin logicians and professional philosophers. On the other hand, Christian theologians, most notably Augustine, use the notion of an inner word in their attempts to make intelligible the assimilation of the divine Logos to the incarnate Christ. Augustine presented an articulated psychology of the inner man as a model of spiritual production, and it was the active nature of the inner word, rather than its linguistic analogies, that mattered to him. These two very different traditions encountered each other in the thirteenth-century Latin-speaking universities, and Aquinas played an important role in their assimilation and reshaping. By the end of the thirteenth century and the beginning of the fourteenth century we find lengthy, sophisticated discussions of the nature of conceptual representation, of the question whether the mental word is an act of mind, a special intentional object, or a thing in the world as thought about, and of the distinction, already present in Augustine, between inner reflection on spoken words and an inner discourse independent of spoken languages.

A rich, sophisticated version of the language of thought hypothesis was developed in the fourteenth century by William of Ockham.[17] Ockham drew a sharp contrast between the terms of conventionally significant spoken languages and the concepts or mental terms to which they were subordinated. These concepts were representative signs, significant by their very nature, and they were the same for all, or, at least, for all with similar sense experiences. Just as the terms of spoken language enter into phrases, propositions, and arguments with a grammatical structure, so mental terms enter into grammatically structured compositions, although mental language does not display all the grammatical features of spoken languages but only those essential for semantic features. Mental nouns need to be singular or plural, for instance, but they do not need to be gendered. At the semantic level, the truth-values of mental propositions are a function of the reference of the subject and predicate concepts, together with the syntactic features of the proposition. Ockham's theory of the language of thought was influential into the first decades of the sixteenth century.[18]

PARONYMY AND ANALOGY

So far the discussion of signification has focused on concrete substantial terms, that is, terms such as *man* and *animal* which constitute an understanding of things within the category of substance. No matter what position was taken on common natures or universals, thinkers agreed that such terms did succeed in picking out types of thing within the actual world and that such terms could be given an essential definition in terms of genus and difference (e.g., "Man is a rational animal"). However, not all significant terms are of this sort. One of the main achievements of later medieval thought was the sophisticated analysis of different types of term. I shall focus on two cases: concrete accidental terms and analogical terms.

Concrete accidental terms are roughly equivalent to Aristotle's paronyms, also called denominatives.[19] They include "literate" (*grammaticus*) and "white" (*album*). The problem with such terms is that they do not fall within an Aristotelian category. They seem to have a double relation, on the one hand to substantial things, for only substances can be literate or white, and on the other hand to the qualities of literacy or whiteness. Moreover, unlike the English adjective, they can be used as the subject of a Latin sentence. The issue was further complicated by the competing authorities of Priscian, who said that a *nomen* (name or noun) signifies substance with quality, and Aristotle, who said that the two categories are distinct and that white signifies only a quality. Anselm's *De grammatico* is the first important discussion of these problems, though his work is in many respects close to that of an anonymous commentator on Priscian from the same period. Anselm solved the problem by drawing a distinction between signification and naming (appellation), and saying that Aristotle was only concerned with signification. Whereas the word *man* principally signifies and names a substance which is qualified in a certain way, *grammaticus* (literate <thing>) signifies a quality directly (*per se*) and names a man, the subject of the quality, indirectly (*per aliud*). Subsequent discussions of the same problem were heavily influenced by the rival views of Avicenna and Averroes, once these became known, and culminate in Ockham's theory of connotative terms, which involves a complete reversal of Anselm's position. For Ockham, *album* primarily signifies a thing, and it connotes the form whiteness which qualifies the thing.

The questions concerning concrete accidental terms are linked with the question concerning the semantic unity of words with the same root. Here an appeal was made to the distinction between the thing signified and the grammarian's modes of signifying, which allowed one to distinguish between abstract and concrete, or between nouns, verbs, and adjectives (these being essential features), or between various genders and cases (these being accidental features). An early example is found in William of Conches, who remarked that *white* and *whiteness* differed not in the thing signified (*res significata*), namely, whiteness, but in modes of signifying. This distinction was very important in the discussion of religious language. Aquinas argued that such words as *wise* and *good* signify pure perfections but have creaturely modes of signifying. That is, they suggest the inherence of a separable quality. Their abstract counterparts, wisdom and goodness, also have the wrong modes of signifying, since they are not normally said of substances. To speak about God, we need to cancel out the creaturely modes of both concrete and abstract nouns.[20] However, the central problem of religious language remains, since the thing signified, the pure perfection, will still not be attributed to God in just the sense that it is attributed to human beings.

The reason for this difference of attribution is found in the doctrines of God's simplicity and transcendence, especially as stated by Augustine and Boethius in their works on the Trinity. They insisted that God transcends Aristotle's categories and that God is absolutely simple, so that no distinctions can be made between God's essence and his existence or between one perfection, such as goodness, and another, such as wisdom, or more generally, between God and his properties. As Boethius wrote (*The Trinity* [86] 19), "When we say of him, 'He is just,' we do indeed mention a quality, but not an accidental quality – rather such as is substantial and, in fact, supersubstantial. For God is not one thing because he is, and another thing because he is just; with him to be just and to be God are one and the same." Twelfth-century theologians such as Gilbert of Poitiers and Alan of Lille, partly under the influence of Pseudo-Dionysius and Scottus Eriugena, took the issue further by employing negative theology. We cannot affirm anything positive about God, because no affirmation can be appropriate to a transcendent being. It is better to deny properties of God, saying for instance that he is not good (i.e., in the human sense), and still better to say that God is not existent but superexistent, not substance but supersubstantial, not good but supergood. These theological doctrines raised the general problem of how we can speak meaningfully of God at all, but they also raised a number of particular problems, especially the problem of how we can say that God is just and that Peter is just as well. By the mid-thirteenth century theologians attempted to solve this problem by appealing to analogy.

The discussion of analogical terms was fitted into the framework of the doctrine of equivocal terms found in logic texts.[21] The original focus of discussion was provided by Aristotle's *Categories*, which opens with a brief characterization of terms used equivocally, such as *animal* used of real human beings and pictured human beings, terms used univocally, such as *animal* used of human beings and oxen, and terms used paronymously, such as *strong* and *literate* (the concrete accidental terms we examined above). In the first case, the spoken term is the same but there are two distinct significates or intellectual conceptions; in the second case, principally that of concrete substantial terms, both the spoken term and the significate are the same. The *Categories* was supplemented by the *Sophistical Refutations*, in which Aristotle discusses three types of equivocation and how these contribute to fallacies in logic.

Another inspiration for doctrines of analogy was metaphysics. One crucial text is found in Aristotle's *Metaphysics* IV 2 (1003a33–35): "There are many senses [*multis modis*] in which being [*ens*] can be said, but they are related to one central point [*ad unum*], one definite kind of thing, and are not equivocal. Everything which is healthy is related to health . . . and everything which is medical to medicine." In this text, Aristotle raises the general problem of the word *being* and its different senses, and he also introduces what is known as *pros hen* equivocation or focal meaning, the idea that different senses may be unified through a relationship to one central sense. Another foundational text is from Avicenna's *Metaphysics*, where he writes that being (*ens*) is neither a genus nor a predicate predicated equally of all its subordinates but is rather a notion (*intentio*) in which they agree according to the prior and the posterior. As we shall see, this reference to the prior and the posterior is particularly important. We should also note that *ens* is one of the so-called transcendental terms, or terms which go beyond Aristotle's categories, in that they can be attributed to things of any category. The other central transcendentals were one (*unum*), good (*bonum*), and true (*verum*), so that the discussion of transcendentals is closely related both to the discussion of pure perfections and to the general problem of concrete accidental terms.[22]

For thirteenth-century authors there were three main types of analogy. In the original Greek sense, analogy involved a comparison of two proportions or relations. Thus *principle* was said to be an analogical term when said of a point and a spring of water because a point is related to a line as a spring is related to a river. This type of analogy came to be called the analogy of proportionality, and was briefly privileged by Aquinas in *Truth*. In the second sense, analogy involved a relation between two things, of which one is primary and the other secondary. Thus *healthy* was said to be an analogical term when said of a dog and its food because while the dog has health in the primary sense, its food is healthy only secondarily as contributing

to or causing the health of the dog. This second type of analogy became known as the analogy of attribution, and its special mark was
being said in a prior and a posterior sense (per prius et posterius).
A third type of analogy, sometimes appealed to by theologians, including Aquinas in his Sentences commentary, involved a relation
of likeness between God and creatures. Creatures are called good or
just because their goodness or justice imitates or reflects the goodness or justice of God. This type of analogy was called the analogy
of imitation or participation.[23] Of the three types, it is the analogy
of attribution that is central to medieval discussions.

From the fourteenth century on, discussions of analogy focused
not so much on linguistic usages as on the nature of the concepts
that corresponded to the words used. Is there just one concept that
corresponds to an analogical term, or is there a sequence of concepts? If the latter, how are the members of the sequence ordered
and related to each other? Moreover, how far should we distinguish
between so-called formal concepts (or acts of mind) and objective
concepts (whatever it is that is the object of the act of understanding)? There were also those, such as Duns Scotus, who rejected
analogy.[24]

Other explorations of ambiguity were less directly related to theology and had to do not with individual terms but with whole propositions. One of the basic tools of propositional analysis was the distinction between compounded and divided senses, which is generally
associated with modal logic but originated in Aristotle's discussion
of the fallacy of composition and division. The basic point concerns
two ways of reading the sentence "A seated man can walk." Interpreted according to its compounded sense, this proposition is de dicto
(about a dictum or "that" clause) and means "That-a-seated-man-
walk (i.e., while seated) is possible." Interpreted according to its divided sense, the proposition is de re (about a res or thing) and means
"A seated man has the power or ability to walk." The proposition
is false in the first sense but true in the second. It became standard
when considering modal inferences, including modal syllogisms, to
distinguish between the compounded and divided senses of premises
and conclusion and to work out the logical results of these different
readings. William Heytesbury's treatise on the subject[25] shows the
variety of problems to which the distinction was applied in the fourteenth century.

REFERENCE: SUPPOSITION THEORY

The most notable new theory that took shape in the twelfth century was supposition theory. Like the theory of analogical terms, it had close links with theological problems, particularly those associated with the doctrine of the Trinity, three Persons in one God. The word *suppositum* had a dual use. In grammar, it meant subject, sometimes syntactic, that is, the noun agreeing with the verb, but more usually semantic, that is, the bearer of the form predicated; in theology, it meant Person, the subject qualified by the divine essence. These senses and those associated with the word *suppositio* (putting as subject) and the verb *supponere* (to put as subject) fed into the new notion of *suppositio pro* or standing for. Thus the word *God* was said to supposit for a person when it stood for a Person of the Trinity, and to supposit for an essence when it stood for the divine essence (Aquinas, *ST* I, q. 39, a. 4). In its developed form, the theory of supposition, along with its ramifications, particularly ampliation and restriction, explored the different types of reference that a subject or predicate term could have in various contexts.[26] The three main types of supposition were material, simple, and personal. A term was said to have material supposition when it stood for itself or for other occurrences of the same term, as in "Man is a noun." Thus material supposition stood in for quotation devices. A term was said to have simple supposition when it stood for a universal, as in "Man is a species." Both material supposition and simple supposition gave rise to controversy, but especially the latter, because of the obvious problem of the ontological status of universals or common natures. Finally, a term has personal supposition when it is taken for its normal referents, as when *man* is taken for Socrates, Plato, and so on.

Some logicians distinguished accidental personal supposition from natural supposition, which allowed a term to have prepropositional reference to all its referents, past, present and future, while others insisted that supposition must be purely propositional and contextual. This debate was linked with the question of how to define supposition: is it a type of signification belonging especially to the subject of a proposition, or is it not a type of signification at all but the acceptance of a term as standing for its referents?[27] It also affects the doctrines of ampliation, whereby the reference of a term can be extended, and restriction (the opposite of ampliation). Parisian logicians, such as Jean le Page, writing *circa* 1235, tended to accept natural supposition and to say (like Buridan in the fourteenth century) that terms had natural supposition in scientific propositions, that is, universal necessary truths, so that no ampliation was necessary. As a corollary, in nonscientific propositions the supposition of terms was restricted in various ways. For English logicians in the thirteenth century, all supposition was contextual, and the notion of ampliation had to be used when the subject of a proposition was to extend beyond present existent things.

The notion of ampliation was particularly important in the analysis of propositions containing tensed verbs, modal terms, and epistemic terms such as *imagine*. Logicians generally held that affirmative propositions with nonreferring terms are false, yet many of the propositions we wish to take as true have terms that refer to nothing currently existent. The doctrine of ampliation allowed reference to extend over past, future, and possible objects. In the later fourteenth century Marsilius of Inghen argued that one should also allow reference to imaginable objects which were impossible. By allowing this kind of ampliation to occur when such terms as *imagine* were used, he could save the truth of "I imagine a chimera," while still holding that "A chimera is an animal" was false.[28]

The three types of personal supposition most often appealed to are determinate, purely confused (*confuse tantum*), and confused and distributive. These types were normally illustrated by means of the descent to singulars. For instance, to say that the subject of a particular affirmative proposition, "Some A is B," has determinate supposition is to say that one can infer the disjunction of singular propositions, "This A is B, or that A is B, or the other A is B, and so on." To say that the predicate of a universal affirmative proposition, "Every A is B," has purely confused supposition is to say that one can infer a proposition with a disjoint predicate, "Every A is this B or that B or the other B, and so on." To say that the subject of a universal affirmative proposition has confused and distributive supposition is to say that one can infer a conjunction of propositions, "This A is B, and that A is B, and the other A is B, and so on." Some people distinguished between mobile and immobile cases. For instance, no descent is possible from "Only every A is B," and so A has immobile supposition. A fourth type of supposition is collective supposition,

as in "Every man is hauling a boat," given that they are doing it together. Here any descent will involve a conjoint subject, as in "This
man and that man and the other man are all hauling a boat."

The theory of personal supposition was used to solve a variety
of problems. One standard problem had to do with promising (or
"owing" in some authors). If I promise you a horse, is there some
horse that I promise you, and if not, how is the original sentence to
be construed? A wide variety of answers was proposed. Walter Burley
suggested that *horse* has simple supposition; Heytesbury took it that
horse had purely confused supposition and that it did not imply
"There is some horse that I promise you," because the new position
of *horse* before the verb gave it determinate supposition. Ockham
preferred to replace the sentence by a more complex sentence, "You
will have one horse by means of my gift."[29]

TRUTH AND PARADOX

Language and logic are concerned with truth, but what is truth? The
question was complicated by the interplay between Aristotle's claim
that "it is because the actual thing exists or does not exist that the
statement is said to be true or false" (*Categories* 4b8–10), the doctrine
of transcendentals according to which one, good, being, and true are
not only identical but come in degrees, and Christ's claim in John's
Gospel 14:6, "I am the way, the truth and the life." In *On Free Choice
of the Will* II 12 Augustine used propositional truth as a stepping-
stone to the conclusion that God is Truth. Since propositional truths
exist, by the Platonic one-over-many principle there must be a truth
in which they participate, and this Truth can only be God. In other
places, Augustine appealed to a paradox, formulated by Bonaventure
(*Disputed Questions* [213] 113) in these words: "If there is no truth,
then it is true to say: 'There is no truth.' But if this is true, then
something is true. And if something is true, there is a first truth."
Anselm made a similar move in *Monologion* 18. In his *De Veritate*
he took up the issue of different senses of the word *truth* and found a
solution which allowed him to reconcile the conflicting authorities.
Truth is fundamentally rectitude, and this notion applies first to
God, but we can also speak of the truth of objects, insofar as they
rightly reflect divine Ideas, and of the truth of statements, insofar as
they rightly reflect the truth of objects.

Unsurprisingly Aquinas rejected the Platonic moves which allowed a progression from seeing the truth of propositions to seeing the divine Truth (*ST* I, q. 2, a. 1, ad 1); and his discussion of different senses of truth began not with God but with the world around him. He took the claim attributed to Isaac Israeli, according to which truth is "the commensurateness of understanding and thing" (*adaequatio intellectus et rei*), and argued that there were two sorts of conformity, that between mind and object and that between object and mind. When we speak of conformity between object and mind we are speaking of transcendental truth, by virtue of which objects are reflections of divine ideas; when we speak of mind and object, we speak of the human mind's conformity to the objects around it whereby judgments are true (*ST* I, q. 16, a. 1; q. 21, a. 2). These two senses are then used to explain that God can be called Truth because in him there is a double conformity, given that his being (*esse*) and understanding (*intelligere*) are the same.

One of the most notorious problems of truth is associated with insolubles or semantic paradoxes.[30] The simplest version is the Liar Paradox, "What I am saying is false," given the *casus* or initial situation that this is all that is said, but complex versions with hypothetical propositions ("God exists, and some conjunctive proposition is false.") or sequences of mutually referring propositions ("Suppose that Socrates says 'Plato says something false,' and Plato says 'Socrates says something true.'") were also discussed.[31] In the twentieth century such paradoxes have been used to cast doubt on the very foundations of semantic theory and have led to elaborate distinctions between levels of language and metalanguage. Medieval logicians, however, show no signs of such a crisis mentality, and while they did employ certain restrictions on self-reference and make certain distinctions between language and metalanguage, these techniques were generally limited to the problem in hand.

INFERENCE AND PARADOX

The notion of inference, or *consequentia*, was at the heart of logic. The enormous amount of writing devoted to problems of signification and reference was intended to help the reasoner avoid fallacious inference. Similarly the many treatises on obligations (the rules to be followed in a certain type of disputation) were intended to give the student practice in following through the logical implications of the propositions he had accepted.[32]

There was considerable debate about the definition of validity. The claim that a consequence is valid if and only if it is impossible for the consequent to be false when the antecedent is true was questioned for two reasons. In the first place, the propositions involved were taken to be occurrent items, whether written, spoken, or mental. They could fail to exist, in which case there is nothing to carry a truth-value. Alternatively, their meaning could be at odds with their actual expression, as in "Every proposition is affirmative, therefore no proposition is negative." Such problems were discussed at length, for example, by Buridan, who solved them by substituting a definition in terms of signification, that is, that a consequence is valid if and only if it is impossible for it to be as signified by the antecedent without its being as signified by the consequent.

The presence of "if and only if" raises the second problem. The truth definition (or Buridan's substitute) may provide a necessary condition for validity, but is it sufficient? If it is sufficient, then we must accept the paradoxes of strict implication, that is, that anything follows from an impossible proposition, and a necessary proposition follows from anything. The debate about these paradoxes began in the twelfth century, and there was a series of attempts to provide a second condition which, with the first, would be sufficient for validity. Abelard had a containment principle by which the dictum of the antecedent should contain the dictum of the consequent, and Robert Kilwardby in the next century, like Strode in mid-fourteenth-century Oxford, said that the consequent had to be understood in the antecedent. Some people in the thirteenth century focused on reality, and argued that a consequence must capture a causal relation and that as a result the antecedent must be about a state of affairs that can at least be supposed to be possible. None of these people could accept the paradoxes as formally valid. On the other hand, the *Parvipontani* or *Adamites* (followers of Adam of Balsham) in the twelfth century and Buridan in the fourteenth were happy to accept the "if and only if" formulation as offering both necessary and sufficient conditions for validity, with all that that implied for the acceptance of the paradoxes.

There are many places other than those mentioned above in which logical and philosophical or theological issues overlap, including discussions of the nature of propositions and of modal logic.[33] A number of these discussions, like those mentioned above, seem to present logic as a study of inference rather than as a search for truth, but as Augustine remarked, "it is one thing to know the rules of inference, another to know the truth of propositions" (*On Christian Doctrine* II 34). He went on to say "Knowledge of inference, definition, and division is a great help to the understanding [*intellectorem*], so long as one does not make the mistake of thinking that having learned them is the same as having learned the truth of the blessed life" (ibid. II 37). For the medieval thinker, logic was a preliminary study, not an end in itself.

NOTES

1. For fuller introductions to logic see I. Hadot [405] and J. Marenbon [465] for the earliest period, P. Dronke *CH12* for the twelfth century, and *CHLMP* for the later Middle Ages. For language, see the articles in S. Ebbesen [460]. For full bibliographies, see E. J. Ashworth [456] and F. Pironet [470]. For texts, see N. Kretzmann and E. Stump *CT* I. Subsequent notes point to further reading.
2. See I. Hadot [405].
3. For grammar, see C. H. Kneepkens [463].
4. See M. A. Covington [458], C. Marmo [466], and I. Rosier [472] and [473].
5. See translation in *CT* I 12–38.
6. See S. Read [47].
7. See especially *On Christian Doctrine, The Teacher,* and *De dialectica.*
8. See E. J. Ashworth [236] and I. Rosier [258].
9. See N. J. Green-Pedersen [461].
10. P. V. Spade, *CHLMP* 188.
11. *CT* I 105.
12. *CT* I 104–05. The translation masks Lambert's use of the term *species.*
13. See G. Pini [298].
14. See J. Biard [457].
15. See G. Dahan [459].
16. See C. Panaccio [469].
17. See C. Panaccio [322].
18. See E. J. Ashworth [455].
19. See N. Kretzmann [41].
20. See E. J. Ashworth [237] and I. Rosier [474].
21. See E. J. Ashworth [235] and chapter 6 in this volume.
22. See J. A. Aertsen [504] and chapter 4 in this volume.

23. See B. Montagnes [467].

24. For discussion, see chapter 6 in this volume.

25. *CT* I 413–34.

26. For a rich array of nontheological texts, see L. M. de Rijk [471].

27. See Lambert in *CT* I 106–07.

28. See E. J. Ashworth [455] for this and other problems of reference.

29. See ibid.

30. See P. V. Spade [475].

31. Albert of Saxony in *CT* I 357, 349.

32. See K. Jacobi [462] and M. Yrjönsuuri [51] for discussions of consequences and obligations.

33. For propositions, see G. Nuchelmans [468]; for modal logic, see S. Knuuttila [464].

4   Philosophy in Islam

Why "Philosophy in Islam"? Why not "Islamic Philosophy" or "Arabic Philosophy"? The simple answers to these questions and the far from simple consequences of those answers provide an entry into the rich world of ideas briefly explored in this chapter. The simple answer to the question "Why not 'Islamic Philosophy'?" is that not all philosophers in lands under Islamic rule in the Middle Ages were Muslim. It is easy to forget how diverse the empire of Islam was and, in particular, that it included numerous lively religious minorities.[1] Among philosophers there were:

- Muslims, such as al-Farabi, Avicenna (Ibn Sina), and Averroes (Ibn Rushd), some of whom were Sunni, others Shiites or Ismaili, as the Brethren of Purity
- Christians, for instance Yahya Ibn 'Ady, a leading disciple of al-Farabi and a well-known Jacobite theologian
- Sabians, such as the physician Thabit ibn Qurra, a translator
- Mazdaeans or Zoroastrians, such as Mani al-Majusi
- Pagans, such as Abu Bakr al-Razi, the famous Rhazes, who denied the very possibility of revelation or prophecy, on the ground that it would favor a particular people and would therefore be incompatible with God's justice
- Jews, such as Ibn Suwar, Halevy, Maimonides, etc.

The great number and importance of Jewish philosophers, including those working in the Latin West after the Reconquista, call for a full chapter devoted to their thought (the chapter following this one), but they, as well as the other non-Muslims listed above, must be considered as participants in a single philosophical conversation carried on from the ninth through the thirteenth century and beyond.

Scholars have sometimes preferred to speak of "Arabic philosophy," to avoid suggesting that there is an "Islamic" way of philosophizing comparable to the conception of "Christian philosophy" advocated, controversially, by Gilson as a way to capture the spirit of medieval philosophy in the Latin West.[2] But there are problems with "Arabic philosophy," too. Leaving aside the case of Judeo-Arabic (Arabic written in Hebrew characters), we need to recognize that not all philosophical texts were written in Arabic, since Avicenna, among others, penned some important treatises in Persian. Besides, the word *Arabic* may be construed as referring not only to the language used by the philosophers but also to their ethnic background, and with the exception of al-Kindi and Averroes, few philosophers were Arab. Avicenna and al-Ghazali, for example, were Persian.

Inclusion of the last-named thinker in my census of philosophers points to yet another complication, for al-Ghazali's chief contribution to philosophy was a powerful critical work, the *Incoherence of the Philosophers*. This raises the question, what is meant by philosophy? Often, one restricts it to *falsafa*, an Arabic word which simply transliterates the Greek *philosophia* and immediately points to the discipline's foreign origin. Most of the *falasifa*, that is, Hellenized philosophers, claimed membership in a school deriving from Aristotle, and Averroes bitterly criticized Avicenna for distancing himself too much from "the first teacher." Others, however, such as al-Razi, criticized Aristotle and invoked Plato or Socrates. Moreover, Islamic theology (Kalam) had already elaborated some philosophical concepts and an ontology – it had developed philosophical reflections, even if its practitioners did not want to be equated with the *falasifa*. Ghazali objects vigorously to the *falasifa*'s exaggerated claims to having apodeictic demonstrations of the existence or nature of God, but his objections were themselves so philosophically acute that Averroes felt called to refute as many of them as he could (while conceding the validity of others). It has been well argued that there is much genuine and original philosophy in Kalam and that Avicenna had more influence on Ghazali than has previously been thought.[3]

"Philosophy in Islam" thus includes the ideas of non-Muslims, non-Arabs, and many thinkers who did not wish to be known as philosophers – and it is none the poorer, philosophically, for all that. It deserves further emphasis here that even those who called themselves *falasifa* were not grounded exclusively in Aristotle and Neoplatonism (or in Neoplatonic texts falsely attributed to Aristotle, such as the Proclean *Liber de causis* and the Plotinian *Aristotle's Theology*[4]). There were other Greek sources, including Christian ones, such as Philoponus's arguments against the eternity of the world. Little is known about how Stoicism came to influence the *falasifa*, but it clearly did. The same goes for the philosopher-physician Galen, who influenced many *falasifa* who were also physicians, such as al-Razi, Avicenna, Ibn Tufayl, and Averroes. And Syriac and Persian sources are not to be ignored, although the great translation movement at the time of the early Abbasids certainly concentrated on Greek texts.[5] With regard to these, however, it must be noted, there is still considerable uncertainty as to what philosophical thinkers in Islam actually had before them. It is not always clear whether we are dealing with translations of a full work or simply of some kind of summary. We have an Arabic version of Galen's *Summary of Plato's "Timaeus"* but do not know of a full translation of the *Timaeus* itself. It is uncertain whether there existed a full translation of Plato's *Laws*.[6] There is a longstanding dispute as to whether Aristotle's *Politics* was translated into Arabic, and even, as in the case of Aristotle's *Nicomachean Ethics*, if a full translation existed, we do not know how much and when it circulated (al-Kindi's references to the work are rather vague, for example).[7]

A final remark to conclude this explication of "philosophy in Islam": although the scope of this chapter will be limited arbitrarily almost entirely to philosophers up to and including Averroes (d. 1198), it must be understood that the supposed death of philosophy in Islamic lands after Averroes is a myth. An Avicennian tradition, the Philosophy of Illumination, introduced by Suhrawardi (1154–91), has been maintained up to the present, particularly in Iran, with philosophers such as al-Tusi (1201–74), Mir Damad (1543–1631), and Mulla Sadra (1571/2–1641).[8] Recently, scholars have edited postmedieval philosophical texts from other areas of the Islamic world, such as the Ottoman Empire, in which, for instance, several scholars wrote *Tahafut*, that is, *Incoherence of the Philosophers* treatises along the same lines as Ghazali's. The 1533 *Incoherence* of Kemal Pasazade (also known as Ibn Kemal) takes into account the arguments of Ghazali, Averroes (contrary to the claim that Averroes had no impact on philosophers in Islam), and of a previous Ottoman scholar, Hocazade.[9] For medievalists, of course,

philosophy in Islam in the Middle Ages is by itself sufficiently en-
grossing to reward study by further generations of scholars, but the
philosophical-critical conversation with which we are concerned in
this chapter continued beyond our period into the present.

PHILOSOPHY, RELIGION, AND CULTURE

It is commonly thought that there was in the Middle Ages (and perhaps still is) a fundamental conflict between philosophy and the
religion of Islam. It is clear from what we have already seen of
the presence of philosophical thought even in the critics of *falsafa*
that the idea of a simple opposition is a misconception. It would be
equally a misconception, however, to imagine that there was a single
dominant positive idea of what philosophy and religion have to do
with one another. Rather, we find a variety of thoughtful and imaginative explorations of the relationship. The fact that none of the discussions we shall consider was strictly homologous with anything
in the Latin West makes these discussions more, not less, fruitful for
cross-cultural understanding.

The importance of cultural context can hardly be exaggerated.
Where Christianity came as a new religion into a Graeco-Latin civilization in which the classical philosophical schools were well represented, the situation was just the opposite in Islam. There philosophy came on the scene in the ninth century as an alien import,
with the task of making a place for itself in a civilization formed
at its deepest levels, both politically and culturally, by the Qur'an
and the law based on it. One of the first debates involving *falsafa*
centered on whether logic itself was truly universal or simply arose
from Greek grammar. Translators and most of the first defenders
of *falsafa* were not Arabic speakers. Their broken Arabic and their
strange coinages to render Greek technical terms puzzled their
Muslim interlocutors, so proud of their language and its importance
as the language of the revelation to Muhammad. Many regarded the
Qur'an itself as uncreated, a claim grounded in its inimitability, the
impossibility of composing verses of such literary artistry. The debate was complicated by the fact that the *falasifa* adopted the view of
the Alexandrian School that Aristotle's *Rhetoric* and *Poetics* are inte-
gral parts of logic, rather than of practical philosophy. They equated
the arguments of the specialists in Kalam with dialectic and those of

the Qur'an with rhetoric and poetical arguments.[10] Once the *falasifa* began to use a more palatable kind of Arabic and to bring stylistic improvements to the translations, some of the misunderstandings dissipated, and logic, often compared to mathematics, was clearly distinguished from Greek grammar, acknowledged as universally valid, and later on found a home in the curriculum of the schools of law. The debate raises vividly the question of what is universally valid in philosophy and what is culturally determined. If logic could be regarded for a while as peculiarly Greek, we should not wonder at the problematic status of metaphysics for some of the thinkers we shall be considering.

As concerns the broader issues in the relation of philosophy with religion, we will do well to begin at the end of our period, with Averroes (1126–98), for an incomplete grasp of his position is a prime source of the belief in a simple and basic philosophico-religious conflict. A fuller understanding of his views will help us to place a number of earlier discussions in context.

Judge Averroes

There is an image of Averroes as a defender of implicitly antireligious Free Thinking and as a forerunner of the Enlightenment[11] that is based largely on a partial reading of his *Decisive Treatise, Determining the Nature and Connection between Philosophy and Religion*.[12] In this work Averroes does indeed praise philosophical insight as the highest form of knowledge. The liberal image is severely cracked, however, if not entirely shattered, when one reads, in Averroes' refutation of al-Ghazali's *Incoherence of the Philosophers*, that "heretics are to be killed."[13] Is there an inconsistency? Not at all. Averroes was not simply a philosopher physician but also a judge and, therefore, an expert on Islamic law. The treatise is presented as an official *fatwa* or juridical decision determining the canonical status of philosophy. "The purpose of this treatise," he declares at the outset, "is to examine from the standpoint of the study of the law [*shari'a*], whether the study of philosophy [*falsafa*] and logic is allowed by the law, or prohibited or commanded either by way of recommendation or as obligatory."

Averroes' judgment is that the studies in question are *obligatory* for an intellectual elite but must be forbidden to ordinary believers.

The *fatwa* presentation and no fewer than nine references to al-Ghazali (1058–1111) show clearly that the latter's *Incoherence of the Philosophers* had had a serious impact throughout the Islamic world. Before providing a lengthy and detailed refutation of al-Ghazali's arguments in his own *Incoherence of the Incoherence*, Averroes here offers a more popular defense of logic and philosophy, but it is a defense couched in terms of Islamic law. He astutely begins with logic, for al-Ghazali himself had defended logic and claimed in his intellectual autobiography that the logic of the *falasifa* was superior to the reasoning of the specialists in Islamic law, and he is said to have convinced the schools of law to include logic in the curriculum. But Averroes carries the justification of logic further. He argues for its usefulness as an instrument for *falsafa*, which he defines as "nothing more than the study of existing beings and reflections on them as indications of the Artisan," that is, God, as the Creator. *Falsafa* thus becomes theodicy, aiming to prove the existence of the creator and to provide a better understanding of God. Averroes thereby seeks to counter al-Ghazali's charge that the *falasifa* do not really prove that the world has an Artisan, since they have reduced that word to a metaphor (*Incoherence*, second and third discussions). A crucial step in Averroes' acculturation of philosophy to the requirements of Islam rests on a shift in terminology in the words translated in English as *philosophy*. Elaborating a parallel between aspects of Islamic law and philosophy, Averroes substitutes "wisdom" (*hikmat*) for *falsafa*. In the Qur'an one of the beautiful names of God is "The Wise," and, therefore, "wisdom" has a qur'anic ring to it, whereas *falsafa* connotes something alien. Averroes then calls "philosophy" (still *hikmat*) the art of arts. He concludes the first section of the treatise by claiming that for every Muslim there is a way to truth suitable to his nature, first quoting Qur'an XVI 125: "Summon [them] to the way of your Lord by wisdom and by good preaching, and debate with them in the most effective manner." The root of the word for "debate," *jadal*, is used to refer to Aristotle's *Topics*, a work concerned with dialectical arguments based on generally received opinions. Averroes will equate this "debate" with Kalam, or Islamic theology. He is then able to present philosophy as one way of fulfilling the qur'anic injunction – a way that is appropriate, and indeed obligatory, for certain individuals:

Thus people in relation to Scripture fall into three classes. One class is those who are not people of interpretation at all: these are the rhetorical class. They are the overwhelming mass, for no man of sound intellect is exempted from this kind of assent. Another class is the people of dialectical interpretation: these are the dialecticians, either by nature alone or by nature and habit. Another class is the people of certain interpretation: these are the demonstrative class, by nature and training, i.e., in the art of philosophy [hikmat]. This interpretation ought not to be expressed to the dialectical class, let alone the masses. ([161] 65)

By thus elliding some of the distinctions between qur'anic language and technical Greek philosophical words and concepts, Averroes is able to claim at the end of the *Treatise* that "philosophy [hikmat but now intended as synonymous with *falsafa*] is the friend and milk-sister of ... law [shari'a]."

Too many interpreters, unaware of these shifts in terminology and of cultural differences, have assumed that Averroes raised questions about the relation between philosophy and religious faith similar to those posed by the so-called "Averroists" in thirteenth-century Paris. Averroes does not in fact refer to religion but rather to the *shari'a* or Islamic law, and the relation he asserts between philosophy and this law is one of accord, but only for a small elite.

Prophecy interprets philosophy (culturally): al-Farabi

Al-Farabi, the "second teacher" (after Aristotle) and an important participant in the early debate about the status of logic,[14] pays lip service to Greek terminology in speaking of the "Ideal or Virtuous City," but indicates that *city* may mean a universal empire with great ethnic, linguistic, and religious diversity. He is fully aware that Islamic rule aims at being universal and that a city-state does not fit the current political and economic situation.[15]

The absolutely perfect human societies are divided into nations. A nation is differentiated from another by two natural things – natural make-up and natural character – and by something that is composite (it is conventional but has a basis in natural things), which is language – I mean the idiom through which men express themselves. As a result some nations are large and others are small. (*The Political Regime* [97] 32)

Al-Farabi is a radical: *falsafa*, which for him reached its peak with Aristotle, is absolutely and universally true, but accessible only to a small intellectual elite. The masses therefore need something they can relate to, that is, religion, which must be adapted to particular cultures. Although there is only one philosophical truth – and in the Alexandrian tradition he claims that Plato and Aristotle are basically in agreement – there must be a plurality of true religions, varying from culture to culture, each of them conveying philosophical concepts by means of appropriate symbols. He explains, for instance, that darkness or chaos in religious texts represents nonbeing or prime matter, the Agent Intellect is represented by the angel Gabriel, and so forth. Philosophy alone uses apodeictic demonstrations, Kalam uses dialectical arguments, and religion uses rhetoric and poetry.[16] Hence, in the *Book of Letters* and in *The Attainment of Happiness* he writes that *falsafa* is prior in time (*sic*) to religion [*"din,"* closer to our conception of religion than Averroes' *shari'a*].[17] Religions are culturally determined imitations of true Aristotelian philosophy. Prophecy is simply an overflow of intelligibles on the imagination and, therefore, subordinated to philosophy. A perfect ruler will be not only a philosopher but also a lawgiver and a prophet or will work in connection with a prophet, to translate philosophical ideas into a more accessible language for the various cultures. Whether al-Farabi actually held these views or used them to flatter and attract prospective *falasifa* may be debated, but he was much respected and died of old age, in spite of his not so hidden assertions of the primacy of philosophy.[18]

The *falasifa*'s overemphasis on "apodeictic demonstration" and their claim that they alone practiced it explains why al-Ghazali delighted in showing that most of their arguments were not apodeictic at all, particularly in metaphysics, but on the contrary manifested an uncritical acceptance of Greek philosophic stances. His forcefulness matches that of al-Farabi's bitter attacks against his intellectual rivals, the specialists in Kalam, whom he ridiculed.

Philosophy culminates in prophecy: Avicenna

Al-Farabi's rationalism and his subordination of religion to the role of local interpreter of Greek philosophy strongly influenced Averroes, but it put *falsafa* on the margins of Islamic culture. Avicenna

(980–1037), as a Persian writing in both Arabic and Persian, engaged positively with the culture of Islam. He was even involved at times in practical politics as vizier of Shams al-Dawla.

Avicenna knew Aristotle's *Metaphysics* by heart, but he could not understand it, he tells us, until a little treatise by al-Farabi revealed to him that metaphysics was not focused on theology, as he had believed, but rather on being *qua* being.[19] But then his own profound thinking led him to modify or abandon some of Aristotle's teachings. Avicenna "completed" Aristotle's understanding of physical causes as causes of motion preceding their effects with an understanding of true or metaphysical causes, which are simultaneous with their effects but operate necessarily and by emanation.[20] The Agent Intellect, the tenth separate intelligence, is not only a source of intellectual illumination but also literally a "giver of forms" for sublunary beings and grounds this causal simultaneity. In other words, Avicenna accepted the challenge to rethink some of the inherited Greek "orthodoxy." Though still philosophizing in the spirit of Aristotle,[21] he took into account Neoplatonic ideas, as well as concepts elaborated in Kalam, and he paid more attention to the circumstances of his own place and time. This may explain why his texts have remained influential in Islamic culture until today, especially in Iran.

Avicenna's best-known metaphysical text, the *Metaphysics of the Shifa'*, ends in Book X, chapters 2–5, with reflections on political philosophy.[22] Here he presents prophecy as the culmination of intellectual development, a grasp of intelligibles, which no longer requires discursive reasoning. In chapter 2 he argues for the necessity of prophecy. Human beings need to form associations, which require a Lawgiver who must convince the masses, and must therefore be a human being (an invidious contrast is intended with the Christian conception of Christ as Son of God). The Lawgiver must be a prophet:

A prophet, therefore, must exist and he must be a human. He must also possess characteristics not present in others so that men could recognize in him something they do not have and which differentiates him from them. Therefore he will perform the miracles ... When this man's existence comes about, he must lay down laws about men's affairs ... The first principle governing his legislation is to let men know that they have a Maker, One and Omnipotent ... that He has prepared for those who obey Him an afterlife of bliss, but for those who disobey Him an afterlife of misery. This will induce the multitude to obey the decrees put in the prophet's mouth by God and the angels. But he ought not to involve them with doctrines pertaining to the knowledge of God, the Exalted, beyond the fact that He is one, the truth, and has none like Himself. To go beyond this . . . is to ask too much. This will simply confuse the religion they have. ([114] 100)

Yet, to incite promising youth to pursue philosophy, the prophet may insert symbols and signs that might stimulate a true philosophical awakening, as is the case in the Qur'an.

Chapter 3 gives a rather rationalistic justification of Islamic prescriptions about worship, such as ritual purification for the official prayers, and the pilgrimage. Chapter 4 rationally justifies other Islamic practices, such as almsgiving, care for the poor, the handicapped and the sick, as well as justifications of marriage customs and the dependency of women on men, since women "are less inclined to obey reason." (It is interesting to note that on such details Avicenna distances himself from al-Farabi, who followed closely Plato's *Republic* in affirming a quasi-equality of women and also in commanding that the chronically ill and the handicapped not be taken care of. Averroes will follow al-Farabi in his neglect of those who are not "useful" to the city, as well as in affirming that "the woman shares in common with the man all the work of the citizens," even if in his own society "they frequently resemble plants," as is the case in bad cities. Their being a burden upon the men is one of the causes of urban poverty.[23])

The concluding chapter of Avicenna's work concerns the Caliph and political organization. Avicenna obviously considers Muhammad the greatest prophet – not simply one among many, as he was for al-Farabi – and he gives rational justification here for the most basic principles of *shari'a*. Avicenna's account of political philosophy and religion is much more Islamicized than al-Farabi's. His position is still fairly rationalist, however, as a small treatise on prayer[24] and the *Proof of Prophecies*[25] clearly attest. A genuinely mystical interpretation of his thought is doubtful.

Exile

Al-Farabi, Avicenna, and al-Ghazali worked in the East, but *falsafa* began to spread to the West of the Islamic lands, to "Andalusia" in particular, where the political situation was both confused and fragmented. In al-Andalus the *falasifa* renounced the Islamicized Platonic ideal of the philosopher-ruler-lawgiver-prophet and advocated "exile" from the "city," perhaps because of the political instability.

Ibn Bajjah, or Avempace (d. 1138), another physician-philosopher, wrote *The Governance of the Solitary*.[26] Abandoning al-Farabi's dream of the virtuous or perfect state, he focuses on the place of the philosopher in an imperfect city.

> It is clear from the situation of the solitary that he must not associate with those whose end is corporeal nor with those whose end is the spirituality that is adulterated with corporeality. Rather, he must associate with those who pursue the sciences. Now since those who pursue the sciences are few in some ways of life and many in others, there even being ways of life in which they do not exist at all, it follows that in some of the ways of life the solitary must keep away from men completely so far as he can, and not deal with them except in indispensable matters and to the extent to which it is indispensable for him to do so; or emigrate to the ways of life in which the sciences are pursued – if such are to be found. This does not contradict what was stated in political science and what was explained in natural science. It was explained there [that is, in natural science] that man is political by nature, and it was explained in political science that all isolation is evil. But it is only evil as such; accidentally, it may be good, which happens with reference to many things pertaining to nature. (*The Governance of the Solitary* [361] 132)

Separate islands

Ibn Tufayl (c. 1116–85) wrote a famous philosophical novel preceded by a technical introduction, *Hayy ibn Yaqzan*, or *The Living, Son of the Wakeful* ("Wakeful" here may refer to the Agent Intellect). In this charming tale Hayy (the Living), having come somehow to a deserted island as a newborn, is raised by a doe. Without contact with other human beings, he discovers by himself not only how to survive but, later, all the principles of *falsafa*. He deduces the existence of God and then, at first, tries to imitate the celestial bodies. He emulates their provision of light and warmth by taking care of the animals; their brightness by cleanliness, perfumes, and dazzling clothes; their circular movements by spinning himself until he loses consciousness, as the "whirling" dervishes or Sufi do, and running around his own house, in a transposition of the pilgrimage ritual around Abraham's house at Mecca; and their contemplation by concentrating his thoughts on the necessary being, or God. Bit by bit, however, he realizes that his environmental concerns and his interest in cleanliness are distracting him from the contemplation of God and his own essence, and so he abandons them and reaches a state that cannot be expressed. On a neighboring island, a man named Asal, a believer in one of the true religions, decides to become a hermit and moves to Hayy's island, which he assumes to be deserted. After Hayy encounters him and quickly learns to speak, Asal discovers that Hayy has reached a much higher level of contemplation than he has himself. On the other hand, Hayy cannot understand why Asal's religion offers only images and parables of philosophical truths. In order to enlighten the people of the other island, Hayy and Asal travel there, but the more Hayy tries to teach them true philosophy, the more restless they become. Finally, Hayy understands that they are not gifted for philosophy and should for their own good be left in peace in their religion. He returns to his own deserted island with Asal, who, despite his best efforts, never reaches Hayy's level of contemplation.[27]

This remarkable tale implies that reason can discover everything on its own, while religions are socially useful for ordinary people but are only pale imitations of *falsafa*.[28] Ibn Tufayl's views are surprising, since he was court physician and vizier of the Almohad ruler Abu Ya'qub, to whom he introduced Averroes. Finding Aristotle's texts difficult, Abu Ya'qub requested that Averroes write commentaries on them, a request with which Averroes complied monumentally and seminally.

The question of philosophy's relation to religion is far from central in the philosophical texts produced in medieval Islam. What was written on this question is nevertheless of considerable interest, especially if we avoid the misconception that there was a single view of the matter – or a single pair of violently opposed positions, one philosophical and purely rational, the other religious and unsystematically dogmatic.

PSYCHOLOGY AND METAPHYSICS

Al-Farabi developed a psychology to fit his views on religion and prophecy. For him, there is only one Agent Intellect for the whole of humankind, the tenth emanated intelligence, which he equates with the angel Gabriel, who transmitted the Qur'an to Muhammad. The intelligibles emanate from the Agent Intellect to all human beings, but most of the intelligibles can be acquired only by the few people who are best prepared to receive them, the *falasifa*, of course.

Those are the first intelligibles which are common to all men, as, for example, that the whole is greater than the part, and that things equal in size to one and the same thing are all equal to one another. The common first intelligibles are of three kinds: (1) the principles of the productive skills, (2) the principles by which one becomes aware of good and evil in man's actions, (3) the principles which are used for knowing the existents which are not the objects of man's actions, and their primary principles and ranks: such as the heavens and the first cause. (*On the Perfect State* [95] 203, 205)

The intelligibles then can overflow on the imagination in the guise of symbols and parables appropriate to the various cultures and languages. Al-Farabi's subordination of prophecy to philosophy explains his claims that not only the first intelligibles for metaphysics but also those for ethics and the various disciplines come by emanation from the Agent Intellect, whereas al-Ghazali, who has less confidence in the intellect than al-Farabi, attributes the discovery of even the basic principles of astronomy and medicine to prophecy. (Interestingly al-Farabi tells us that his teacher, the Christian Ibn al-Haylan, and his fellow Christians were forbidden to read Aristotle's *Posterior Analytics*, known in Arabic as *The Book of Demonstration*.) Emanation of the first intelligibles from the Agent Intellect ensures the validity of the putatively apodeictic demonstrations characteristic of the *falasifa*. Neoplatonism grounds Aristotelianism.

Avicenna considered it necessary to abandon some of Aristotle's tenets, not only to develop his account of prophecy, but also to ground his conception of a purely spiritual afterlife and to provide a more sophisticated human and animal psychology for the present life. In his famous *De anima* of the *Shifa'* (Book I, chs. 1–3) he argues that the rational soul is not the form of the body but a full substance on its own. He then constructs a thought experiment – "the flying man" – to prove that self-consciousness is immediate and not a result of reflection. The text reminds us, retrospectively, of Descartes's *Cogito*.

The one among us must imagine himself as though he is created all at once and created perfect, but that his sight has been veiled from observing external things, and that he is created falling in the air or the void in a manner where he would not encounter air resistance, requiring him to feel, and that his limbs are separated from each other so that they neither meet nor touch. He must then reflect as to whether he will affirm the existence of his self. He will not doubt his affirming his self existing, but with this he will not affirm any limb from among his organs, no internal organ, whether heart or brain, and no external thing. Rather, he would be affirming his self without affirming for it length, breadth and depth. And if in this state he were able to imagine a hand or some other organ, he would not imagine it as part of his self or a condition for its existence. ([129] 387)

Avicenna gives a much more detailed account than Aristotle of the inner senses.[29] More germane to the themes of the present chapter are his conception of the Agent Intellect and his distinction of four "intellects" within the human soul. With most Greek Aristotelian commentators, he holds that there is only one Agent Intellect for the whole of humankind and follows al-Farabi in claiming that it is the tenth Intelligence, which rules the sublunary world. But within the soul Avicenna posits: (1) a purely potential intellect; (2) an actual intellect, which has received the primary intelligibles (such as the principle of noncontradiction and the notion that a whole is greater than any of its parts) from the Agent Intellect; (3) an habitual intellect, which conserves secondary intelligibles and can use them at will; and (4) the acquired intellect, when it is actually thinking the intelligibles and knows that it is doing so. Since the soul is a spiritual substance for Avicenna, and not, as Aristotle held, a form impressed in matter, it survives the body after death. The afterlife is purely spiritual, but people who have not reached full and immediate self-consciousness, not being able to conceive of themselves without the body, will recreate for themselves an imaginary body, in which they will experience the "physical" rewards or punishments of the afterlife, as they are described in the Qur'an.[30]

Since Avicenna, contrary to al-Farabi, does not subordinate prophecy to philosophy, he indicates that some individuals have a very powerful potential intellect and can therefore get in touch with the Agent Intellect easily and do not need much instruction or reasoning to acquire new knowledge. Some do not need any discursive process at all, but only intuition, and their habitual intellect becomes a divine or holy intellect, which immediately grasps all intelligibles at the same time. Syllogisms are no longer necessary. In that case these intelligibles overflow into the imagination, which translates them into symbols, parables, and so forth. Such an intellectual faculty is the highest human faculty and the prophet's privilege.[31]

It is clear that Avicenna is trying to do more than accommodate Greek philosophy to his political and religious circumstances. He finds food for his own distinctive thought wherever he can. He is famous for arguing in the *Metaphysics of the Shifa'* I 5 that being is "the first concept." In that chapter he holds that the other primary concepts are "thing" (known in Latin as the transcendental *res*), and "necessary."[32] Aristotle had spoken of some notions as pertaining to all being as such (for example, "one," "true," and "good"). Avicenna derived the need for "thing" as a primary concept from the Kalam's ontological commitments. He argued that the concept was required to ground the distinction between essence and existence, as well as the distinction between the contingent and the necessary-through-itself.[33]

Since I have relied mostly on the *Shifa'*, a text clearly in the Aristotelian tradition, for all its originality, I must point to three problems of Avicennian interpretation. First, the Latin versions of Avicenna's works do not always match the Arabic. This led Rahman to wonder whether Avicenna really claimed that existence is accidental to essence, as Thomas Aquinas understood him to have done.[34] Since the Latin manuscripts are often older than those we have in Arabic, the Latin text may sometimes be more correct than the Arabic. Besides, recent studies show that Avicenna's psychological and epistemological conceptions evolved and that he does not always take the same position in every text.[35] Second, Avicenna sometimes speaks of an "Oriental" philosophy, which some hold to be his own philosophy and quite different from his "Aristotelian" texts, while others deny this.[36] The third difficulty stems from the fact that at some stage in Avicenna's career he and other *falasifa* began to adopt the language of the mystics or Sufi, perhaps to provide some disguise for their unconventional rationalist views. Several small texts were published a century ago as *Avicenna's Mystical Treatises*, among them the rather rationalist approach to Islamic prayers we referred to earlier.[37] His lasting influence on Latin scholasticism, greater than that of Averroes, certainly comes from his rationalism, but it is a rationalism that modified some Aristotelian tenets by integrating aspects of Neoplatonism with them and that developed theologically fruitful distinctions between essence and existence and between contingency and necessity.[38] Avicenna's distinction between metaphysical and physical causes is at the heart of Duns Scotus's distinction between essentially and incidentally ordered causes, central to his famous proof for the existence of God.

Al-Ghazali, debunking the *falasifa*'s claims to apodeictic demonstrations, focused his attack on al-Farabi and Avicenna and their conception of causation. His intellectual autobiography shows that he was fully aware that this was the core issue in his condemnation of two of their central positions: eternal creation and the denial of God's knowledge of particulars.[39] Emanation, which he attacks brilliantly, makes creation an eternal necessity for God. Al-Ghazali insists that only God is a true Agent and that agency requires the ability to distinguish between two indiscernible temporal instants. It therefore requires knowledge of particulars, as well as choice. Whether al-Ghazali, under Avicenna's influence, allows some efficacy to secondary causes remains a disputed question.[40]

Strikingly, al-Ghazali spends little time on the *falasifa*'s views on the intellect, whereas those views were to cause much commotion in thirteenth-century Paris. Al-Ghazali simply indicates that the *falasifa* fail in their attempt to prove that the human soul is a substance capable of subsisting after death. On this issue he may have been happier with Aristotle's conception of the human soul as the form of the body, since in Islam resurrection is complete recreation, and there is no conception of a soul surviving the body's death. Al-Ghazali simply deplores the *falsafa*'s denial of the resurrection of the body and, therefore, the reality of physical rewards and punishments at the resurrection.

Averroes claims that there is not only a single Agent Intellect for the whole of humankind, but also only one "material" or passive intellect. The so-called "Material Intellect" is in fact immaterial, but in intellection it plays a role similar to that of matter in hylomorphic composition. His position seems to deprive human beings of their own capacity to think and to act freely, since they themselves do not really think, but the common Material and Agent Intellects think in them and feed them intelligibles. Such views caused an uproar at the University of Paris, where some members of the arts faculty adopted them with enthusiasm. In late 1270 Thomas Aquinas felt the need to write his *On the Unity of the Intellect Against the Averroists* to refute such views and to criticize Averroes' interpretation of Aristotle as a betrayal. It has recently been argued, however, that some of Aquinas's criticisms are misguided and that Averroes can in fact give a coherent account of our awareness of our acts of understanding as being our own acts.[41] The argument depends on the correct reading of Averroes' *Long Commentary* on the *De anima*, which is known only through a medieval Latin translation, although a few fragments of the Arabic have recently surfaced.

It is not easy to determine exactly what Averroes' position is on the Material Intellect.[42] Not only is the text of the *Long Commentary* very difficult, but scholars working on the original Arabic text of Averroes' *Epitome* of the *De anima* have shown that in that text he does not claim that there is only one Material Intellect for the whole of humankind. They therefore argue that such a strange position must come from errors in the Latin translation. In fact, there are two versions of the *Epitome*, and more recent research has shown that Averroes revised his text at a later date. It is, therefore, true that Averroes did not at all defend this position in his first version of the *Epitome*, but, later on, he felt the need to develop it. He indicates in his preface to the revised *Epitome* that his earlier exposition rested more on the commentators than on the text of Aristotle. Once he really focused on Aristotle's own text, his views changed.[43] Even if we limit ourselves to the commentaries on the *De anima* and do not touch on the various positions defended in other texts,[44] there are still some thorny issues. First, it has only slowly been recognized that Averroes changed his mind on various philosophical issues and went back to correct some manuscripts of his own previous works. Second, whether the *Middle Commentary*, which is a paraphrase of Aristotle's text but includes a long excursus on the Material Intellect, precedes the *Long Commentary* is disputed.[45] The situation may become clearer when R. C. Taylor publishes his English translation of the *Long Commentary*.[46]

ETHICS

Little scholarly attention has been paid to philosophical ethics in Islam.[47] The focus on *falsafa* as mainly Aristotelian has contributed to this neglect, for although the *Nicomachean Ethics* and a summary of it known as the *Summa Alexandrinorum* were translated into Arabic, they did not circulate widely or quickly. Few ethical texts in the Aristotelian tradition have survived, including some known to have been written, such as al-Farabi's *Commentary on the Nicomachean Ethics*. Averroes' *Middle Commentary on the Ethics* still awaits a complete critical edition. There exist, however, a number of interesting texts from a Hellenistic, more popular tradition of spiritual medicine.

The *falsafa* tradition was much influenced by the Alexandrian School, which developed a curriculum requiring that students first acquire the habits of character necessary for serious philosophical studies. The *falasifa* distinguish, therefore, between a "reformation of character" or "spiritual medicine," as prerequisite to the study of logic and philosophy, and a "scientific ethics" grounded in metaphysics (as we saw in our reflections on Avicenna's *Metaphysics of the Shifa'* X).

Scholars in Hellenistic philosophy have shown that Stoics, Skeptics, and Epicureans wrote "therapies of the soul" intended to cure students' passions, or at least curb them, in order to liberate the soul for the study of philosophy. Emotions, passions, or desires are considered to be either false beliefs or the effects of such beliefs, and they can therefore be cured or curbed by substituting more appropriate beliefs. Literary artistry makes the arguments more appealing for budding philosophers, and, generally, there is a progression from rhetorical to dialectical and truly philosophical arguments, since stages in the healing process allow for greater and greater philosophical sophistication.[48]

One of the longest treatises of al-Kindi (c. 801–66) is *The Art of Dispelling Sorrows*, in which he moves from "gentle remedies," that is, Stoic arguments, to "stronger remedies," that is, metaphysical Neoplatonic arguments. There are striking similarities to Boethius's *Consolation of Philosophy*, since both are deeply rooted in the same Hellenistic tradition.[49]

Al-Razi, the nondenominational Persian philosopher-physician (c. 864–925 or 932), wrote a charming *Spiritual Medicine*, much grounded in Galen, which incites the reader to reform his character and begin studying logic and philosophy.[50] A critic of Aristotle, al-Razi took Plato's views on transmigration literally and elaborated a very original conception of the soul, in which animals are endowed with some sort of reason and choice. This allows al-Razi to elaborate a purely rational normative ethics, based on a consideration of God's basic attributes of intelligence, justice, and compassion. A detailed environmental ethics is included, as well as a case study of the type, "Who should be saved first?"[51] Since God is merciful and tries to diminish pain, al-Razi attacks the ascetic practices of various religions:

> The judgment of intellect and justice being that man is not to cause pain to others, it follows that he is not to cause pain to himself either. Many matters forbidden by the judgment of intellect also come under this maxim, such as what the Hindus do in approaching God by burning their bodies and throwing them upon sharp pieces of iron and such as the Manichaeans cutting off their testicles when they desire sexual intercourse, emaciating themselves through hunger and thirst, and soiling themselves by abstaining from water or using urine in place of it. Also entering into this classification, though far inferior, is what Christians do in pursuing monastic life and withdrawing to hermitages as well as many Muslims staying permanently in mosques, renouncing earnings, and restricting themselves to a modicum of repugnant food and to irritating and coarse clothing. Indeed, all of that is an iniquity towards themselves and causes them pain that does not push away a preponderant pain. ([383] 232)

Al-Razi also accepts the Alexandrian distinction between a prephilosophic "reformation of character" and a scientific ethics based on metaphysics.

Since al-Farabi's *Commentary on the Nicomachean Ethics* is lost, we turn to his popular *Reminder of the Way to Happiness* (not to be confused with *The Attainment of Happiness*), which advocates character reformation and invites its readers to the study of logic (carefully distinguished from grammar). For al-Farabi there are ethical first intelligibles, such as the existence of human freedom, emanating from the Agent Intellect. In his *Long Commentary on Aristotle's De Interpretatione*, he mounts a scathing critique of specialists in Kalam who, according to him, hold that there is no human freedom.[52] Here again, a "scientific ethics" rests on psychology and metaphysics.

Al-Farabi's Christian disciple, Yahya ibn 'Ady (893–974) also wrote a *Reformation of Character*, which includes barbed attacks against clerics who abuse their flock.[53] Trying to defend Christian monks from the attacks of al-Razi and Muslim thinkers who considered celibacy excessively ascetic and detached from community life, he argues that it allows the monks to prepare better apodeictic syllogisms. This surprising view helps us better to understand how much the philosophers emphasized their monopoly on demonstrative reasoning.

Among Muslims, this tradition continues in Ibn Miskawayh (d. 1030). His *Reformation of Character* reverses the traditional order and begins with a systematic presentation of ethics, much influenced by the *Nicomachean Ethics*, but ends by prescribing medicine for the soul. Its first part lays down a foundation, with a study of the faculties of the soul and reflections on the good and happiness and on virtues and vices. After discussing character and human perfection and its means, Miskawayh surveys in more detail the good and happiness. He focuses the fourth part of his treatise on justice and in the fifth deals with love and friendship. Finally, medicine for the soul is provided, with references to Galen and al-Kindi. Miskawayh here analyzes different diseases of the soul, such as anger, fear of death, and sadness; determines their causes; and suggests appropriate treatment. His *Treatise on Happiness* relies heavily on al-Farabi's *Reminder* and belongs entirely to the "medicine of the soul" genre.

This tradition imbues al-Tusi's (d. 1274) *Nasirean Ethics*, written in Persian.[54] No religious community was immune from the genre: the Muslim religious writer, Ibn Hazm of Córdoba (994–1064), wrote a *Book on Character and Behavior*, and the Jewish writer Ibn Paqudah (c. 1050–80) penned a *Guide to the Duties of the Heart* inspired by this tradition.

Avicenna, though subscribing to the Alexandrian tradition of a double ethics, that is, a prephilosophic one and a scientific one, wrote little on ethics but, as we have seen, concludes his *Metaphysics of the Shifa'* with a rational justification of the basic prescriptions of the *shari'a*.[55]

This brief and vastly incomplete presentation of philosophy in Islam shows that there is much pioneering work yet to be done. Since 1950 much has happened in the field. Exciting discoveries have been made. English translations of key texts, such as Avicenna's *Metaphysics of the Shifa'* by M. E. Marmura and Averroes' *Long Commentary on the "De anima"* by R. C. Taylor are eagerly awaited. Critical editions of other important texts are still needed, however, as well as analyses of arguments and works of interpretation. It would be wrong to exaggerate the contribution to current controversies about "western" and "Islamic" values that might be made by scholarly research in the material presented in this chapter, but it can at least be said that a deeper understanding of philosophy in medieval Islam, including a more nuanced awareness of the issues debated concerning the very existence of *falsafa* in Islamic culture, can only improve our insight into the nature and role (and perhaps the limitations) of philosophy in general.

NOTES

1. J. L. Kraemer, for instance, has admirably shown the cultural interchanges in Baghdad at the end of the tenth century and the first half of the eleventh century between people of various religious and ethnic backgrounds [492].
2. E. Gilson, "What is Christian Philosophy?," in [635] 177–91, and E. Gilson [628]. F. Van Steenberghen defended the autonomy of philosophy and argued that strictly speaking there can be no specifically Christian philosophy in [637].
3. See R. M. Frank [487–89].
4. See C. D'Ancona Costa [477] and J. Kraye *et al.* [18].
5. See D. Gutas [490]. Gutas shows how, then as now, political ideologies sometimes dictated the choice of the texts that were translated.
6. D. Gutas [102] and T.-A. Druart [100] doubt it, but J. Parens [105] affirms it.
7. H. A. Davidson in [483] shows admirably the Greek origins of arguments on those topics, as well as the Kalam sources, and their transformation and integration at the hands of philosophers in lands under Islamic rule.
8. See the second part of H. Corbin [10], called "From the Death of Averroes to the Present Day." Corbin also highlighted that philosophy persisted among Sunni and Shiite, as well as Ismaili.
9. M. Aydin [478].
10. See D. Black [480], in particular the chapter on the imaginative and poetic syllogism, pp. 209–41.
11. E. Renan [172].
12. Also known as *The Harmony Between Philosophy and Religion*. My translation is based on that of G. F. Hourani [161]. Most of the texts I shall refer to in this section were not translated into Latin during the Middle Ages and, therefore, had little impact on the scholastics, even if they gained popularity with the Enlightenment (see G. A. Russell

[497]) and in our own time, particularly among the disciples of Leo Strauss.

13. *Incoherence of the Incoherence*, discussion 17, that "heretics be killed" [165] I 322.

14. Al-Farabi was famous for his Long Commentary on Aristotle's *De interpretatione* and his epitomes of Aristotle's Organon, including the *Poetics*. He carefully distinguished logic from grammar, and though he is a rationalist, his language and vocabulary are influenced by religious terminology.

15. See R. Walzer's translation [95].

16. M. Galston [101] and J. Lameer [103] highlight the link between logic and political philosophy in al-Farabi.

17. See *The Attainment of Happiness* in *Alfarabi's Philosophy of Plato and Aristotle* [96].

18. M. Mahdi in particular has highlighted al-Farabi's rationalism in [104], and C. E. Butterworth has recently published translations of the *Selected Aphorisms, The Book of Religion*, and *The Harmonization of the Opinions of the Two Sages: Plato the Divine and Aristotle* in [98].

19. *The Life of Ibn Sina* [117] 30–35.

20. *Shifa's Metaphysics* VI 1 and 2. Medieval Latin translation [116] II 291–306. English translation [113].

21. See D. Gutas [124].

22. Trans. [114].

23. *Averroes on Plato's "Republic"* [164] 101 and 59.

24. In *Avicenna on Theology* [120].

25. Trans. [22] 112–21. Curiously, Roger Bacon (c. 1210–92) adapted the end of Avicenna's Book X to Christendom in his *Opus maius*, Part VII.

26. Very partial English translation in [22] 123–33.

27. Partial excellent English translation [22] 134–62; full translation [368].

28. In the Middle Ages Ibn Tufayl's novel was translated into Hebrew (with a Hebrew commentary by Moses Narboni). It was translated into Latin only in 1671, by Pocok, and into English in 1708 under the title *The Improvement of Human Reason Exhibited in the Life of Hai Ebn Yokdhan, In which is demonstrated, by what methods one may, by the meer light of nature, attain the knowledg of things natural and supernatural; more particularly knowledg of God, and the affairs of another life.* The English text is illustrated and provided with an appendix, intended to protect the faith of Christian readers, "in which the possibility of Man's attaining the true knowledg of God, and things necessary to salvation, without instruction, is briefly consider'd" [367]. The Latin and English translators both read the tale as a purely rationalist account, although some have interpreted it as a mystical allegory.

For interpretations of the text, see L. I. Conrad [369]. There is some dispute whether Pocok's translation could have influenced the author of *Robinson Crusoe*, and simplified forms of the tale are still sometimes told as a fairy tale to Middle Eastern children. See also H. Daiber [481].

29. On this see chapter 9 in the present volume.

30. See J. Michot, *La Destinée de l'homme selon Avicenne* (Louvain, 1981).

31. Partial English translation in F. Rahman [119].

32. Trans. [49] 219–39. Also see M. E. Marmura [131] and Thomas Aquinas, *Truth*, q. 1, a. 1.

33. R. Wisnovsky [134]. Marmura pointed earlier to differences between Avicenna's philosophy and the Kalam [130]. For the immense influence of these distinctions in Latin philosophy, see chapter 6 in this volume.

34. F. Rahman [132].

35. See D. Gutas in [133] 1–38 and D. N. Hasse in [133] 39–72.

36. S. H. Nasr argues for the "originality" of the Oriental Philosophy in [11] 247–51, whereas D. Gutas claims there is no such thing [123].

37. A. F. Mehren, *Traités mystiques d'Avicenne*, 4 fascicles (Leiden, 1889–94). H. Corbin, too, highlighted a "mystical" aspect in Avicenna [10]. But if mysticism there is, it is a very rationalistic one.

38. See J. F. Wippel [261].

39. Trans. [149].

40. R. M. Frank says yes in [487], and M. E. Marmura denies it in [151] and [150].

41. See D. Black [166].

42. H. A. Davidson has remarkably retraced the general history of this issue among both the Greek commentators and the *falasifa* in [482].

43. Averroes seems first to have followed Alexander of Aphrodisias, then to have adopted the position of Ibn Bajjah (Avempace) [360], and finally, after rereading Themistius, to have decided that there should be one Material Intellect for all humankind. In the *Long Commentary* he somewhat rhetorically accuses Ibn Bajjah of having led him into error.

44. Such as *The Epistle on the Possibility of Conjunction with the Active Intellect* [160].

45. A. L. Ivry, who edited and translated the *Middle Commentary* (Arabic edition in 1994 and with English translation in 2002), maintains that it is posterior to the *Long Commentary*, whereas H. A. Davidson considers that it preceded it (Ivry [170], Davidson, with Ivry's response, in [167]).

46. The articles by A. Hyman, A. L. Ivry, and R. C. Taylor in [168] offer much useful material on these difficult questions.

47. Except for G. F. Hourani [491] and M. Fakhry [486].

48. See M. C. Nussbaum [494] and [495].

49. See T.-A. Druart [92] and [485].

50. Trans. [384].

51. See his autobiography *The Book of the Philosophic Life*, trans. C. E. Butterworth [383], and T.-A. Druart [385] and [386].

52. Trans. [94] 76–84. See also T.-A. Druart [99].

53. Trans. [366].

54. Trans. G. M. Wickens [390].

55. Mehren (note 37 above) had attributed to him a treatise on the *Fear of Death*, but, in fact, this text comes from the concluding section of Miskwayh's *Reformation of Character*.

5   Jewish philosophy

If medieval philosophy is strange to the modern reader, medieval Jewish philosophy is even stranger. To the extent that medieval philosophy has been recognized as philosophy rather than dismissed as theology, its boundaries have been strictly drawn, geographically and doctrinally, around Christian western Europe. This excludes both Islamic and Jewish philosophy, so that even significant philosophical activity in southern France and Islamic Spain has remained invisible to the modern western tradition. When activity beyond the prescribed boundaries has been acknowledged at all, it has been by the few historians of medieval philosophy and then, as a rule, only to the extent that its influence on major Christian thinkers could not be ignored. The significance of work beyond the boundaries has thus been determined almost exclusively by relevance to the interests of Christian philosophers. Except for a few specialists, therefore, the general view of medieval philosophy remains unduly narrow. Whether one reads Hegel's lectures on the history of philosophy, or Heidegger's, or Russell's, one could only conclude that there were no medieval Jewish philosophers – and this despite the fact that the period in question is esteemed by scholarly Jews as a golden age.

Rather than attempting to remedy this neglect by a comprehensive survey of medieval Jewish philosophers, I will focus on four figures whose importance for later philosophy, Jewish as well as Christian, is especially great: Saadiah Gaon, Solomon Ibn Gabirol (Avicebron), Moses Maimonides, and Gersonides (Levi ben Gerson). To give some unity to the consideration of the diverse styles and concerns of these thinkers, I will give major attention to a single philosophical question: is the universe eternal or created? In order to suggest the distinct contribution of Jewish philosophy and to situate it in relation

to other medieval philosophy, I will take account of three sorts of
influence: (1) the philosophical and other literary traditions that informed each philosopher's thought; (2) the influence each had upon
subsequent Jewish thought; and (3) the influence each had upon subsequent Christian philosophy. For one of our four selected thinkers,
strangely, influence of the second kind is nil, while influence of the
third kind is quite extensive.

THE ROOTS OF KNOWLEDGE – SAADIAH GAON (882–942)

Although we have no direct evidence regarding Saadiah's education,
his writings reflect extensive knowledge of Greek philosophy and
science, the influence of Islamic theology (Kalam), and a familiarity with Christian doctrine and various forms of eastern philosophy. While Saadiah's work was unknown to the Christian West,
its influence on Jewish philosophy was (and is) extensive. Saadiah
was the first Jewish philosopher, as distinct from a philosopher who
happened to be Jewish, his foremost concern being the relation between philosophy and the Hebrew Bible and tradition. As a result,
subsequent Jewish philosophers had to respond to his work, even if
critically.

Saadiah's writings were of three kinds, all of them, however, with
the single aim of educating the Jewish community at a time when
Hebrew literacy was in decline and when, among the literate, confusion and error were rampant: polemics;[1] pedagogical works concerned with the preservation of knowledge of the Bible and Jewish
tradition; and two predominantly philosophical works, *The Book of
Creation* and *The Book of Doctrines and Beliefs*.[2] Since *The Book
of Creation* has had little influence on subsequent Jewish thought,
while *The Book of Doctrines and Beliefs* is still studied as a major
work in Jewish religious philosophy, I will discuss only the latter.

In *The Book of Doctrines and Beliefs* Saadiah sought to demonstrate a fundamental harmony between philosophy and biblical
revelation. As a basis for exhibiting this harmony with regard to particular disputed questions (and after outlining hindrances to knowledge and cautioning at length about the proper order of inquiry), he
argued for the soundness of four roots of human knowledge. From the
outset, Saadiah repeatedly argued that these roots must be cultivated

in successive stages. In one of his most interesting arguments he presented this view of knowledge as appropriately progressive, rather than perfect from the beginning, in response to an objection to the existence of a perfect creator: such a creator, the objection ran, would have been able to create a perfect world with perfectly rational creatures. Saadiah, following Aristotle, insists that the perfection of one root is a necessary condition for development of the next. Differently stated, and in a manner that anticipates subsequent Aristotelian philosophy, he formulated the difference between types of self-evidence as a difference between what is most evident to us (sensible knowledge) and what is most evident in itself (first principles). The first three roots are philosophical, the fourth, traditional. Together these roots sustain Saadiah's theory of biblical interpretation as well as the more strictly philosophical side of his harmonizing project. The four roots are as follows.

(1) *Sense perception* (literally: sensible science). Provided the sense organ is healthy and the individual is not deluded, belief derived from sensation is sound and is the basis for all subsequent knowledge. Saadiah points out that only a very few radical skeptics reject this root and claims that in so doing they also reject the second and third roots, since the further knowledge is from sensation, the more it is subject to doubt. "The reason for this unequal distribution of views lies in the fact that the second type of knowledge is more hidden than the first and likewise the third more hidden than the second. Naturally, one is more readily inclined to deny what is hidden than what is obvious" ([106] 37).

(2) *Reason*. Saadiah holds that some truths are intrinsically (necessarily) evident or knowable *per se*. His description of this sort of knowledge shows his unqualified confidence in the natural powers of human reason, provided that it is properly trained: "As to the knowledge of reason [literally: the intelligibles], we hold that every conception formed in our mind when it is free from defects is undoubtedly true knowledge, provided we know how to reason, complete the act of reasoning, and guard against illusions and dreams" ([106] 38). He adds, however, that those who believe in the rational status of dreams and illusions do so in order to safeguard sensible knowledge, confusing, as it were, sense perception and imaginative representation. Assuming that dreams derive directly from sense perceptions, they believe that to deny the rational status of dreams is

simultaneously to deny the sensible origins of human knowledge. Saadiah's explanation for trust in dreams is both novel and striking. On the one hand, he uses it to bolster his own claim for the close relation between sensation and reason. On the other hand, he uses it to safeguard the rational status of prophetic revelation in dreams, claiming that they "contain a flash of inspiration from above in the form of hints and parables" ([106] 39, trans. modified). That is, provided that proper distinctions are recognized among the different types of representation, sensible, imaginative, and rational (which requires proper training), there is no fear of confusing wakeful states with dream states and no need to doubt the veracity of sense perception. Saadiah's twofold account of dreams is thus a bold argument that implicitly posits revelation both as the culmination of the natural process of human cognition and as a divine aid that circumvents the slow temporal process of perfection, ensuring that those who are intellectually weaker would not be bereft of religious faith.

(3) *Inference*, when it yields propositions that cannot be denied without simultaneously denying propositions derived either from sense perception or from reason. Inference is necessary when neither sensory nor rational evidence is sufficient to account for a phenomenon, for example, when we perceive smoke without perceiving fire or, most significant, when we perceive the universe but not a cause for it. Or again: "We are compelled to admit that man possesses a soul, although we do not perceive it by our senses, so as not to deny its obvious functions. Similarly, we are compelled to admit that the soul is endowed with reason, although we do not perceive it by our senses, so as not to deny its obvious function" ([106] 36).

Saadiah outlines seven rules for inference in either philosophy or the interpretation of the biblical tradition. These again confirm the authority of reason. Inference should not contradict (1) sense perception, (2) reason, or (3) some other truth, and (4) it should not be self-contradictory or (5) involve greater difficulties than those we seek to resolve. The sixth and seventh rules enjoin caution, so as to avoid hasty conclusions. Provided the interpreter exercises proper care, according to Saadiah, the first four rules should be applied to all biblical interpretation.

(4) *Reliable tradition*. Saadiah refers here primarily, but not exclusively, to the revealed tradition. He argues that this root is in fact based upon both sense perception and reason. Certainty concerning

the status of prophetic instruction is derived from the prophet's performance of miracles that is witnessed by others and cannot be explained otherwise. Thus, both sense perception, in the form of witness, and inference to a cause of an event that cannot be explained
otherwise serve to verify the status of prophecy.

Saadiah offers two justifications for a speculative approach to religion, an inquiring approach that makes use of sense perception, reason, and inference and does not simply take the tradition as given.
First, speculative inquiry turns into real, intrinsic knowledge what
God has revealed as extrinsic, prophetic instruction. Second, taking
advantage of every basis for knowledge enables the believer to refute those who deride religious belief. Maimonides was to question
Saadiah's overwhelming confidence in the power of human reason
as a misguided form of Kalam.

According priority in biblical interpretation to sense perception
and reason over tradition would not be surprising when applied to
many questions. It is striking that Saadiah maintains this priority
even when dealing with the question of creation. And since, as he
notes at the beginning of his discussion, sense perception provides
no data on this question (if it did, there would be no disagreement
about it), he in fact proceeds on the basis of reason and philosophical
speculation. Maimonides will be especially vehement in his critique
of Saadiah here.

Saadiah offers four proofs for the divine creation of the universe.[3]
In a manner that became standard later, these proofs use Aristotelian
cosmological or natural principles in order to reach conclusions that
are intended to refute Aristotle's conclusion that the world is eternal. And in contrast to Aristotle's statement in the *Topics* (I 11,
104b13–17) that the origin of the world can only be investigated dialectically, Saadiah claims that creation is demonstrable. His proofs
proceed from the finite nature of the universe, the composite nature
of bodies, the nature of accidents inhering in bodies, and the nature
of time. In outline, they run as follows. (1) Since the heaven, earth,
and all celestial bodies are finite in magnitude, the force that preserves them must be finite as well. Hence, the world must have had
a beginning and would have an end. (2) Since the world comprises
well-fitting composite bodies, they must be "the skillful work of a
skillful artisan and creator" ([106] 54) – a version of the argument
from design. (3) Since natural substances and the accidents inhering

in them are finite and contingent (that is, do not exist necessarily), they must have been brought into existence by a creator. (4) Since the infinite cannot be traversed in thought or in reality, time must be finite. Were time not finite, finite beings could not have been generated. Finally, having concluded that the world had a beginning and that time is finite, Saadiah claims that were creation not *ex nihilo*, finite beings would create themselves, which is impossible. Consequently, all beings must have been created by an external, eternal, all-powerful being.

There is a central inconsistency in Saadiah's proofs for creation that will be vehemently criticized by Maimonides, namely, that although he denies that sense perception can provide data about the origin of the world, he bases his proofs upon the perceived nature of actually existing finite beings. In view of Saadiah's unfailing belief in the power of human reason, the greatest irony about Maimonides' criticism is that he accuses Saadiah of the error for which Saadiah accused others: pseudo-reason.

UNIVERSAL HYLOMORPHISM – IBN GABIROL (AVICEBRON) (c. 1021–c. 1058)

It was discovered only in 1859 that the man known to the Jewish tradition almost exclusively as Solomon Ibn Gabirol, a poet who composed hundreds of liturgical and secular poems, was the thinker known to the Christian tradition as Avicebron, the supposedly Muslim philosopher who composed the *Fons vitae*, the *Fountain of Life*. Of Ibn Gabirol's philosophical works, only two are extant, the *Fons vitae* (Hebrew: *Mekor Hayim*) in a twelfth-century Latin translation from the original Arabic, and *Tikkun Midot ha-Nefesh* (Improvement of the Moral Qualities). Since the latter work on practical ethics exerted little influence on subsequent philosophy, Jewish or Christian, I shall restrict my discussion to a brief overview of the *Mekor Hayim*, in which the more significant philosophical elements of the *Tikkun Midot ha-Nefesh* are, in any case, repeated.

Mekor Hayim reflects its author's education in the rich Judeo-Arabic intellectual culture, philosophical, scientific, and literary, of Islamic Spain at its height. The work is written in the form of a dialogue between a teacher and his disciple. It is divided into five books, preceded by an introductory summary of its intention and structure.

The intention is to inquire into the nature of universal matter and universal form as they are manifest in composite corporeal substance as well as simple spiritual substance. The structure of the work is described as follows.

In the first treatise, we shall treat those things which ought to be posited about universal matter and universal form in order to assign the matter and form in composite substances. In the second we shall treat the substance sustaining the corporeality of the world. In the third we shall treat the reality of simple substances. In the fourth we shall treat the science of understanding the matter and form of simple substances. In the fifth we shall treat universal matter and form in themselves. ([135] 1; trans. mine)

Although Ibn Gabirol's account of the relations between matter and form is not consistent,[4] it is evident that by "simple substance" he never means something indivisible, lacking all composition. His most original and influential contribuition to philosophy is in fact his hylomorphism, according to which all substances are composed of matter and form, with matter hierarchically ordered from the highest general spiritual matter to the lowest prime matter. Whatever his sources – Aristotle, the Stoics, Proclus, Isaac Israeli, and Pseudo-Empedocles have all been suggested – Ibn Gabirol develops an original Neoplatonic hierarchical system of Being that is seamlessly unified, bound by the being of God at its apex and that of prime matter at its nadir.

In Ibn-Gabirol's two emanationist accounts of it, creation is atemporal. In one account, matter originates in the essence of God, whereas form originates in the divine will; in the other, both matter and form originate in the divine will.

Mekor Hayim is a unique work in medieval Jewish philosophy, in that it lacks any internal evidence that could identify it as a work written by a Jewish philosopher; it contains no reference to the Hebrew Bible or to any other Jewish source, traditional or philosophical. It is not surprising, therefore, that, in contrast to its significant positive as well as critical[5] reception by Christian philosophers, especially Franciscans, such as Bonaventure and Duns Scotus, *Mekor Hayim* exerted little influence on Jewish philosophy. This strange destiny can best be understood in light of the harsh criticism leveled against Ibn Gabirol by the twelfth-century Jewish Aristotelian, Abraham Ibn Daud, who accused him of addressing his work to all nations, rather than to the Jewish people; focusing at too great a length on a single subject (matter and form); lacking a scientific method and using false (imaginative) premises to reach false conclusions; and misleading the Jewish people greatly.

THE LIMITS OF REASON – MOSES MAIMONIDES (1138–1204)

Moses Maimonides is without doubt both the best known and the most controversial medieval Jewish philosopher. Although there is disagreement about his preeminent merit, none will deny that his influence on subsequent philosophy, both Christian and Jewish, has been the most extensive and enduring. Like many of his medieval contemporaries, especially in the Jewish and Islamic tradition, Maimonides was trained as a physician, jurist, and philosopher. On the basis of our knowledge of the education of other prominent Jews of this time, it is reasonable to assume that he first studied the Torah, the Talmud, mathematics, and astronomy with his father and subsequently was educated by Arab masters in the natural sciences, medicine, and philosophy. From his own testimony in a letter to Samuel Ibn Tibbon, the translator from Judeo-Arabic into Hebrew of his major philosophical work, *Dalalat al-Ha'irin* (Guide of the Perplexed), we know that, in addition to Aristotle, whom he held in the highest esteem, Maimonides was influenced by philosophers in the Islamic world, especially al-Farabi.

Maimonides' prominence as a spiritual authority is evidenced by his extensive *Responsa* to legal, religious, and philosophical questions sent to him by Jewish communities in both Islamic and Christian lands and by the *Mishneh Torah*, a work written in Hebrew in which he sought to present a clear systematic exposition of the Oral Law in order to make it fully accessible to all Jews. His prominence as a physician is attested by his medical writings and by his appointment as court physician to al-Fadil, Salah al-Din's vizier.

The *Dalalat al-Ha'irin* (henceforth, the *Guide*) has as its explicit aim the resolution of perplexity at the apparent tension between philosophy and revelation, a perplexity felt most acutely by those educated in both the Torah and philosophy. It is to this audience that the *Guide* is addressed. Maimonides diagnoses the source of his readers' perplexity as, on one hand, a strong intellectual desire, leading to an inordinate haste in the pursuit of knowledge, and, on the other hand, improper instruction in divine matters given by the Jewish Mutakallimun, such as Saadiah. Since the perplexity with which the *Guide* is concerned is occasioned by improper interpretation of the Bible in relation to philosophy, I shall begin with the problem of interpretation and proceed to the three topics most susceptible to error: divine unicity, creation, and providence.

The apparent contradiction between the Torah and philosophy arises, according to Maimonides, from the misguided interpretation of biblical speech by applying to it the criteria and methods proper to the natural sciences. The Bible does not proceed demonstratively or in a linear fashion, and neither will the *Guide*. Maimonides holds that his method, which deliberately intertwines dialectics and indicative hints, is pedagogically most expedient, because it follows both biblical prudence, which counsels great caution in disclosing divine matters, and philosophical prudence, which teaches by developing the student's capacity for similar independent pursuit. He instructs his reader:

> If you wish to grasp the totality of what this Treatise contains... you must connect its chapters one with another; and when reading a given chapter, your intention must be not only to understand the totality of the subject of that chapter, but also to grasp each word that occurs in it... even if that word does not belong to the intention of that chapter. For the diction of this Treatise has not been chosen at haphazard, but with great exactness and exceeding precision and with care to avoid failing to explain any obscure point. And nothing has been mentioned out of its place, *save with a view to explaining some matter in its proper place.* (*Guide* I, introduction [178] 15; emphasis mine)

After outlining other difficulties pertaining to the philosophical interpretation of the Torah, Maimonides presents the most fundamental one, namely, the natural limitations of human reason for apprehending divine science. By divine science, Maimonides means the intellectual instruction contained in the Torah, as distinct from its moral teachings. He immediately reassures the reader, however, that divine and natural science are complementary, and that true knowledge of the latter is necessary for true knowledge of the former. For although revelation may give believers true opinions about divine subjects, they can understand these subjects only when they have gained a knowledge of natural science. That is why, according to Maimonides, the Bible commences with the "Account of the Beginning" and philosophers commence their study with physics. Initially, there is no difference in understanding between the vulgar and the elite. Neither group can see the apparent contradictions within the Bible or the apparent contradictions between philosophy and revelation that are occasioned by the Bible's parabolic form of speech. The vulgar, however, are content with the letter of the biblical text, whereas the potentially wise are prompted by the Bible to pursue additional knowledge. But after study of the natural sciences, the elite experience perplexity and must seek genuine understanding of the mysteries of divine science, that is, true understanding of the Torah. Such understanding will sometimes amount to understanding clearly that full insight and philosophical demonstration are beyond us. "You should not think that these great *secrets* are fully and completely known to anyone among us. They are not. But sometimes truth flashes out to us so that we think that it is day, and then matter and habit in their various forms conceal it so that we find ourselves again in an obscure night, almost as we were at first" (*Guide* I, introduction [178] 7).

The major principle of interpretation derivable from Maimonides' introductory remarks and repeated throughout the *Guide* is Aristotelian. Following Aristotle's dictum in the *Nicomachean Ethics* (I 2; 1094b24–27), that "it is the mark of an educated man to look for precision in each class of things just so far as the nature of the subject admits," Maimonides does not seek demonstrative proofs where these are inappropriate, namely, in divine science and in subjects which derive their principles from it. The less a subject admits of demonstration, the greater the disagreement it engenders. Thus, according to Maimonides, the greatest disagreements are encountered in metaphysics, lesser ones in natural science, and none in mathematics.

Since the express purpose of his work is the resolution of perplexity occasioned by errors, Maimonides focuses primarily on questions where biblical interpretation or philosophical argument is most likely to go astray. Hence, he devotes the bulk of each inquiry to refutation and only subsequently articulates his own position. The *Guide* is thus dialectical (precisely in the sense of Book I of Aristotle's *Topics*) and does not shy away from criticism of other Jewish thinkers. Maimonides often proposes the teachings of the philosophers, especially Aristotle, as superior to those of his coreligionists. For attaining human perfection, the elimination of error is most critical with respect to the following: (1) divine incorporeality, (2) creation, (3) providence, (4) divine law, and (5) human perfection. Concerning the first, fundamental subject, the philosophical and revealed teachings are in complete agreement. Apparent disagreement about God's incorporeality is the result of vulgar misunderstanding of revelation. With respect to the other subjects, some disagreements between the two traditions are apparent, others real. When the disagreements between philosophical and revealed teachings manifest real conflicts, Maimonides' position is always an adaptation of the revealed tradition that is philosophically reasonable, though often indemonstrable.

The proper understanding of God's incorporeality and unicity, according to Maimonides, is the primary purpose of the entire Torah, since true human perfection is impossible without such an understanding. Hence, despite the great difficulty in attaining it and despite the esoteric nature of the subject, all Jews must attain some understanding of God's incorporeality and must reject the contrary conception. On this issue, Maimonides takes a radical, uncompromising position, one which eventuates in a strict negative theology. The most adequate knowledge of God accessible to human reason is the understanding of what God is not, of the radical distinction between God and creatures. Thus Aristotle, "prince of the philosophers," could demonstrate that God exists but no more; he denied the possibility of human knowledge of the essence or *whatness* of the supralunar realm and especially of the prime mover. Maimonides entirely agrees:

Know that the description of God, may He be cherished and exalted, by means of negation is the correct description...I shall make it clear to you that we have no way of describing Him unless it is through negations and not otherwise...It has already been demonstrated that God, may He be honored and magnified, is existent of necessity and that there is not composition in Him...and that we are only able to apprehend the fact that He is and cannot apprehend His quiddity. (*Guide* I 58 [178] 134–35)

Consequently, Maimonides insists on a figurative interpretation of the letter of the Torah and the tradition in every instance where corporeality may be suggested. In so doing, he challenges the beliefs of most Jews and the teachings of some of his predecessors, notably Yehudah ha-Levi. Unlike many previous Jewish thinkers, who considered anthropomorphic language necessary for the religious instruction of the majority even while denying the ultimate veracity of such attributions, Maimonides holds that all anthropomorphisms are conducive only to idolatry. Accordingly, he discusses divine incorporeality not only in the philosophically framed *Guide* but also in his *Commentary on the Mishnah* and in the *Mishneh Torah*. He bases five of the thirteen beliefs he considers necessary for gaining access to the "world to come" (i.e., to immortality) on the affirmation of divine unicity and incorporeality. Conversely, he insists that belief in divine corporeality, and thus in a literal understanding of biblical verses implying it, entails exclusion from the community of Israel and from the world to come. Consequently, most of Book I of the *Guide* is devoted to an explanation of anthropomorphic biblical terms that leads to Maimonides' celebrated (or notorious) denial of meaning to positive divine attributions and his denial of any positive knowledge of God by analogy, however remote. Attributes of action, that is, characterizations of God from effects in the created world, are permissible, but even these are, strictly speaking, untrue. They are acceptable because they are the best exemplars for human actions to imitate, but they do not articulate anything true about God.

Following Aristotle and the Islamic philosophical tradition, Maimonides provides four demonstrative proofs for the existence of God. All of them are causal, beginning from observed physical phenomena and concluding that, since infinite regress of causes is impossible, there must be an uncaused first cause or prime mover of the entire chain of causality. Following Avicenna, Maimonides identifies Aristotle's prime mover with the singular necessary being whose existence is identical with his essence, unlike every other being, in all of which existence is distinct from essence and is possible rather than necessary. Maimonides departs from Avicenna, however, regarding creation. Where Avicenna held that other beings come from God by a necessary emanation, Maimonides denies that causal necessity extends to God. God is the cause of necessity in the universe rather than being bound by it.

Precisely because Aristotle recognized the limitations of natural human reason, Maimonides can substitute revealed teachings for some of the Philosopher's speculations on subjects inaccessible to demonstration. Thus, on subjects which Maimonides considers fundamental in the Torah, such as creation and providence, subjects on which Aristotle and the Bible disagree, Maimonides seeks to establish the greater probability of revealed teaching over the philosophical. Concerning both creation and providence, Maimonides first exposes the weaknesses of the philosophical position and then attempts to show that revealed teachings are more plausible, either by being more congruent with the requirements of logic or better as explanations of sensible experience.

> Do not criticize me for having set out doubts that attach to his [Aristotle's] opinion...However, we shall treat this philosopher as his followers have enjoined us to treat him. For Alexander [of Aphrodisias] has explained that in every case in which no demonstration is possible, the two contrary opinions with regard to the matter in question should be posited as hypotheses, and it should be seen what doubts attach to each of them: the one to which fewer doubts attach should be believed. Alexander says that things are thus with respect to all the opinions regarding the divine that Aristotle sets forth and regarding which no demonstration is possible. (*Guide* II 22 [178] 320)

In investigating the question of creation, Maimonides outlines three main positions that seem tenable: that of the Torah, that of Plato, and that of Aristotle. The first affirms creation *ex nihilo* by an act of God's will; the second affirms an act of creation out of a prime matter coeternal with God; the third affirms a prime mover of a world coeternal with itself, as well as with time and motion. Having outlined the three positions, Maimonides argues that although Plato's position does not undermine the foundation of the Torah, while Aristotle's destroys it, both philosophical positions can be refuted as if they were one – and he in fact proceeds to treat them as such. The conflation of these distinct philosophical positions and Maimonides' admission that neither the philosophic nor the revealed position is demonstrable have led scholars to speculate that in upholding the position of the Torah Maimonides is hiding his true opinion, which is contrary to the Torah, namely, belief in the eternity of the world. It is, however, possible to explain Maimonides' position in a way that not only honors his stated opinion but is also more cogent philosophically than such speculation allows. The proposed explanation is as follows. Although the Platonic position does not destroy the foundations of the Torah for unphilosophical believers, it still restricts divine power in a manner that compromises the revealed notion of God. This is because the coeternal existence of anything prior to creation (e.g., prime matter), with the necessity of such matter for the very act of creation, restricts the creative act, insofar as it ontologically determines to some extent (however small) what God can or cannot do. Consequently, that coeternal matter is also a codetermining principle in the created world. Simple believers cannot recognize the difference between creation *ex nihilo* and creation out of coeternal prime matter, and hence, for them, the Platonic position is consistent with the Torah's affirmation of creation. But the perplexed philosophers, the audience of the *Guide*, can see the difference. Moreover, to the perplexed but believing philosophers the Platonic position is attractive, since it allows them simultaneously to affirm creation and explain it, whereas the Torah's position places creation beyond explanation. By adopting the Platonic position, however, these thinkers must admit a principle of change and decay independent of the divine will, an admission with grave consequences for the possibility of human perfection, let alone divine justice.

The central question is thus whether or not the origin of the world is demonstrable. Since Aristotle attempted to resolve the question philosophically, while Plato proposed his view as only a "likely story," it is Aristotle's arguments that pose a real threat to the Torah and hence require careful investigation. If they are shown to be based on conjecture rather than on demonstrative principles, then the position of the Torah can be proposed as, at the very least, equally plausible. Maimonides therefore takes great pains to show that whereas Aristotle's teachings are true with respect to sublunar physics, with respect to celestial physics, let alone metaphysics, they are not only uncertain and contrary to Ptolemy's physics, but also violate some of Aristotle's own logical precepts. Moreover, he points out on numerous occasions that Aristotle himself concluded that the question of the world's origin is beyond demonstration and that it is only the later Aristotelians, for example, Saadiah, who believed an answer to be demonstrable.[6] To underscore this conclusion, Maimonides argues for the indemonstrability not only of unobserved, unique, extranatural events, but of all unobserved phenomena:

No inference can be drawn in any respect from the nature of a thing after it has been generated, has attained its final state, and has achieved stability in its most perfect state, to the state of that thing while it moved toward being generated. Nor can an inference be drawn from the state of the thing when it moves toward being generated to its state before it began to move thus. Whenever you err in this and draw an inference from the nature of a thing that has achieved actuality to its nature when it was only *in potentia*, grave doubts are aroused in you. Moreover things that *must exist become impossible in your opinion*, and on the other hand things that are *impossible become necessary in your opinion*. (*Guide* II 17 [178] 295; emphases mine)

Maimonides provides here a counterfactual example to show the impossibility of deducing the necessary conditions for existence from existence itself. He imagines the incredulity of a man who, having grown up without any association with females, human or animal, cannot believe that human birth occurs as it does.

Once the philosophical position on the origin of the world proves doubtful and the position of the Torah on this question is accepted as equally valid, all the teachings of the Torah, including miracles and prophecy, can be shown to be philosophically reasonable. Nonetheless, it is important to emphasize that, according to Maimonides, if there were to be a demonstration concerning the origin of the universe, its conclusion would have to be accepted even if it contradicted the *letter* of the Torah.

Maimonides' argument for the indemonstrability of the origin of the world, which denies the extension of causal necessity to God, pertains only to divine acts. It is not a rejection of natural, necessary teleology but only limits it to the actually existing universe in its formed state, though without excluding the possibility of free, undetermined divine intervention in it. This possibility, according to Maimonides, is made immanent in nature in virtue of the creative act. Thus, a miraculous event does not constitute a disruption of the natural order. Rather, miracles are virtual, unactualized possibilities in nature and are a constitutive part of the original plan of creation. Likewise, it is precisely because of the cognitive and voluntary nature of the creative act, precisely insofar as it is not necessitated, that God can be said to be provident and omniscient, rather than the divinity described by Aristotle as indifferent to the sublunar world. God's knowledge of the world of generation and decay is general, whereas his knowledge of potentially immortal things – of human beings insofar as they are intellects and thus made in the image of the divine intellect – is particular. The sublunar extension of particular providence solely to human beings is not merely a concession to the Torah, nor is it the result of excessive intellectualism (two opposed accusations brought against Maimonides). Rather, insofar as it makes no claims to individual immortality,[7] this position is the only one that can be held consistently, once both free voluntary creation and natural causality are affirmed. Those beings that are subject to the laws of necessary causality are known only as species, as subject to the universal laws originating in God, since it is only as species that they possess permanence and thus can be truly known. On the other hand, intellectual beings, who do not act necessarily but can choose to act or refrain from action (where action proper is understood to be consequent upon intellect), to that extent actualize their proper perfection, attain their permanence, and can be known as distinct individuals rather than as essentially identical members of a species.

It is beyond the scope of this chapter to inquire whether Maimonides thought God could be said to know individual human beings who do not actualize their intellects. It is more likely that he would have denied it. What is important to recognize for Maimonides is that (1) *qua* human, all individuals possess a freedom to act which strictly natural beings do not, and (2) human beings were given the Law, by means of which they can act according to intellect (the divine as well as their own) and which they can choose, or refrain from choosing, to make their own. Whereas irrational creatures attain their proper perfection according to the necessary universal laws of their nature, human beings are free to attain their perfection through the "intellectual" revealed law. Failure to do so is a willed corruption of human natural perfection and thereby reduces the individual to a rank of being lower than the rational. "Know that this single soul, whose powers or parts are described above, is like matter, and the intellect is its form. If it does not attain its form, the existence of its capacity to attain this form is for nought and is, as it were, futile" (*Eight Chapters* 1 [177] 64). On the other hand, by observing divine law and seeking to understand it, all human beings are capable of attaining "a portion in the world to come."

Maimonides' influence on subsequent philosophy, both Jewish and Christian, can scarcely be overemphasized. His influence on

Christian philosophy is most evident in Thomas Aquinas, whose frequent references to the views of "Rabbi Moyses" are highly respectful, even when he disagrees with the Rabbi.[8]

A PURER ARISTOTELIANISM – GERSONIDES (LEVI BEN GERSHOM) (1288–1344)

Gersonides was born in Provence, is believed to have resided in Orange most of his life, and clearly spent a considerable amount of time in Avignon. It is generally agreed that his knowledge of Greek philosophy and science was obtained through Hebrew translations of Greek and Arabic texts, but there is disagreement as to whether he could read Latin. In any case, his works exhibit familiarity with both the substance and style of scholastic philosophy,[9] and there is direct evidence of his interaction with Christian thinkers and with the papal court, where he was highly regarded as a mathematician and astronomer.

Although Maimonides' fame and influence as a Jewish Aristotelian far exceeds that of Gersonides, it is Gersonides who is the more thorough and consistent Aristotelian. In this light, it is ironic – though not surprising given the turbulent ethos of the times – that Gersonides' philosophical works have remained unknown to the Christian philosophical tradition,[10] while in the Jewish tradition they have been maligned or pointedly ignored. His *magnum opus*, *The Wars of the Lord* (*Milhamot ha-Shem*), was indeed vilified as "Wars against the Lord," while his numerous commentaries on Averroes' commentaries on Aristotle were ignored. With the exception of an English translation of his *Supercommentary on the Prior Analytics* and an unpublished partial translation of his *Supercommentary on the Epitome on the De Anima*, they still remain hidden in manuscript form. Since, despite their intrinsic interest, the supercommentaries exerted no influence on subsequent philosophy, Jewish or Christian, I will focus strictly upon the *Wars*.[11]

In the introduction to the *Wars*, Gersonides lists six great problems that must be addressed in order to achieve human perfection, both intellectual and political. Each of the six *aporiae* is the subject of a separate book: (1) whether the soul is immortal; (2) the nature of dreams, divinations, and prophecy; (3) whether or not God knows individual existents; (4) the nature of divine providence; (5) the nature and motion of heavenly bodies (astronomy); and (6) whether the universe is eternal or created. Although the final question is last in order of investigation, Gersonides explicitly states that it is first in order of importance. It is the fundamental principle and difficulty from which all others follow. He also asserts at the outset that the only possible proof concerning the origin of the universe is an *a posteriori* one and that no proof can be derived from "the essence of the first cause" (an implicit critique of Saadiah's position):

> It is important to realize that on this question we cannot derive proofs from that which is prior to the world, e.g., from the First Cause; for our knowledge of the essence of the First Cause is very slight. Hence, we cannot make it a premise from which we can construct proof for this question. Indeed, the kind of proof available to us in this inquiry is the *a posteriori* proof, which is based on phenomena posterior to this generated entity [the universe], if it is the case that the world is generated. (*Wars*, introductory remarks [323] 92)

Insofar as the difficulties of a question are philosophical, Gersonides says he will proceed through an examination of the strengths and weaknesses in the different opinions on it in order to derive principles from them as well as to distinguish the true from the false and eradicate doubt. In a manner that is more challenging than Maimonides', Gersonides announces that his concern is to help "the man of inquiry," not those who attempt to prohibit inquiry, for philosophical inquiry is an "imitation of God," and "the Torah is not a *nomos* [law/custom/tradition] that forces us to believe falsehoods but rather directs us toward the attainment of truth to the extent possible" (*Wars* I, introductory remarks [323] I 98; translation modified).

Maimonides, as we have seen, endorses the position of the Torah on some subjects after claiming that they exceed rational demonstration. In sharp contrast, Gersonides argues that the *natural* desire for knowledge of these subjects that is evident from the philosophical investigations that have been devoted to them (including those of Maimonides) indicates such knowledge is *naturally* attainable. Foremost among these subjects are the origin of the universe and God's knowledge of individual existents, the topics on which I will focus in what follows. On both matters, Gersonides' conclusions challenge Maimonides' claims and do so on philosophical grounds.

In his investigation of the origin of the universe, Gersonides first outlines the diverse ways in which two basic contradictory positions on the question have been understood and defended. Creation can be interpreted either as the successive generation of many worlds or as the creation of a single one, and each of these interpretations admits of two possibilities, namely, creation *ex nihilo* and creation out of primordial matter. Likewise, eternity can be interpreted either as the eternal existence of the world or as God's eternal emanation of the world. From his preliminary analysis, Gersonides concludes that only three of the various opinions merit further investigation: Aristotle's arguments for eternity, Maimonides' arguments for creation *ex nihilo*, and Plato's arguments for creation out of primordial matter. He further claims that all of the arguments advanced thus far in favor of these positions are inadequate. He finally defends a version of the Platonic position, but does so on the basis of essentially Aristotelian scientific considerations.

What is most striking about Gersonides' position is not simply that he argues for atemporal creation out of a primordial absolutely formless matter, according to the laws of physics, but that his reasons for holding this position on the question of origins also ground his conviction that the world is indestructible and everlasting. He further claims that his position is fully consistent with the Torah, including its teachings on miracles, for miracles always involve a change in already existing matter. In Gersonides' view, creation out of *absolutely* formless matter (the void and primeval water in Genesis 1) in no way circumscribes the divine will, because formless matter has no potentiality whatever for motion or change until it is endowed with form, which is precisely what constitutes creation. Like his account of the world's creation, Gersonides' arguments for the world's indestructibility are based on the laws of physics, especially on what is naturally necessary, possible, and impossible. His investigation of this question begins with an examination of the causes of destruction. These are either natural or voluntary. Natural destruction is possible only by virtue of matter rather than of form, for "form is what *strives* to preserve the determinate [that is, formed] existent in existence to the extent possible" (*Wars* VI; translation mine).[12] Although it is possible that an individual existent considered in itself can be destroyed if it is acted upon by powers that are naturally contrary to and greater than its powers of action, this contrariety does not pertain to heavenly bodies, whose form is perfect. Moreover, insofar as the perfect form of the heavenly bodies is what endows sublunary existents with form and perfects them, it is not possible that the forms (species) of changeable existents will cease to exist. Hence, Gersonides concludes, there is no natural cause of the world's destruction. Is the world destructible, then, by an act of will, purposefully? Gersonides dismisses this as absurd. For if the forms of existing things strive to preserve and perfect them, all the more so does God. To suppose that God has the power, let alone the will, to destroy the world amounts to ascribing to God a capacity for performing base and deplorable acts. On the same grounds on which he has rejected various alternative scenarios for creation (the creation of successive worlds, of possible other worlds, and creation *ex nihilo*), Gersonides has now defended the eternity *a parte post* of the one world created out of primeval matter.[13]

The same consistent philosophical naturalism animates Gersonides' discussion of God's knowledge of individuals. The problem, once again, is to reconcile philosophy and religion. The philosophers, who are not concerned with divine justice *per se*, which requires knowledge of individuals as individual, deny divine knowledge of individuals in order to ascribe to God only such knowledge as genuinely deserves the name, that is, an intellectual grasp of the universal and necessary. The theologians, however, whose foremost concern is divine justice and providence, insist on God's knowledge of individual, contingent beings and actions. Both positions, however, seem to compromise human freedom – the first, by leaving individual human acts and events to chance and hence, futile; the second, by regarding all individual human actions as subject to a strict determinism. Judging the different formulations of both views (including Maimonides' attempt to reconcile them) as philosophically inadequate, Gersonides holds that God does not have *knowledge* of individuals as individual. Nonetheless, rather than simply endorsing the philosophers' view and rejecting that of the theologians, Gersonides reformulates both views in a noncontradictory manner. Following the philosophers, he argues that, properly speaking, knowledge (science) as such is of the universal and necessary, whereas "knowledge" of individuals is not knowledge but sensation. God does not know individuals as individuals precisely because they are *sensible* and as such cannot *be* known. Nonetheless, God *knows* individuals in another respect, namely, insofar as they are ordered by an intellect.

For we have claimed that God's knowledge of particulars as ordered is based on the intelligible order pertaining to them which is eternally inherent in His intellect and is not based upon these contingent things. For God does not acquire His knowledge from them; rather they acquire their existence from His knowledge of them, since their existence is an effect of the intelligible order pertaining to them inherent in the divine intellect. (Wars III 5 [323] 133)

Precisely because this kind of knowledge reflects (or even grounds) the understanding of necessary natural laws, it also entails an understanding of what is really or naturally possible, including the kinds of events and actions to which choice and freedom pertain. Thus, although God knows that certain sorts of events and actions will always occur, God does not (cannot) *know* that this or that individual will act in this or that way at this determinate time. "God's knowledge of future events does not imply that the events foreknown will necessarily occur; rather its opposite is still possible ... They remain contingent by virtue of the factor of choice" (Wars III 5 [323] 133).

The most radical aspect of Gersonides' philosophical writings, and the one that best explains their exclusion from the Jewish and Christian philosophical canons, is also the one that makes manifest his kinship with Spinoza. For Gersonides, our scientific knowledge of the universal and necessary (in contrast with sense perception of the individual and contingent) is not different in kind, but only in degree, from God's knowledge. Hence, the more individual human beings understand the natural, necessary order of things, the more they "share" a dimension of God's knowledge and the freer they are.

JEWISH–CHRISTIAN INTERACTIONS

Three types of interaction, differing in both form and content, characterize medieval Jewish–Christian intellectual relations: (1) polemical disputations, written and oral; (2) unilateral scholarly consultation on biblical interpretations; and (3) mutual philosophical exchanges or influences. Considering the philosophical focus of this chapter and in light of the forced conditions under which the first two kinds of interaction occurred, I will say little about these types beyond noting some important differences within and between them.

Although the political context of every disputation was one in which the Jews were a persecuted minority, the early polemics (roughly up to the thirteenth century) generally took the form of written dialogues which, despite their straw-man's presentation of an antagonist's views, exhibit familiarity with the other tradition's sources and are not coerced. Conversely, the later disputations (including those that were subsequently recorded in written form) were public events initiated by the ecclesiastical authorities, in which Jews "participated" under threat of forced conversion or death. In neither case, however, is there evidence of genuine influence, let alone a reciprocal one.[14]

Jewish–Christian interaction and influence with respect to biblical interpretation occupies a middle ground between polemic and philosophy. On one hand, Christian exegetes and philosophers sought the expertise (grammatical, philological, and philosophical) of Jewish interpreters. On the other hand, these exchanges were not only one-sided, but often the same Christian thinkers who sought such Jewish expertise, advocated toleration, and secured the protection of Jews from expulsion and other forms of violent persecution did so for reasons that justified violent and oppressive policies, albeit short of elimination (e.g., Robert Grosseteste, Alexander of Hales, Roger Bacon, Thomas Aquinas, John Duns Scotus, and others).[15]

In contrast to the preceding two forms of interaction, there were, from the thirteenth century on, reciprocal philosophical interactions between Jews and Christians that are relatively (though far from entirely) independent of repressive ecclesiastico-political concerns and at times implicitly opposed to them. Among the factors responsible for this change in the nature of Jewish–Christian interactions, the most important for our purpose are (1) the Latin translations of Greek, Arabic, and Judeo-Arabic scientific and philosophical texts in Toledo during the latter half of the twelfth century; (2) the translation of Greek, Arabic and Judeo-Arabic scientific and philosophical texts into Hebrew and the foundation of scholarly communities whose primary philosophical languages were Hebrew (rather than Judeo-Arabic) and at least one of the Romance languages and many of whose members were also versed in Latin; (3) the vibrant community of Jewish and Christian scholars and translators established in Naples by the Emperor Frederick II in the first half of the thirteenth century, a community whose discourse was independent of ecclesiastical censure; and (4) the Latin translation of Maimonides' *Guide*, which gave rise to extensive scholarly cooperation between Jewish and Christian scholars in Italy.

An early and exemplary interaction at the imperial court was that between Jacob Anatoli, the emperor's physician, who translated philosophical and scientific works from Arabic and Latin into Hebrew and most likely assisted in translations of Hebrew and Arabic texts into Latin, and Michael Scott, a renowned translator of Arabic works into Latin. Anatoli's testimony to the nature of their relation is remarkable in at least two respects. First, he bestows the highest possible praise on a Christian thinker in the introduction to his major work, *Malmad ha-Talmidim* (The Goad of Students), a text devoted to sermons on the *Torah*. Second, he attributes to Michael Scott a superior ability as a biblical exegete. In addition, in a manner that is strikingly similar to Maimonides' exhortation to the reader of his *Introduction to Avot* (*The Eight Chapters*) to "hear the truth from whoever says it," Anatoli enjoins the traditional Jewish reader of *Malmad ha-Talmidim* to appreciate truth, irrespective of the religious affiliation of its proponent.

The translations and cooperation begun in the imperial court created a common philosophical corpus that made possible, for the first time, genuine Jewish and Christian dialogue and mutual influences, especially in Italy. Thus, complementary to Maimonides' extensive influence on Christian philosophy, there is clear evidence of influences of scholastic and Neoplatonic Christian philosophy on Jewish philosophy. These influences are evident in both Maimonidean and anti-Maimonidean Jewish philosophers. Thus, for example, in his commentary on the *Guide* as well as other texts, Moses of Salerno (d. 1279) employed scholastic terminology and method, while Hillel of Verona and Immanuel of Rome were heavily influenced by Dante.

In contrast to the relative independence from doctrinal concerns and ecclesiastical oversight of the philosophical exchanges in Italy initiated by the imperial court, reciprocal influences were not openly acknowledged in Spain and Provence. On the contrary, although the writings of Jewish philosophers clearly exhibit familiarity with Christian philosophy, especially with the works of Thomas Aquinas, Duns Scotus, William of Ockham, Peter Aureol, Nicole Oresme, and the like, little research has thus far been devoted to the nature and extent of such influences. The exception is Shlomo Pines' seminal essay, "Scholasticism after Thomas Aquinas and the Teaching of Hasdai Crescas and His Predecessors" [256]. Despite the astounding parallels between the works of Jewish and Christian philosophers noted in this chapter, and despite the intrinsic unlikelihood of the texts in question being independent of one another, Pines could only offer his evidence and conclusions regarding influences tentatively.[16]

The precarious nature of Jewish-Christian philosophical interactions, especially those that are explicitly acknowledged, is poignantly evident in the Renaissance. This fragility also makes evident the extent to which Jewish-Christian philosophical interactions are a special case of the tenuous status of philosophy in relation to ecclesiastico-political power. Elijah del Medigo (1460–96) is a vivid example. Born in Crete under Venetian rule, del Medigo was an Averroist Aristotelian, fluent in Hebrew, Arabic, Greek, Latin, and Italian, who was the head of the Padua Yeshiva, where he lectured on philosophy. Among his numerous Christian admirers and patrons was Pico della Mirandola, who viewed him as his mentor in philosophy and Jewish mysticism. When, at the invitation of the Venetian government, del Medigo was asked to serve as an arbiter in a heated philosophical conflict, his determination in favor of one school of thought sparked the animosity of the other. For similar reasons, stemming from his Averroism, he came into conflict with the Jewish Rav of Padua. Consequently, after Pico's death in 1494, having lost his powerful Christian patron, del Medigo was compelled to return to Crete, where, ironically, he remained highly esteemed by both Jews and Christians.

NOTES

1. Saadiah's major polemic was against the Karaite sect which had a significant following in the Islamic world toward the end of the tenth century. The Karaites rejected Talmudic Judaism and sought to establish a Judaism based strictly on the Hebrew Bible without its legal and interpretative tradition.

2. Of Saadiah's works only two are available in English translation, *The Book of Doctrines and Beliefs* [106] and his *Book of Theodicy* [107].

3. Saadiah adds that there are other proofs as well. Since the four proofs he presents are based on the standard Kalam proofs for creation, of which

Maimonides presents seven, Saadiah's reference must be understood to include at least these.

4. At times he presents matter and form as undifferentiated, at others, as opposed. Likewise, at times, he draws a distinction between the origins of matter and form respectively in the divine essence and divine will, at others, he claims that both originate simultaneously in the divine will. The inconsistency about the status of matter can be traced back to Plotinus.

5. E.g., Thomas Aquinas's criticism (*De substantiis separatis* 5–8) of Ibn Gabirol's positing of spiritual matter.

6. See above, p. 125 and note 3.

7. It should be noted that, for Maimonides, sublunar individuation can occur only through matter. God's knowledge of human beings *qua* intellects is knowledge of the agent intellect in which different individuals participate in proportion to their understanding.

8. See, for example, *Quaestiones de anima*, q. 3, obj. 6 and ad 6; q. 8, obj. 19 and ad 19. Aquinas often follows Maimonides. See, for example, *Expositio super librum Boetii De Trinitate*, q. 3, a. 1; *ST* IaIIae, qq. 101–02, *passim*; *Quaestiones disputatae de potentia*, q. 3, *passim*. On Aquinas and Maimonides in general see J. I. Dienstag [190], D. Burrell [121, 189, and 500], I. Dobbs-Weinstein [191], and W. Dunphy [183] and [192].

9. See *The Wars of the Lord* I 1, last paragraph, which reflects Aquinas's position.

10. The exception is Book V of *The Wars of the Lord*, which was translated into Latin as an independent work on astronomy.

11. It must be noted that, even though ignoring the supercommentaries makes our task simpler, it also thereby overlooks the ways in which the discussion of the same questions in them may modify and enrich our understanding of Gersonides' *philosophical* positions. This is especially important in light of the fact that in the supercommentaries Gersonides is not constrained by the need to harmonize philosophy and biblical teachings.

12. The terminological differences notwithstanding, Gersonides' arguments are strikingly similar to Spinoza's, including the language of striving (*hishtadlut*).

13. It should be noted that Maimonides too argued that the world is eternal *a parte post*. See *Guide* III 25 [178] 502–06.

14. See S. W. Baron [499], especially 55–134.

15. Robert Grosseteste, Letters 5 and 7 [194] and *De cessassione Legalium* (1232), discussed in L. M. Friedman [198] 21–23; Alexander of Hales, *Summa Fratris Alexandri* II ii. 8, 1 [358]; Roger Bacon, *Compendii studii Philosophiae*, in Bacon, *Opera quaedam hactenus inedita*, ed.

J. S. Brewer (London, 1859), p. 472; Thomas Aquinas, *ST* IaIIae, q. 10 (cf. Cajetan's Commentary in the Leonine edition), as well as *Opusculum ad Ducissam Brabantiae*; John Duns Scotus, *Quaestiones in librum quartum Sententiarum*, d. 4, q. 9.

16. W. Kluxen, a pioneer in the research of medieval Jewish–Christian philosophical influences, is even more cautious. See [193].

6   Metaphysics: God and being

Ancient Greek philosophers have much to say about God or the gods; some of them also have much to say about being (whether being as predication or identity, expressed by "X is Y," or being as existence, expressed by a bare "X is" or "there is an X"). They do not systematically connect the two topics, however, and neither do many modern philosophers. But many medieval philosophers did. Can thinking about being help us understand God? Can thinking about God help us understand being? I will explore some connections that medieval philosophers saw between the two topics, and also some difficulties that they encountered. I will focus not so much on particular philosophers as on central ideas that many different philosophers took up, illustrating these ideas from the work of philosophers who set them out in especially interesting or accessible ways, and noting challenges that different philosophers answered in different ways. Many of these ideas and challenges begin with Muslim authors and are then taken up by Christian authors from the thirteenth century on. I will go back and forth between Muslim and Christian sources.

PHYSICAL AND METAPHYSICAL PROOFS OF GOD

The proofs of the existence of God are an obvious place to begin. Thomas Aquinas, in *Summa theologiae* I, q. 2, a. 3, says that God's existence can be proved in five ways. Thomas's first way, arguing from causes of motion, and his second, from efficient causes, are physical arguments, taken from Aristotle; his fifth way, from teleology, is equally physical, derived ultimately from the Stoics. But the third and fourth ways seem to be *ontological* arguments, by which I mean not that they resemble Anselm's famous argument, which

Thomas rejects (*ST* I, q. 2, a. 1, ad 2), but simply that they start from the fact of being (in the sense of existence), and not from contingent facts about the physical world.

The fourth way turns on the "degrees" according to which things are said to be more X or less X:

More and *less* are said of different things as they are differently close to something which is *most*: thus something is hotter which is closer to what is most hot. There is therefore something which is truest, and best, and noblest, and consequently most *being* [or most *real*]: for the things which are most true are most real, as [Aristotle] says in *Metaphysics* II. But what is said to be most thus-and-such, in any genus, is the cause of all things in that genus, as fire, which is most hot, is the cause of all hot things, as [Aristotle] says in the same book. Therefore there is something which is the cause of being, and goodness, and any other perfection, to all beings; and this we call God. (*ST* I, q. 2, a. 3)

Thomas is claiming that as fire, which is most hot, is the cause to other hot things of the fact that they are hot in their lesser degrees, so God, who is most being, is the cause to other beings of the fact that they *are*, in their lesser degrees. There are obvious objections to Thomas's proof as a proof; but supposing Thomas is right, how are we to understand the situation he is describing? In what sense are there degrees of being? Is "being" said differently of God and of creatures – are they somehow of different logical types? As Thomas is well aware, Aristotle says that "being" is not said univocally of substances and of accidents: an accident "exists" in a derivative and diminished sense, since for whiteness to exist is just for some substance to exist and be white. Is there a similar difference between the existence of God and of created substances? Even if so, how does God communicate a lower degree of existence to other beings? Presumably not the way that a substance communicates existence to an accident, by being the substratum of that accident; nor the way fire communicates heat to iron, by being mixed in with the iron. But is there another model for this metaphysical connection between God and the world?

The advantage of a "metaphysical" proof of God's existence, if it could be made to work, is that it would lead us, by thinking through the questions about God and being that it raises, to a deeper conception of God, and of God's causal connection to other things, than simply conceiving him (say) as the first cause of motion.

At least since Avicenna, there has been a sharp debate over whether this strategy could work. John Duns Scotus – himself a defender of Avicenna – puts it as follows.

There is a controversy between Avicenna and Averroes. Avicenna claimed that not God, but something else, such as being, is the subject of metaphysics. For no science proves the existence of its own subject, yet the metaphysician proves that God and the separate [i.e., immaterial] substances exist. In his final comment on Book I of the *Physics*, Averroes criticizes Avicenna: assuming Avicenna's major premise (common to them both), that no science proves the existence of its subject, he infers that God is the subject of metaphysics and that God's existence is proved not in metaphysics but in physics, since no kind of separate substance can be proved to exist except through motion, which pertains to physics. (*Reportatio parisiensis*, prologue, q. 3, a. 1; Latin with translation (modified here) in Scotus [286] 9–10)

This is not simply a disciplinary boundary dispute over what metaphysics should study or over which science has the privilege of proving the existence of God. Avicenna and Averroes are envisaging quite different kinds of proofs, yielding quite different (though not necessarily incompatible) ways of thinking about God and God's relation to the world. Averroes is defending the traditional Aristotelian procedure of arguing from sublunar things to the eternally constant motions of the heavenly spheres as their governors, and then from these motions to their movers, the first of which is God. Avicenna, by contrast, wants to give a proof of the existence of God that does not depend on facts about the physical world, but argues from being to God as the first cause of being. Avicenna is here trying to make good what he sees as a disappointment in Aristotle's *Metaphysics*. While Averroes thinks that metaphysics is purely a science of immaterial things, God and the other movers of the heavenly spheres, Avicenna, following Farabi, thinks that Aristotelian metaphysics is also about being in general and its universal attributes (which are "immaterial" in the sense that they do not depend on matter and apply to immaterial as well as to material beings). Avicenna sometimes says that metaphysics has being as its *subject* and God as its *object* – that is, starting by investigating being, it ends by establishing God as the first cause of being.[1] But Aristotle's *Metaphysics* is disappointing as an execution of this project, since it establishes God only as the cause of the rotation of the outermost sphere – and this procedure shows so little about God that it is not even clear how God is superior to the "intelligences" or "angels" moving the other spheres. Avicenna wants to make good the promise of the *Metaphysics* by establishing God as the first cause of being to all beings, both material and immaterial. To do this, however, he needs more of an argument than Thomas's "fourth way," which simply assumes there will be a single *most* being, which will be a cause of being to all beings. We might wonder why there cannot be an infinite regress to ever higher causes of being. Or, even if an infinite regress is impossible here, why shouldn't there be several independent "first" beings, each of which needs no cause of being beyond itself? The answer cannot be that *every* being requires a prior cause of being, since God himself does not. If a being X has not always existed but came-to-be in time, we can see why it would require something prior to cause its existence: if we use this premise, however, we are beginning not from the fact of being but from the fact of coming-to-be or motion. And why couldn't there be several independent *eternal* beings? These difficulties are among the reasons many philosophers, including Averroes, conclude that Avicenna's metaphysical way of proving God's existence does not work and that we must argue from physics instead.

AVICENNA'S ARGUMENT AND SOME CHALLENGES TO IT

One way Avicenna presents his argument begins from modality. If X exists, then its existence is either necessary or contingent.[2] More precisely, either X's existence is necessary *through X itself* (disregarding the causality of any other objects) or it is contingent as far as X itself goes. If X exists, then there must be a sufficient reason for X's existing. If X is necessarily existent through itself (*wajib al-wujud bi-dhatihi*), then X itself contains the sufficient reason for its own existence. But if X is contingently existent through itself (*mumkin al-wujud bi-dhatihi*), and if X in fact exists, then it requires some further cause. If Y contains a sufficient reason for X's existence, then X's existence is no longer contingent: so Avicenna says that, although X is contingently existent through itself, it is necessarily existent through something else (*wajib al-wujud bi-ghayrihi*). Avicenna's first task in proving the existence of God is to prove there is something that is necessarily existent through itself. Perhaps this is all there is to proving the existence of God; or perhaps it is not a proof of *God's* existence until we have shown that there is only one such being and that it has at least some of the traditional attributes of God.

In any case, to accomplish this first task, take any actually existing thing X (say, yourself). If X is necessarily existent through itself, the task is completed. If X is contingently existent through itself, it is necessarily existent through something else, say Y. Y is either necessarily existent through itself or necessarily existent through something else; and so on. But why should there not be an infinite regress? Avicenna does not deny the possibility (as an Aristotelian, he believes the world and all biological species in it are eternal, so you have an infinite series of past ancestors). But even if there is an infinite series of causes of X, "each one of the causes is either contingent in itself or necessary in itself. If it is necessary, it would not need a cause, and if it is contingent, then the whole [composed of all the causes in the series] is characterized by contingency. And every contingent thing requires a cause beyond itself; so the whole [series] requires a cause outside itself" (as stated in Ghazali, *The Incoherence of the Philosophers* [148] 82, translation modified; cited in Averroes' *Tahafut al-Tahafut* [165] I 163). To put it another way, if we take the *complete* (perhaps infinite) series of causes of X, by definition this series cannot have a cause external to itself; so the whole series is not contingent in itself; so it cannot be composed entirely of things that are contingent in themselves; so it must contain some term that is necessary in itself; since this cannot have a cause, it must be the first uncaused cause within the series.

Avicenna is perhaps in greater trouble with his argument for the *uniqueness* of a being necessarily existent through itself. But his argument for the *existence* of such a being was already controversial. Ghazali, in his *Incoherence of the Philosophers*, rejects the argument. More surprisingly, when Averroes comes to the defense of philosophy in his *Incoherence of the Incoherence*, he "defends" this argument only with serious qualification. In fact, his modified version of the argument, although verbally it sounds similar, works only by turning Avicenna's metaphysical argument back into the Aristotelian physical argument that Avicenna was trying to escape.

Ghazali criticizes Avicenna's inference from "each term in the series of causes is contingent in itself" to "the whole series of causes is contingent in itself." Ghazali's critique is particularly interesting, because it turns on a critical examination of Avicenna's notion of contingency. Ghazali says:

The expressions "contingent" and "necessary" are obscure expressions, unless by "necessary" is meant what has no cause for its existence, and by "contingent" what has a cause for its existence. If this is what is meant, let us go back to this expression and say "each [cause in the series] is contingent, in the sense that it has a cause beyond itself, but the whole [series] is not contingent, in the sense that it does not have a cause beyond itself and outside itself." If by "contingent" is meant something other than what we mean, we do not understand it. (*Incoherence of the Philosophers* [148] 82, trans. modified; Averroes, *Tahafut al-Tahafut* [165] I 164)

Avicenna will reply that it is impossible for a necessary whole to be composed of contingent parts, and this seems plausible if necessary and contingent beings belong to two different logical or ontological types. But Ghazali says that if there are such ontological concepts, Avicenna has not made them clear to him; Ghazali suspects that "contingent" and "necessary" are just high-flown phrases for "caused" and "uncaused" (which are extrinsic, relational concepts, not something intrinsic to a thing's mode of being), in which case his paraphrase exposes the fallacy in the argument. Ghazali concludes that Avicenna's attempt to avoid infinite regress arguments fails, and that the only way to establish the existence of God is to assume that no infinite causal regresses are possible; which, he thinks, is possible only if we give up the Aristotelian thesis of the eternity of the world (and of species within it), and hold, with the *mutakallimun*, that the world was created in time.[3]

Averroes, in his response to Ghazali, tries to reconstruct a defensible version of Avicenna's argument, and thus to argue for God without giving up the eternity of the world. His way of doing this turns on a distinctive response to Ghazali's challenge about the meaning of "contingent" and "necessary." Averroes' version goes:

Contingent beings must have causes which precede them, and if these causes again are contingent it follows that they have causes and that there is an infinite regress, and if there is an infinite regress there is no cause, and the contingent will exist without a cause, and this is impossible. Therefore the series must end in a necessary cause, and this necessary cause must be necessary either through a cause or without a cause, and if through a cause, this cause must have a cause and so *ad infinitum*; and if we have an infinite regress here, it follows that what was assumed to have a cause has no cause, and this is impossible. Therefore the series must end in a cause which is necessary without a cause, i.e., necessary by itself, and this must be the necessary being. (*Tahafut al-Tahafut* [165] I 165, trans. modified)

This is thus a two-stage argument, first from contingent beings to a necessary being, and then from a necessary being to a *causeless* necessary being, or being "necessary through itself." Averroes, like Ghazali, thinks that Avicenna uses the world "contingent" too broadly, to mean "what has a cause" (*Tahafut al-Tahafut* [165] I 164): Averroes thinks that, for the argument to be demonstrative, we must begin from what is contingent in a stricter sense, or, as Averroes says, "truly contingent."

What Averroes means by "truly contingent" becomes clear from Thomas's "third way," which closely parallels Averroes' argument:

We find some things that are capable [*possibilia*] both of existing and of not existing, since some things are found to be generated and corrupted, and therefore to be capable both of existing and of not existing. But it is impossible for everything of this kind to exist always, since what is capable of not existing, at some time does not exist. Therefore, if all things are capable of not existing, at some time no thing existed. But if this is true, even now nothing would exist, since what does not exist does not begin to exist except through something [else] which exists; so that if no being existed, it would be impossible for anything to begin to exist, and thus nothing would now exist, which is plainly false. Therefore, not all beings are contingent [*possibilia*]; there must exist some thing which is necessary. But every necessary [being] either has a cause of its necessity from elsewhere, or it does not. But it is not possible to proceed *ad infinitum* in necessary [beings] which have a cause of their necessity, just as [this was not possible] in efficient causes, as was proved [in Thomas's second way]. Therefore, it is necessary to posit something which is necessary through itself, not having the cause of its necessity from elsewhere, but is the cause of necessity to other things; which is what everyone calls God. (*ST* I, q. 2, a. 3)[4]

The key point is that for Averroes and Thomas, if X is contingent, then at some time X has not existed, whereas Avicenna thinks that everything other than God is intrinsically contingent, even the heavenly bodies and their movers, which as a good Aristotelian he takes to be eternal. For Averroes, the only "truly contingent" things are those that do not always exist, that is, sublunar things: he answers

Ghazali's challenge to spell out an intrinsic sense of "contingent" by saying that something is contingent if it is material and therefore capable of generation and corruption. Likewise, a "necessary" being is something that always exists, because it has no matter and therefore is not capable of generation and corruption (the heavens, for Averroes, are not composed of matter and form, although their substance can broadly be called a "matter," capable of changing place but not of generation and corruption). So, although Averroes' argument sounds a lot like Avicenna's, it means something quite different. When Averroes argues from something contingent to something necessary, he is arguing from generable and corruptible material things to something eternal, which could perfectly well be the heavenly bodies. To turn this into a proof of the existence of God, Averroes adds a second stage, arguing from a "necessary" – that is, eternal – being to an *uncaused* necessary being; and since the heavens are moved, and so need some cause to move them, this gets us to some cause beyond the heavens. The crucial point here is that, in trying to salvage a version of Avicenna's argument from contingency against Ghazali's criticisms, Averroes has essentially turned it back into an Aristotelian physical argument. As a result, all the reasons one might have for being dissatisfied with Aristotle's original argument will apply equally against Averroes. Can Avicenna's ontological alternative be saved?[5]

ESSENCE AND EXISTENCE

Contingency is supposed to be an intrinsic property that explains *why* contingent things need causes in order to exist; if, as Ghazali suspects, it is merely a synonym for "caused," then an infinite series of contingent causes need not be contingent, and Avicenna's proof for God breaks down. In fact, Avicenna has an answer to this challenge. It turns on the distinction between a thing X and its being or existence (*wujud*), that is, that through which X is existent (*mawjud*).

One way this distinction arises is through the analysis of creation, as distinguished from other kinds of change. Aristotle recognizes four basic kinds of change: alteration (change in quality), augmentation and diminution (change in quantity), locomotion (change of place), and generation and corruption. In the first three kinds of change, there is a persisting substance that loses one accident and acquires another. In generation or corruption, there is not properly a substance that persists, but only the matter, which loses one substantial form and acquires another; in such a case, Aristotle says that the substance (the matter–form composite) "comes-to-be absolutely" (rather than X merely coming-to-be Y), but it does not come-to-be *out of nothing*, and Aristotle does not believe that coming-to-be out of nothing is possible. However, medieval writers think that God *created* the world, in some way other than by generating it out of a preexisting matter. The *mutakallimun* in Islam, and most Christian writers, think that God created things out of nothing at the beginning of time, when before that moment only God existed. Even the *falasifa*, who do not believe in a beginning of time, think the world is causally dependent on God in a deeper way than simply by having been generated by him out of some preexisting matter in the past: rather, the world is *always* being created by God. The language of essence and existence gives a way to explain what creation is. When God *creates* something, no part of it previously existed: God is not taking a preexisting matter and giving it a form, but giving existence to something that did not previously exist. As the Qur'an puts it, "when God wishes to create a thing, he says to it 'be!' and it is" (Qur'an XVI 42). But what status do these things have prior to their existence? Since the results are different when God tells a horse "be!" and when he tells an ostrich "be!," there must be some difference between a horse and an ostrich even before they exist. Before an individual horse exists, the *essence* of horse – what a horse is, or what it is to be a horse – already grounds propositions such as "the horse is a quadruped." For Avicenna, it is this essence to which God adds existence.

This analysis of creation does not depend on creation happening in time. Even if God creates a star or an angel from eternity, he is still adding existence to an essence. Even if the essence never lacks existence, it does not contain existence of itself, but needs it supplied, by God or by some proximate cause. One way to think about essence and existence is given by medieval realist semantics. According to medieval realists, in the sentence "Socrates is white," the subject term signifies Socrates and the predicate term signifies whiteness, and the sentence is true when whiteness is *in* Socrates: whiteness is the (formal) cause, to Socrates, of his being white. Thus, at least in normal cases, a sentence is true if there is an inherence structure in the world corresponding to the predication structure of the sentence. (There are abnormal cases: in "Socrates is Socrates" the subject and the predicate signify the same thing; in "[the] white [one] is Socrates" the significatum of the subject inheres in the significatum of the predicate rather than vice versa; in "[the] white [one] is musical" the significata of the subject and of the predicate both inhere in a third thing.) Likewise, "Socrates is human" is true when humanity inheres in Socrates, and "Socrates exists" or "Socrates is existent [*mawjud/ens*]" is true when existence or being (*wujud/esse*) inheres in Socrates. To say that X is contingently existent through itself is just to say that the essence of X does not include existence: what makes X X, or what it is for X to be X, does not include what makes X existent, or what it is for X to exist. If such an X does exist, it is because some other cause, external to X, gives existence to X. By contrast, to say that X is necessarily existent through itself is to say that the essence of X does include existence: for X to be X is already for X to exist, and no further cause is needed for its existence.

The essence–existence distinction thus allows Avicenna to discern an intrinsic difference, indeed a difference of logical type, between things that need causes for their existence and things that do not. It also allows him to answer Ghazali's challenge that an infinite series of contingent causes might collectively be necessary: an infinite number of essences, none of them intrinsically possessing existence, still do not possess existence, unless something from outside gives it to them. The ultimate sufficient reason for the existence of those things that do exist can only be some being (or beings) whose essence includes existence. So, if Avicenna can sustain his metaphysics of essence and existence, he can defend his proof of something necessarily existent through itself – whether or not we are willing to call this a proof of the existence of God.

Note that this Avicennian proof is not an "ontological" argument of the form: the concept or essence of God involves existence, therefore God exists. Avicenna's argument is causal, arguing from effects, contingent beings, to the conclusion that they have some cause whose essence involves existence. As Thomas Aquinas says,

This proposition, "God exists," is, in itself, self-evident, because the predicate is the same as the subject, since God *is* his existence ... but because *we* do not know what God is, it is not self-evident *to us*, but needs to be demonstrated through things which are more evident to us but less evident by nature, namely, by [God's] effects. (*ST* I, q. 2, a. 1)

Thomas's denial that we have knowledge of God's essence was controversial (Scotus, for one, thinks we do have such knowledge), but he is right to warn that the concept "essence which involves existence" is not by itself a concept of some determinate essence X, such that X involves existence: it is merely the concept of a property which might turn out to be satisfied by many essences or by none.

ONLY ONE NECESSARY BEING?

Both Avicenna and Thomas argue, not only that there must be at least one being that is necessarily existent through itself, but also that there can be only one. Their arguments start from an argument of Farabi's. Farabi begins his *Principles of the Opinions of the People of the Perfect City* by proclaiming: "the first being [*mawjud/ens*] is the first cause of being [*wujud/esse*] to all other beings [*mawjudat/entia*]" ([95] 56). Farabi takes for granted that he does not have to worry about infinite causal regresses, so he does not waste time proving that there is such a first being. Rather, he is concerned to establish its attributes. His argument is generally of the form, "the first being must be F, because if it were non-F, there would be some other being causally prior to it." In particular, Farabi argues that the first being must be entirely simple, that is, lacking any kind of composition, because if it were composite, its components (and the cause bringing them together) would be causally prior to it. Farabi then infers from the *simplicity* of the first cause (it is internally one) to its *unicity* (there is only one of it): the reason is that two simple beings cannot have anything to differentiate them. If there were two "first" things, they would have something in common, and each would also have some distinguishing differentia, so that we could analyze A as X + Y and B as X + Z. Or perhaps B contains some differentia, beyond the shared element, to distinguish it from A, so that we could analyze B as X + Z, with A being distinguished from B only by not having Z, not by any positive differentia. Either way, at least one of the assumed "first" beings would be composite, and so could not be first: there would have to be something causally prior to it.

Farabi makes this argument without having the notion of essence–existence composition or the Avicennian distinction between necessary and contingent beings. Avicenna, using these notions, develops a more elaborate argument for the unicity of the first being (*Shifa'*, *Metaphysics* I 7). Here I will sketch Thomas's less complicated treatment (there are also good discussions by Ghazali and Averroes at *Tahafut al-Tahafut* [165] I 170–81). Immediately after the *quaestio* on the existence of God, Thomas gives a long *quaestio* on God's simplicity (*ST* I, q. 3), arguing that God is not composed in any way: he is not composed of quantitative parts (as a body is), or of matter and form, substance and accident, genus and differentia, essence and *suppositum*, or essence and existence. Thomas supports these conclusions both by arguing that any composite has something prior to it (for Farabi's reasons, so especially q. 3, a. 7) and by arguing that any of these kinds of composition involve potentiality, whereas the first being must be pure actuality (following the Aristotelian principle of the priority of actuality to potentiality, *Metaphysics* IX 8, cited in *ST* I, q. 3, a. 1). In the case of essence–existence composition, if God were not his own *esse*, then his essence would be of itself in potentiality to existence, and so God could not be the first being (q. 3, a. 4); again, if God were not his own *esse* but merely *had esse*, he would be a being only by participation and so could not be the first being (q. 3, a. 4). God is thus an "*esse* without addition" (q. 3, a. 4, ad 1) or "subsistent *esse*," not an *esse* inhering in some essence other than *esse*. Thomas then argues that there could not be two such *esses*, because, being simple and "without addition," they could not have anything to individuate them. "There can be only one subsistent *esse*, just as, if [a] whiteness were subsistent [rather than inhering in a substratum], there could only be one, since whitenesses are multiplied according to their recipients" (q. 44, a. 1). This modification of Farabi's argument for the unicity of the first being allows Thomas to avoid an objection to Farabi, namely, that the two supposed "first" beings need not have a common element and a distinguishing element, since they may have nothing in common except being "first" and "simple" (i.e., uncaused and uncomposed), which are mere negations. Thomas, by contrast, can specify a common nature that the two beings would have to share – *esse* itself.

CHALLENGES TO ESSENCE–EXISTENCE COMPOSITION

Thomas's argument breaks down, however, if you deny Avicenna's theory of essence–existence composition. Avicenna and Thomas think that, if X is intrinsically contingent, "X exists" or "X is existent [*mawjud/ens*]" is saying something about X that is not contained in "X is X," and they conclude that the existence (*wujud/esse*) of X is something present in X, beyond the essence of X. But some medieval thinkers reject this analysis. They deny that "existent [*mawjud/ens*]" is *paronymous* (or *denominative*) from "existence," as "white" is paronymous from "whiteness":[6] here something is named paronymously from Z if it is not called "Z," but is called by some name grammatically derived from "Z" (Aristotle, *Categories*, ch. 1). It seems dubious to say that "white" is grammatically derived from "whiteness" rather than vice versa (this is more plausible in Greek and Arabic than in Latin or English), but the deeper issue is logical or causal: something is called "white" *because* there is a whiteness in it. Ockham, despite his attack on realist semantics, concedes the point in the case of "white." As he puts it, "white" is a *connotative* term, *connoting* whiteness: "white" does not always signify the same things, but signifies something only on the condition that there is a whiteness in it. But (says Ockham) "being" or "animal" always signify the same things, and there is no reason to think they connote a further beingness or animalness: so there is no reason to think that either the existence or the essence of the animal Bucephalus is anything other than Bucephalus.

Ockham grants that "Bucephalus exists" (or "the essence of Bucephalus exists") is not a necessary truth. But, he says, "Bucephalus is Bucephalus" (or "the essence of Bucephalus is the essence of Bucephalus") is also not a necessary truth: any of these sentences is true only when Bucephalus exists. So "there is no more reason to imagine that essence is indifferent to being [*esse*] or not being than that it is indifferent to being an essence or not being an essence": sometimes Bucephalus exists and sometimes he does not, but this is not because there is an essence lying around from eternity and waiting to receive existence. Ockham grants that, because "Bucephalus exists" is contingent, there is something beyond Bucephalus through which Bucephalus exists, but this is just Bucephalus's external causes, not an *esse* inhering in Bucephalus. And "God exists" is necessary, not because God's essence is or includes *esse*, but because God exists without a cause.[7]

But if this analysis is right, the whole Farabian-Avicennian way of proving the unicity of God breaks down. If there were two gods, there would be no reason why they had to be either pure *esse* or *esse* plus a distinguishing differentia. Each might be a single simple nature, with no common component at all. We could still give an *a posteriori* physical argument that there is only one God (the world is too ordered and integrated to be the work of several separate first causes; this is the third of three arguments Thomas gives at *ST* I, q. 11, a. 3). But this argument is at best plausible, not demonstrative, and Ockham concludes that we cannot demonstrate the unicity of God. Perhaps this means we cannot demonstrate the existence of God either. We can demonstrate that there is a first (i.e., uncaused) cause, but not that there is only one such cause, and so not that there is some one cause of all things. Depending on how strong a sense you attach to the word *God*, this may mean we cannot demonstrate that there is a God. Ockham leaves the linguistic decision up to you.[8]

Few Christian thinkers will admit to believing in essences waiting to receive existence. If such an essence is not itself created, we are denying that everything but God is created by God. If God created it, did he do so by giving existence to some prior essence, and so back *ad infinitum*? But if an essence can be created without a prior essence, why not suppose that Bucephalus is created without a prior essence? We might maintain (as Thomas does) that God creates the essence of X just when he gives it existence (i.e., when he creates X) and that there are no *prior* essences. This avoids the difficulties mentioned, but it undercuts much of the original reason for drawing the essence–existence distinction. And it leads many Christian thinkers to conclude that essence and existence cannot be really distinct, as one thing (*res*) is distinct from another, since whenever there are two *res* other than God, God should be able to create either of them without the other.[9]

CHALLENGES ABOUT GOD AND *ESSE*

The essence–existence distinction must also confront another infinite regress challenge. Whenever X is a contingent being, X exists through the existence of X, which is something other than X. But the existence of X also exists. Does it exist through a further existence, and so *ad infinitum* (as Averroes asks in *Tahafut al-Tahafut* [165] I 180–81)?[10] But if it exists through itself – that is, if its essence includes existence – then on Avicenna's analysis it is an intrinsically necessary being, and Avicenna claims to have proved that there is only one such being, namely God.

Thomas tries fending this off by denying that existence itself exists.[11] But some medieval thinkers take the bull by the horns and accept that, for any X, the *esse* of X is God, so that just as "running [*currens*]" or "runs" in "Socrates is running" or "Socrates runs" signifies running (*currere*), so "existing [*ens*]" or "exists" in "Socrates is existing" or "Socrates exists" signifies God. This view is taken by many Muslim writers who combine Avicennian philosophy with Sufism. In Christendom it is taken most famously by Eckhart in his *Prologues to the Opus tripartitum*, whose key formula is "*esse est Deus*." But earlier, independently of Avicenna, it was often thought to be the view of Boethius, and it seems also to be Anselm's view. Behind all these figures stands Proclus, who identifies (his second) God with a Platonic Form of being, in which all things must participate in order to be.[12]

Thomas is well aware of this Platonizing view. He often comes close to its terminology. He says that, since God is the only subsisting *esse*, "all things other than God *are* not their *esse*, but *participate* in *esse*," and he infers "that all things which are diversified according to their participating diversely in *esse*, so that they *are* more or less perfectly, are caused by one first being which *is* most perfectly. Hence Plato said that it is necessary to posit a unity prior to every multiplicity" (*ST* I, q. 44, a. 1). Anything that *is* by participation needs some cause in order to be, and this cause must be a being not-by-participation, and thus must be God. Thomas *almost* always avoids saying that creatures participate in God; but God is "just *esse* [*esse tantum*]" or "*esse* without addition" (q. 3, a. 4, ad 1), and God is the cause of other things' participating in *esse*, "as fire, which is most hot, is the cause of all hot things" (q. 2, a. 3; "fourth way," cited above).

Nonetheless, Thomas hotly denies that the *esse* of creatures is God. God is not *esse*-in-general (*esse commune*): he is "just *esse*," but not all *esse* is God. Both God and *esse*-in-general are "*esse* without addition," but differently (q. 3, a. 4, ad 1): *esse*-in-general is *neutral* with respect to different additions, like animal-in-general, which is neutral to rationality, whereas God is an *esse* that *excludes* any addition, like irrational-animal. God's quasi-differentia, corresponding to "irrational," is to *not* be the *esse of* any essence.[13]

In *Summa contra Gentiles* I 26 Thomas gives an extended polemic against the view that God is the "formal *esse* of things," that is, "that through which, formally, they *are*," as Socrates is white formally through his whiteness. (Certainly things *are* through God, but only as their efficient cause, not as their formal cause, not as what is signified by the predicate "are.") Thomas's arguments often seem to assume that his opponents think God *inheres* in things, and is therefore dependent on them, like an accident in a substance or a form in matter. This makes his opponents look like pantheist eccentrics, when in fact they were quite mainstream. They thought, not that God is a form inhering in things, but that he is an *extrinsic* formal cause of the fact that they *are*, like a Platonic Form. (So, when X perishes, X's *esse* does not perish – it just ceases to be X's *esse*.) Or, to formulate it within an Aristotelian context, things other than God are denominated beings (*entia*) by *extrinsic denomination*, that is, by denomination/paronymy from a form outside them, not from one inhering in them. (An animal is called "healthy" by intrinsic denomination, but a diet or urine is called "healthy" by extrinsic denomination, as being a cause or a sign of health in an animal; Socrates is called "known" by extrinsic denomination, not from knowledge in him but from knowledge in someone who knows him.)

Thomas, and probably most scholastics after his time, take it as absurd for something to *be* by extrinsic denomination. What could be more intrinsic to a thing than its very being? To say that something exists only by extrinsic denomination seems close to saying that it does not genuinely exist.[14] And indeed Eckhart infers that "God alone properly speaking exists."[15] It may help here to consider the phrase *wahdat al-wujud*, "unity of existence," used in the Arabic discussions. This phrase could be taken to mean either the claim that "there is only one existence [*wujud*]" or the claim that "there is only one existent [*mawjud*]." If the existence of each existent X is God – as the infinite regress argument seems to show – then this implies *wahdat al-wujud* in the first sense. But it may also be hard to avoid *wahdat al-wujud* in the second sense. Certainly, if we say that Socrates exists, we must mean it in a different sense than when we say that God exists. To say that Socrates exists is only to say that he has a certain relation to God, who alone exists in the full sense.

UNIVOCITY, EQUIVOCITY, ANALOGY

Eckhart is perhaps the only major scholastic after Thomas's time to hold that the *esse* of creatures is God. But a kindred view can be found in Henry of Ghent. As we have just seen, if the *esse* of creatures is God, then to say that Socrates exists is to say that he has a certain relation to God. This suggests that we should say, not that the *esse* of Socrates is God, but that it is some relation he has to God; this relation would be intrinsic to Socrates and so would avoid the objections against making the being of a thing extrinsic to it. The obvious relation would be "passive creation," that is, Socrates' being-created-by-God. Henry's view adds a complication. Instead of distinguishing between Socrates' essence and his existence as two *things* (res), Henry distinguishes between *esse essentiae* and *esse existentiae* as two modes of being that Socrates enjoys. Socrates' *esse existentiae* is his actual existence, which is his being-created-by-God, or his relation to God as efficient cause. His *esse essentiae* is that by which he is eternally said to be a human, an animal, and so forth, whether he actually exists or not. This, Henry says, is Socrates' relation to God as formal or exemplar cause, which is his distinctive way of imitating the divine perfections.[16]

On Henry's view, as on Eckhart's, existence means something quite different when said of creatures than when said of God, just as it means something different of accidents than of substances (the *esse* of whiteness is its being somehow related to a substance, namely, its *inhering* in the substance, that is, the substance's being white). But Henry's view involves the difficulty that we cannot without circularity explain "creating Socrates" as "causing *esse* to Socrates," since *esse*, as said of Socrates, just means being-created. Perhaps we should just accept "creating" as an undefined primitive; but there is a deeper difficulty. The diminished, parasitic *esse* of creatures consists in their being somehow related to God; but, likewise, the diminished, parasitic *esse* of a fictive being, say a goatstag, consists in its being somehow related to creatures (to a goat and a stag, or to the mind that imagines it). What is remarkable about God, though, is that he can give *real esse* to the objects he creates, where a human mind gives only *fictive esse* to the objects it imagines. On Henry's account, or Eckhart's, there seems no way to explain the difference, and so again it is hard to avoid the consequence that nothing but God really exists.

This is one reason for Scotus's insistence, against Henry, that being must be said univocally of God and creatures (also of substances and accidents, since accidents also really exist). It is sometimes said that Scotus overreacted against Henry's extreme view, that being is said *equivocally* of God and creatures, and that if he had been aware of Thomas's moderate view, that being is said *analogically* of God and creatures, he would not have had to rush to the opposite extreme, univocity. But Henry too says that being is said analogically of God and creatures, and the mere word *analogically* does not solve the problem. Being is also said analogically of creatures and fictions, and we want to explain why creatures, unlike fictions, exist properly and not just metaphorically.[17] What is needed is what later scholastics call a single "objective concept" or *ratio* of being, such that God first possesses this *ratio* himself and then communicates the same *ratio* to other things. (The "formal concept" of horse is the mental act or habit of thinking "horse." The "objective concept" is what the formal concept is a concept of, the *ratio* or nature of horseness shared by the different individual horses.) While many later scholastics defend against Scotus the traditional view that being is said analogically of God and creatures (and of substances and accidents), they are concerned to show why creatures properly exist, and often they defend the unity of the objective concept of being.

Medieval writers often say that the name *being* applies primarily to God and secondarily to creatures. A minimalist reading of this claim is that God exists prior to other things, is a perfect or infinite being, and is the cause of being to finite beings. But priority, causal dependence, and different degrees of perfection are compatible with univocity. Thus although triangles are prior to other polygons, which cannot exist without them and are proved to have many of their geometrical properties *because* of their constituent triangles, nonetheless they are all called "polygons" univocally, because "they are equal with regard to the *ratio* of this name, although one can be prior or posterior to another in actual existence" (Aquinas, *Truth*, q. 2, a. 11).[18] For "being" to be said analogically, we need that "being itself, however abstractly and confusedly it is conceived, of its own force [= meaning] requires this order, so that it should belong primarily and *per se* and as-it-were completely to God, and that through this it should descend to other things, in which it is not present except with a relation [*habitudo*] and dependence on God," whereas "a univocal is of itself indifferent, in such a way that it descends to its inferiors [the species or individuals that fall under it] equally and without any order or relation of one to another" (Suárez [619] Disp. 28, §3, para. 17). For there to be a single objective concept of being, the sense of "being" that applies to creatures must also apply to God, so it cannot just mean "dependent on God." But, Suárez is saying, dependence on God is not just a further fact about creatures, in addition to the fact that they exist. The *way* that the common concept of being applies to them involves a relation of essential dependence on the prior way that it applies to God. Can this middle position be explained and defended?

Different writers, often following different suggestions in Thomas, try to explain the inferiority of the *esse* of creatures in different ways. Cajetan and some other Thomists say that being is said of different things by an *analogy of proportionality*. X exists through X's *esse*, Y exists through Y's *esse*, and both are said analogically to exist, because X's *esse* is to X's essence as Y's *esse* is to Y's essence. Each *esse* is the actuality of the essence, and there will be different degrees of *esse* as there are different potentialities to actualize; the highest *esse* will be God, an actuality not limited by any potentiality to receive it. Suárez, however, while agreeing that there is such a proportionality, says it does not imply that being is said analogically. Indeed, he holds that proportionality is consistent with univocity (surely being is said univocally of cats and dogs, despite this proportionality). Suárez's conditions for the different kinds of analogy can be put schematically as follows. If S and T both have the predicate P, and if S is P through a form F existing in S, and T is P through a form G existing in T, in such a way that G does not denominate T as P through what G is in itself, but only because G is to T as F is to S, then T is called P through an *analogy of proportionality* to S. (If G would still denominate T as P, disregarding any relation to S and F, then there is a proportionality but not an analogy, for S and T may both be called P univocally.) If S is P through a form F existing in S, and T is P through the form F existing in S (T is thus not denominated P intrinsically, but extrinsically, through a form in something else to which T is somehow related) then T is called P through an *analogy of extrinsic attribution* to S: this is the way diet or urine is called healthy by attribution to the animal. Where P is said by analogy of extrinsic attribution, there is not a single objective concept of P that applies both to S and to T, and Suárez says, this is what led Scotus to deny that being is said by analogy of attribution. But Suárez tries to show how being can be said by analogy of attribution, while preserving a single objective concept, by distinguishing intrinsic from extrinsic attribution. If S is P through a form F existing in S, and T is P through a form G existing in T, in such a way that G involves a relation of essential dependence on the form F existing in S, then T is called P through an *analogy of intrinsic attribution* to S. Perhaps the most convincing example is the way that health is said of an organ of the body. The heart, unlike urine, is healthy through an intrinsic form, namely the proper functioning of that kind of natural thing, just as an animal is healthy through the proper functioning of that kind of natural thing. But the health of the organ involves an essential dependence on the health of the whole animal: for the heart to function properly is just for it to contribute in the appropriate way to the proper functioning of the whole animal. Suárez thinks that, if being were said of creatures by an analogy of proportionality or extrinsic attribution to God, then creatures would not really and intrinsically exist. He offers intrinsic attribution as a way to save both the reality of creatures and their essential dependence on God in their existence. His difficulty will be to explain why it is not just a further fact that creatures exist because God creates them, but is constitutive of their *esse*. Perhaps the example of the health of the heart offers a model.[19]

We are brought around again to the questions raised at the beginning, coming out of Thomas's fourth way for proving God's existence. Thomas says that God is most being, as fire is most hot, and that God is a cause to other things of their diminished degrees of being, as fire is the cause to other things of their diminished degrees of being hot. Thomas does not make it clear enough (certainly not in this text) how the degrees of being, or the causing of being, are to be understood. Avicenna's essence–existence distinction, and the analysis of creation as giving existence to an essence, give a hope of clarifying these concepts, but involve further difficulties. So do the conception of God as a Platonic Form of being; or as the only thing that *is* in the full sense, so that for other things to "be" is just to be somehow related to God; or as an *esse* not limited by being the *esse of* any essence. The late scholastic discussions of the analogy of being, like the earlier and sometimes wilder positions on God and *esse*, are a continuous struggle with the problems posed by connecting theology and ontology, as Avicenna and Thomas had proposed to do. Each position offers its difficulties and leads to further discussions. I have not tried here to solve the difficulties, but rather to set them out as they presented themselves to medieval thinkers.

NOTES

1. For Avicenna on the object of metaphysics, see the *Metaphysics* of his *Shifa'* I 1–4 [111]. Avicenna speaks in his *Autobiography* ([124] 28) of his frustration with Aristotle's *Metaphysics*, his inability to discover the primary "aim" or "object" of this treatise and this science, and his discovery of the solution on reading al-Farabi's *On the Aims of the Metaphysics* [93].

2. The word *mumkin* is often translated as "possible" in English translations of Arabic philosophical texts, following Latin translators who render it by *possibile*. But the correct translation is "contingent," since it is opposed to "necessary" (*wajib*) just as much as to "impossible."

3. On Kalam and *falsafa*, see p. 98 in this volume.

4. Thomas's main immediate source for his "third way" is in Moses Maimonides, *Guide of the Perplexed* II 1 [178] 247–48. But on some points Thomas is closer to Averroes' argument, and he seems to be directly influenced by Averroes' texts as well (not by the *Tahafut*, which had not yet been translated into Latin, but by related discussions in the *Physics* and *Metaphysics* commentaries). Either Maimonides is following Averroes, or they are both offering the same radical reconstruction of Avicenna's argument and bringing it back much closer to Aristotle's physical argument. Both Maimonides and Averroes interpret "necessary" as "eternal," and "contingent" as "generable and corruptible," whereas for Avicenna everything that actually exists is necessary, although everything but God is contingent *in itself*. For an extended discussion of Avicenna's proof and al-Ghazali's reactions to it, see H. A. Davidson [483] (Maimonides, and Thomas's third way, at 378–85). On Thomas's proofs of the existence of God and their context in his thought, see now J. F. Wippel [262] (controversies about the sources and interpretation of the third way at 462–69). Obviously the step "if all things are capable of not existing, at some time no thing existed" is problematic.

5. Averroes' argument requires him to distinguish between permissible and impermissible causal regresses. He claims that there cannot be an infinity of things existing simultaneously, but only of things existing successively. Since all necessary beings exist eternally, this means that there cannot be infinitely many necessary beings; and since every cause of a necessary being is necessary, no necessary being can have an infinite series of causes. On the other hand, a contingent being, for example, an animal, can and does have an infinite series of contingent causes, namely its ancestors, who do not all exist simultaneously. So why must it also have a necessary cause? Averroes says that your father is not the *per se* cause of you, that is, not the cause of your being, because

if he were, he would have to be continually present to supply being to you: this means that at each moment that you are alive, your father would have to be alive, and so would your grandfather, and so on, and there would be an impermissible simultaneous infinity. So an infinite regress is possible only in *per accidens* causes, not in *per se* causes; and Averroes thinks that the whole series of animals in the species, being contingent and perishable, must also be sustained in being by a *per se* cause – immediately by the sun, whose periodic motions regulate the life cycles of sublunar species, and ultimately by the unmoved movers producing the sun's constant motion.

Averroes' response to Avicenna and Ghazali led to interesting arguments about what kinds of infinite regress are permissible and about *per se* and *per accidens* causes. It is disconcerting to be told that that the sun is a *per se* cause of you and your parents are not; Averroes says that your parents are instruments that the sun uses to make you, as a carpenter might use an axe in making another axe, then throw the first one away or recycle its parts for later use; the sun would be like an immortal carpenter who has been recycling his sublunar tools from all eternity. John Duns Scotus in his *De primo principio*, the most thorough medieval discussion of different kinds of causal series, gives a reconstruction of Averroes' argument that avoids these implications. For Averroes' argument and his confrontation with Avicenna and Ghazali, see *Tahafut al-Tahafut* [165] I 156–70. For Scotus, see A. B. Wolter's edition and translation of *De primo principio* [287].

6. So already Farabi, *Kitab al-Huruf* (Alfarabi's Book of Letters), ed. M. Mahdi (Beirut, 1990) 110–17, taken up by Averroes against Avicenna, *Tahafut al-Tahafut* [165] I 235–41.

7. Ockham's discussion of essence and existence at *Summa logicae* III, tract. 2, ch. 27, is given with translation in Ockham [311] 92–95; quoted passage at 94 (translation modified). For his theory of connotation in general, see Ockham [316], especially chs. 5–10 and the chapters on individual categories; Ockham [315] ch. 11; and in this volume pp. 86 and 205.

8. For Ockham on whether God's existence can be proved, see the texts collected in [311] 115–26; for Ockham's claim that God's unicity is unprovable, and the question whether this implies that God's existence is also unprovable, see especially pp. 125–26.

9. A good and accessible discussion is the thirty-first of Suárez's *Metaphysical Disputations* [trans. in 618]. Suárez disposes of the idea of essences *prior* to existence in section 2. For an opposing scholastic approach to essence and existence, see D. Banez [238].

10. The same point (along with some of the other difficulties about the essence–existence distinction) is noted by Suhrawardi [388] 45–47.

11. In his commentary on Boethius's *Quomodo substantiae* in [229] II 396, cited and discussed by J. F. Wippel [263] 122.

12. For Eckhart see his *Parisian Questions and Prologues* [363]. Note, however, that the *Parisian Questions* take a very different approach to the question of God and being than the *Prologues to the Opus tripartitum* (see A. Maurer's discussion in his introduction); note also that we have no *Opus tripartitum* apart from its *Prologues*, although we have various other works of Eckhart's that were undoubtedly supposed to be incorporated into it. Among Muslim writers, Ibn al-'Arabi is often credited with working out the theory according to which "exists" always signifies God; this account is worked out more fully by later writers, most famously Mulla Sadra (Sadr al-din Shirazi). The most accessible presentation in English is a short treatise by al-Jami [370]. For Boethius see "How Substances are Good in Virtue of their Existence without being Substantial Goods" in [86]. For Anselm see his *Monologion* 1–3. For Proclus see his *Elements of Theology* [381]. Proclus's distinction between the Form of being and the highest God (the Form of unity or goodness) is collapsed by his Christian and Muslim followers, such as the (Muslim) *Liber de causis* (Book of Causes) [373] and the (Christian) Pseudo-Dionysius the Areopagite. Thomas in *ScG* I 26 says that some people justify this view of God and *esse* by citing Pseudo-Dionysius's *Celestial Hierarchy* 4, "the *esse* of all things is the supersubstantial divinity."

13. Thomas's phrase "just *esse*" (*esse tantum*) corresponds to Avicenna's phrase *wujud mutlaq*, whose interpretation is disputed by Muslim philosophers in the same way. Thomas does on occasion speak of creatures as participating in God: the texts are collected and discussed in J. F. Wippel [263] 142–48. While for Avicenna it is apparently sufficient for God to be the *ultimate* cause of any contingent being's existing, Thomas insists that God is always an *immediate* cause of existence; see *ST* I, q. 45, a. 5. Thomas is here following the *Liber de causis* against Avicenna.

14. So explicitly Suárez, *Disputationes metaphysicae*, Disp. 28, §3, para. 15 and Disp. 32, §2, para. 14 [619].

15. Meister Eckhart, *Parisian Questions and Prologues* [363] 79. The *Prologues* and the appendix given in this volume give a good presentation of this whole way of thought, and show how deeply rooted Eckhart is both in Avicenna and in the pre-thirteenth-century western metaphysical, logical, and grammatical traditions. However, note that this volume persistently mistranslates the expression (e.g.) *esse album* as "white existence," when it should be "being-white."

16. For this view see Henry of Ghent, *Quodlibet* I 9 [219], especially V 53–55, and *Quodlibet* X 7–8 [219], especially XIV 151–75. In some passages Henry sounds close to Eckhart. Perhaps surprisingly, Ockham

cites with approval a similar view of the existence of creatures (though one with fewer metaphysical commitments) from Robert Grosseteste (Ockham [311] 94).

17. For Scotus on being as univocal, see [286] 4–8 and 19–22. For Thomas on being as analogical see, e.g., *Truth*, q. 2, a. 11; *ST* I, q. 13, a. 5; *ScG* I 32–34. For being as said analogically of God and creatures, of substance and accident, and of real and fictive beings, see Henry of Ghent, *Quodlibet* VII 1–2 [219] XI 26–30. Even Scotus's summary of Henry's position at [286] 17–19 admits that Henry thinks being (and so on) are predicated analogically, not purely equivocally, of God and creatures.

18. Thomas's example is in fact "number," which I find less clear. Both "number" and "polygon" are Aristotelian examples of things that are said, not equivocally or analogically, but of some things first and of others afterwards.

19. For Suárez on the analogy of being see [619] Disp. 28, §3 and Disp. 32, §2 (also, on the formal and objective concepts of being, see Disp. 2, §§1–3). For an opposing late scholastic view, see Tommaso de Vio Cajetan [596] and John of St. Thomas [608]. Scholastic terminology on the kinds of analogy is confusing. Sometimes the scholastics count analogous terms as a special kind of equivocals, sometimes as midway between equivocals and univocals; sometimes it is linguistic items and sometimes their significata that are equivocal or univocal or analogous; sometimes only things that are analogous by proportionality, rather than things that are analogous by attribution, are called analogous. Worse, the types of analogy that I (following Suárez) have contrasted as analogy of attribution versus analogy of proportionality are sometimes contrasted as analogy of proportion versus analogy of proportionality, and sometimes as analogy of attribution versus analogy of proportion (thus the phrase "analogy of proportion" can stand in different writers for *both* sides of the contrast; I have avoided the term altogether). The example of the heart is mine, but I think Suárez would accept it.

7   Creation and nature

Natural philosophy was "the most widely taught discipline at the medieval university."[1] We may get an idea of the extent of the subject in what has been called its classical century, 1277–1377,[2] by looking at the contents of John Dumbleton's mid-fourteenth-century *Summa of Logic and Natural Philosophy*. After a first part on logic, the major headings are[3]

II. First principles, matter and form; opinions about substantial forms; how qualities are intended and remitted.

III. On motion in the categories of place, quality, and quantity. On the causes of motion. How velocity is produced and caused. How alteration and augmentation are measured. The definitions of motion and time.

IV. On the nature of the elements and their qualities. If each element has two qualities in the highest degree. The action and reaction of elements on each other. The relations of elemental and qualitative forms. Density and rarity and their variation. How the powers of natural bodies depend on their magnitudes. The relative weights of pure and mixed bodies.

V.   On spiritual action and light. Whether light belongs particularly to some element or compound. On the nature of the medium receiving spiritual action, such as light. On the variation of spiritual action in a medium. Whether spiritual agents act instantaneously or in time.

VI. On the limits of active and passive powers. On the difficulty of action. On the limits of the powers of natural bodies by their natural places. Do the powers of elemental forms seek rest as well as motion? On the motion of the heavens and their movers. On the limits of size of natural bodies. How some bodies are moved by an intrinsic mover [ex se] and some are not.

VII.   On the cause of individuals and species of generable and corruptible things with regard to their numbers and the potencies of matter and agent. Whether the Prime Mover is of infinite power and whether it has been proved by a physical argument that the world and motion had no beginning.

VIII. On the generation of substances by like substances and animals by complete animals and by putrifaction. On the numerical unity of the soul with respect to the sensitive and intelligible and on the operations of the nutritive soul.

IX.   On material related to *On the Soul*, Book II, concerning the five senses.

X.   On universals which are called "Ideas" by the Platonists and on the passive intellect. On the simple and complex operations of the human intellect. [This part may never have been completed.]

Thus the curriculum of natural philosophy in Dumbleton's *Summa* ranges from physics through a study of the elements and their interactions, optics, biology, and psychology. Parts VIII and IX, on biology and psychology, take up almost 40 percent of the entire work. The basic framework is Aristotelian, but in the emphasis on light and in the missing Part X there are Platonic elements. To this basic framework, Dumbleton added instruction in the basic tools of natural philosophy that John Murdoch has called "analytical languages" – inquiries into the intension and remission of forms, maxima and minima, proportions of velocities in motion, and so forth.[4] Elements of the fundamental logical approach of medieval natural philosophy are explained in Part I of the *Summa*.

Even a cursory account of all of Dumbleton's topics is out of the question in a short chapter. In what follows, after a brief look at what happened before the thirteenth century, I will consider the relations between natural philosophy and astronomy and then developments in later medieval natural philosophy, both those that originated mainly within arts faculties and those that seem to have arisen out of its interactions with theology. But first something should be said about a presupposition of essentially all of medieval natural philosophy, namely, that the world is God's creation.

CREATION

An important background assumption for the subject of this chapter
is the belief that the natural world and we ourselves are creatures –
not self-made or self-subsistent beings, but products of a transcendent mind or reason. So Boethius wrote in his *Consolation of
Philosophy* (III 9):

> Oh Thou, that dost the world in lasting order guide,
> Father of heaven and earth, Who makest time swiftly slide,
> And, standing still Thyself, yet fram'st all moving laws,
> Who to Thy work wert moved by no external cause:
> But by a sweet desire, where envy hath no place,
> Thy goodness moving Thee to give each thing his grace,
> Thou dost all creatures' forms from highest patterns take,
> From Thy fair mind the world fair like Thyself doth make.
> Thus Thou perfect the whole perfect each part dost frame.

The metaphysics of creation provided medieval thinkers with
many topics for reflection, some of which are discussed elsewhere
in this volume.[5] For present purposes, it is important to bear in
mind that not only the heavens and earth, physical elements, animal species, souls, and angels, but also time and space, were typically regarded as created. There was thus no time "before" creation.
Augustine's treatment of this theme in *Confessions* XI is a classic
text for the early Middle Ages. Later, medieval Aristotelians, following Aristotle's definition of time as the number of motion with
respect to before and after (*Physics*, IV, 10–14), argued that time began with the creation of the cosmos – without the cosmos there are
no moving bodies and no minds capable of numbering their motions
in days or years, and so forth, and hence before the cosmos existed
there was no time. Analogously, in a typical medieval view, there is
no space outside the last sphere of the finite cosmos, because there
are no bodies there whose extensions might be measured. But just
as God exists eternally "before" the creation of the cosmos, so God
is ubiquitous "outside" the cosmos, existing wholly at every point.
Fourteenth-century discussions of God's ubiquity outside the cosmos by the likes of Thomas Bradwardine and Nicole Oresme have
been shown to have connections with Isaac Newton's concept of
absolute space.[6]

The account of creation in Genesis was authoritative for medieval Jews and Christians, but this did not lead them to reject such

understanding of the world as could be gathered from observation and logical or rational analysis. In his *Letter to the Grand Duchess Christina* in the early seventeenth century, Galileo famously defended his own approach to reconciling the Bible and science by quoting Augustine's *The Literal Meaning of Genesis*. In doing so, Galileo was not misrepresenting Augustine's position. Nearly every sentence of the creation story in Genesis was difficult to interpret, and exegetes suggested a wide range of interpretations that might shed light on the sacred text while not conflicting with established knowledge of nature. Augustine in particular returns repeatedly to the question of how one should use science or natural philosophy in biblical hermeneutics. From the very beginning of his commentary he suggests many alternative interpretations (I 1 [61] I 19–20), and he warns against dogmatic adoption of readings that may be contradicted by experience and reason:

That would be to battle not for the teaching of Holy Scripture but for our own, wishing its teaching to conform to ours, whereas we ought to wish ours to conform to that of Sacred Scripture... Usually, even a non-Christian knows something about the earth, the heavens, and the other elements of this world, about the motion and orbit of the stars and even their size and relative positions, about the predictable eclipses of the sun and moon, the cycles of the years and the seasons, about the kinds of animals, shrubs, stones, and so forth, and this knowledge he holds to as being certain from reason and experience. Now, it is a disgraceful and dangerous thing for an infidel to hear a Christian, presumably giving the meaning of Holy Scripture, talking nonsense on these topics; and we should take all means to prevent such an embarrassing situation, in which people show up vast ignorance in a Christian and laugh it to scorn... If they find a Christian mistaken in a field which they themselves know well and hear him maintaining his foolish opinions about our books, how are they going to believe those books in matters concerning the resurrection of the dead, the hope of eternal life, and the kingdom of heaven, when they think their pages are full of falsehoods on facts which they themselves have learnt from experience and the light of reason? (I 18–19 [61] I 41–43)[7]

NATURE AS EPIPHANY: NATURAL PHILOSOPHY THROUGH THE TWELFTH CENTURY

For knowledge of the natural world, the early medieval West was largely dependent on such texts as Pliny the Elder's *Natural History* and Seneca's *Natural Questions*. Derivative from these and other Roman writings were such medieval encyclopedic works as Isidore of Seville's *On the Nature of Things* and *Etymologies* and the Venerable Bede's *On the Nature of Things*. Neoplatonic works such as Macrobius's *Commentary on Cicero's Dream of Scipio* and Martianus Capella's *Marriage of Philology and Mercury* must also be mentioned. Works such as these supplied empirical facts about nature that might be investigated philosophically, but they were not always in themselves accurate or rationally structured. With the disappearance from view of Aristotle's works, the most significant text in natural philosophy available in Latin before the twelfth century was doubtless Calcidius's translation of and commentary on Plato's *Timaeus*, sections 17A–53B.[8] Equally influential, although not as thoroughly natural, was Boethius's *The Consolation of Philosophy*. In mathematics there were some texts translated by Boethius from Greek and later calendrical works (*computus*). In Scottus Eriugena's *Periphyseon*, God is so intimately present in nature as to raise the charge of pantheism, although for all his emphasis on theophanies Eriugena presents little by way of physical detail.[9]

In the twelfth-century cathedral schools, natural philosophy in the form of ideas taken from Plato's *Timaeus* had an efflorescence in interpreting Genesis on the six days of creation (the *hexaëmeron*). Such twelfth-century works have been said to involve "the discovery of nature."[10] Assimilating what Genesis said about the first day of creation to Plato's statement in the *Timaeus* that in the beginning there was chaos or unformed matter, Thierry of Chartres, in his *Treatise on the Works of the Six Days*, supposes that the world soul of the *Timaeus* is the same as the Holy Spirit and is referred to where Genesis says, "and the spirit of God hovered over the waters [*Spiritus Dei superferebatur aquas*]."[11] The oneness of the cosmos precedes it and comes from God, who is everywhere. From the number one, Thierry goes on to examine other mathematical rather than physical aspects of the cosmos.

Other twelfth-century authors such as William of Conches, Bernard Sylvester, Adelard of Bath, and Hermann of Carinthia are also worthy of natural-philosophical attention.[12] They have much more to say about details of the natural world than can be found in Eriugena's *Periphyseon*. Adelard of Bath's *Questions on Natural Science*, for instance, begins with the topics, "The reason why plants grow without a seed being sown beforehand" and "In what way some plants are to be called hot, when they are all more earthy than fiery" ([355] 85). Like Thierry, Adelard thinks that the heavenly bodies are animate ([355] 219). Indeed, it is his opinion that "Whoever thinks they are inanimate, is himself rather without a soul." He argues energetically for his own view of the stars and planets, "partly from their position, partly from their composition, and partly, too, from their action." It would be the height of folly, he thinks, to suppose that the bright and unpolluted celestial realm does not participate in the movement of soul and the excellence of mind. Again, "If their action is the cause of the death and life of lower animals, what should be thought about these stars?...To believe that what provides the effect of life for others is itself without life, can only be the belief of a frivolous jester."

As compared to later medieval natural philosophy, twelfth-century natural philosophy is more literary or descriptive and less analytic. Cosmological works have a heavy infusion of Plato's *Timaeus*, of the book of Genesis, of Cicero's *On the Nature of the Gods*, and so forth. There is much more said that could be assimilated to the Platonic Ideas (albeit interpreted as the Word of God) and much more attention to spiritual or intellectual creatures than would be the case later. Importantly, all of these twelfth-century works assume that nature exhibits regularity, starting with God and then the heavens, which are most regular, and, through the influence of the heavens, to the diversity of the sublunar realm. So Hermann of Carinthia refers to the "law of a certain universal condition" as involved in the very definition of nature and to "the natures of things" as the basis for their specific properties:

All movements of secondary generation are administered by a certain relationship of nature (by the decision, of course, of the Author of all things)... and since every order of things which are living is perpetuated by a law of a certain universal condition which in common speech is called "nature," from nature itself it seems most appropriate to begin...It is customary for the term "nature" to be used for two concepts...(i) [as] Seneca...says: "What is nature other than God and divine reason inserted into the whole universe and its parts?"...(ii) But the other is that by which Plato composes the soul of the universe...By taking up *this* "nature" natural scientists even attempt to describe individually the natures of all bodies – both of the heavens and of the lower world...What, then, appears to me to be the most accurate description possible is this: nature is a certain perpetual property of universal *genitura* [generated things] of propagating and conserving itself, as far as this is inherent [*quantum in ipsum est*]...This is close to the last of the definitions which Boethius supports – i.e., that the natures of things are, themselves, the things' proper species, since the property of every *genitura* depends on its species. (*De essentiis* [365] 151–55)

ASTRONOMY AND ASTROLOGY

Most medieval thinkers assumed that the motions of the heavenly bodies affect the course of nature in the sublunar realm. Until the twelfth century, Latin knowledge of the heavens came largely from the late Roman works mentioned earlier, all of which were not only nonmathematical but often inconsistent or at least highly fanciful.[13] When, however, Arab astronomy began to be known in Europe, bringing with it a knowledge of Greek mathematical astronomy, the situation changed dramatically. In many medieval cosmologies, God uses the celestial realm as the instrument or intermediate cause of all terrestrial effects (Hermann of Carinthia's *De essentiis* is structured on this assumption). Diversity of day and night, the seasons, the weather, growth of plants and animals, and so forth are explained, first, by the obliquity of the ecliptic or apparent path of the sun, moon, and planets relative to the apparent rotation of the sphere of the fixed stars, and then by the individual motions of the sun, moon, and planets through the zodiac. Insofar as these supposedly important causal circumstances could be reliably known, physicians attempted to take account of them in explaining human illnesses and in determining the appropriate timing of medical procedures. Alchemy also assumed the effect of heavenly emanations on the development of metals. Such theories are less evident in later university works, perhaps because they were thought to call freedom of the will dangerously into question, but even so eminent a thinker as Albert the Great took the principle of celestial causation quite seriously.[14]

How was one to think of the science built on this view of the heavens? In Islam, Avicenna had initiated a tendency to categorize astrology as natural philosophy and astronomy as mathematics,[15] a move that raised significant questions about the relations of the two disciplines to one another. Astrology became the discipline that addressed the physics of the heavens, as well as applying this physics of heavenly influences on earth. It was thus through the translation of Abu Mashar's *Introductorium maius in astronomiam*, an astrological work, that the Latin West was first introduced to Aristotelian physics.[16] On the other hand, astronomy built mathematical models to track the positions of the planets (hence providing the forecasts of lunar, solar, planetary, and stellar positions needed for applied astrology), but it often built these models unconstrained by considerations of physical plausibility.

From the time of Plato, most natural philosophers were agreed that a spherical heaven (with concentric shells rather like an onion) surrounds a spherical earth, although they differed about the details. Aristotle had posited a set of such spheres, each with its own uniform motion but each also carried with the movement of the spheres surrounding it, meant to account for the observed positions of the planets through the year. From the time of Hipparchus and Apollonius, however, many mathematical astronomers lost hope of accurately "saving the phenomena" of planetary motions using models containing only concentric uniformly rotating spheres. They therefore proposed models in which spheres rotated around centers that were not the center of the cosmos (epicycles, eccentrics) or even changed their rates of rotation (equants). This led to a division of labor over the centuries between natural philosophers seeking physically realistic theories of the heavens and mathematical astronomers proposing theories that accurately predicted planetary positions,

This break between mathematical astronomy and natural philosophy led to many methodological or epistemological discussions, as well as to many efforts, over the years, to reintegrate the science of the heavens. Did mathematical astronomy take its premises from natural philosophy at least in assuming that all heavenly motions are circular because they are the motions of spheres made up of aether for which such motion is natural? Or could mathematical astronomy be an autonomous science that did not need to look to natural philosophy, but could simply build mathematical theories to fit observations? J. Ragep has argued that in Islam astronomy was sometimes treated as purely mathematical in order to assure that it did not challenge theological doctrine.[17] Nasir al-Din al-Tusi (1201–74) "made clear in the *Tadhkira* that an astronomer should prove most cosmological matters using 'proofs of the fact' (that simply establish their existence using observations and mathematics) rather than 'proofs of the reasoned fact' (that 'convey the necessity of that existence' using physical and/or metaphysical principles)."[18]

The difficulty with Tusi's proposal, however, was that astronomers had known since the time of Hipparchus that the same planetary motions can be accounted for equally well in different ways: a model with an eccentric may give the same predictions as a model with a deferent and epicycle. In mathematics proper, such as arithmetic or geometry, the foundations are axioms that are better known to the mathematician than the theorems proved on the basis of these foundations. But in astronomy that is not necessarily the case. Ali al-Qushji (fifteenth century), who wrote a commentary on Tusi's "Epitome of Belief," "admitted that as far as saving the phenomena of astronomy were concerned there was no way to differentiate between a model in which the earth rotates and one in which everything else rotates around an unmoving earth."[19] Nevertheless, astronomy was not dependent on natural philosophy, al-Qushji claimed, because its premises are only reasonable suppositions, not claimed to be absolutely true.[20]

It is worth pondering that the whole of Aristotelian natural philosophy was built on the observation or "empirical fact" that the heavens rotate once a day, carrying around the stars and planets. It was by inference from this universally observed "fact" that Aristotle and Aristotelians, following a reasonable and empirical scientific method, concluded that the heavens must be composed of a fifth element, aether, moved in eternal rotation by immaterial unmoved movers. The ongoing existence of systems of mathematical astronomy in which it was apparent that the process of reasoning from observations to higher level general theory could not guarantee that the higher level theory was uniquely true, even if its predictions were accurate, no doubt served to inject a degree of ongoing caution into natural philosophy's epistemological claims. At the same time it meant that medieval natural philosophy never became a truly mathematical science, as physics after Newton would be.

SCHOLASTIC NATURAL PHILOSOPHY

Medieval natural philosophy underwent significant changes when Aristotle's scientific works were translated into Latin and eventually became the standard textbooks of university arts faculties. Without abandoning the presupposition of divine creation of the universe, natural philosophy now focused more on the natures things had in themselves – on the specific "inner principles of motion or rest" of *Physics* II 1 – than on creatures as signs of their maker. According to Aristotle, the goal of natural philosophy is to develop a deductive science (modeled on the axiomatic format of Greek geometry), which explains observed physical phenomena through their essential causes, proximate and remote. Starting from the observation that all things move, physicists were expected to work analytically (or *quia*, by proofs of the fact) to discover the principles of nature (analogous to the definitions, axioms, and postulates of geometry). They would then explain natural processes using these principles as the basis for demonstrations *propter quid*, or of the reasoned or caused fact.

Thus Aristotelian science is empirical – it begins from experience, but – and this is essential – the method of getting from experience to theory is not to collect more data, but rather to think analytically about some small body of experience in order to gain insight into it. So, for instance, one might reason that wherever there is motion there must be a mover, and then inquire what the mover might be. The preeminent tools of scholastic natural philosophy are not experimental or mathematical, but logical. As commentators on the works of Aristotle, medieval natural philosophers sometimes assumed that Aristotle had produced a finished scientific system, but they could not help but notice that in the works they were commenting on, Aristotle did not lay out a synthetic deductive system, but rather worked dialectically to discover the principles of such a system. In their own contributions to natural philosophy, then, scholastic natural philosophers were not the dogmatists of the later stereotype, but quite often open to new ideas and arguments and might characterize their own solutions to problems as "probable" rather than certain.

In their lectures in the arts faculties of universities, natural philosophers expounded and explained Aristotle's texts chapter by chapter and line by line, suggesting improvements to Aristotle as seemed necessary.[21] Complementing lectures on texts as core activities of medieval universities were disputations, in which masters and students might take part. In written commentaries on Aristotle including *quaestiones* (questions followed by arguments on opposing sides and determinations or solutions), some questions are those that a master teaching students about Aristotle's text might want to bring up. For instance, it might be asked whether it is true, as Aristotle argued, that place is the innermost unmoving boundary of the surrounding body (*Physics* IV 1–5, definition at 212a20–21). Other questions appearing in Aristotelian commentaries concerned issues about which there was significant contemporary difference of opinion. Such questions on natural philosophy could also have been part, not of disputations linked to one or the other of Aristotle's works, but of disputations on sophismata, problems, or anything at all (quodlibetal disputations).[22]

The written works by thirteenth-century natural philosophers – for instance, the work of Roger Bacon, Albert the Great, and Thomas Aquinas – are more often expository or synthetic (much of Aquinas's work was simply exposition of Aristotelian texts), while the fourteenth-century approach was more often analytic and in the form of *quaestiones* – for example, the work of Ockham, the Oxford Calculators, John Buridan, and Nicole Oresme. One factor that differentiated scholastics who aimed for a (single) synthetic Aristotelian-Christian science from those scholars who took a more analytic approach was their view on the status of the principles of one science, say physics, relative to the principles and conclusions of another, say metaphysics. For those who took a synthetic view, the principles of natural philosophy or physics might ideally be proved by deduction from the higher science of metaphysics (or the lower science would simply add some new principles to the principles of the higher science). Ultimately, on this view, all science might be deduced from self-evident principles, and the lower sciences would be integrated with the higher ones. On the other hand, there were those, like Boethius of Dacia, who claimed autonomy for natural philosophy or physics, arguing that the principles of physics were neither self-evident nor proved by metaphysics, but established *a posteriori*, from the analysis of experience[23] – and that physics and its principles need not be synthesized with such Christian beliefs as the creation of the world in time.[24]

Scholastic natural philosophers followed Aristotle in assuming that natural effects have not only an efficient cause, but also material, formal, and final causes (Aristotle, *Physics* II 3; *Metaphysics* I 3–10). On this conception, natural philosophy explains only those effects that have all four of these causes. Besides effects that follow their causes regularly and for a purpose, there are effects that occur rarely or accidentally through the concurrence of causes, but natural philosophers did not expect to be able to explain such irregular or chance events, which have no final cause. Some scholastic natural philosophers, for instance Nicole Oresme, attempted to enlarge the range of phenomena for which natural philosophy could discover the causes to include what was considered marvelous or magical.[25] Others, for instance John Buridan, concluded that except for miracles and human free will, everything in the universe is subject to natural laws.[26]

The assumption that the world has a final cause or purpose intended by God led some natural philosophers to assume that they might be able to reason out how the world must be because it is right or good that it be so. Boethius's picture of the world as in some sense a "perfect whole" did indeed persist through the Middle Ages. But there was also concern to respect God's freedom. Fourteenth-century "voluntarists" were especially insistent that God was not compelled to create the world in what humans might consider the best or even a good way. He could have done or do anything that does not involve a logical contradiction. According to H. Oberman, this view reinforced arguments for empiricism: since God was free to create the world in different ways, we must use observation to determine what is in fact the case.[27]

Thus the conception of the world lying behind much late medieval natural philosophy allowed that it contained more contingency – though this might not be the aspect of nature that could become a part of science – than is sometimes supposed in discussions of medieval theories of science.[28] And if there is contingency in the cosmos, then things could be other than they are. Pierre Duhem, one of the great pioneer historians of medieval natural philosophy in the early twentieth century, famously argued that the Condemnation at Paris in 1277 of 219 heretical propositions led medieval natural philosophers to consider alternatives to Aristotelian natural philosophy by requiring them to accept the proposition that God can do anything that does not involve a logical contradiction. By stimulating natural philosophy to go in new and fruitful directions, Duhem wrote, the Condemnation of 1277 brought about the birth of modern science.[29]

If Duhem was right, then theology impacted natural philosophy (perhaps for the best) through the Condemnation of 1277, but it is arguable that before 1277 natural philosophers had already been moving in the direction of concluding that the cosmos is contingent, and that many states of affairs are possible that are not in fact the case. Moreover, a common scholastic philosophical move that had a similar impact on natural-philosophical reasoning – one that is not necessarily tied to the Condemnation of 1277 – was the habit of reasoning *secundum imaginationem*, that is, of posing counterfactual situations and asking what would happen in such a case. In the disputations *de obligationibus* and *de sophismatibus* that played so prominent a role in medieval arts education, the student was trained, above all, to reason logically from an arbitrary hypothesis to whatever followed consistently from it. This was a perfect preparation for reasoning *secundum imaginationem*.

To pursue his program of ontological minimalism, William of Ockham frequently asked whether it might be possible that one thing exist without another. If, for instance, quantity is thought to be something real and distinct from substance and quality, what would happen if one supposed that God removed the quantity from a substance while leaving the substance unmoved – wouldn't it still fill the same volume? In this way Ockham argued that substances and qualities alone, without anything independent corresponding to words falling under the categories of quantity or motion (action and passion), could explain whatever needed to be explained.[30] By thus arguing *secundum imaginationem*, Ockham adopted a minimalist ontology. But such arguments could work in more than one way. John Buridan, for instance, argued, *contra* Ockham, that local motion must be some sort of inherent quality. What would happen, Buridan said, if God rotated the whole cosmos and every body in it? Would that situation be any different from what is now thought to be the case? It must be different, he believed (his intuition thus being the opposite of Ernst Mach's later). It followed that local motion must correspond to an inherent quality, even if there are no fixed reference points by which to judge it. Thus late medieval natural philosophers frequently reasoned *secundum imaginationem* or supposed that God might do something not found in the normal course of nature, but, even after they did so, there was considerable leeway for coming to differing conclusions.

Historians of science have been particularly interested in seeing how thirteenth- and fourteenth-century natural philosophers introduced mathematics into natural philosophy.[31] The influence

of Robert Grosseteste was especially important here.[32] More pervasive, however, was the introduction of an armamentarium of analytic
tools, partly from mathematics but mostly from logic, for unravel-
ing any given problem. In particular, Ockham and his followers defined science as propositional knowledge about the world and then
used supposition theory to analyze the ways in which the propositions of science mapped on to the things of the world.[33] In disputations on sophismata, university students, particularly at Oxford,
were trained in critical thinking, with sophismata sentences and the
related cases often coming from natural philosophy. How this happened can be seen in William Heytesbury's *Sophismata* and *Rules for
Solving Sophismata*, in Richard Swineshead's *Book of Calculations*,
in many works on the intension and remission of forms, on maxima
and minima, on first and last instants, on continuity and infinity,
and so forth.[34] J. Murdoch has argued, indeed, that these analytical languages created a methodological unity between late medieval
philosophy and theology, by means of which theology became much
more philosophical than was the case at other times.[35]

It should perhaps be noted here, in light of the communality of
methods, that in the later Middle Ages the boundary between natural philosophy and theology (or metaphysics) was not as sharp as one
might expect, given the Aristotelian conception of sciences as self-
contained deductive systems, because theologians had developed a
theory of natural theology according to which natural theology, like
natural philosophy, begins from experience.[36] On this theory, the
knowledge that human beings derive from sense experience of natural things is the basis for human knowledge of the being of God – by *a
posteriori* demonstrations *quia*, not *a priori* demonstrations *propter
quid*.

The possibility of a vacuum

According to John Buridan, the question of the possibility of a vacuum inside the cosmos is a question clearly relevant both to natural
philosophy and to theology.[37] Medieval natural philosophers generally agreed that the entire universe or cosmos is a spherical plenum,
with nothing outside it, not even empty space, and no empty spaces
within it. Aristotle had worked very hard to show that the ancient
atomists' conception of an empty three-dimensional space was

incoherent; instead, as we have seen, he had defined "place" as the innermost unmoving surface of the surrounding body. By Aristotle's definition a vacuum, if it existed, would be an extension capable of receiving a body, but in which no body was present. Aristotle had argued, by contrast, that extension is always to be measured on or by a body on which, so to speak, different reference points can be established. If there were empty space, there would be no reference points within it by which a longer or a shorter extension could be measured.

In the way of thinking about God's absolute power supported by the Condemnation of 1277, it should not be denied that God could create a vacuum unless to do so would involve a logical contradiction. Is there, then, a logical contradiction in supposing that God *de potentia Dei absoluta* could annihilate everything inside the sphere of the moon? Most people thought not, but they had different ways of construing the situation that would result. For some, the result would be in effect to cut a sphere out of the cosmos, so that no body could occupy a place inside the emptied sphere of the moon, just as there was no space there, and likewise no body could be in place outside the cosmos as a whole. According to Buridan, if God annihilated everything inside the sphere of the moon, then there would be no determinate dimension there – a body placed inside the sphere could move at a high velocity in a straight line for a long time and never get any closer to or farther from any particular part of the sphere of the moon.[38] On the other hand, according to Buridan, God could *de potentia Dei absoluta* create measurable extension in three dimensions separate from any body (what we might call Euclidean space) inside the sphere of the moon. For Aristotle, extension without an extended body was impossible. Here, however, the development of scholastic theology had brought such impossibility into question. Aquinas had held, for instance, that after transubstantiation the extension of the former bread now filled the role of substance as subject of the qualities formerly inhering in the bread (this is discussed further below).

For Buridan, then, if God *de potentia Dei absoluta* annihilated everything inside the sphere of the moon, there was nothing logically contradictory in supposing that God also created within the sphere of the moon quantitative extension not inhering in any body: this was something known to be possible – albeit miraculously – because it was the case in the transubstantiated Eucharist. Then if a body were placed within the incorporeal dimensions inside the sphere of the moon, it could move away from one part of the sphere of the moon and toward another part. In such a situation, the kinematics would be no different from the kinematics of ordinary natural motion. It would be necessary, however, to reconceptualize dynamics. In Aristotelian dynamics, velocity was supposed to depend on the forces causing motion and the resistances they encountered. On this view, a greater weight falling in the same medium would fall faster than a lesser weight, while the same weight falling in a less resistant medium would fall faster than it would fall in a more resistant medium.

If a body were moving in a vacuum, first of all it would be necessary to determine if the motion was natural (like the fall of a heavy body) or violent (like the motion of a projectile). One could suppose that in a vacuum there would be no "up" or "down," so that bodies in a vacuum would not move to their natural places, or one could assume that somehow positions in a vacuum would continue to be identified by the natural places of fire, air, water, or earth formerly there. In either case there would be no medium resisting the motion. Then it followed, according to normal Aristotelian dynamics, that the velocity of a body moved by any force whatsoever would exceed all finite velocities. But, according to the usual line of reasoning, an actually infinite velocity is a logical contradiction, since the body would arrive at the end of its motion immediately, and it would not reach the midpoint of a given path before it reached the end. Aristotle had, in fact, used the logical contradiction of an actually infinite velocity as one of his arguments for the nonexistence of any vacua in the cosmos. But if proper regard to the omnipotence of God required that God could *de potentia Dei absoluta* create a vacuum, and if God could put a body in motion in that vacuum, then it followed that an infinite, self-contradictory velocity could not result from the lack of external resistance. A finite velocity must result. How can this be understood? One might argue that distance alone, without resistance, is sufficient to explain why motion takes time. Dynamics might be changed to argue that any given force will cause only some finite maximum velocity, which is decreased by the resistance of any medium. Mathematically one might suppose that velocities are proportional to $F - R$ or to $(F - R)/R$, where F is force and R resistance. Or, thirdly, one might suppose that a ball thrown in such a vacuum would be moved by its "impetus" (normally thought to be proportional to its mass and velocity or MV) in such a way that impetus is not a force in the normal sense. By reasoning like this, medieval natural philosophers like John Buridan concluded that projectiles in general, and not just those in unnatural situations supposed to result from the absolute power of God, were moved by impetus, considered to be a quality inhering in the projectile.[39]

Medieval natural philosophers had little natural philosophical motivation for investigating the possibility of a vacuum inside the universe other than the fact that Aristotle argued against it, making it an issue that every master teaching Book IV of the *Physics* would rehearse in expository questions. They likewise had little reason to care about the motion of projectiles, except that Aristotle's theory of the cause of projectile motion was strained and unconvincing. Scholastic theology also had little reason to care about the possibility of vacua or about the cause of projectile motion. This is a case, then, in which the technique of reasoning *secundum imaginationem* or of calling upon the absolute power of God in order to distinguish between natural and logical impossibilities served to move natural-philosophical thinking. Insofar as the result was movement away from Aristotle's ideas and toward those of Galileo or Newton, it has been considered progressive. While others may blame medieval natural philosophers for being excessively rational (spinning webs like spiders) and for having devoted too little time to making new observations, we might rather praise them for the rational construction of Aristotelian natural philosophy as an empirical and demonstrative natural science.

INTERACTIONS OF NATURAL PHILOSOPHY AND THEOLOGY

In her investigations of later medieval natural philosophy, Anneliese Maier studied theological as well as natural-philosophical works, but when she used such texts she usually set aside the theological context of a discussion in order to concentrate on topics of interest in relation to the later history of science. To understand the dynamics of intellectual change in later medieval natural philosophy it is essential, however, not only to retrieve such discussions but also to look at the theological problems that gave rise to them.

It is sometimes debated whether medieval natural philosophy was inherently theological (because it was essentially God-oriented) or, on the other hand, whether it was completely dissociated from theological concerns.[40] It would seem, however, that the situation was more complicated than either of these positions in its pure form would allow. Theology did have a significant influence on medieval natural philosophy, but this did not prevent natural philosophy from being scientific or from being good philosophy. In some cases the influence was scientifically beneficial. And sometimes influence ran in the other direction. Masters teaching in theology faculties frequently called upon natural philosophy to help resolve theological issues. There were thus "theologian-natural philosophers,"[41] who knew as much as anyone else about natural philosophy as well as theology. Problems with the relative dating of the philosophical and theological work of such thinkers as Aquinas, Scotus, and Ockham make it difficult to prove which context was the controlling one. Nevertheless, it would appear that the motivation for innovation often came from a particular theological problem, such as that of giving what might be called a physically accurate account of the transubstantiation of bread and wine into the body and blood of Christ, which was believed to occur, by God's action, in the Eucharist.[42]

Transubstantiation and ontology

After God miraculously transubstantiated the bread of the Eucharist into the body of Christ, it was held that the appearances (*species*) of bread continued to be present, although they did not inhere in any body. The conflicting descriptions of this situation given by various theologian-natural philosophers brought differences of ontology with them that had implications for natural philosophy itself. For Thomas Aquinas, in the Eucharist the quantity or extension of the former bread now took the place of its substance, with the qualities that had formerly belonged to the bread now inhering in this extension. For William of Ockham, on the other hand, the qualities of the former bread by themselves occupy an extended place, within which is the body of Christ to which they are not in any way related.[43] To explain how Christ could be "really" in the Eucharist, theologians used Aristotelian concepts as far as possible. But when the theological doctrine seemed to require a modification of Aristotelian conclusions – to allow, for instance, that in the Eucharist a quantity or quality might exist without inhering in a substance – they suggested and frequently adopted modifications to the Aristotelian view. Some, like Aquinas, developed a special "sublimated" natural philosophy to explain the existence of the quantitative and qualitative "accidents" of bread and wine in the Eucharist without any bread or wine. On the other hand, the tendency of a philosopher like William of Ockham was to avoid such sublimated physics and instead to say either that the situation was totally miraculous or, alternatively, to modify ordinary natural philosophy itself in light of the theological special case. Thus Ockham did not try to give a natural explanation of how the transubstantiated Eucharist could move or act and be acted on (since, for example, it has no substantial form it would seem to have no natural place and likewise no natural resistance to violent motion), but instead suggested that God may cause a miracle at every instant of the Eucharist's motion. On the other hand, when Ockham denied the separate existence of quantity in connection with the mode of Christ's presence in the Eucharist, he consequently denied the separate existence of quantity throughout all of natural philosophy.

It seems that in cases like this, Aristotelian natural philosophy had a greater impact on theology than the reverse. But after the theologian-natural philosophers had finished trying to describe transubstantiation using the tools of natural philosophy, their results also had an impact within natural philosophy proper. Thus many fourteenth-century natural philosophers accepted the conclusion that a quantity or quality can exist without inhering in a substance (it happens in the Eucharist) and that quantity is not something separate from substance and quality (it is not separate in Christ as he exists in the Eucharist). These were theories that philosophical theology gave back to natural philosophy. Such theories were often reasonable and consistent in themselves. Indeed, historians have sometimes praised the new theories as representing progress within natural philosophy, paying no attention to the evidence that they were developed to solve theological problems.[44]

The physics of angels

The interactions of theological discussions of the place and motion of angels in commentaries on the *Sentences* with discussions of the natural motions of the elements in commentaries on the *Physics* provide another telling example of the ways theology and natural philosophy cross-fertilized in the fourteenth century. Just as twelfth-century natural philosophers had identified the Holy Spirit with Plato's world soul, so natural philosophers after the recovery of Aristotle's scientific works assumed that Aristotle's prime movers were to be identified with angels, both supposed to be immaterial substances. This identification may explain why in the later Middle Ages angels were thought to be intrinsically immaterial and without bodies, while in earlier Neoplatonic theories they were often assumed to have ethereal or aerial bodies or vehicles, not to mention one or more sets of wings.[45]

In the typical later medieval conception, angels are a part of creation, perhaps referred to as "heavens" in the Genesis statement that on the first day God created "the heavens and the earth." Natural philosophers wanted to understand how the prime movers or angels move the heavenly spheres (obviously part of natural philosophy), but they also wanted to explain how the same or very similar sorts of entities (immaterial substances) could be sent by God to earth as messengers. With regard to the "place" of angels, Thomas Aquinas argued that angels are only in place by their actions, and that they may occupy a larger or smaller finite volume depending upon the action they exert. Interestingly, one of the propositions condemned in 1277 was the proposition "that without an operation a substance is not in place." Mentioning this condemnation (*Ordinatio* II, d. 2, qq. 1–2, para. 200 [281] VII 244), Scotus argued that angels are in place by their substance and not only by their action. The differences between Aquinas and Scotus here had consequences for a question commonly asked in *Sentences* commentaries: can an angel move from point A to point B without traversing the distance in between? It was assumed that angels are normally in the empyrean heaven at the outside of the cosmos. When they are sent to earth, then, must they traverse all the ether spheres before arriving here? Not necessarily, according to Aquinas's theory. If an angel did not act along the path from heaven to earth, then it could leave point A and appear at point B without ever being in the extension in between the two points. Indeed, if angels could only be present where they intended to act and if they were, in themselves, indivisible, then it seemed to follow that their motion would necessarily be discontinuous – some theologians, including Henry of Ghent, therefore argued that angels are in a sort of atomic or quantum time (see Scotus, *Ordinatio* II, d. 2, part 2, q. 7, para. 497).

In Duns Scotus's view, if angels are sent as messengers within the natural world, while here they probably act naturally:

It is not unreasonable to suppose that an angel, insofar as it participates in the corporeal condition (that is insofar as there is something of the same nature [*ratione*] in it and in a body), that it also participate in some way in the measure of body. But insofar as it is moved locally, it participates in place [*ubi*], which is a corporeal passion in some way, of the same nature in it and in a body. Therefore it can also be measured by the measure of the motion of the first body [i.e., the motion of the heavens, which is the primary measure of time]. (*Ordinatio* II, dist. 2, part 2, q. 7. *Utrum angelus possit moveri in instanti*, para. 501 [281] VII 380)

To the next question, whether an angel can move from extreme to extreme without traversing what is in between, Scotus answered:

It seems probable that the angel cannot, because the order preestablished by the superior agent seems to be necessary to any inferior agent that acts with regard to such ordered [*ordinata*] things. For example: the order of natural forms succeeding each other in natural generation is determined by the establisher of nature [*instituente naturam*]. And therefore with respect to any natural agent it is necessary, just as no natural agent can make vinegar immediately unless from wine. Therefore, since the order of the principal parts of the universe comes from God, for any created agent and created power this order seems to be necessary when it is supposed to act on those things which have this order. Therefore an angel, when it moves itself through bodies which have this order, cannot, without any order, make itself to be immediately in one given place from any other given place, for then no distance would seem to impede its action. (*Ordinatio* II, dist. 2, part 2, q. 8, para. 515 [281] VII 386–87)

Thus Scotus supposed that angels sent to earth, although they may be indivisible, become part of the natural order.

In the *Physics*, Aristotle had argued that indivisibles cannot move. This was one step in his argument that the only eternal motion in the cosmos is the rotation of the heavenly spheres, all other motions necessarily being interrupted by moments or periods of rest. The argument against the motion of an indivisible body was part of this chain of arguments. But, as any late medieval theologian-natural philosopher would say, we know from the Bible that angels move.

Only think of Gabriel's annunciation to Mary. It follows that Aristotle must be wrong in arguing that an indivisible cannot be moved. What should a commentator on this section of Aristotle's *Physics* do? By the early fourteenth century, Christian natural philosophers had a number of things to think about in commenting on Aristotle and a number of possibly inconsistent motivations. First, insofar as Thomas Aquinas and others used Aristotle's proof of the existence of a prime mover as all but the last step of a cosmological argument for the existence of God, a commentator would presumably not want to undermine Aristotle's proof of a prime mover. On the other hand, Aristotle's proof of the prime mover was highly interwoven with his supposed proof that the world is eternal. So a Christian commentator on Aristotle might want to preserve the proof of the existence of a prime mover, while calling into question the proof of an eternal world. The argument that indivisibles cannot move was one step in Aristotle's larger argument.

Entering further into Aristotle's arguments of Books VII and VIII of the *Physics*, then, the commentator would come to Aristotle's argument that everything that is moved must be moved by something else (with all motion ultimately traceable back to one or more unmoved prime movers). In attempting to demonstrate this case by case, Aristotle denied that even animals and human beings move themselves. A Christian wanting to protect human free will would be inclined to balk at the argument that humans are not responsible for their own actions or motions. Building up to the case of animals and humans, moreover, Aristotle argued that even the elements in natural motion do not move themselves. This apparently contradicted his earlier account of "natural" motion as a having a source internal to the thing in motion (as against "violent" motion, where the source of change is external), but it was necessary to his argument.

Faced with these problems, Aquinas quite ingeniously saved Aristotle's argument in Book VIII of the *Physics* by saying that what causes the natural motion of elemental bodies is the generator of the body and the remover of the impediment to its motion. Thus elements have only a passive potentiality to be moved in natural motion not an active potentiality. From Duns Scotus on, this argument was rejected on the very plausible grounds that whenever an effect is produced there must be a cause that is present and acting.

While a heavy body is falling, its generator and the remover of the impediments to its motion may have ceased to exist. So Scotus, and following him John of Jandun, Buridan, and many others concluded that in the natural motion of elements the cause is a form inhering in the body, either its substantial form or its weight acting as the instrument of the substantial form.

What motivated Scotus's conclusion that an element can move itself in natural motion? There are, indeed, strong arguments in favor of this conclusion, but it cannot be denied that it subverts the main chain of argument of Books VII and VIII of the *Physics*. Most likely, Scotus first worked out the pattern of reasoning leading to this conclusion in order to explain the motion of angels. Although the chronology of Scotus's works is not known with certainty, the editors of his commentary on the *Metaphysics* argue that the books in which he deals with the motion of angels were written after his commentaries on Peter Lombard's *Sentences*. And in the *Ordinatio* in the Balić edition, between the introduction of the question of the motion of angels and the conclusion, there is a large section (twenty-two pages) devoted to the natural motion of the elements. Thus, the new theory of the motion of the elements likely came into existence as an aid to explaining the motion of angels.

In sum, it is probable that late medieval discussions of angels had a significant impact on natural philosophy. But if theorizing about angels affected medieval natural philosophy, it should also be recognized that most of the basic principles used in that theorizing had come originally from natural philosophy – as we have seen, Scotus assumes that angels sent as messengers fall under the normal laws of nature. In the discussion of angels, then, we can see in detail the effects of the decision within medieval universities that theologian-natural philosophers should develop a Christian-Aristotelian natural philosophy no less rigorous and detailed in its way than what mathematical science would become in the early modern era.

NOTES

1. E. Grant [514] 148.
2. A. Maier [521] V 382.
3. Cf. E. Sylla [378] 133–34 for Parts II and III.
4. J. Murdoch [524], 280–87.

5. In this volume, on the relation of God's eternity to time, see chapter 1; on creation as a major topic in Jewish philosophy, see chapter 5; on the ontological dependence of creatures on God (whether or not the world is thought to have a finite past), see chapter 6.
6. See E. Grant [516] 173–75.
7. See W. P. Carvin [506] 44–45 for Thomas Aquinas's very similar point of view.
8. See T. Gregory in *CH12* 54.
9. Scottus Eriugena [90]; J. Marenbon [3].
10. M.-D. Chenu [507], ch. 1; T. Gregory in *CH12* 63–64; B. Stock [533].
11. [89] 564–65.
12. See *CH12*.
13. See B. Eastwood [511].
14. See J. Hackett [204] 114–15; P. Zambelli [202].
15. J. Ragep [531] 52. The same assumption appears in Hermann of Carinthia's *De essentiis*; see C. Burnett [365] 6–10.
16. R. Lemay [519]; C. Burnett [365] 8–9.
17. J. Ragep [531] 50, 53–63.
18. Ibid. 59.
19. Ibid. 62.
20. Ibid. 62, 70.
21. See C. Leijenhorst *et al.* [42] for eight reasons why scholastic Aristotelian natural philosophers went beyond mere interpretation of Aristotle's texts.
22. See E. Grant [517] 199–210 for lists of questions on Aristotle's natural works, and E. Grant [516] 681–741 for questions on cosmology from a wider range of works including commentaries on the *Sentences*.
23. E. Sylla [534].
24. On Boethius of Dacia see chapter 11 in this volume and E. Grant [516] 53–55. On the "Latin Averroism" of Boethius and others as implying a "double truth," see A. Maier [521] iv, part I.
25. See B. Hansen [350].
26. See A. Maier [521] iv, part V. On the metaphysics of freedom, see chapter 9 in this volume; on moral freedom, see chapter 10.
27. See H. Oberman [530] 408–11.
28. E. Serene *CHLMP* 496–517; C. Schabel [307] on God's foreknowledge.
29. See J. Murdoch [527, 528, and 523] for summaries of the argument first made by P. Duhem in vol. ii (1909) of [509] 412 and vol. iii, viii. For a short statement see E. Grant *CHLMP* 537–39.
30. See chapter 8 in this volume.
31. J. Murdoch [525].
32. See A. C. Crombie [197].

33. See chapter 3 in this volume.
34. E. Sylla *CHLMP* 540–63 and [377]. See A. Maier [521] II; E. Sylla [536]; R. Sorabji [532] for intension and remission of forms; J. Longeway [348] and C. Wilson [349] on maxima and minima; N. Kretzmann [518] and J. Murdoch [529] for first and last instants; J. Murdoch in *CHLMP* 564–91 and E. Sylla [340] on infinity and continuity.
35. J. Murdoch [524].
36. S. Marrone [522], ch. 15.
37. See E. Grant [517] 50–51.
38. E. Sylla [343].
39. See A. Maier [521] III, chs. 4–5.
40. See A. Cunningham [508] and E. Grant [513] for a recent round in this debate.
41. E. Grant [512] 174–75.
42. The doctrine of transubstantiation was promulgated in canon 1 of the Fourth Lateran Council in 1215. See H. Denzinger [24] 260, no. 802.
43. E. Sylla [535].
44. See A. Maier [521] IV, Part III, and E. Sylla [535] 364.
45. Cf. http://www.newadvent.org/cathen/01485a.htm

8 Natures: the problem of universals

Aristotelian science seeks to define the essential nature of a thing and then to demonstrate the features the thing must have because of that nature. A philosophically inevitable question thus arises for Aristotelians: what *is* a nature? Is it a reality over and above (or perhaps "in") the things whose nature it is? Is it a mental construction, existing only in our understanding of things; if so, on what basis is it constructed? This is the medieval problem of universals, or at least one way of thinking about the problem. In a classic formulation, Boethius states the problem in terms of the reality of genera and species, two main types of universals involved in an Aristotelian definition of essential nature (as in "a human being is a reasoning/ speaking animal," which places us in the genus of animals and marks off our species by reference to our "difference" from other animals in reasoning or using language): "Plato thinks that genera and species and the rest are not only understood as universals, but also exist and subsist apart from bodies. Aristotle, however, thinks that they are understood as incorporeal and universal, but subsist in sensibles."[1] A rigorous tradition of, mainly Aristotelian, discussion originates from Boethius's tentative exploration of the problem thus stated. But a more Platonic solution had been put into play about a century before Boethius by Augustine, and this, too, would have a rich development.

EXEMPLARIST REALISM: UNIVERSALS AS DIVINE REASONS

Augustine did not regard universal natures as mind-independent entities, in the way Plato conceived of Forms, but as existing in the *divine* mind. Accordingly, these natures still serve as models for their singulars, insofar as they are the universal exemplars of creation. In a passage often referred to by medieval authors, Augustine introduces his position in the following manner:

In Latin we can call the Ideas "forms" or "species," in order to appear to translate word for word. But if we call them "reasons," we depart to be sure from a proper translation – for reasons are called *"logoi"* in Greek, not Ideas – but nevertheless, whoever wants to use this word will not be in conflict with the fact. For Ideas are certain principal, stable, and immutable forms or reasons of things. They are not themselves formed, and hence they are eternal and always stand in the same relations, and they are contained in the divine understanding.[2]

Augustine could in fact claim to be reconciling Plato and Aristotle, for, in terms of Boethius's formulation, he held that universality resided in an understanding, the divine understanding. Nevertheless, this conception can still do justice to the Platonic intuition that what accounts for the necessary, intelligible features of the ephemeral particulars of the visible world is the presence of some universal exemplars in the source of their being; for, existing in the *divine* mind, the ideas serve as archetypes of creation, by which God preconceives his creation in eternity. Indeed, this also points the way for us to a more certain kind of knowledge than any we can gain from sensory experience. As Augustine continues:

And although they neither arise nor perish, nevertheless everything that is able to arise and perish, and everything that does arise and perish, is said to be formed in accordance with them. Now it is denied that the soul can look upon them, unless it is a rational one ... not each and every rational soul ... but [only] the one that is holy and pure ... What devout man imbued with true religion, even though he is not yet able to see these things, nevertheless dares to deny, or for that matter fails to profess, that all things that exist, that is, whatever things are contained in their own genus with a certain nature of their own, so that they might exist, are begotten by God their author, and that by that same author everything that lives is alive, and that the entire safe preservation and the very order of things, by which changing things repeat their temporal courses according to a fixed regimen, are held together and governed by the laws of a supreme God? ... All things are set up by reason, and a man not by the same reason as a horse – for that is absurd to suppose. Therefore, single things are created with their own reasons. But where are we to think these reasons exist, if not in the mind of the creator? ... Whatever exists comes to exist, however it exists, by participation in them. But among the things set up by God, the rational soul surpasses all [others], and is closest to God when it is pure. And to the extent that it clings to God in charity, to that extent, drenched in a certain way and lit up by that intelligible light, it discerns these reasons... By this vision it becomes most blessed. These reasons, as was said, whether it is right to call them Ideas or forms or species or reasons, many are permitted to call [them] whatever they want, but [only] to a very few [is it permitted] to see what is true.[3]

A major metaphysical problem generated by Augustine's position was that of reconciling the multiplicity of divine ideas ("all things are set up by reason, and a man not by the same reason as a horse") with the simplicity of God's nature.[4] Another issue, more pertinent to our present discussion, was the accessibility and role of divine ideas in human cognition. As we can see from the passage just quoted, Augustine makes recognition of truth dependent on divine illumination, a sort of irradiation of the intelligible light of divine ideas, which is accessible only to the few who are "holy and pure." But this seems to go against the experience that there are knowledgeable nonbelievers or pagans and also against the Aristotelian thesis that we can acquire the first principles needed for scientific demonstrations from experience by a purely natural process. Later Augustinians therefore argued for a less morally charged view of illumination and a less exclusively illuminationist account of knowledge. For example, Matthew of Aquasparta (c. 1238–1302), recapitulating Bonaventure, writes that it is a mistake to hold that "the entire essence of cognition comes forth from the archetypal or intelligible world and from the ideal reasons," for "if that light were the *entire* and *sole* reason for cognition, then the cognition of things in the [divine] Word would not differ from their cognition in their proper kind, neither would the cognition of reason differ from the cognition of revelation." On the other hand, the view that "the entire essence of cognition is caused and comes from below, through the senses, memory, and experience, [working together] with the natural light of our active intellect," is also defective, for it "destroys the way of wisdom."[5]

What is the contribution of the exemplars or ideal reasons on this sort of view? Henry of Ghent provides an interesting answer to this question. He first distinguishes cognition of a true thing from the cognition of the truth of the thing. Since any really existing thing is truly what it is (even if it may on occasion *appear* something else), any cognition of any really existing thing is the cognition of a true thing. But cognition of a true thing may occur without the cognition of its truth, since the latter is the cognition that the thing adequately corresponds to its exemplar in the human or divine mind. By the exemplar in the human mind, Henry means the concept of a thing we can acquire for ourselves through experience. "But," he insists, "by this sort of acquired exemplar in us we do not have the entirely certain and infallible cognition of truth." This is impossible for three reasons, taken respectively from the thing from which this exemplar is abstracted; the soul, in which this exemplar is received; and the exemplar itself that is received in the soul about the thing:

The first reason is that this exemplar, since it is abstracted from change-able things, has to share in the nature of changeability... And this is why Augustine... says that from the bodily senses one should not expect the pure truth [syncera veritas]... The second reason is that the human soul, since it is changeable and susceptible to error, cannot be rectified to save it from swerving into error by anything that is just as changeable as itself, or even more; therefore, any exemplar that it receives from natural things is necessarily just as changeable as itself, or even more, since it is of an inferior nature, whence it cannot rectify the soul so that it would persist in the in-fallible truth... The third reason is that this sort of exemplar, since it is the intention and species of the sensible thing abstracted from the phantasm, is similar to the false as well as to the true [thing], so that on its account these cannot be distinguished. For it is by means of the same images of sensible things that in dreams and madness we judge these images to be the things, and in sane awareness we judge the things themselves. But the pure truth can only be perceived by discerning it from falsehood. Therefore, by means of such an exemplar it is impossible to have certain knowledge and certain cognition of the truth. And so if we are to have certain knowl-edge of the truth, then we have to turn our mind away from the senses and sensible things, and from every intention, no matter how universal and ab-stracted from sensible things, to the unchangeable truth existing above the mind.[6]

Henry holds that direct intuition of the divine ideas is had only by angels and the souls of the blessed in beatific vision; it is granted in this life only in rare, miraculous cases, in rapture or prophetic vision. In more typical cases of genuine insight, it is only necessary "that the unchangeable truth impress itself into our concept, and that it transform our concept to its own character, and that in this way it inform our mind with the expressed truth of the thing by the same similitude that the thing itself has in the first truth" (*Summa quaestionum ordinarium*, a. 1, q. 2 [222] fol. 7 I).

Henry's point can be put this way. Since the external thing itself is just a (more or less defective) copy of the divine exemplar, the still more defective copy of this copy that we obtain from experience (the human exemplar) can only be improved by means of the original exemplar, just as a copy of a poor reproduction of some original picture can only be improved by retouching the copy, not on the basis of the poor reproduction, but on the basis of the original. Since the external thing is fashioned after its divine idea, the "retouching" of our empirical concept by the impression of that idea yields a better representation of the truth of the thing – so much better, indeed, that the "retouched" concept enables us to judge just how well the thing realizes its kind. For example, the rough idea of a circle I acquire from experience in learning to use the term *circle* may serve for telling circular shapes apart from noncircular ones, but when I come to understand that a circle is a line every point of which is equidistant from a given point, I will see clearly what it was that I originally conceived in a vague and confused manner in my original concept. The "flash" of understanding, when I realize that it is *necessary* for *anything* that *truly* matches the concept of a circle to be such as the definition describes, would be an instance of receiving illumination without any particular, miraculous revelation.

Even granting, however, that the concepts initially acquired from sensible objects need to be further worked on in order to provide us with a clear understanding of the natures of things, we may wonder whether this further work could perhaps be done by the natural faculties of our mind, assuming only the general influence of God in sustaining the mind's natural operations, but without performing any direct and specific "retouching" of our concepts "from above." Using our previous analogy of the acquired concept as the faulty copy of a poor reproduction of an original, we may say that if we have a number of different poor, fuzzy reproductions that are defective in a number of different ways, then through a long and complex process of collating them, we might still be able discern the underlying pattern of the original and thus produce a copy that is actually closer to the original than any of the direct reproductions, without ever being allowed a glimpse of the original.

This was the Aristotelian approach, which increasingly dominated medieval discussions of universals from the time of Abelard in the early twelfth century.[7] In this approach, divine illumination would consist of creating a human mind capable of illuminating experience on its own. As Aquinas put it, God has created us with "a certain likeness of the uncreated light, obtained through participation," namely, the agent intellect (*ST* I, q. 84, a. 5), a power capable of abstracting from experience universals that were quite adequate for a science of natures and their properties.

COMMON NATURES, SINGULAR EXISTENTS, ACTIVE MINDS

The Aristotelian project of explaining universality in human cognition without illumination from a transcendent source generated questions of its own. For in this approach it is natural to ask exactly what the abstracted universals in the mind are, what it is for them to exist in the mind, how they are related to their particulars, what their real foundation in those particulars is, what their role is in the constitution of our universal knowledge, and how they contribute to the encoding and communication of this knowledge in the various human languages. These questions give a new aspect to the problem of universals, namely, a *semantic* aspect.

The most important influence on Latin discussions in the thirteenth century and later was Avicenna's distinction of the absolute consideration of a universal nature from what applies to the same nature in the subjects in which it exists. The distinction is neatly summarized in the following passage:

Horsehood, to be sure, has a definition that does not demand universality. Rather it is that to which universality happens. Hence horsehood itself is nothing but horsehood only. For in itself it is neither many nor one, neither is it existent in these sensibles nor in the soul, neither is it any of these things potentially or actually in such a way that this is contained under the definition of horsehood. Rather [in itself it consists] of what is horsehood only.[8]

In his little treatise *On Being and Essence*, Aquinas explains the distinction in greater detail:

A nature, however, or essence ... can be considered in two ways. First, we can consider it according to its proper notion, and this is its absolute consideration; and in this way nothing is true of it except what pertains to it as such; whence if anything else is attributed to it, that will yield a false attribution ... In the other way [an essence] is considered as it exists in this or that [individual]; and in this way something is predicated of it *per accidens* [nonessentially], on account of that in which it exists, as when we say that a man is white because Socrates is white, although this does not pertain to man as such.

A nature considered in this way, however, has two sorts of existence. It exists in singulars on the one hand, and in the soul on the other, and from each of these [sorts of existence] it acquires accidents. In the singulars, furthermore, the essence has several [acts of] existence according to the multiplicity of singulars. Nevertheless, if we consider the essence in the first, or absolute, sense, none of these pertain to it. For it is false to say that the essence of man, considered absolutely, has existence in this singular, because if existence in this singular pertained to man insofar as he is man, man would never exist, except as this singular. Similarly, if it pertained to man insofar as he is man not to exist in this singular, then the essence would never exist in the singular. But it is true to say that man, but not insofar as he is man, may be in this singular or in that one, or else in the soul. Therefore, the nature of man considered absolutely abstracts from every existence, though it does not exclude any. And the nature thus considered is what is predicated of each individual.[9]

What is most striking in this passage is the way Aquinas talks about *the same* nature existing in different things, as well as being "considerable" apart from existing in anything. It is clear that the sameness in question cannot be the numerical unity of a single existent, since it is precisely existence that is abstracted from in the absolute consideration of a nature.[10] The scholastics often referred to the sameness of the same nature in this passage as a "less-than-numerical unity." We might say that it is the unity of something that is *not strictly the same* but *recognizably the same* in multiple instances, as the sameness of a book existing in multiple copies, or in general, the sameness of some common information content carried by several copies, possibly in various media. It is this notion of sameness that is operative in counting items as distinct only when they are distinct in kind (which, of course, is only to say that it is the sameness of a universal – but a universal that "subsists," to use Boethius's language, in particular existing things and is a universal only as it is "understood"). For example, the number of publications of an author is the number of his different published writings, and not the number of the different copies of one and the same work. The same work is just one work on the list, but this one work may exist in multiple copies, indeed, in different editions, encoded in different media (say, paper, CD-Rom, e-book, or Internet website), and may have radically different accidental attributes in those different "incarnations." Yet this does not mean that there exists some one "universal book" over and above its singular realizations in these different media. On the contrary, we can talk about this *one book* as one and the same work only by abstracting from its different realizations, in different forms of existence in those various media.

This account gives rise to a further question, however. Aquinas said that the absolute consideration of a nature abstracts both from its being in extramental singulars and from its being in the mind. But, apparently, precisely according to this consideration it has to be in the mind, for it can be recognized as common *only* when the mind considers it in abstraction from its individuating conditions in the singulars. So how can we say that it is abstracted from being in the mind, when it can be abstract, and hence a universal, only if it is in the mind?

What is required here is care in distinguishing between what we can say about *the same nature as such* and what we can say about *the same nature on account of its conditions* as it exists in this or that subject. Such care is obviously required in recognizing that the same book can have quite different accidental features in its printed edition (where it may have 200 pages, for example) and in its electronic edition (where it may have no pagination at all). Similar care is required in recognizing that the same nature is a universal insofar as it is in this or that mind and that it is *only* as being in a mind that it is properly called a universal. As Aquinas remarks:

When we speak about an abstract universal, we imply two things, namely, the nature of the thing itself, and abstraction or universality. So the nature itself to which it is accidental that it is thought of, or that it is abstracted, or that the intention of universality applies to it, exists only in the singulars, but the nature's being abstracted, or its being thought of, or the intention of universality is in the intellect. And we can see this by the similar situation in perception. For sight sees the color of an apple without its smell. Thus, if it is asked: Where is the color that is seen without the smell? . . . it is obvious that it is nowhere else but in the apple. But that it is perceived without the smell happens to apply to it [*accidit ei*] on account of sight, insofar as in sight there is a similitude of color but not of smell. Similarly, humanity that is thought of exists only in this or in that man; but that humanity is apprehended without its individuating conditions (which is nothing but for it to be abstracted, which confers on it the attribute of universality) is an accidental feature of humanity [*accidit humanitati*] in virtue of its being perceived by the intellect, in which there is a similitude of the nature of the species but not of the individuating principles.[11]

So, although *the universal nature*, namely, *that which is predicable of several singulars*, is nothing but the common nature as such, considered absolutely, still, *that it is predicable of several singulars* pertains to the same nature, not according to its absolute consideration, but only on account of its being conceived by the abstractive intellect, that is, insofar as it is a concept of the mind.

Even if such a response is tenable, it shows what sort of problems this conceptual framework is bound to generate. Speaking about the same nature possibly receiving contrary attributes in its several instances and different modes of being constantly risks inconsistency, unless we keep track of what can be said of what according to what actual criteria of identity and distinctness. Accordingly, it is no wonder that authors working in this framework, which came to be referred to as the *via antiqua*, elaborated further distinctions regarding the properties accruing to natures in their being in minds[12] and the properties accruing to them in their being in the world.[13]

COMMON TERMS, SINGULAR NATURES

Anyone who wanted to escape the metaphysical complexities of the *via antiqua* had to go to their roots, which lay in the semantic framework within which they arose. This was the tack taken by William of Ockham, the pioneer of a radically new conceptual framework, the *via moderna*. According to Ockham, the *via antiqua* conception would entail that

a column is to the right by to-the-rightness, God is creating by creation, is good by goodness, just by justice, mighty by might, an accident inheres by inherence, a subject is subjected by subjection, the apt is apt by aptitude, a chimera is nothing by nothingness, someone blind is blind by blindness, a body is mobile by mobility, and so on for other, innumerable cases.[14]

But this stems precisely from the root of all errors, namely, "multi-plying beings according to the multiplicity of terms...which, however, is erroneous and leads far away from the truth."[15]

Whether intentionally or not, Ockham no doubt exaggerated the logically driven ontological extravagance of the *via antiqua*. His aim, however, was not just to get rid of the real or perhaps merely apparent unwanted ontological commitments of his opponents, but rather to simplify the entire conceptual apparatus, together with its available yet rather complicated ways of getting rid of such commitments. Accordingly, Ockham based his program on a radical reinterpretation of the fundamental semantic relationships.

As in the *via antiqua*, Ockham's universals exist only in the mind (or in utterances or written expressions), and extramental existents are all singular. But for Ockham, that is all there is to it. There are no common natures or essences "in" either the mind or the world. At one stroke, therefore, as if by magic, all questions of the form "*How* does this or that essence subsist in this or that particular?" vanish. There are no essences capable of being considered "absolutely" and accruing different accidents in their existence in the mind or outside it.[16]

Furthermore, the number of fundamentally different sorts of real things is reduced by Ockham to just two: substances and qualities. If we provide the appropriate analyses of complex concepts in the other categories in terms of the simple concepts of the categories of substance and quality, all that we want to say about the world in terms of quantities, relations, and the other Aristotelian categories can be said without positing any distinct further realities in the things themselves.[17]

Much of the weight of Ockham's program therefore rests on the process by which we form our simple universal concepts, for these are the concepts that anchor our entire conceptual edifice in reality. This process yields the key terms in a mental language which is somehow the same for all human beings and to which spoken or written terms are conventionally subordinate. The universals in Ockham's mental language are natural, furthermore, in meaning. The mental term *human* naturally and directly signifies, "indifferently," all and only human beings, past, present, future, and merely possible – and this in spite of the facts (1) that the term is formed from experience of a minuscule sample of the individuals it signifies, and (2) that there is no single human nature all these things have in common which could be directly represented by the term. Not surprisingly, Ockham's claim to having a language adequate for scientific purposes, when he has, in effect, bypassed the question of what there is about things that causes (i.e., in some way *justifies*) our grouping them the way we do, did not meet with universal acceptance. The *via antiqua* in its Thomist and Scotist forms continued to attract adherents in the later Middle Ages, and even followers of the *via moderna* sometimes had difficulty staying on Ockham's straight and narrow path. Buridan, for example, when arguing against contemporary skeptics about our ability to acquire simple concepts of substances, resorts in his epistemology to some old ways of thinking about abstraction that he could not quite consistently afford in his semantics.[18] The nominalists' semantic innovations, while they avoided the realists' ontological problems, led directly to a number of new epistemological problems. The *via moderna* thus helped push the interests of philosophers in a direction which became their major preoccupation in the modern period.[19]

NOTES

1. *Commentary on the Isagoge of Porphyry* (itself an introduction to Aristotle's *Categories*) in P. V. Spade [20] 25.
2. *On Eighty-Three Different Questions*, q. 46, 2 in P. V. Spade [6] 383.
3. Ibid. Also see *On Free Choice of the Will* II, where Augustine argues that we can recognize the imperfections of objects of a certain kind in our experience (for example, objects that are not perfectly equal, or objects that are not absolutely one, since they are many in their parts), only if we already know what it would be like for objects to be perfectly equal or perfectly one. But since these perfect instances are not given in experience, it seems to follow that we can only have these concepts from a source other than sense experience, from a Truth within but above the mind.
4. I briefly discuss Aquinas's solution to the problem in "The Medieval Problem of Universals" [543]. Cf. Aquinas, *ST* I, q. 15, a. 2; I *Sent.*, d. 36, q. 2, aa. 1–3; Henry of Ghent, *Summa quaestionum ordinariarum*, 2, a. 65, q. 5 [222]; John Duns Scotus, *Ordinatio* I, d. 35, q. un. [281]; Thomas of Sutton, *Quodlibeta*, IV, q. 5 [389]. For a modern discussion, less sophisticated than the preceding, see C. Hughes [242].
5. Bonaventure *et al.* [215] 94–96.
6. Henry of Ghent, *Summa quaestionum ordinariarum*, a. 1, q. 2 [222] fol. 5 F.

7. But exemplarist realism makes an impressive comeback in John Wyclif's *On Universals*, ch. 2 [352], especially pp. 14–15.

8. Avicenna, *Metaphysica* V 1 [116] II 228; trans. [6] 461.

9. *On Being and Essence* 2.

10. For more on Aquinas's conception of the relationship between the notions of unity and being, see G. Klima [244].

11. *ST* I, q. 85, a. 2, ad 2.

12. For example, the distinctions between impressed and expressed species and between formal and objective concepts. The impressed species is the intelligible content abstracted by the agent intellect from sensory representations of singulars, the phantasms. This intelligible species, impressed by the agent intellect upon the potential intellect, serves as the principle of the act of concept formation of the latter, called *formatio*. The result of this act is the expressed species, which is nothing but the formal concept, the universal concept as existing in this singular mind. See Cajetan [594] 163 and J. Poinsot [380] 170, 255–68. The objective concept is the representational content of the formal concept, the common nature of singulars insofar as it exists in the mind as its immediate, abstract, universal object. See Suárez [619] 360–61 and Cajetan [594] 67–71, 121–24.

13. The metaphysical problems most closely connected with discussions of universals were (1) the problem of individuation and (2) the distinction between (or "composition of") essence and existence. The first called for an answer to the question: what is it in this or that cow that makes it "this" or "that" cow, rather than a congeries of universals? On this, see J. Gracia [541–42]. On essence and existence, see chapter 6 in this volume. Differing accounts of universals were also involved, more or less closely, in debates about the unity or plurality of substantial forms and the ontological status of Aristotelian categories other than substance. On substantial form, see chapter 9 in this volume. On the other categories, see chapter 3 in this volume.

14. Ockham, *Summa logicae* I 51 [308] *OPh* I 169.

15. Ibid. 171.

16. See P. V. Spade [20] 114–231 and *Ockham's Theory of Terms* [316] 77–88. For a sympathetic but ultimately inconclusive exposition, see M. M. Adams [318] 3–141. Also see my article and those by Spade and Karger in *CCOck*.

17. *Ockham's Theory of Terms* [316] 126–88; M. M. Adams [318] 143–313.

18. See J. M. M. H. Thijssen [544] and G. Klima [342].

19. For a fuller treatment of some of the matters discussed here, see G. Klima [543].

9   Human nature

Nothing in medieval philosophy was more fiercely contested than the topic of human nature. Among the many questions discussed were the nature of the soul, the relationship between the soul and the mind, the workings of sense and intellect, the role of the passions, the limits to human freedom, and the extent of our dependence on divine grace and illumination. Yet these disputes, though wide-ranging, were fought in the context of general agreement on a number of basic issues. There was general agreement that human beings have a soul but are not merely souls – that they are composites of soul and body. There was also agreement that the human soul is immaterial and created by God; it does not come into existence naturally, as the souls of other animals do. Likewise, almost all agreed that the soul does not preexist the body,[1] that God brings it into existence once the fetus has sufficiently developed, and that, once created, the soul will exist forever – that it is incorruptible. The story of medieval thinking on human nature concerns how this general framework was developed in various and conflicting ways and how these various theses could be proved philosophically – if indeed they could be proved at all.

MIND AND BODY AND SOUL

It is hard to imagine a more impressive start to medieval thinking about human nature than the writings of Augustine. "Refuse to go outside," he advised. "Return to yourself. Truth dwells within" (*Of True Religion* 39.72). Remarks like these announced a major shift in philosophical thought. Rather than looking to the physical world for fundamental truths, or to an abstract realm of Forms, Augustine proposed a first-person method. Look within.

The truth Augustine sought was not only truth about ourselves. By looking within, he thought, we could gain some understanding of the nature of God as this was professed in the Christian doctrine of the Trinity. The distinctness of memory, understanding, and will, combined with their mutual inclusion of one another, made the mind an image, albeit a distant one, of the three Persons that are God (*Trinity* X–XV). In striving toward this height, however, Augustine established fundamental conclusions about our own nature. What is a body? Something that occupies space in such a way that a part of it occupies less space than the whole (X 7.9).[2] What is the mind? Those fixated on the senses and images of the physical world suppose that the mind is some kind of body, or perhaps a harmonious state of the body. For our mind to suppose this is for it to confuse sensory images with its very self, to add something physical to what it knows itself to be. "Let it set aside what it *thinks* itself to be, and discern what it *knows*" (X 10.13). What the mind knows – what every mind knows – is that it is a thing that thinks:

Who would doubt that he lives, remembers, understands, wills, thinks, knows, and judges? For if he doubts, he lives; if he doubts, he remembers why he doubts; if he doubts, he understands that he doubts; if he doubts, he wants to be certain; if he doubts, he thinks; if he doubts, he knows that he does not know; if he doubts, he judges that he should not rashly consent. (X 10.14)[3]

In knowing all this about itself, the mind knows its very self. Whereas others suppose that willing and understanding are qualities inhering in some further substance, Augustine insists that the mind grasps its own nature with certainty: "a thing is not said to be known in any way when its substance is unknown" (X 10.16). Hence we know what the mind is, simply by looking within ourselves: our mind just is our own thinking, willing, and understanding. This inward-directed method dominated western thought for centuries. In 1077 Anselm began his famous proof for the existence of God with the injunction to "enter into the chamber of your mind; exclude everything but God and what helps you to search for him, and then search for him, with the door closed" (*Proslogion* 1). For Bonaventure in 1259 the mind's journey to God begins with the external world and then leads us "to reenter ourselves – that is, into our mind, in which the divine image shines" (*Itinerarium mentis in Deum* 3.1). Despite Bonaventure's best efforts, however, philosophy changed course dramatically in the thirteenth century, as it absorbed new influences from Aristotle and Islamic thought. Although authors such as Thomas Aquinas and John Duns Scotus labored mightily to meld Augustine and Aristotle, the two approaches to human nature could hardly have been more different. In place of Augustine's introspective method, which tended to leave the body behind in focusing on the *mind*, the Aristotelians made an essentially biological notion of *soul* the model for their understanding of our nature as well as that of other animals. Instead of treating thought as the essence of mind, they treated it as merely its activity, and took mind to be a faculty of the human soul. As for the soul itself, its nature was said to be unknown, or at least unavailable to introspection. As Thomas Aquinas put it, "The human intellect neither is its understanding, nor has its own essence as the first object of its understanding. Instead, something external, the nature of a material thing, is its first object" (*ST* I, q. 87, a. 3).

This is not to say that scholastic Aristotelians regarded the soul as a complete mystery. It was axiomatic for them that the soul is the *first principle of life* – that is, the most basic internal explanation for why plants and animals are alive (see Aristotle, *De anima* II 1). To be alive, on this account, just is to engage in the operations that characterize all or some living things: taking nourishment, growing, reproducing, moving, perceiving, desiring, and thinking. Hence the soul was conceived of as having assorted powers for producing these various functions and was divided into functional parts: five, according to Aristotle, or three in Avicenna's more standard account: vegetative (= nutritive), sensory, and rational. (Aristotle added appetitive and locomotive.[4]) The soul actualizes the body, which is to say that soul and body are related to one another as form to matter. Encouraged by Aristotle's remark that "It is not necessary to ask whether the soul and its body are one, just as we do not ask about wax and its shape" (*De anima* II 1, 412b6–7), scholastic authors supposed that this kind of hylomorphic (that is, matter–form) framework could solve the perennial problem of unifying soul and body. The diversity of plans for doing this suggests that the solution was not self-evident.

Scholastic accounts of the soul–body relationship fall into two broad classes. First, there were those that treated human beings as composites of matter and a series of forms, so that the initial unformed matter (prime matter or, more literally, "first matter") is shaped by a corporeal form, and this form–matter composite is at the same time shaped by a further form, all the way up to the ultimate form, the rational soul. Among early scholastic authors, it was standard to follow the eleventh-century Jewish philosopher Ibn Gabirol (Avicebron) in supposing that human beings are composed of many such essential or substantial forms: corporeal, nutritive, sensory, rational, and perhaps still more (*Fons vitae* IV 3). For later authors like Henry of Ghent and Duns Scotus, a human being is composed of just two substantial forms: a corporeal form for the body, plus the rational soul.[5] A second class of theories held that the rational soul is the only substantial form of a human being, that it both shapes the body and gives rise to all the capacities associated with life. This unitarian account was first articulated by Thomas Aquinas. It was perhaps his most original and most divisive contribution to philosophy. One critic, Peter John Olivi, referred to it as a "brutal error," and it was condemned by successive archbishops of Canterbury.[6]

There were several reasons why the issue was so controversial. First, the substantial form was thought to fix the identity conditions of whatever it informs. That is, a body remains the same body only as long as it retains the same form. But if a human being has only one substantial form, then the body goes out of existence at the moment of death, when soul and body separate. Aquinas wholly endorsed this result, remarking that "Just as one does not speak of an animal and a human being once the soul has left – unless equivocally, in the way we speak of a painted or sculpted animal – so too for the hand and eye, or flesh and bones" (*ST* I, q. 76, a. 8; cf. Aristotle, *De anima* II 1, 412b19–22). In addition to raising various theological problems,[7] this result struck many as absurd. Ockham, for instance (*Quodlibet* II 11), wondered what could possibly explain why something new (a corpse) comes into existence at death with all (or virtually all) of the physical qualities possessed by the living body. Surely it is much easier to suppose that the same body endures through death. But this can be so only if it has its own substantial form, apart from the soul.

Underlying this debate was a further and more general worry about the cogency of Aquinas's account. As noted already, all sides agreed that the rational soul is immaterial. But how can it be immaterial and at the same time the form of the body? This was an issue that all scholastics had to confront, especially after 1312 when the Council of Vienne declared it heretical to hold that "the rational or intellective soul is not *per se* and essentially the form of the human body."[8] But the problem was especially pressing for Aquinas and his followers, because they needed the rational soul to give shape to the body, to give rise to the body's nutritive operations, to be the inner principle behind sensation, *and at the same time* to be immaterial. How can the soul do all of those things and yet be immaterial? Aquinas's solution (*ST* I, q. 77) rests on a distinction between the soul's essence and its powers. In its own right, the soul is a substantial form, whose essence is unknown or at least hidden. What we can know of the soul is what we can observe of its operations, which leads us to infer that the soul has certain powers. These powers "flow" from the soul's essence, but they are not that essence. Hence the human soul gives rise to our ability to digest food, which is as physical a process as anything in nature. But the human soul also gives rise to our capacity for thought, which all agreed is not a physical process. Since Aquinas distinguished the soul and its powers, he saw no difficulty in reconciling these roles. His opponents, adhering more closely to Augustine's conception of mind, refused to distinguish the soul's essence and its powers, a stance made easier by their pluralism regarding substantial form.

By identifying the rational soul as a human being's only substantial form, Aquinas made considerable trouble for himself and his followers. But he claimed one notable advantage for his account: its contribution to solving the soul–body problem. What exactly was this problem? In contrast with early modern thinkers, medieval philosophers did not regard the soul–body problem as a problem about causality. The notion of an immaterial being acting on matter was considered unproblematic, and although causation in the other direction was generally not allowed, causality in one direction was enough to explain interaction. For the body to act on the soul's immaterial powers – intellect and will – bodily information was simply transformed by the intellect into an immaterial state.[9] The medieval version of the soul–body problem was instead the problem of how to reply to Platonic dualism. Although almost none of Plato's writings were known at first hand, authors like the fourth-century Nemesius of Emesa had described how Plato "did not hold that an animal is made up of soul and body, but that it is the soul using the body and (as it were) wearing the body." As Nemesius observed, "This claim raises a problem: How can the soul be one with what it wears? For a shirt is not one with the person wearing it" (*De natura hominis* 3 [375] 51–52). Augustine had insisted that a human being is soul *and* body (*City of God* XIX 3), but he had little to say about how the two parts of the soul–body pair were bound together. Aristotelian hylomorphism saw the soul as actualizing a potentially living body, but this did not by itself solve the problem of the unity of the individual human being. Scotus, who pursued metaphysical questions farther and deeper than anyone else in the Middle Ages, simply granted that "there is no cause for why this actuality and that potentiality make one thing *per se*...except that this is potentiality with respect to that, and that is actuality" (*Ordinatio* IV.11.3.53 [282] VIII 652–53). Nothing more can be said.

Aquinas could say something more. As noted earlier, the substantial form supplies the identity conditions for a body and each of its parts. Each part exists just as long as it is actualized by the form of the whole of which it is a part. Moreover, the substantial form was understood to play a causal role in sustaining all the intrinsic properties of a substance. Substances have the enduring characteristics they do because of their distinctive underlying form.[10] This conception of form yields an exceptionally clear account of substantial unity: since its form is what individuates and causally sustains all the parts of a substance, none of them can exist or endure apart from it. Therefore, if the human soul is the one substantial form of the human being, body turns out to be indivisible from soul in the strongest sense. Unsurprisingly, given its explanatory force (and the way it still leaves room for the soul to exist apart from the body), Aquinas's unitarian account would become the dominant view by the end of the era.[11]

COGNITION

Among the various ancient schools of philosophy, none posed a more serious challenge to Christianity than skepticism. One might be a Christian and a Platonist, like Augustine, or a Christian and an Aristotelian, like Aquinas, or conceivably even a Christian and a

Stoic. But it is hard to see how the beliefs of a Christian could be reconciled with a skeptic's suspension of all belief.[12] Augustine described in the *Confessions* how he fell under the sway of skepticism for a time, becoming someone who had "lost all hope of discovering the truth" (VI 1) and "believed it impossible to find the way of life" (VI 2). He quickly came to reject this stance, diagnosing the skeptic as someone who mistakenly holds out for the wrong standard of certainty: "I wanted to become as certain about things I could not see as I was certain that seven and three are ten . . . I desired other things to be just like this" (VI 4). Those who limit their beliefs to what meets this test will be doomed to withhold assent in almost all cases. But why should this be the standard for adequate justification? Why is that kind of certainty the only acceptable kind? We have already seen Augustine appeal to self-knowledge for one kind of certainty. In other cases he defends a more relaxed standard of justification, one that leaves a prominent place for the evidence of the senses and, crucially, the authority of others:

> I considered the innumerable things I believed that I had not seen, events that occurred when I was not present . . . many facts concerning places and cities that I had never seen, many things accepted on the word of friends, many from physicians, many from other people. Unless we believed what we were told, we would do nothing at all in this life. (VI 5)

If this holds true in everyday life, it holds all the more true where religious belief is concerned. In this way, Augustine turns the challenge of skepticism to the advantage of Christianity, arguing that the lack of certainty that threatens theistic belief in fact threatens all our beliefs. If we have good reasons for rejecting global skepticism, then we should consider whether these might also be good reasons for rejecting religious skepticism.[13]

Later thinkers seem to have regarded Augustine's treatment of these issues as decisive. Skepticism simply ceased to be a prominent topic of discussion until the end of the Middle Ages. Instead, attention was focused on how knowledge is acquired. Here the issue was not how to define knowledge – the question that Plato originally posed and that dominated later twentieth-century epistemology – but how to understand the cognitive operations that generate it. The complex and sophisticated theories of cognition developed in the thirteenth and fourteenth centuries had various roots. Most obviously, there were Aristotle's brief remarks on the intellect and his more detailed discussion of sensation. Equally important were Augustine's extensive observations on mind and perception, in the *Trinity* and elsewhere. A third major source was the Islamic tradition, particularly Alhazen's influential treatise on optics and Avicenna's brilliant and original development of Aristotle's thought.

All medieval work on cognition takes as its basis a fundamental distinction between sense and intellect. The sensory powers were indeed regarded as powers of the soul, but they were taken to be powers that require physical organs, and that we share with nonrational animals. Writing a half-century before Descartes's depiction of lower animals as nonsentient machines, Francisco Suárez noted a similar tendency in some of his contemporaries. "This view is intolerable and enormously paradoxical," he wrote (*De anima* I 5), given that we have the same sensory organs inside and out, the same kinds of behavior in response to stimulus, and the same ability to store memories of particular impressions. In all, Suárez argued, we have as much evidence for sensation in animals as we do in infants and the severely retarded.

Human beings are special among the animals, for medieval thinkers, because we have a mind, a cognitive power that is not part of the brain or in any way physical. Such immateriality was taken to explain how the mind could engage in abstract, conceptual thought. Whereas the physical senses were limited to the apprehension of particular images and objects, the intellect was regarded as unlimited in its representational scope, able to grasp not just a particular quality but the very nature of the quality, a nature that was the same in all individuals possessing the quality.[14] Hence the mark of the mental was not intentionality but conceptualization, and the divide between the physical and the nonphysical was located not at the boundary of consciousness but at the boundary of abstract thought.

Medieval philosophers devoted primary attention to the mind, but the senses were not ignored. Avicenna proposed a distinction that became fundamental between two kinds of sensory objects, forms and intentions (*Liber de anima* I 5 [115] 86). In general, a form is the kind of sense object that the five external senses are suited to grasp: color, size, shape, sound, and so forth. An *intention* is a characteristic of the object that gets conveyed by the object's form but that cannot be detected by the five senses themselves. This terminology allows

Avicenna to distinguish two levels of sensory processing, which he describes as the external and the internal level. The external senses are the familiar five senses, which have particular sensory qualities as their objects. There are likewise five internal senses (*Liber de anima* I 5, II 2, and IV I [115] I 87–90 and 117–19, II 1–11; *Najat* II 6 §3 [119] 30–31):

- common sense (also called phantasia), which collects impressions from all five of the external senses
- imagination (also called the formative power), which retains the images collected in the common sense
- the imaginative power (in human beings: the cogitative power), which composes and divides sensory images
- the estimative power, which makes judgments that go beyond external appearances (the sheep recognizes it should flee the wolf)
- the power for memory (in human beings: recollection), which retains impressions formed by the estimative power

This terminology is drawn largely from Aristotle, augmented by a complex earlier Islamic tradition.[15] But Avicenna goes well beyond Aristotle's uncertain suggestions by collecting these disparate faculties under the heading of internal senses and giving them specific locations in the brain and definite functions. Later medieval authors – notably Averroes (*Liber de medicina* II 20), Albert the Great (*De homine*, qq. 35–41), and Aquinas (*ST* I, q. 78, a. 4) – would develop their own accounts of the internal senses, building on Avicenna's suggestions and modifying the terminology in complex ways.

A theory of sensation requires some account of sensory representation. Within the internal senses the perceptible properties of bodies were said to be represented by *phantasms*. More generally, information from the external world was said to be passed to the senses and into the intellect through a series of forms or "*species*." Augustine had spoken of four such species: in the object, in the sense, in memory, and in the mind (*Trinity* XI 9.16). The most important medieval work in this area came from an eleventh-century Islamic author, Alhazen (Ibn al-Haytham), whose *Optics* has to count as the most impressive premodern account of perception. In careful detail, Alhazen studied the physical and psychological underpinnings of vision, tracing the propagation of visual forms through the medium and into the eye and exploring the ways in which we thereby acquire information about the various sensible properties of the object, such as its color, distance, shape, size, motion, and so forth. Latin authors, led by Roger Bacon, studied this work in the thirteenth century, and it quickly became standard to conceive of cognition as the product of a multiplication of forms or species through the air, into the sensory organs, and ultimately into intellect.[16]

There was general agreement that all such species, even the abstract "intelligible" species, represent objects in virtue of somehow being likenesses of them. Beyond this, however, there was considerable disagreement about how species play their representational role. Among thirteenth-century authors, for example, Robert Kilwardby followed some remarks of Augustine's in holding that sensible qualities make a physical impression on the sensory organs, producing a species there, and that sensation occurs when the immaterial sensory soul then perceives those impressions (*On Imagination*, ch. 3).[17] Aquinas, in contrast, took a more Aristotelian line, holding that the sensory organ's reception of a species just is the sensation.[18] On this kind of view, sensation is a physical event, a passive informing of the sense organ from outside. Later in the thirteenth century Olivi attacked views of this second sort for their passivity and attacked views of the first sort for making the internal impression the object of perception. On Olivi's own view, perception occurs in virtue of the mind's "virtual attention" outward to the objects themselves.[19] The mechanisms of this account are obscure, but it is clear that Olivi wanted to eliminate both sensible and intelligible species in favor of a direct grasp of the object itself. Although Aquinas insisted that the species is not the thing perceived, but that *by which* external things are perceived (see, e.g., *ST* I, q. 85, a. 2), Olivi claimed that a species must inevitably "veil the external thing and impede its being attended to in itself as if present" (II *Sent.*, q. 58, ad 14 [271] II 469). This debate went on through the Middle Ages and began again with Locke and his critics, this time over the role of *ideas*.

Some issues regarding the senses had parallels for intellect. Those who rejected sensible species, such as Olivi and later Ockham, also rejected intelligible species.[20] Aquinas's account of sensory passivity also held at the intellectual level: "Our intellect's operation consists in being acted on in a certain way" (*ST* I, q. 79, a. 2) – it consists, in other words, in receiving intelligible species. There were also enormous differences between the sensory and intellectual levels. Most significantly, philosophers in the Aristotelian tradition distinguished between two intellectual powers, the agent intellect and the possible intellect (or, more aptly, the active and receptive intellects). The possible intellect starts out as a *tabula rasa*, building up conceptual knowledge through sensory input. The agent intellect is responsible for transforming that sensory data into something intelligible. This is to say that the agent intellect, through the process of abstraction, takes information that is material and particular and makes it into something immaterial and abstract. In this way, the perception of a black cat can give rise to the concept *black* or the concept *cat*.

Everything about the agent intellect was obscure and controversial. It was supposed to perform its transformative operation by abstraction, but there seems to have been little understanding of how that would work.[21] One possible reason for the neglect of this issue is that medieval energies were focused on a more basic question: is the agent intellect even a part of the human soul? Aristotle's remarks on this topic (*De anima* III 5) were cryptic, and later medieval authors were confronted with a confusing jumble of philosophical authorities. Avicenna, whose views were particularly influential, conceived of the agent intellect as a separate substance, related to the human soul as the sun is related to our eyes (*Liber de anima* V 5 [115] II 127). This view was endorsed by prominent Christians, including Roger Bacon (*Opus tertium*, ch. 23; *Opera...inedita*, ed. J. S. Brewer [London, 1859]) and Henry of Ghent (*Quodlibet* IX 15). Just as influential, and much more controversial, was Averroes, who sometimes seems to have thought that both the agent intellect and the possible intellect are separate substances (e.g., *Commentarium magnum de anima* III 5). This peculiar sounding doctrine of *monopsychism*, according to which one intellect is shared by all human beings, was embraced by some arts masters in the thirteenth century – in particular, Siger of Brabant (see his *Questions on De anima* III) – but was fiercely rejected by theologians such as Bonaventure and Aquinas. Bonaventure, writing in the early 1250s, held that "however one dresses up [*coloret*] this view, it is bad and heretical: for it goes against the Christian religion... against right reason... and against sensory experience" (II *Sent.* 18.2.1).[22]

How could anyone believe that all human beings share a single intellect? The theory sounds less odd when considered in its broader context. First, Aristotle's brief remarks on the intellect have struck many as inviting such a conclusion.[23] For Christians, moreover, this separate intellect could be identified with God, a line of thought that might seem to mesh with the Augustinian conception of divine illumination. Augustine had famously argued that at least some human knowledge is attainable only if we are illuminated by God:

When we deal with things that we perceive by the mind, namely by the intellect and reason, we are speaking of things that we look upon immediately in the inner light of Truth, in virtue of which the so-called inner man is illuminated and rejoices...When I'm stating truths, I don't even teach the person who is looking upon these truths. He is taught not by my words but by the things themselves made manifest within when God discloses them. (*The Teacher* 12.40)

Although Augustine never supposed that human beings lack their own intellects, he so stressed our dependence on a light of truth above the mind as to make the mind itself seem incomplete.

Divine illumination held a central place in medieval epistemology until the thirteenth century, when it was gradually displaced by Aristotelian empiricism. Bonaventure staunchly remarked that "the light of a created intellect does not suffice for a certain comprehension of any thing without the light of the eternal Word" (*Christ our one teacher*, n. 10, CT III 84). He was well aware, however, that Aristotle's influence had to be acknowledged, and so he sought a compromise:

Although the soul is, according to Augustine, tied to the eternal laws, because it somehow attains that light through agent intellect's highest focus and through the higher part of reason, nevertheless it is undoubtedly true, in keeping with what the Philosopher says, that cognition is generated in us through the senses, memory, and experience, from which the universal is assembled in us, which is the source of art and knowledge. (*Christ our one teacher*, n. 18, CT III 88)

This is striking not only because Bonaventure leaves room for the empiricism of *Posterior Analytics* II 19, but also because even the Augustinian language of the first few lines has been infected with the Aristotelian agent intellect. By the end of the thirteenth century the next great Franciscan master, Duns Scotus, had dispensed with illumination entirely. When it comes to knowledge of "infallible truth, without doubt and deception," Scotus insisted that human beings "can achieve this, by purely natural means" (*Ordinatio* I, d. 3.1, q. 4, n. 258). God does in a sense illuminate the mind, but he does so by making the world intelligible, giving it a structure and coherence such that our minds, on their own, can grasp truths in science, mathematics, and philosophy.[24]

The twilight of illuminationist epistemology coincided with renewed interest in skepticism. Henry of Ghent, still defending the theory of illumination in the 1270s, began his influential theological *Summa* with a series of articles on skepticism and illumination. The first article considers ancient skepticism at length, arguing to the contrary that human beings can apprehend a thing "as it is, without any mistake or deception" (*Summa quaestionum ordinariarum*, art. 1, q. 1, *CT* III 97). If this is what it means to know a thing, then Ghent concludes that human beings can have knowledge. But he goes on in the very next question to qualify this claim dramatically, remarking that if we limit ourselves to natural means then "it is altogether impossible for us to have an altogether certain and infallible cognition of truth" (q. 2, *CT* III 119). In this way, Henry continues to find a place for divine illumination.

By the fourteenth century illumination was no longer a topic of serious investigation. Disputes over skepticism and the limits of human knowledge now occurred most often in the context of a distinction between two types of cognition: abstractive and intuitive. Scotus introduced this terminology as a distinction between cognition that "abstracts from all existence" and cognition that "can be of a thing insofar as it is present in its existence" (*Lectura* II, d. 3.2, q. 2, n. 285). Imagination, then, counts as abstractive, whereas perception is ordinarily intuitive. Innocuous as this distinction seems, it became enormously influential and controversial. There were, in particular, disputes over how to define the two kinds of cognition and disputes over whether there could be intuitive cognition of nonexistent objects. This in turn led philosophers and theologians to take more seriously the possibility of sensory illusion and intellectual error, issues that had not been seriously pursued since Augustine's era.[25]

The high-water mark of medieval skepticism came with Nicholas of Autrecourt. Writing to the Franciscan Bernard of Arezzo in the 1330s, Autrecourt begins with Bernard's definition of an intuitive cognition as that "through which we judge that a thing exists,

whether or not it does exist." Autrecourt argues that it follows from
this definition that one can never be certain that a perception is
veridical. Consequently, contrary to Aristotle's claim that "sensa-
tions are always true" (*De anima* III 3, 428a11), Autrecourt concludes that "you are not certain of the existence of the objects of
the five senses" (first letter, n. 11). Moreover, "you are not certain
whether anything appears to you at all" (n. 12), and indeed "you
do not know whether your own intellect exists" (n. 15). In a second letter Autrecourt goes even farther, arguing that the principle of
noncontradiction is the only firm footing for certain knowledge. But
since virtually nothing of what passes for philosophical knowledge
can be derived from that principle, "Aristotle in his entire natural
and theoretical philosophy possessed such certainty of scarcely two
conclusions, and perhaps not even of one" (second letter, n. 23).

WILL, PASSION, AND ACTION

It is sometimes said that the will is a medieval discovery and that
ancient theories of human nature were developed in the complete
absence of any such faculty. This is controversial,[26] but what seems
clear is that Augustine was the first major philosopher to give a
detailed account of the will in something like its modern sense.
Fittingly, given Augustine's methodology, he first did so through reflection on his own case, in the *Confessions*, analyzing his tortured
path toward religious conversion. The opening chapters of that autobiography trace his intellectual journey from careless adolescence
through Manichaeism, skepticism, and Neoplatonism, and finally to
complete acceptance of Christianity. But the real drama begins only
at the point where "all doubt left me" (VII 10). This, he had supposed, would be the end of the story. But he came to discover that –
contrary to Socrates in the *Protagoras* – knowing what is right is not
sufficient for doing what is right. What was the problem?

I was held fast not by the iron of another but by my iron will. The enemy
had a grip on my will and from there made a chain for me and bound me.
From a distorted will comes lust, and servitude to lust becomes habit. When
there is no resistance to habit, necessity follows. By these links, as it were,
connected to one another (hence my term a chain), a harsh servitude held
me under constraint. (VIII 5)

Although Augustine was intellectually ready to change his life, his will was not willing. How could this be? All that was necessary at this point was an act of will: "Not just the going but also the arriving there would have required nothing other than the willing to go" (VIII 8). What could prevent him from willing that which he wanted? The problem was that his will was split in two. What was necessary was "willing strongly and wholly, not the turning and twisting one way and another of a will half-wounded, struggling with one part rising up while the other part falls down" (VIII 19).

Later medieval authors debated at length the relationships between will and intellect and between will and the passions. What is perhaps most significant in these discussions is the conception of will as a faculty subject to complex dispositions. Just as we commonly think of the mind as acquiring beliefs and memories over time, Augustine conceives of the will as shaped by habitual decisions. In the *Nicomachean Ethics*, Aristotle had described how acquiring the right sort of habit from an early age "is very important, indeed all-important" (II 1, 1103b25). Augustine was no student of Aristotle, but he develops much the same point and situates it within his theory of the will. This would be crucial to later medieval ethics, according to which the all-important virtues of charity and justice are dispositions of the will.[27] Moreover, it was this conception of the will that shaped Augustine's theory of grace. Just as genuine understanding requires that the intellect be illuminated by God, so moral goodness requires that the will be infused with virtue. A will that has been badly habituated from a young age – like his own – can find itself in the iron grip of necessity. Such necessity made it literally impossible for Augustine to convert on his own. "The labor is beyond me until you open the way" (*Confessions* XI 22). As he grew older, Augustine came to put ever more stress on the role of grace, arguing that even the free acceptance of grace requires grace. In the end, he succeeded in having the contrary view of his contemporary Pelagius regarded as a heresy. These questions were destined to remain at the forefront of medieval thought. In the fourteenth century Thomas Bradwardine was so disturbed by some modern views that he composed an extensive treatise *On God's Cause against Pelagius*, arguing that "no philosophical or moral virtue is a true virtue, absolutely right or just, without charity and grace perfecting it." Without these, "every such action is in some way a sin" ([339] 327C).

Overshadowed by these notorious debates over grace was some very subtle late medieval work in action theory. Aquinas's theory of action – to take the most studied instance – is standardly said to involve twelve discrete steps on the way to a voluntary act.[28] Among the most pressing questions in this area was the relationship between reason and the passions. St. Paul had famously described how "The flesh lusts against the spirit and the spirit against the flesh. They are in conflict with one another, and so you do not do the things you want" (Galatians 5:17). Augustine saw his own early years as an illustration of such remarks (cf. *Confessions* VIII 5). He came to analyze the phenomenon as a failure of will – not so much weakness of will, as we now call it, but a flawed disposition of will, making it impossible to will "strongly and wholly" in a way that would be efficacious.

Although the Pauline text suggests that spirit and flesh are matched in an even fight, medieval authors tended to view the relationship between the will and the passions as asymmetrical, inasmuch as only the will (*voluntas*) could give rise to voluntary actions.[29] If the passions were literally to conquer the will in the way Paul suggests, the resulting action would be an involuntary one, for which the agent would not be directly responsible. (Such cases would be exceedingly rare. Even then, one might be indirectly responsible for being disposed to have such overwhelming passions.) Moreover, most later medieval authors identified the will as "rational appetite," meaning that it chooses what the intellect has judged to be good. This makes the conflict between will and passion still more puzzling, since the passions now seem ineligible to influence the will. Yet, of course, we do all suffer temptation. Indeed, Adam and Eve's original sin was thought to have made such temptation an inescapable part of this life. Thus not even St. Paul could keep his flesh from lusting against his spirit. To make sense of this influence, the flesh was viewed as doing its work indirectly, by shaping how the mind conceives of a situation.[30]

The description of will as rational appetite did not go unchallenged. One of the most interesting critiques was that of Scotus, who proposed two kinds of inclinations within the will. Developing a suggestion made by Anselm (*On the Fall of the Devil* ch. 14; *The Harmony of the Foreknowledge, the Predestination, and the Grace of God with Free Choice* ch. 19), Scotus distinguished between an inclination for one's own advantage (*affectio commodi*) and an inclination for justice (*affectio justitiae*). The first explains our inclination toward what is good for ourselves; this is the aspect of our will that Scotus thinks is captured by the phrase *rational appetite*, in virtue of which we pursue that which most contributes to our own happiness. We are also inclined, however, to do what is good regardless of whether it has any connection to ourselves. This inclination for justice explains our freedom to resist pure self-interest. In Scotus's view, it grounds our crucial capacity to love God for his own sake rather than for our own reward.[31]

FREEDOM AND IMMORTALITY

Differing conceptions of human nature lead directly to disagreements in ethics and political theory, the focus of the next three chapters in this volume. Two convictions were of fundamental importance to medieval authors in this regard: that human beings are free, and hence worthy subjects of praise and blame; and that human beings are immortal, and hence subject to eternal happiness or suffering. Though philosophers differed in how they analyzed and argued for these propositions, there was almost universal belief in their truth. Even Bradwardine, for all his anti-Pelagianism, acknowledged that "All the theologians, all the logicians, all the moral philosophers, and almost all the natural philosophers unanimously testify that free decision[32] must be posited" (*On God's Cause* [339] 443D). There was controversy, nevertheless, as to how freedom of will could be reconciled with divine providence, grace, and foreknowledge, on one hand, and with the determining influence of intellect, on the other. In the latter connection, it is common to speak of a theory being more or less intellectualist or voluntarist, depending on whether it gives a greater or lesser role to intellect or will. This is, however, not a very useful way to understand the debate, because all agreed that the will is crucial for free decision. The central question was *how* the will performs its crucial task. Specifically, how and to what extent is it determined by intellect and other forces? Philosophers today distinguish between *compatibilists*, who believe that the will can be free even if determined by outside factors, and *libertarians*, who argue that the will can move itself spontaneously. Much the same issues were in play during the Middle Ages, when the kind of determinism in question was typically God's grace and providence or the intellect's judgment regarding what is best. Augustine once again was influential, but although his remarks on free will were extensive (see, e.g, *On Free Choice of the Will* III and *City of God* V 10), his views on the crucial issues are often hard to determine.[33] Anselm's views are likewise difficult to interpret, but he seems to come closer to something like compatibilism. He explicitly denies that free will requires the dual ability, at a single moment, to choose or not choose a thing, arguing that someone so upright as to be unable to sin is more free than someone who is able to either sin or not sin (*On Freedom of Choice*, ch. 1). Elsewhere he considers the case of an angel created in stages, who has been created up to the point of being "ready to will but not yet willing anything" (*On the Fall of the Devil*, ch. 12). This angel could not move itself to that first act of willing, Anselm claims, because "whatever moves itself to willing, first wills itself so to move." Since the angel, *ex hypothesi*, does not will anything, it cannot move itself to will, and so it needs something else to move it. Anselm thus seems to deny that the will has the power to move itself spontaneously.[34]

Scholastic philosophers debated this issue vigorously. Aquinas did not clearly defend either side (at any rate, scholars disagree on the point),[35] but the next generation of philosophers took clear positions. Henry of Ghent, Olivi, and Scotus defended a libertarian-style account. Godfrey of Fontaines and later John Buridan were in effect compatibilists.[36] Godfrey, writing in 1289, proposed that in discussing free will "We should not deny what is first and most certain because of ignorance and doubt about what is secondary." One such certain principle is that nothing can move itself.

> Therefore if it seems to someone that, on the supposition that the will does not move itself, it is difficult to preserve the freedom that on his view he wants to posit in the will, in the way he likes, he should not on the basis of this secondary claim proceed to deny prior and more certain claims. Rather, on account of the certainty of the prior claims that he has to suppose, he should study how to make these compatible with the secondary claims. (*Quodlibet* VI 7 [275] 170)

In other words, rather than abandon a basic principle of metaphysics – that nothing can move itself – we should reconsider our assumptions about what freedom requires. Others would question this alleged principle of metaphysics. Scotus, the most influential defender of the will's spontaneity, distinguished between two ways in which a thing might be indeterminate: either because it is insufficiently actualized, or because it has a "superabundant sufficiency" that allows it to move itself in any one of various ways (*Quaestiones super libros Metaphysicorum* IX 15.31–32 [285] 152–55; [284] 610). The will is special because it is indeterminate in this second way. So, given its exceptional nature, "it seems truly stupid to apply universal propositions about active principles to the will" (*Quaestiones* IX 15.44 [285] 158–59; [284] 614). As for why the will has this capacity, Scotus remarked – much as he had regarding the unity of body and soul (see above) – that there is no further explanation to be had. "There is no other cause to be given for why it chooses in this way except that it is such a cause... There is no other cause except that it is the will" (*Quaestiones* IX 15.24, 29 [285] 150–53; [284] 608, 610).[37]

Still, despite such disagreements, medieval authors were in broad agreement on the importance of the will and the reality of human freedom. The reason they could agree on this point was that they agreed on the connection between freedom and moral responsibility. Aquinas was merely stating a truism when he remarked that "Without free decision there could be no merit or demerit and no just punishment or reward" (*Truth*, q. 24, a. 1). Medieval views about just punishment and reward were, however, typically projected beyond the present life. In a sermon on the Apostles' Creed, Aquinas remarked that without the hope of a better life to come, "death would without doubt be dreaded intensely, and a human being would do anything bad before suffering death" (*In symbolum apostolorum* 11.1001). So while free will made moral responsibility possible, personal immortality gave such responsibility its force, by opening up the prospect of eternal salvation or damnation.

There was little disagreement about the fact of human immortality, but extensive debate over whether it could be proved. Aquinas believed it could be. His central argument depended on showing that the human soul has a function – thought – that it exercises without any bodily organ. He then reasoned that if the soul has such a function, it can exist without a body, and that the body's corruption would therefore not bring about the soul's corruption (see, e.g., *ST* I, q. 75, a. 6). This does not yield the conclusion that *human beings* are immortal. Full human immortality would require the resurrection of the body, something that was not generally considered provable.

Even the demonstrability of the soul's immortality was rejected by many later authors, including Scotus (*Opus Oxoniense* IV 43.2 [286] 149), Ockham (*Quodlibet* I 10), and even Cajetan, Aquinas's great Renaissance commentator (*In de anima* III 2).[38] Scotus argued as follows. Even if the intellect functions without any bodily organ, this does not show that the intellect's function could endure without a body, because there might be other ways in which the intellect's function depends on the body. In fact, Aquinas and Scotus were in agreement that our intellect does need the body for its normal operation. Both held that the intellect must constantly turn toward sensory images (phantasms) in the course of thinking abstractly. So, even for a meaningful immortality of the soul, Aquinas needed to establish something further. He needed to establish that the soul would take up a new mode of cognition once apart from the body.[39] He was in fact prepared to argue just that. He thought that our soul, once separated from the body, would think like the angels, albeit in an inferior way (*Quaestiones disputatae de anima*, qq. 15–21; *ST* I, q. 89). Not surprisingly, there was doubt about whether this could be proved. As scholastic philosophy became increasingly rigorous in its methods, such debates over *provability* became increasingly common.

NOTES

1. Some early Christians, such as Origen, held that souls were created before their bodies were created. Augustine left open this question (see, e.g., *Confessions* I 6). By the time of Aquinas, however, preexistence was no longer treated as a serious option, and there was an almost universal consensus that the soul is infused well after the point of conception. For a survey of thirteenth-century views, see R. Dales [545].

2. This careful definition allows Augustine to say that the mind, although not a body, is extended throughout the body in a special way: "it is a whole in the whole body, and a whole in each part of the body" (*Trinity* VI 6.8).

3. See also *Trinity* XV 12.21, *On Free Choice of the Will* II 3, and *City of God* XI 26. For further discussion of Augustine's first-person method, see G. Matthews [73], chs. 3–4 and chapter 12 in this volume.

4. See Avicenna, *Liber de anima* I 5 [115] I 79–80; Aristotle, *De anima* II 3, 414a31–32. For an early scholastic description of the soul's powers, see *CT* III 9–34, an anonymous work dating from around 1225.

5. For the early thirteenth century, see, for example, Philip the Chancellor, *Summa de bono* IV 8 [379] 284. The most notable later pluralists are Henry of Ghent (*Quodlibet* IV 13), John Duns Scotus (*Ordinatio* IV, d. 11, q. 3 [282] VIII 604–56), and William of Ockham (*Quodlibet* II 10–11), all three of whom disagree among themselves in various ways (see M. M. Adams [318] 647–69). For a detailed survey of views in this area, see R. Zavalloni, *Richard de Mediavilla et la Controverse sur la Pluralité des Formes* (Louvain, 1951).

6. Aquinas articulates his view in various places: for a concise statement, see *ST* I, q. 76, arts. 3–4. For Olivi, see II *Sent.*, q. 71 [271] II 637. On the Oxford condemnations, promulgated first by Robert Kilwardby in 1277 and then by John Pecham in 1284, see D. A. Callus [239] and J.-P. Torrell [260] 304–05.

7. Discussion focused on the real presence of Christ in the Eucharist and the endurance of Christ's body in the tomb. For a brief account, see M. M. Adams [318] 650–52.

8. See H. Denzinger [24] no. 902. The target of this condemnation was the aforementioned Olivi, who took the rational soul to inform a certain *spiritual matter* that was distinct from the corporeal matter we call the body (see II *Sent.*, q. 51, and R. Pasnau [274]). This decree would be reaffirmed by the Lateran Council of 1513, making trouble for a whole new generation of Catholic philosophers in the early modern era.

9. For scholastic authors, this transforming role was standardly played by agent intellect (see, e.g., Aquinas, *ST* I, q. 79, a. 3; q. 84, a. 6). Augustine seems to have thought that even sensation required this sort of spiritual transformation (*The Literal Meaning of Genesis* XII 16). Ockham, at the other extreme, was idiosyncratic in believing that the material could act on the immaterial. See, e.g., *Reportatio* II 12–13 [308] *OTh* V 275.

10. See, e.g., Aquinas: "every natural body has some determinate substantial form. Therefore since the accidents follow from the substantial form, it is necessary that determinate accidents follow from a determinate form" (*ST* I, q. 7, a. 3).

11. See the discussion in D. Des Chene [546] ch. 4. For a late scholastic exception to this consensus, see Jacob Zabarella, a sixteenth-century Paduan philosopher, [622] 395.

12. For information on ancient skepticism, see M. Burnyeat [38].

13. For further discussion of Augustine's methodology, see N. Kretzmann [71]. Augustine returns to these issues in many places, including *Against*

the Academicians, *The Advantage of Believing*, *Trinity* XV, and *City of God* XI.

14. See, e.g., Aquinas, *ST* I, q. 14, a. 1; q. 84, a. 2.

15. See H. A. Wolfson [553]; D. L. Black [479].

16. On the role of Bacon in developing earlier Islamic theories, see K. Tachau [552] ch. 1.

17. Augustine suggests this account in various places, e.g., *On Music* VI 5, trans. R. C. Taliaferro (New York, 1947); *The Magnitude of the Soul*, trans. J. J. McMahon (New York, 1947) 23–24; *The Literal Meaning of Genesis* XII. For discussion see G. O'Daly [75].

18. See, e.g., *ST* I, q. 85, a. 2, ad 3: "There are two operations in the sensory part. *One occurs solely in virtue of an impression; in this way the operation of a sense is completed by its receiving an impression from something sensible.* The other operation is the forming in virtue of which the imaginary power forms for itself an image of an absent thing, or even of something never seen." Cf. Aristotle, *De anima* II 11, 423b32: "To sense is to be affected in a certain way."

19. See II *Sent.*, q. 23; q. 58, ad 14; q. 72, q. 74, and R. Pasnau [551] chs. 4–5.

20. Such claims also extended to the mental word (see chapter 3 in this volume), which Olivi identified as the act of thought (see *CT* III 136–51). For Ockham, see E. Stump in *CCOck* 168–203, as well as the text translated in A. Hyman and J. J. Walsh [17] 670–79.

21. See P. King [549] for discussion of this point.

22. For another fierce reply to the theory, see Aquinas's short treatise *De unitate intellectus*. For an anonymous defense of monopsychism by an arts master at the University of Paris, see *CT* III 35–78.

23. Most famous is *De anima* III 5, speaking of agent intellect: "This intellect is separate, unaffected, and unmixed, being in essence activity . . . It is not the case that it sometimes thinks and at other times not. In separation it is just what it is, and this alone is immortal and eternal" (430a17–23).

24. For text and translation of the key question, see John Duns Scotus [286] 96–132. For further discussion of divine illumination, see R. Pasnau [550].

25. Particularly important were the views of Peter Aureol and William of Ockham. For Aureol see *CT* III 178–218. Ockham's view has been the subject of extensive discussion and disagreement in modern times. See, most recently, E. Karger in *CCOck* 204–26. For a striking instance of skepticism's influence in the early 1330s, see the selection from William Crathorn at *CT* III 245–301. For Scotus on intuitive and abstractive cognition, see R. Pasnau in *CCScot* 285–311.

26. A. Dihle [547] stresses the importance of Augustine. T. Irwin [548] argues for will in Aristotle; C. H. Kahn [69] gives a good sense of the complexity of the whole issue.
27. See B. Kent [558] and chapter 10 in this volume.
28. See A. Donagan in *CHLMP* 642–54.
29. See, e.g., Anselm, *On Freedom of Choice*, chs. 5–7; Aquinas, *ST* IaIIae, q. 77, a. 1.
30. For Aquinas's views in this area, see P. King [243] and N. Kretzmann [247].
31. See Scotus [288] 179–81 and 469–73; for discussion, see A. Wolter [301]. How are these two inclinations to be weighed? That it is *rational* for us to love God more than ourselves was defended by Aquinas (III *Sent.*, d. 29, q. un., a. 3), Godfrey of Fontaines (*CT* II 271–84, 301–06), and, it would seem, by Ockham (*CCOck* 273–301).
32. "Free decision" translates *liberum arbitrium*, which was the standard medieval phrase for what we call free will, from Augustine through Anselm and into the scholastics. It was not customary among medieval authors to speak of the *will* as being free, although many authors concluded in the end that free decision is a capacity belonging to the will. Still, the medieval terminology is useful because it leaves open the question of whether our capacity for free decision really is the product of our faculty of will.
33. See C. Kirwan [70] and E. Stump in *CCAug* 35–78.
34. See S. Visser and T. Williams [147], who read Anselm as a kind of libertarian.
35. For three very different accounts, see E. Stump [259], S. MacDonald [249] and R. Pasnau [255].
36. See the selections in Henry of Ghent [221] and the discussion of Olivi in R. Pasnau [273]. For Buridan, see J. Zupko [345] and Buridan in *CT* II 498–586. In [21] I, O. Lottin presents many interesting texts, in Latin, from throughout the thirteenth century.
37. For discussion, see P. King [296] and T. Williams [299].
38. See chapter 13 in this volume for discussion of the dispute among Renaissance scholastics.
39. On the turn toward phantasms in Aquinas, see *ST* I, q. 84, art. 7 and R. Pasnau [255] ch. 9. For Scotus, see *Lectura* II, d. 3.2, q. 1, n. 255; *Lectura* I, d. 3.3, q. 1, n. 300; *Ordinatio* I, d. 3.3, q. 1, n. 392; *Ordinatio* I, d. 3.1, q. 3, n. 187. On Aquinas's difficulties in establishing the soul's immortality, see J. Owens [254].

10　The moral life

From the dawn of the Middle Ages to their end, moral theorists struggled to explain what makes a person good by human standards, what it takes to merit happiness in the afterlife, and what, if anything, the two have to do with each other. Some inveighed against the worldly ethics of ancient philosophers; others praised the ancients for important moral insights. Yet every leading medieval thinker worked to develop an account of the moral life far more comprehensive than most professors of philosophical ethics or moral theology today would attempt. The idea that a serious theologian could dismiss classical ethics as unworthy of study and debate was no more acceptable than the idea that a serious philosopher could dismiss questions about the immortality of the soul and the nature of God as irrelevant to moral life in human society.

I shall begin by sketching Augustine's pioneering work in ethics, along with some of the puzzles it creates. After a look at respectful but significant revisions of Augustine by Anselm of Canterbury, I turn to the brave new world of universities, where the pagan Aristotle soon emerged as an authority to be reckoned with. Beginning in the mid-thirteenth century, efforts to weave together his insights with Augustine's became at once highly complex and the occasion for passionate academic dispute. Less than a century old, universities were already embroiled in their first stormy experiment with "multiculturalism."

What kind of freedom does moral agency require? Do we always act in pursuit of happiness, always seeing our own actions as in some way good? Is it possible to choose an act we know full well to be wrong? What does it mean to love God above all, and who is able to do so? Reflecting upon and debating such questions, Thomas

Aquinas, Duns Scotus, William of Ockham, and others joined in producing a fine-grained analysis of human motivations that may still be unequaled. In laboring to work out what it means to love God, medieval moral theorists thought long and hard about what it means to love anyone.

AUGUSTINE AND CLASSICAL ETHICS

Augustine shares with ancient philosophers the conception of ethics as an inquiry into the supreme good: that which we seek for its own sake, never for the sake of some further end, and which makes us happy.[1] He also shares the conviction that all human beings by nature want to be happy, agreeing that happiness is a condition of objective well-being, not merely the pleasure a person might gain from satisfying whatever desires she happens to have, however deluded or self-destructive. Beginning within this shared framework, Augustine's thinking leads him far afield from classical ethics. He argues that happiness is possible only in the afterlife, in the company of God and the saints. We cannot make ourselves happy; we can at most hope to merit the reward of happiness in the afterlife. As happiness is a gift of God's grace, so, too, is virtue a free gift, not one we can earn by our own natural resources or independent merits. Finally, Augustine contends that all true virtues are rooted in God-given charity, the kind of love extolled by St. Paul in I Corinthians 13 (Latin: *caritas*; Greek: *agape*). Because pagans lack charity, all of their apparent virtues are vices, and all of their actions are sins.[2]

Of course, pagans can promote the good of other individuals, even the good of their community, thereby acquiring what Augustine calls "civic" virtues. But far from accepting such virtues as genuine but second-rate, he pronounces them vices. This disparaging view plainly requires some explanation.

Suppose that a Christian with charity, awakened at 4 a.m. by the cries of her infant son, chooses to comfort him, instead of ignoring the child and going back to sleep. Suppose that a pagan mother behaves in precisely the same way. Augustine would praise the Christian because she recognizes God as the highest good, the only good to be loved strictly for his own sake and above all else. She knows that the value people have, just because they are human, must never be considered independent of God as the creator of human nature. She knows, too, that whatever virtue she herself has is God's gift, hence to be exercised with appropriate humility. When she comforts her son, she acts for the sake of eternal happiness, from a love of the child as belonging to God, and with gratitude for God's grace.

Augustine would fault the pagan mother for aiming at only some earthly end and acting from bad motivations. If she acts from love of the child just because he belongs to her, she favors him as something akin to private property. (Why consider this virtuous when even animals demonstrate tender concern for their own offspring?) If she simply enjoys taking care of babies, she acts from a desire for her own pleasure or satisfaction. The pagan mother will fare better in Augustine's judgment if she happens to be a Stoic sage; so let us suppose that she is. Like Augustine, she believes that virtues lie wholly in the mind, but that anyone who does have a virtuous mind will perform, or at least try to perform, a wide range of physical actions. Say she believes, too, that a virtuous person would rise at 4 a.m. to comfort a crying child even if he belonged to a total stranger. As a Stoic, however, she also believes that happiness comes exclusively from a virtuous mind, so that virtue and happiness both lie wholly within the individual's control. Augustine retorts:

A virtuous mind is something very praiseworthy...A great thing, an admirable thing; admire it, Stoic, as much as you can. But tell me: From where does it come? It is not precisely your virtuous mind that makes you happy, but the one who has given you the virtue, who has inspired you to desire it, and granted you the capacity for it...It is a good thing that it pleases you. I know you are thirsty for it; but you cannot pour yourself a drink of virtue. (Sermon 150, §9)[3]

However much their actions might benefit others, even society as a whole, Stoics grossly overestimate how much lies within human control – and not, in Augustine's view, owing to some simple factual mistake. They exaggerate human power and self-sufficiency because they want credit for making themselves both virtuous and happy.

This analysis of motivations reflects Augustine's view of human nature's present condition, damaged by original sin. After Adam's fall, all human beings are born with the inordinate self-love Augustine calls "pride." Only through God's gift of charity can we love God, others, and even ourselves as we should: according to their intrinsic value, neither more nor less than deserved. Without God's liberating grace, our motivations and value judgments remain incurably self-centered (*City of God* XII 8, XIV 28, XV 22).

Augustine's theocentric moral theory carries forward St. Paul's attack on the elitism and intellectualism of classical ethics. In Paul's and Augustine's view, virtues are no longer moral dispositions achieved by only a select few, through many years of learning and practice beginning in childhood. No matter how bad one's upbringing and education, no matter how undistinguished one's native intelligence, nobody ever stands beyond hope of life-changing moral improvement. With God's grace, the greatest sinner might be converted to virtue. As nobody in this life is ever beyond hope, neither is anyone beyond danger of degeneration. Even the saints among us must continue struggling to resist temptation.

Emphasizing always our shared, flawed humanity, Augustine's moral doctrine envisions what is aptly described as "a lifelong process of convalescence."[4] The process cannot even begin until we admit that we are impotent to control our own lives and place our faith in a power greater than ourselves. I imagine, then, that Augustine would award high marks to Alcoholics Anonymous and programs modeled on it, only expressing regret that recovering addicts are among the few members of our society humble enough to recognize what he believed were truths applicable to everyone and to the whole of moral life.

In replacing wisdom with charity or love as the foundational virtue Augustine shifts western ethics away from the standard classical focus on reason or intellect. Virtue comes to require above all a good will. Note, too, that we are no longer assured that virtuous character will protect us from misery, let alone make us happy, amidst the pervasive evils and injustices of human society. Dismissing as grandiose lies the classical treatments of virtue as constitutive of the happy life, Augustine recasts virtue as that by which one merits happiness after death: "By means of these divinely bestowed virtues, we now live a good life and afterward are granted its reward, the happy life, which must be eternal. Here these same virtues are in action, there in effect; here they are working, there they are paid; here their function, there their end" (Letter 155, §16).

Open questions

Augustine's works raised many questions in the minds of later philosophers and theologians: about how his account of the moral life went in detail, whether it needed revisions to be coherent, and whether he was simply wrong on certain points.[5] Consider, for instance, the thesis that all human beings naturally want to be happy. In itself this poses no problem for Christian moral thought. It does, however, pose problems when combined with what I shall dub "the eudaimonist principle": that everything we will, we will for the sake of happiness. If our every action is motivated by the desire for happiness, it would seem impossible for someone to choose an act mainly, let alone exclusively, because she believes it the right thing to do. Is the eudaimonist principle even compatible with love? When we act to promote the well-being of friends and family even at high expense to our individual well-being, are we still pursuing our own happiness, albeit in an expanded, enlightened way, or can we sometimes set aside concern for our own happiness and act mainly from love for someone else?[6]

Further puzzles arise from the notion of virtue as that by which we merit happiness. Is God somehow bound to reward virtue with happiness? Would he be unjust if he did not? How does the merit/reward schema square with the conception of both happiness and virtue as gifts of grace? Toward the end of his life, as Augustine became embroiled in disputes with Pelagians, references to human merit virtually disappeared from his writings. The merits he emphasized were the merits of Christ. At this stage he sought chiefly to establish that virtue itself is a "free gift" of grace, which God is not bound to reward with happiness. If God in any way owed us happiness, grace would not be grace. Indeed, if happiness were given in accord with human merit, grace would not be grace (*Answer to Julian* IV 15; *Answer to the Two Letters of the Pelagians* II 3; IV 19).

HAPPINESS AND MORALITY

Anselm of Canterbury agreed that fallen humanity, without grace, cannot help but sin. He diverged from Augustine chiefly in his analysis of rational nature as God created it. In his view, a creature naturally able to will nothing but happiness could not be either morally good or evil, just or unjust. In attacking the eudaimonist principle Anselm initiated a controversy in western ethics that continues in various forms to this day. Even within Anglo-American circles, philosophers are so divided that some believe the eudaimonist principle beyond reasonable doubt, whereas others believe it both false and a threat to morality. As we shall see, the medieval debate has little to do with the physical actions human beings are able to perform. It centers instead on the kinds of motivations we have in doing whatever we do.

Justice for its own sake

Anselm breaks new ground in distinguishing sharply between two basic inclinations (*affectiones*) of the will: one for justice or rightness, the other for happiness or what is advantageous. (The distinction here is between two kinds of goods, not between the good inclination for justice and some wicked penchant for selfishness or injustice.) Anyone who wills justice, Anselm argues, must will justice for its own sake. Someone who wills an act for the sake of happiness, such as giving money to the Salvation Army for the sake of a tax deduction, wills nothing other than happiness. So if happiness is, by a creature's God-given nature, the sole end it has the capacity to will, the creature remains at the amoral level of an animal – able to care about others, as a dog cares about its puppies or its master, but only from a natural inclination to include the welfare of others in one's own pursuit of happiness or self-realization. On the other hand, a creature whose nature lacked the inclination to happiness but included the inclination to justice, so that it could not will anything other than justice, would again remain at the amoral level. Given that human beings and angels are by nature capable of sinning, as evidenced by God's punishment of Adam and Satan, Anselm concludes that God created rational nature with both inclinations of the will. The will for justice was intended to temper the will for happiness, so that the individual would be able to keep it within limits but likewise able to transgress (*The Fall of the Devil*, chs. 13–14).

At present, however, human nature suffers from the damage done by Adam's fall. Retaining the capacity for free choice (*liberum arbitrium*) that makes us moral agents, we have lost the inclination

to justice necessary for using this capacity and can now recover it
only through God's grace.[7] Without the inclination to justice, a person becomes psychologically akin to an addict. Deeply unhappy, yet
enslaved to his own desire for happiness, he cannot will anything
else: "Having abandoned justice, [the will] remains as regards its own
power a servant of injustice and unjust by necessity. For it is unable
by itself to return to justice; and without justice the will is never free,
because without justice, the natural freedom of choice is useless"
(*The Harmony of the Foreknowledge, the Predestination, and the
Grace of God with Free Choice* III 13).

Willing under the aspect of the good

From the mid-thirteenth century onward, Aristotle's works did much
to shape scholastic debate about the will, happiness, and morality.
Some authors came to regard the will as an "intellectual appetite,"
determined to act for the sake of happiness and deriving its freedom from the intellect's freedom to interpret and judge happiness
in one way or another.[8] However alien to Augustine's thought this
new conception of the will was, it at least agreed with his apparent
endorsement of the eudaimonist principle. A second controversial
principle, often attributed to Aristotle, declared that whatever we
will, we will "under the aspect of the good" (*sub ratione boni*). One
need look no farther than the writings of Aquinas to find both principles staunchly defended.[9]

Aquinas opens the second part of his *Summa theologiae* by arguing that all human actions are for the sake of an ultimate end,
and there is only one such end, which we seek under the aspect
of the good. This single ultimate end is happiness (*ST* IaIIae, q. 1,
aa. 6–8; q. 8, a. 1). Even when we behave self-destructively, we are
seeking fulfillment – seeing our behavior as somehow good for us,
if only in satisfying some twisted appetite for pleasure. In claiming
that we necessarily will happiness and that everything we will, we
will for the sake of happiness, Aquinas does not mean to deny that
people have very different conceptions of happiness. Nor does he
mean to suggest, as Aristotle believed possible, that someone can
reach a point of no return in moral development, so that from then
on, she is determined to pursue the same conception of happiness
that she has in the past. Only if offered the perfect happiness of the

beatific vision, says Aquinas, are we moved of necessity to will it. Offered anything else, we can consider its good aspects and will it, but equally consider the ways in which it lacks perfect goodness and refuse it (q. 10, a. 2).

In contrast to Augustine, Aquinas recognizes two kinds of happiness: the imperfect happiness of earthly life, attainable through our own natural resources, and the perfect, supernatural happiness of the afterlife, attainable only with God's grace. The disagreement with Augustine should not be dismissed as purely verbal. Neither, however, should it be overstated. What Aquinas calls imperfect happiness differs in kind, not merely in degree, from the perfect happiness possible with God. Thomistic moral theory leaves no doubt that the sole ultimate end, the only happiness that can entirely satisfy us, lies in the afterlife (ST IaIIae, q. 1, a. 7; q. 5, a. 5).

How does Aquinas reconcile the eudaimonist principle with the command to love God more than oneself, one's neighbors, or anything else in the universe? Two distinctions are worth noting: First, between the "thing" we desire to attain, that is, that which makes us happy – God, the absolutely perfect good – and happiness, that is, our "use, or attainment, or possession" of that thing (ST IaIIae, q. 2, a. 7). Second, between seeking one's own good strictly as an individual and seeking the shared, "common" good, which by nature is greater than any individual's good. "From charity," Aquinas writes, "a person ought to love God, who is the common good of all, more than himself, because happiness is in God as in the common well-spring for all who are able to share this happiness" (ST III, q. 26, a. 3).

Having chosen Aquinas as my representative "intellectualist," I should add that he was actually quite moderate by contemporary standards in his embrace of the idea of choice as always determined by the apprehension of some good. Others at Paris worked much harder to present and defend what they considered the unexpurgated Aristotle. Even late thirteenth-century theologians, notably Godfrey of Fontaines, sometimes faulted Aquinas for straying from Aristotle's teachings in awarding the will too large a role in our moral lives. At the same time, other theologians worried that uncritical devotion to Aristotle's teachings posed a serious danger to morals. If everything we will is willed for the sake of happiness, and we are determined to choose in accordance with what we judge, in any given situation, will promote our happiness, all wrongdoing appears to result from some intellectual mistake in judging the course of action that would in fact promote our happiness.

The principle that everything we will, we will under the aspect of the good, triggered especially bitter controversy. If all this means is that we cannot choose an act unless we judge it in some way desirable, the principle might be taken as true but hardly worth mentioning. Even Peter Olivi, perhaps the most anti-Aristotelian thinker of the late thirteenth century, was prepared to accept the principle so construed. But what difference could it conceivably make to morals? The same act, Olivi reasons – such as fornicating right now, in these particular circumstances – can be regarded as desirable in one respect and undesirable in another. Correctly regarding the act as immoral (*inhonestus*), the agent would be unable to choose it; correctly regarding it as pleasurable to the senses, he surely could choose it. He could even see the act in both ways at the same moment, for there is nothing contradictory in judging an act both pleasurable and immoral. The individual sees it in one way or the other and chooses accordingly because he wills to do so, not because he is ignorant or because his mind must somehow have lost sight of the salient moral facts (II *Sent.*, q. 57, ad 15).

Inalienable freedom

As worried as Olivi by intellectualist trends, Duns Scotus saw fit to revive Anselm's theory of the will's dual inclinations, albeit with a crucial difference. Where the Anselmian inclination to justice is lost through original sin and recoverable only through God's grace, it becomes in Scotus's ethics the root of the will's innate, inalienable freedom. All human beings, just because we have wills, have both inclinations: the natural inclination to desire one's own fulfillment and seek what is good for oneself, as well as the inclination to love goods for their intrinsic worth and for their own sake. There is nothing reprehensible about the inclination to seek happiness or self-realization. Not only is it part of our God-given nature, it forms the psychological basis for the virtue of hope. On the other hand, the inclination to justice forms the psychological basis for charity, a greater virtue than hope (*Ordinatio* III, supplement d. 26; trans. [288] 178–80). Through this inclination we are liberated from our natural drive to seek self-realization above all. We are able to love God and other human beings primarily for their own sake, instead of primarily because they return our love, make us happy, or in some other way prove advantageous.

Attacking the notion of will as intellectual appetite, Scotus argues that a creature can be highly intelligent in judging what promotes its happiness, choosing and acting accordingly; but if it is so constructed that the quest for happiness is its sole motivation, it does not have the freedom necessary for moral responsibility. It lacks what is properly called a will, for a being with a will can act against the natural desire for its own well-being (*Ordinatio* III, d. 17; II, d. 6, q. 2; [288] 180–82, 464–70). Scotus believes we know introspectively, from experience, that we are never, in fact, determined to choose the course of action we regard as best promoting our happiness. Acting always for the sake of happiness further suggests that, in choosing an act, we must always be weighing the expected consequences for our own happiness (*Quaestiones in Metaphysicam* IX, q. 15; *Ordinatio* IV, supplement d. 49, qq. 9–10; [288] 152, 194). If this is true, the common assumption that the very actions most revelatory of an individual's character are often spontaneous acts of kindness – or, on the opposite side, spontaneous acts of meanness – would appear mistaken.

In the final analysis, though, Scotus does not reject the eudaimonist principle because he believes it disproved by purely descriptive, empirical psychology. He rejects it because he considers it ruinous to morals, hence intolerable as a principle of moral psychology.[10] A moral agent must perforce have an inclination for justice in order to control the natural appetite for what he believes most advantageous to himself:

This inclination for justice, which is the primary moderator of the inclination for the advantageous – inasmuch as it is not necessary that the will actually seek that to which the inclination for the advantageous tends, and inasmuch as it is not necessary that the will seek this above all else (namely, to the extent the inclination for the advantageous disposes it) – this inclination for justice, I say, is the freedom innate to the will, because it is the primary moderator of the inclination for the advantageous. (*Ordinatio* II, d. 6, q. 2; [288] 468)

Convinced that if we are ever determined to choose the act we do by our natural desire for happiness, our status as moral agents stands on shaky grounds, Scotus argues that we could be presented with the perfect, eternal happiness of the beatific vision and yet not will it. Granted, we are so determined to willing happiness that we would be unable to refuse (*nolle*); but – contrary to Aquinas and his followers – we could simply not will (*non velle*) the happiness offered (*Ordinatio* IV, supplement d. 49, qq. 9–10; [288] 192–94).

Does Scotus aim to banish the natural desire for happiness from the moral life, as if there were something morally reprehensible about trying to be happy? Not at all. He always describes the inclination for justice as checking, moderating, or keeping within appropriate limits the inclination for happiness, not as eradicating it.[11] This becomes especially clear in Scotus's account of how the good angels differed from Satan. The good angels were neither able to refuse happiness nor did they want to, but they willed God's well-being even more than their own. Satan sinned, not in willing his own happiness, but in willing it immoderately. Because he had an inclination for justice, he was able and obligated to keep his desire for happiness within bounds, instead of seeking happiness above all else, or willing to have it only for himself, or willing to have it too soon, or willing to have it without working to merit it (*Ordinatio* II, d. 6, q. 2; [288] 468–74).

Love and pleasure

Ockham goes even farther than Scotus in spurning the eudaimonist principle. No matter how great the happiness offered, he argues, the will can outright refuse it. Our freedom to refuse happiness extends even to the perfect happiness of the beatific vision. What reason, one wonders, could a person conceivably have for refusing? Ockham suggests that one might regard God as disadvantageous and refuse on those grounds. Of course, one would be mistaken in such a judgment; but as long as such a judgment is possible, the will could act in accordance with it. The physical suffering experienced by Christ is offered as evidence that God could be seen and rejected under the aspect of the disadvantageous, even by someone with a clear vision of his essence (*Ordinatio*, d. 1, q. 6 [308] *OTh* I 503–06).

Examining the thesis that whatever we will, we will under the aspect of the good, Ockham sees a need for clarification. If all one means by "good" is that which is desired or desirable, of course we always will under the aspect of the good. Thus interpreted, the Thomistic position becomes true but trivial. On the other hand, if one means by "good," either moral (*honestum*), useful, or pleasurable, the thesis must be rejected as false. A person can will an act she regards as good in none of these ways, even one that she herself correctly judges to be evil, such as worshiping false gods (*Quaestiones variae* 8 [308] *OTh* VIII 442–44).

Many philosophers would grant that someone can will an act he does not regard as morally good, useful, or pleasurable to the senses, yet insist that he must regard it as pleasurable in some other way, else he would have no motive whatsoever in acting. Ockham takes a very different view: that the pleasure we experience in willing X is an effect, not a cause, of willing X. We experience pleasure in loving someone precisely because we love. Although love and pleasure usually come combined, they are in reality separable (*Ordinatio*, d. 1, qq. 3 and 6; *Quodlibet* II, q. 17; [308] *OTh* I 403–28, 486–507; IX 186–88).[12] Far from needing the motivation of pleasure to love someone, we can love and continue loving without feeling pleasure. Once again Satan serves as a useful example. This fallen angel sinned by loving himself to excess, and he continues to love himself. The hell in which he lives forever is one where even self-love produces no pleasure (*Ordinatio*, d. 1, q. 3; [308] *OTh* I 411).

Ockham argues that the thesis, whatever we will, we will under the aspect of the good, must also be rejected because it undermines a distinction endorsed by all theologians, the distinction between sins done from ignorance and sins done from evil (*malitia*). Some might describe an ignorant sin as one done from ignorance of a moral principle; others might describe it as one done from ignorance of how the principle applies to the particular situation in which the agent finds himself. But if we cannot sin with knowledge of both the relevant principle and its present application, how is it possible to sin from evil (*Quaestiones variae*, q. 7, a. 3 [308] *OTh* VIII 365–66)?[13]

In his own account of sins from evil Ockham moves into much-contested territory. By 1285 the Paris theological faculty had officially approved the proposition: "There is no *malitia* in the will unless there is error or some lack of knowledge in reason."[14] Despite official approval, the proposition continued to trigger heated debate even at Paris. Perhaps some brief remarks about scholastic moral vocabulary can help to shed light on the conflict.

EVIL, BADNESS, VICE, AND SIN

In translating the *Nicomachean Ethics* Robert Grosseteste did his best to preserve the range of meaning of Aristotle's Greek. The words *hamartia* and *hamartema* are a case in point. They signify "missing the mark," falling short of a goal, or not measuring up according to some norm. The departure from the norm might be deliberate and deserving of moral reproach. Then again, it might be a technical misstep, such as an archer's failure to hit the target – evidence that he falls short of excellence as an archer, but in no way evidence that he falls short as a human being. Grosseteste's choice of *peccatum* as a translation was reasonable because the Latin word, too, can signify a nonmoral deviation from the norm. Using the term in this way, Aquinas called even a musician's mistake in performance a *peccatum*. He treated as morally bad acts only the subset of *peccata* through which the agent incurs guilt (*culpa*).[15] Other theologians, such as Ockham, who used *peccatum* in a more restricted, specifically moral sense, still applied it to a wide range of actions. All would agree (say) that someone who takes ballpoint pens from the office for her private use at home, sincerely but mistakenly believing that she is not stealing, has committed a *peccatum*, if only from ignorance. Someone with disordered appetites who succumbs to the temptation to eat more than he judges appropriate would likewise be seen as committing a *peccatum*, if only from weakness or passion.

Most of today's English-speakers either avoid the word *sin* entirely or they reserve it for deliberate, heinous moral offenses, typically involving injury to others. The conventional translation of *peccatum* as "sin" therefore tends to mislead, even in its strictly religious meaning. Recognizing that Cicero had written much about what is and is not a *peccatum* – even before Grosseteste's Aristotle entered the picture – medieval authors saw themselves as continuing and extending a moral dialogue begun in antiquity, not as changing the topic to one that only Christians, Jews, and Muslims could understand and believe worth debating.

Scholastics classified sins in many different ways. They distinguished between the original sin all humans inherited from Adam and the actual sins one commits strictly as an individual. They divided sins according to seriousness and related punishment, distinguishing venial ("pardonable") sins from the mortal sins that represent a decisive turning away from God, break the relationship with him, and result in damnation unless God chooses to renew the relationship. They distinguished between ignorance, passion, and *malitia* – in increasing order of gravity – as internal, psychological sources of sin. Finally, they distinguished between sins and vices, treating the first as actions and the second as the settled dispositions that incline a person to such actions.

In translating the Greek *kakia*, an abstract noun derived from the adjective *bad* (*kakos*), Grosseteste again sought to preserve the non-moral sense of the word. He opted for the Latin *malitia*, an abstract noun derived from the adjective *bad* (*malus*), probably intending it to be read as "badness" or perhaps as "evil" in the widest sense of the word.[16] His readers had no trouble recognizing natural badness (or evil, as in the evils of sickness or natural disasters), as well as the badness of moral character. They divided sharply, however, on Aristotle's account of sinning from *malitia*. Some supported the thesis that everyone who sins from *malitia* is somehow ignorant of what he ought to do. Others believed this was so much intellectualizing neopaganism. The denial that we can do wrong knowingly was judged tantamount to the denial we can sin from evil. To will evil without the urging of passion or any error whatsoever by the mind was, in Scotus's words, "the fullest meaning of sin" (*Opus Oxoniense* II, d. 43, q. 2; [288] 478).

The seven deadly sins

In the form best-known today, the list of seven deadly sins runs: "pride, covetousness, lust, anger, gluttony, envy, and sloth." Presumed to be a roster of sins leading to damnation, it might appear to prove that people in the Middle Ages had bizarre values. Why are gluttony and sloth included when far better candidates, such as treachery and injustice, are not? Why this particular order, where lust ranks after only pride and covetousness for deadliness?[17]

Even thirteenth-century professors found the list perplexing, although they had the good fortune to receive an older, more coherent version of it. The version most familiar to them, developed by Gregory the Great and included in Peter Lombard's *Sentences*, names principal or capital vices, not deadly sins, and runs from "spiritual" vices, considered the most serious, to vices somehow related to the flesh.[18] Pride, envy, and anger come first, covetousness, gluttony, and lust at the end, with the vice of *acedia* (alias "sloth") in the middle. Dante's *Purgatory* follows exactly the same order.

The expression "deadly sins" most often appears in medieval popular literature, sermons, and guides for confessors. After 1215, when the church required laypeople to make an annual confession, they needed instruction in identifying and remembering their sins. The scheme of seven, originally developed for monastic education, was adapted for this wider practical purpose and enjoyed a long, successful career – except in universities, where it was found so hard to rationalize that by the early fourteenth century the effort was mostly abandoned.

Objections already suggested by Bonaventure's commentary on the *Sentences* (1250–52) became fairly standard in the late thirteenth century. The seven capital vices cannot be modeled on "capital" crimes, for if these were the vices most deserving of punishment, faithlessness would be among them. The list of seven, however, includes no vice opposed to the virtue of faith, just as it includes none opposed to the virtue of hope. Considering vices as extremes of excess and deficiency, pairs opposed to some virtuous "mean," the list of seven capital vices still makes no sense. Why does it include covetousness (or greed: *avaritia*) but not prodigality? Why seven vices instead of fourteen (II *Sent.*, q. 42, *dubium* 3)?

Trying to rationalize the scheme of seven, Bonaventure suggests that a vice is called "capital" because it gives rise psychologically to a great many sins, like a prolific head of family. He proceeds with an account of how each of the seven vices warps the soul's response to some perceived good. Aquinas, too, appeals to psychological fecundity, offering his own account of distortions (*ST* IaIIae, q. 84, a. 4). Alas, neither these nor other proposed rationales could resolve the greatest problem with the scheme of seven. At a time when moral theorizing was virtue-centered, the list of seven vices simply did not correspond with any list of seven virtues agreed to have special importance. The list reflected an older approach: identifying troublesome vices, then presenting virtues as remedies for them. Despite its continued popularity with preachers, the idea of virtues as correctives for vices had lost favor in theological circles. Floating free of the virtue-centered framework and pinned only to dubious claims about psychological causality, the seven capital vices did not survive much longer as a topic of even perfunctory academic interest.

VIRTUES, THEOLOGICAL AND OTHER

Augustine's view of all true virtues as gifts of grace itself fell from grace in the twelfth century. Peter Abelard was apparently the first to challenge it. Influenced by Cicero's writings and Boethius's commentary on Aristotle's *Categories*, Abelard revived classical talk of virtues as dispositions (*habitus*): qualities that human beings develop gradually, from practice in exercising our natural powers, so that they become "second nature" and very difficult to change (Abelard, *Ethics* II). I say classical "talk" because both Abelard and later twelfth-century theologians extended the concept of a disposition to include virtues given by God, even to infants through the sacramental grace of baptism.[19] By the late thirteenth century, when Grosseteste's translation of Aristotle was required reading in the universities, professors routinely classified all virtues as dispositions – not only the virtues that even pagans can acquire through many years of practice, but also virtues like charity, divinely "infused" in Christians as gifts of grace.[20] This peculiar concept of a disposition, alien to classical philosophy, became entrenched in scholastic moral theory.

Although the list of acquired virtues came to include virtually all of those discussed by Aristotle, theologians often followed the Stoics and the church fathers in awarding special status to the "cardinal" virtues of prudence, justice, temperance, and fortitude. Accepting Aristotle's division of virtues into the "intellectual" and the "moral," scholastics treated prudence as the sole intellectual virtue among the cardinals. The three infused virtues most discussed were faith, hope, and charity, all called "theological" virtues because of their direction to God and the happiness of the afterlife.[21] Aquinas and his followers posited infused prudence and moral virtues in addition to the infused theological virtues. Scotus, Ockham, and others, while faulting Thomists for positing virtues beyond necessity, themselves ventured to posit naturally acquired faith and charity.

Why so many kinds of virtues? Later medieval theologians sought to explain what makes someone morally good in the present life as well as what it takes to "merit" the complete happiness possible only with God in the afterlife. All agreed that nobody merits eternal happiness in the way that a good, hard worker would merit his wages. All agreed that God's grace, in one form or another, constitutes the indispensable foundation for merit. There nonetheless remained ample room for debate about different forms of grace and related forms of merit. The grounds for debate were all the wider because even those with serious reservations about Aristotle's teachings usually incorporated some of his insights into their own work.[22] Attempts to develop a synthesis of ancient and Christian moral thought became the norm, with much controversy about how the theory should go but relatively little about whether the effort was worthwhile.

Far from trying to end the synthetic project, the episcopal condemnation at Paris in 1277 left academic theorists free to continue working on it. The bishop's wrath was directed mainly at young philosophy professors who highlighted conflicts between ancient and Christian ethics, giving the impression that Christian teachings were either erroneous or to be accepted purely on faith. Thus we find among the 219 propositions condemned: "That happiness is had in this life and not in another"; and "That happiness cannot be caused directly by God." The first leaves open the possibility that happiness is had both in this life and in another, as the second leaves open the possibility that happiness is directly caused both by God and by the human agent.[23]

Augustine would have worried that the condemnations were far too weak, leaving the university open to the siren song of pagan ethics. He would have had grounds for worry. The medieval church never adopted wholesale the moral doctrines of Augustine's anti-Pelagian writings. Not until the late sixteenth century did Rome clarify its official position on pagan virtues. By that point the sharp dichotomy between Christians under grace and everyone else had become strongly associated with the Protestant reformers, Martin Luther and John Calvin, and their growing ranks of disciples. The medieval tradition, shaped by Aquinas and Scotus, distinguished between the moral goodness even pagans might have and the meritorious goodness dependent strictly upon God's grace. Pope Pius V accordingly condemned a Catholic theology professor for teaching, "All the deeds of unbelievers are sins, and all the virtues of philosophers are vices."[24]

Even when they agreed that we can develop true virtues without God's saving grace, scholastics often disagreed about the place of these naturally acquired virtues in a full account of the moral life. A brief sketch of the different positions taken by Aquinas and Scotus may serve as an introduction to some of the issues that arose in the effort to explain what, if anything, good moral character has to do with attaining happiness in the company of God.

Aquinas: God-given moral virtues

Like virtually all professors of the period, Aquinas considered original sin less morally debilitating than Augustine had. Aquinas never doubts that human beings can develop true virtues without God's gift of charity. On the other hand, a close reading of the *Summa theologiae* reveals that these naturally acquired virtues play a far more modest role than one might expect. Consider, for example, Aquinas's treatment of a standard textbook definition of virtue: "Virtue is a good quality of the mind, by which we live rightly, of which no one makes bad use, which God works in us, without us."[25] Aquinas supports the definition, but with two suggested revisions: that "disposition" be substituted for "quality," and that the last phrase be omitted, to make the definition cover all virtues, both acquired and infused (*ST* IaIIae, q. 55, a. 4). Both revisions, especially coming after a treatise on dispositions heavily indebted to Aristotle's work, might lead readers to assume that acquired virtues figure prominently in Aquinas's own moral theory. Only later in the *Prima secundae* do we learn that Aquinas regards the infused virtue of charity as the "form" of all the virtues and that he posits an entire set of moral virtues infused by God together with charity. God-given moral virtues are virtues without qualification. Naturally acquired moral virtues are inherently imperfect (or incomplete: *imperfectus*), virtues in merely a relative, analogous sense. They differ in kind from God-given moral virtues (q. 63, aa. 3–4; q. 65, aa. 2–3).

It would be difficult to exaggerate the difference between these two kinds of moral virtues. Acquired moral virtues are directed to the imperfect happiness of earthly society and make one morally good in human terms. Infused moral virtues are directed to, and make it possible to merit, the perfect happiness of the afterlife. Acquired moral virtues measure desires and actions according to the rule of human reason, observing a mean determined by prudence. Infused moral virtues measure according to divine rule, observing a "mean" appointed by God. (For example, where human reason dictates that we eat in such a way as to avoid harming our bodies or impairing our ability to reason, God decrees that we mortify the flesh by abstinence.) Acquired moral virtues make related actions easier; infused moral virtues do not. Acquired moral virtues are lost only through a series of bad actions; infused moral virtues can be destroyed by

a single act. As acquired moral virtues are developed naturally, so
they can be increased naturally, through our own efforts. Infused
moral virtues, supernaturally caused by God, can be increased only
by God. Nobody can acquire a single moral virtue without prudence,
nor can one acquire prudence without all of the moral virtues. The
only unqualified moral virtues, however, are gifts of grace rooted in
charity, not prudence. A Christian might have all of these infused
virtues without acquiring any moral virtues through her own natural resources (*ST* IaIIae, q. 63, a. 4; q. 65, aa. 2–3; IIaIIae, q. 23, aa. 7–8;
De virtutibus in communi, q. 10, ad 14).

Aquinas considers charity essential for unqualified moral virtue
on teleological grounds. A person lacking charity can never attain the
ultimate end of perfect happiness. At the same time, Aquinas follows
Augustine in relating the need for charity to the self-centeredness of
fallen humanity. Original sin has so corrupted human nature that,
without grace, we inevitably favor our private goods. Even when
we perform virtuous acts, we perform them from inferior motives,
not from the kind of love possible for human nature in its original
condition. Without charity, then, no one can keep the commandment
to love God above all else (*ST* IaIIae, q. 109, aa. 3–4).

Believing that we need charity to transform our moral characters,
Aquinas argues that this virtue must be a God-given disposition, not
simply the Holy Spirit working in us. If there were no change in the
agent's disposition, he reasons, human acts of charity would be involuntary, with God as the sole efficient cause and the human being
as merely an instrument of God's will. Acts of charity would then
be God's acts and in no way the human individual's own. By the
same token, it would be impossible for someone to perform charitable acts with ease and pleasure. An individual can experience ease
and pleasure only when acting as she is internally disposed to act,
when the actions are "second nature," even if the second nature was
itself supernaturally caused (*ST* IIaIIae, q. 23, a. 2).[26]

Scotus: perfectly moral pagans

As we have seen, Scotus believes that the ability to love others according to their intrinsic worth belongs to the inalienable freedom
of the human will. He believes, too, that "ought" implies "can."
Because fallen human beings without grace are still obligated to love

our neighbors as ourselves and God above all, we must be able to do so, even if we cannot do so as perfectly as someone can in the afterlife. Scotus offers as evidence for his position the willingness of pagans to die in battle for the good of their countries. Someone acting according to natural reason can correctly judge the public good to be a greater good than his own life, can simply love it more and will more to preserve it than his own life. In the same way such a person could judge God the greatest good and love God above all else (*Ordinatio* III, supplement d. 27; [288] 434–40).[27]

True, naturally acquired moral virtues are imperfect in the absence of infused charity in the sense that they do not lead to the end of perfect happiness. On the other hand, Scotus argues, they can still be perfect as moral virtues. One does not need God-given charity to become a perfectly moral human being, only to become a perfectly happy one. However good we make ourselves, eternal happiness remains, as Augustine taught, a free gift of God (*Ordinatio* III, supplement d. 36; [288] 414–16).

Why does moral theory even need to posit virtuous dispositions infused by God? As Scotus sees no reason why one should need such a disposition to perform a charitable act, so he sees no reason why one should need it to perform a charitable act with promptness, ease, and pleasure. Nor is there anything in our experience to prove the existence of some God-given charity, for the same actions and motives might be explained by the naturally acquired virtue of friendship. If the aim is to explain why God grants some persons rather than others eternal happiness, the correct answer, to Scotus's mind, is just that God chose to do so. Infused virtues cannot explain why God chose these persons, because the virtues themselves are free gifts of grace. If God has in fact ordained that infused virtues are necessary to merit salvation, he could have, by his absolute power, dispensed with them. There is nothing about such virtues that makes them intrinsically necessary for salvation. They have the status of secondary causes through which God has chosen to operate, so that their causal role arises strictly from the covenant he freely chose to make with humankind.[28]

Should one protest that God has, on this account, chosen a more elaborate scheme of salvation than he had to choose, Scotus would gladly agree: God often acts more generously than frugally. Ockham repeated and expanded Scotus's arguments against the theoretical necessity of positing virtuous dispositions infused by God. He, too, declared it possible to love God above all through one's own natural resources. He, too, labored to show that no infused virtuous disposition is intrinsically or ontologically necessary. God-given charity is necessary only because of the covenant God chose to make, but could have, by his absolute power, refrained from making (III *Sent.* q. 9 [308] *OTh* VI 279–82). Again, the aim was to emphasize God's generosity in making a covenant that he can be relied upon to keep – not because he would be unjust to violate it, as if he "owed" it to us, but because God is consistently generous, so that he "owes it to himself" to keep the promises he has made.[29]

Martin Luther, trained in the theological tradition associated with Ockham, would later conclude that infused virtues are not even *de facto* necessary for salvation. He would dismiss the whole theoretical apparatus of God-given dispositions as so much more evidence of the disastrous influence of Aristotle, that spawn of Satan, on the whole of scholastic theology. Scotus and Ockham have accordingly come to be cast as paving the way for Lutheranism, notwithstanding such obvious differences from Luther as that both scholastics developed theories heavily shaped by their belief in the inalienable human freedom to make ourselves morally good (albeit not happy), which Luther went so far in denying that even Aquinas ends up looking, by comparison, like a quasi-Pelagian defender of the "virtuous pagan."

NOTES

1. See chapter 11 in this volume.
2. *City of God* V 19–20, XV 22, XIX 1–4, 25; *Answer to Julian* IV 19–23 [57]. My summary rests mainly upon Augustine's later writings. P. Brown's biography [66] remains the best account of how Augustine's thinking developed over the course of his long, tumultuous life.
3. *PL* 38, 808–14. All translations in this chapter are my own. For this sermon, cf. Augustine, *Sermons*, trans. E. Hill (New Rochelle, 1992), 30–39.
4. R. Markus [418] 54.
5. B. Kent *CCAug* 205–33 provides a more detailed treatment of Augustine's moral thought. See J. Rist [76] for a good survey of his views on issues beyond those directly related to morals.
6. W. O'Connor [74] offers insightful analysis of Augustine's perspective on these questions.

7. Anselm's argument that the capacity to sin or not to sin essentially requires the freedom to choose either happiness or justice should not be misread as claiming that the freedom to choose either happiness or justice essentially requires, let alone is, the capacity to sin or not to sin. Believing that God is both free and unable to sin, Anselm firmly rejects the second thesis. However much Scotus and Kant differ from him (and each other), both follow Anselm in defending the first thesis while rejecting the second.

8. See chapter 9 in this volume.

9. See S. MacDonald [250].

10. See J. Boler [290].

11. See M. Ingham [295].

12. Cf. A. S. McGrade [319].

13. See also Ockham [317] 124–27, 242–43.

14. Drawn from the works of Giles of Rome, the proposition was regarded as one that Aquinas had also defended. See Giles of Rome [269] 110–17 and 179–224 for an account of related controversies at Paris.

15. *ST* IaIIae, q. 21, a. 1; *De malo* q. 2, a. 2. D. Gallagher [241] gives a clear explanation of both Aquinas's terminology and relevant conceptual distinctions.

16. English translations of the *Nicomachean Ethics* are more misleading in this respect. Even when they present the Greek *arete* as "excellence," instead of "virtue," they routinely present *kakia* and related words as "vice." This mysterious fondness for the word "vice" tends to obscure the continuity between Aristotle's teachings on nature and his teachings on ethics, a continuity evident to scholastic readers of Grosseteste's translation.

17. Scholarly literature on the seven deadly sins has lately grown to be quite extensive. "Classic" studies include M. Bloomfield [554] and S. Wenzel [563–64]. Wenzel's work is especially helpful in tracing the development of what came to be called, in the English of the King James Bible, the failing of "sloth."

18. See Gregory's *Moralia in Iob*, XXXI, ch. 45, *PL* 76, 620–23 and Peter Lombard, II *Sent.* d. 42, ch. 6.

19. See O. Lottin [21] III, section 2, part 1; C. Nederman [560]; and M. Colish [555].

20. The chief scriptural basis for infused virtues was Romans 5:5. In discussing how we are "justified" by faith, Paul says that "God's love has been poured [*diffusus*] into our hearts through the Holy Spirit which has been given to us." Although scholastics adopted *infusus* as the standard adjective, the watery imagery was the same. Hence Aquinas's description of God as the "common well-spring" of happiness quoted above.

21. See Paul's moving description in 1 Corinthians 13, ending: "So faith, hope, love [*caritas*] abide, these three; but the greatest of these is love."

22. For explanation of later medieval debates about moral goodness and merit I recommend the work of D. Janz [556] and A. McGrath [559] I 12–16, 40–50, 100–19. McGrath is exceptionally good at explaining conceptual changes and tensions, especially between Aristotle's notion of justice and Christian-theological accounts of "justification."

23. See B. Kent [558] 68–79 for references to primary sources and further discussion of condemned propositions related to ethics, including those concerning the freedom of the will.

24. The condemnation of Michael du Bay, reported in H. Denzinger [24] 427–37 (see especially no. 1925), makes for interesting reading. A good many of his errors can be found not only in Augustine's works but also in Paul's Epistles. Du Bay could hardly have chosen a less auspicious juncture to disdain the scholastics and call for a return to the teachings of Paul and the Fathers.

25. The definition, included in Peter Lombard's *Sentences* (II, d. 27, c. 5), is pieced together from various remarks by Augustine.

26. Secondary literature on Aquinas's moral thought often leaves much to be desired in both accuracy and interest. R. McInerny's book [252] and the essays in S. MacDonald and E. Stump [251] seem to me among the most philosophically engaging of recent contributions. S. Pope [257] provides helpful guidance in reading *Summa theologiae* II. This anthology includes an explanation of structure and method, as well as a series of expository essays on this long, difficult text.

27. Later medieval disputes about the natural ability to love God often include fascinating discussions of self-love, self-sacrifice, and other knotty topics in moral psychology. For a good example see the exchange between Godfrey of Fontaines and James of Viterbo in *CT* II 271–306.

28. *Ordinatio* I, d. 17, part 1, qq. 1–2 [281] I, especially 200–03, 215; *Quodlibetal Questions* 17.30–34 [283] 397–98.

29. There is now a wealth of scholarly literature on the later medieval background for Luther's theology. Works by P. Vignaux [562] and H. Oberman [561] are classics in the field. A. McGrath [559] figures among more recent contributions of substance.

11   Ultimate goods: happiness, friendship, and bliss

Reflection upon human happiness was pursued by a number of the greatest thinkers of the Middle Ages, working sometimes as theologians, primarily at least, and sometimes as philosophers, though in more than one sense of the word. The most notable theories of what happiness is and how human beings may obtain it were formulated by three very great minds: Augustine of Hippo, Boethius, and Thomas Aquinas. I will explore the ideas of each of these and will also examine a short treatise on happiness and the philosophical life by Boethius of Dacia (*fl.* 1270), since it strikes a note of contrast with its most notable predecessors. Other significant writers and thematic developments will also be touched on.

Friendship belongs intimately to happiness. All ancient schools of philosophy would have maintained this, even though each one placed the emphases just as seemed appropriate in view of its own characteristic approach to philosophy. Thinkers of the medieval period would not have disagreed about the close connection between friendship and happiness. Sometimes that relationship was made explicit (in particular by Augustine and Aelred of Rievaulx), but sometimes it was left unthematized. The account given here will be led by the texts. I will discuss happiness and friendship together in examining the thought of Augustine, who interrelates the two themes on more than one notable occasion. In considering Boethius and Aquinas, I will for the most part treat each topic separately.

Both themes came to medieval thinkers from two different sources, ancient philosophy and Christianity, and there was no secret about that. To take an example: Augustine was fully alive to the difference between the biblical notions of happiness developed in Psalms or in the Beatitudes (Matthew 5), on the one hand, and the treatises on the highest good/happiness and the highest evil written by Varro or Cicero, on the other. For his purposes (e.g., pastoral autobiography in *Confessions* or Christian apologetic in *The City of God*) he felt free to develop his thought in reliance upon both kinds of source. If Augustine thus felt the influence of each – the ancient pre-Christian wisdom search and biblical, especially New Testament, faith – it should not be assumed either that he intended to make a syncretistic hybrid out of his source reading, or that he wound up doing so. The notion of critical discernment fits better the outcome of his reflection.

AUGUSTINE AND THE UNIVERSAL DESIRE FOR HAPPINESS

Happiness is one of Augustine's lifelong themes. The topic recurs in most of his writings, in different literary genres, with new aspects and perspectives, or with retouches made to already familiar thoughts. His two most insistently recurring ideas are that all human beings without exception desire to be happy, whatever their circumstances, choices, or commitments, and that everything each one does is prompted by this deepest of desires and expresses it in some way. His second overriding conviction is that no thing and no person can fulfill one's desire for happiness; no experience, no object of desire, even when attained, can make one completely, reliably happy – not even the highest ideal open to humankind, such as the search for wisdom and the love of it. His earliest reflections on *beatitudo* are to be found in a dialogue written in 386, *On the Happy Life (De beata vita)*. The theme turns up in three of the four great works of his maturity: *Confessions*, *Commentary on the Psalms*, and *The City of God*. I will focus upon his discussions of happiness and friendship in *Confessions* and *The City of God*.

Happiness and truth as a priori ideas

Confessions, Book X is a search for God, who is both beyond and within the creation. The action that connects the transitions which Augustine makes is expressed repeatedly by the verb *transibo*: "I will go beyond" – in order to search for God, the absolute goal of love. The created world in its beauty cries out: "He made us!" (X 6). The soul, however, is superior in its nature to the world, since it is the source of life for the body (X 7). *Transibo*: above the life-giving power of the soul, and beyond the capacity to perceive which it confers on the body (a capacity which is shared with the souls of animals), there is the mind, or the self (X 7). In the memory are stocked images of all kinds, which have been brought in by sense perception. There I meet myself "and recall what I am, what I have done, and how I was affected when I did it" (X 8). Memory is a power that contains more than the images of sense perception. Ideas, mathematical objects, affective experience, and even forgetfulness are all somehow present in it (X 16). "Great is the power of memory . . . a power of profound and infinite multiplicity. And this is my mind, this is I myself!" (X 17).

But *transibo*! "As I rise above memory where am I to find You?" What is it that lies at the very bottom of mental and affective life, at the deepest preconscious level? What *a priori* forms or ideas shape all that one does? Augustine believes that two quasi-ideas, happiness and truth, give coherence to our entire mental and affective life, in ways of which we are not fully conscious and which it does not lie in our power to alter. Everything we think, desire, or do is structured by these two primal instincts and is expressive of them. When they come together, when we find "joy in the truth" (*gaudium de veritate*), the presence of the absent, transcendent God becomes tangible (X 23). This is the nonlocative "place" (*locus non locus!*) which God occupies within every mind, he who is "immutably above all things" (X 25). Once God is revealed by his own power as "the Beauty ever ancient and ever new," he is recognized by the memory as the transcendent presence that comes to fill the space created within the mind and memory by "joy coming from the truth" (X 27).

Augustine's meditation on memory is a spiritual exercise through which he seeks to mount within the contents of consciousness, from level to level, in order to identify the presence of God within the soul by means of self-knowledge. The better he knows himself, the more he appreciates God's transcendence of his creature. Yet God has left at the deepest point of human self-consciousness a distinctive mark of presence that corresponds to his transcendence, namely that joy in the truth which is completely ineradicable (Augustine believes) from the human mind and memory.[1]

Friendship and happiness

The themes of friendship and happiness are conjugated by Augustine in two writings, the *Confessions* and *The City of God*. Friendship is depicted as a source of intense happiness, and at the same time the space of misery and grief when a friend dies, or of anxiety for the living who are vulnerable to all kinds of insecurity and prey to many evils and sufferings. Augustine brings out the positive value of the classical ideal and practice of friendship (he even uses Cicero's definition of *amicitia* as "agreement in all things, divine and human, together with good will and affection"), but he believes that the Christian values of trust in God, belief in providence, acceptance of the inevitability of death, concern for the good of people who are not particularly virtuous or strong, readiness to forgive, and firm hope in true happiness in the heavenly vision of God reveal a higher way. He therefore proposes a practice of friendship that would be free from illusion regarding moral vulnerability and physical death, exempt from any idolization of the persons we love, realistic about tragedy, and ready to show goodwill in some way to all, out of a sense of humility and of common vulnerability. In these ways he at once acknowledges the classical friendship ideal, which he had lived out in his early years, and at the same time develops a Christian theory of friendship and love in which faith, hope, and charity are accorded their fullest value.

Friendship, happiness, and death are interwoven in the narrative of Augustine's life and loss at around age 20, when he experienced the death of a close friend of the same age. Looking back as autobiographer, twenty-five or so years later, he concluded that the terrible misery of grief he underwent, his depression and his nihilistic sense that death destroys all human value, were due to his "having loved a mortal as though he would never die" (*Confessions* IV 6). Happiness should, he thought, lie in loving friends with a sense of mortality that alone allows the precious value of each present moment to be savored. Such happiness, he considered, cannot be had without faith in God's providential love and in eternal life. He composed a personal beatitude out of phrases of Scripture. "Blessed is the person who loves you, and his friend in you, and his enemy because of you" (IV 9). Friendship, happiness and misery, and mortality are again interrelated at *Confessions* VI 16.

Book XIX of *The City of God* considers the different and contrasting ways in which the final end of human life was delineated
by the ancient philosophers (whose views on the matter Augustine
knew through Varro and Cicero) and by Christianity. Is the highest
goal of human accomplishment and striving to be found in pleasure,
or virtue, or some combination of the two; in an active life or one
of contemplation, or again a mixture of the two? Varro set out, in
all, 298 variations on these notions of happiness. Augustine, on the
other hand, insisted on the vulnerable and contingent nature of life
and happiness. How many ills and misfortunes there are, such as injustice, war, personal miseries and mistakes, sickness and insanity,
that infiltrate insecurity into the center of human experience! The
"unfeigned loyalty and mutual love of true friends" (XIX 8) is the best
source of happiness that this life offers, yet even here, happiness and
misery mix and mingle in the most ambiguous way. No utopia of
peace and contentment is available this side of self-deception and
illusion. The more friends we have the more concern we experience
regarding the ills that may afflict them, or that may cause us hurt
and heartbreak through them. At the death of each of them solace
and delight turn to sadness and grief. The lesson Augustine wants
to teach is, not to become unfeeling toward friends and live in a
castle of self-protection, but rather to affirm all reality, in both joy
and pain, as the expression of an only partially visible providential
order, within which the city of God, at present wayfaring on earth,
is being prepared for everlasting peace. If we accept that we are pil-
grims on a way of faith and hope, then we can be reasonably happy
despite all that may befall us, partly because life has so many good
things to offer, but mostly because we have the hope of unshakeable,
unconditional blessedness to look forward to (XIX 20).

Readers of *The City of God* throughout the Middle Ages and the
early Renaissance (Erasmus, Thomas More) absorbed its message
about happiness, friendship, and the life of the blessed. The happiness of heaven may be thought of as the fullness of friendship,
the Cistercian monk Aelred of Rievaulx (d. 1167) suggested (*Spiritual Friendship* III 79), while friendship in the present life, despite
its limitations, offers an experiential foretaste of the joys of heaven.
He developed here an authentically Augustinian idea. His contemporary, Anselm of Canterbury, thought along the same lines (*Proslogion*
25). Aelred referred to the joys of heaven using *felicitas* and *beatitudo* synonymously. In the later Middle Ages the former term would

tend to be employed somewhat more frequently in philosophical discussion as the general term for happiness, under the influence of the Latin version of Aristotle's *Nicomachean Ethics*, while *beatitudo* tended to be used more specifically for the ultimate blessedness of eternal life.

The strength of Augustine's thought lay in his capacity to be true to experience, especially in its affective heights and depths. He tried to remove all the brackets that had been placed around portions of experience (in particular, of his own) and to acknowledge the ambivalence of choice with regard to good and evil. When writing about friendship and love he thought also about misery, obsession, and illusion. His reading of the human condition is clear-sighted regarding the fragmented and wounded state of the heart, but hope is sustained by the conviction that creation is good and that suffering can have a redemptive meaning.

BOETHIUS: PHILOSOPHY HAS ITS CONSOLATIONS

"Augustine was an African, a psychologist and a saint; Boethius was a Roman and a scholar."[2] Manlius Severinus Boethius (d. 524) was imprisoned during the last year of his life by the Germanic ruler of Italy on a false accusation of high treason. His *Consolation of Philosophy* is one of the greatest examples of prison literature. Boethius spent his imprisonment under the threat of death and was eventually brutally executed. He sought, through writing, to obtain "consolation" (*consolatio* was a genre which traditionally offered solace to the *friends* of the dead). In this connection he appealed to the memory of Socrates and of certain Roman Stoics, whom he regarded as innocent fellow-victims of tyranny. Thomas More would in turn recall the *Consolation* when suffering similar tribulation.

The work is a sustained meditation upon the unjust suffering of the innocent. How is it possible, if indeed it is possible, to be happy while imprisoned and awaiting death? Boethius sought comfort in philosophy, "whose house I had from youth frequented" (I 3). He made an extensive and very artistic survey of all that was best and noblest in ancient philosophy: artistic, because conceived in alternating passages of prose and meter. The work takes the form of a dialogue between Philosophy, who appears to him in the form of a majestic woman, and Boethius's own mind. Philosophy is at first obliged to reacquaint the suffering, complaining prisoner with the

messages he has forgotten – through forgetfulness of his real self
(I 2). True freedom cannot be abolished by manacles, for it is internal.
The real blessings of life (family and friends) are not to be forgotten
in adversity but are a source of happy memories. Happiness does not
lie outside the person in the goods of fortune, but within a free mind
that is in command of itself and that in turn cannot be overpowered
by any outside force.

In Book II the question of true happiness (*felicitas*) is centrally addressed. Philosophy argues that happiness is "the good which once
a man obtains it leaves room for no further desires" (III 2), since
all goods are gathered together in it. The good is often thought to
lie in wealth, honor, power, glory, or pleasure (or else in some ad-
mixture of these five sources of satisfaction). Philosophy challenges
each one of these. The possession of wealth does not exclude anxiety. Honor and advancement are not instillers of virtue (but how
can there be happiness without virtue?). Power, as Boethius himself
needs no reminding (III 5), and even the power of kings, is insecure,
and it attracts only fair-weather friends. Glory is deceptive: it does
not lead to wisdom or self-knowledge. Pleasure is shared by man
with the beasts. There is no happiness in these vain promises. On
the other hand, full happiness will combine all these five imperfect
goods by including them (III 9, prose). But where is such happiness
to be sought? Not within this universe or world. Boethius prays for
God's help in the search, as Plato frequently did in his dialogues. In
the poem concluding III 9, the most beautiful passage in Boethius's
writings, the message of the *Timaeus* is set out. Cosmos and soul are
both expressions of the transcendent, divine Good. Happiness will
consist in participating in the Good, which is God:

> Grant, Father, to my mind to rise to your majestic seat,
> Grant me to wander by the source of good, grant light to see,
> To fix the clear sight of my mind on you.
> Disperse the clouding heaviness of this earthly mass
> And flash forth in your brightness. For, to the blessed, *you*
> Are clear serenity and quiet rest: to see *you* is their goal,
> You, at once beginning, driver, leader, pathway, end.

The rest of the book is occupied by a lengthy argument to show
that the universe is ruled by God and that God can do no evil. Book IV
examines the apparent triumph of vice over virtue, and power over

goodness, but shows that this cannot be the final truth. Boethius takes up the argument of Plato's *Gorgias* (507C). He becomes reconciled, through the use of reason in dialogue with Philosophy, to the conclusion that providence rules the whole universe and extends to the individual. Book V is devoted to the discussion of the highest questions about providence and human freedom.

We can see here a movement from Stoic to Platonic themes and dialectic. Book III forms the hinge. There is a parallel movement from virtue to contemplation ("seeing") as the central element in happiness. Boethius knew the texts of Plato and Aristotle at first hand, and he was well read in later Greek Neoplatonism. His *Consolation* draws upon all these sources and seeks to produce a unified thought that would take in all the highest ethical and metaphysical developments of Antiquity.

But why did that believing Christian, when examining the problem posed by innocent suffering, of patience, providence, and fulfillment, not consider in the first place Job, or Jesus Christ? Why is there no explicitly Christian element in the *Consolation*? Various considerations suggest that he was working according to a program and following out his own early training in philosophy at Athens. Some words used in the *Consolation* do seem to resonate with the Latin versions of the Bible, even though no quotation is made from that source. The work amounts to an apology for providence and the divine government of the universe and human affairs, but one that takes place nevertheless entirely within the ambit of ancient philosophy.

It was in the ages of faith that the *Consolation* was most deeply and constantly appreciated. The favorable reception of this work of pure philosophy throughout the medieval period had the effect of suggesting that there is a single, true account of man and the universe under a provident God, the validity of which rests in all essentials upon principles of reason developed by the ancient philosophers. In this regard Boethius had a huge impact on the faith–reason problematic of the medieval schools.

THOMAS AQUINAS

Aquinas discussed happiness, together with the other great questions of philosophy and theology, in several different works, including his

Sentences commentary and the *Summa contra Gentiles*. His ideas on the subject are set forth in their most mature form in *Summa theologiae* IaIIae, qq. 1–5, written in his last years. This set of five questions concerns the general nature of life's ultimate purpose (q. 1) and the particular conception of complete happiness (*beatitudo*, blessedness, bliss) which Aquinas proposes as meeting the requirements for such a purpose (qq. 2–5). We have here a relatively self-contained treatise that is arguably the most coherent account of its subject produced in medieval times or possibly in any past age. In it Aquinas made rigorous use of philosophical method in continuity with the best traditions of the ancient Greek and Latin philosophers. The setting of the treatise is, however, theological. *Beatitudo*, or the last end, is held to be the beatific vision of God. Like Augustine writing in *The City of God*, Aquinas thus produced a remarkable piece of Christian apologetics using tools fashioned by ancient philosophy.

It is being increasingly recognized that virtue ethics is central to Aquinas's moral thought and to his consideration of the characteristic capacities and achievements of human nature. His study and appreciation of the virtues links him firmly to Aristotle. Thomas endeavors to relate happiness to the moral and speculative virtues, arguing that *beatitudo* does not lie in bodily or material goods such as pleasure or wealth, but rather that the highest happiness attainable by human beings lies in the contemplation of truth.

Each of the questions in *ST* IaIIae 1–5 contains eight articles, so that in reality forty questions in all are asked and answered, together with the usual objections and replies that make up the dialectical character of Aquinas's thought. He sought to make clearer the reasonableness of the positions he adopted and to enrich his own grasp of truth by the deliberate inclusion of whatever truth was present in the objections put to him, or chosen by him.

Question 1 deals with the presupposition of all that follows, the assumption that there must in fact be a final end (goal, point) of human existence. Aquinas discusses here the distinctively human intentional and purposive activity in which our free attempts to identify and obtain the good unfold. He argues that everything humans will is willed for the sake of the good. Nothing can be desired or willed for being bad, but only for being an apparent (or subjectively registered) good. At the most general level, then, we necessarily seek

an ultimate good. In the following questions he takes up the ancient Platonic and Aristotelian inquiry into the true nature of that
good.

In the eight articles of question 2 he asks: does happiness lie (1)
in riches, (2) in honors, (3) in fame and glory, (4) in power, (5) in
bodily endowment, (6) in pleasure, (7) in any endowment of soul, or
(8) in any created good? In articles 1, 3, 4, and 6 it is from Boethius
that the authoritative view (*sed contra*) is drawn. Happiness cannot
consist in riches, because money is made for us, not we for money,
Aquinas argues. It cannot lie in honors because (with Aristotle) honor
is external to the person receiving it. Nor can happiness be identified
with glory, which is something extrinsic to the real worth of the
person. Power does not define it either, being morally ambivalent
and dependent upon virtue for its good use. The human body exists
for the sake of the soul and its specifically human activities, and so
it cannot in itself be the focus of happiness any more than sensory
pleasure can be. Happiness cannot be realized in any created good,
since by definition the latter cannot include everything the human
being can desire. It is, not surprisingly, to Augustine that Aquinas has
resort to express the conviction that only God, the complete good,
can satisfy the innate desire for *beatitudo*.

For Aquinas, however, the essential respect in which God constitutes our blessedness is in a direct vision of the divine nature, a
supreme *cognitive* activity, and here he must deal with an objection
from the standpoint of traditional Christian Platonism. The objection is that *beatitudo* must consist, not in an act of intellect but in
an act of the will, that is, in love. In article 4, Aquinas brings forward
five arguments for this position, two of them naming Augustine and
one of these quoting his claim that "Happy is he who has whatever he desires, and desires nothing amiss." As a basis for replying
to these arguments, Aquinas develops his own position as follows
(with a characteristic reappropriation of Augustine for his own view
at the end):

As stated above two things are needed for happiness: one, which is the
essence of happiness: the other, that is, as it were, its proper accident, i.e.,
the delight connected with it. I say, then, that as to the very essence of happiness, it is impossible for it to consist in an act of will. For it is evident
from what has been said that happiness is the attainment of the last end.
But the attainment of the end does not consist in the very act of the will. For

the will is directed to the end, both absent, when it desires it; and present, when it is delighted by resting therein. Now it is evident that the desire itself of the end is not the attainment of the end, but is a movement toward the end: while delight comes to the will from the end being present, and not conversely – a thing is not made present by the fact that the will delights in it. Therefore, that the end be present to him who desires it, must be due to something else than an act of the will.

This is evidently the case in regard to ends perceptible by the senses. For if the acquisition of money were through an act of the will, the covetous man would have it from the very moment that he wished for it. But at that moment it is far from him; and he attains it by grasping it in his hand, or in some like manner; and then he delights in the money got. And so it is with an intelligible end. For at first we desire to attain an intelligible end; we attain it, through its being made present to us by an act of the intellect; and then the delighted will rests in the end when attained.

So, therefore, the essence of happiness consists in an act of the intellect: but the delight that results from happiness pertains to the will. In this sense Augustine says that happiness is *joy in truth*, because, to wit, joy itself is the consummation of happiness. (*ST* IaIIae, q. 3, a. 4)

The value of friendship enters the discussion at the end of question 4. "Does happiness call for the companionship of friends?" (a. 8). Aquinas respects common sense in such matters. He maintains that for the conditional sort of happiness one can hope for during earthly life (where health of body and soul and some degree of possessions are relevant conditions) friends are indeed necessary, since we need to love. If on the other hand we are thinking of perfect, heavenly *beatitudo*, in that state the love of the infinite, divine good requires no supplement. Friendship will not be in any sense a condition of perfect beatitude but its accompaniment.

It was from William of Auxerre that Aquinas and others of his time inherited the distinction between "perfect beatitude, which the saints will have in the future state, and the imperfect beatitude of the present life."[3] Aquinas could have emphasized the misery and unhappiness of earthly life, as many had done before him, but he chose to value and recommend those experiences and achievements in it which are related in a positive way to perfect happiness. He wisely regarded the happiness attainable in this life as being imperfect at best, but clearly held that it is happiness in an analogical, not merely an equivocal, sense.

Is happiness intellectual or does it come from the will?

The intellectualist account of beatitude put forward by Aquinas met with criticism on the part of John Duns Scotus, and their respective followers remained divided during the later Middle Ages by what is known as the intellectualist-voluntarist controversy. Scotus located human dignity at its height not so much in the formulation of concepts or the act of intellectual vision but rather in the free movement of the will, in that act of loving which embraces with enjoyment (*fruitio*) some object truly worthy of love for its own sake, and not simply as a means to be used (*uti*). Although the controversy was a theological one about how perfect *beatitudo*, the unlimited happiness of heaven, is enjoyed (is it through the intellect's apprehending God and thus opening to the will some access to the divine reality? or is it by the will's freely giving its love, knowledge being only a condition *sine qua non* of enjoyment?), it involved philosophical differences of some magnitude.

Aquinas adopted and refined Aristotle's moral epistemology. The will, he held, is determined by good and only by good but is blind as to what is good. It falls exclusively to the intellect to identify objects of affection and possible action, and to inform the will of them. Within the light thus offered it, the will deliberates and makes a choice. Even an objectively bad choice still reveals the basic determination of the will, which can only choose something as good (but can of course get proportions wrong by preferring a lesser good to a greater, or a merely apparent good to a real one).

Scotus, on the other hand, admired the Augustinian emphasis on the will as self-caused (*"voluntas est voluntas,"* he remarked concerning God). He moved toward ethical indeterminism in his view that what God commands or forbids is right or wrong simply because God commands or forbids it. Scotus agreed with Thomas that desire or delight cannot make up the center of happiness, since desire reveals the absence of the latter whereas delight supposes it already present. He accorded prior importance not to the respective order in which acts come about – for the act of the intellect is certainly prior to that of the will – but to the order of intrinsic worth, where the free act of the will bringing forth love is of unequaled and unrivaled value, bearing as it does within it the entire essence of free commitment.[4]

HAPPINESS IN THE INTELLECTUAL LIFE

Were there intellectuals in the Middle Ages? If we mean by that term someone whose highest reward and deepest satisfaction lies, beyond pleasure, in the realm of pure thought, then we can find many medieval thinkers who indisputably were intellectuals. More than that, we can find authors who gave forceful expression to this dimension of their experience and aspirations. Two contrasting examples of the intellectual will be given here.

Eriugena

John Scottus Eriugena in his masterpiece, *Periphyseon*, only once uses the first person in the presence of his reader:

The reward of those who labor in Sacred Scripture is pure and perfect understanding. O Lord Jesus, no other reward, no other happiness, no other joy do I ask of you except to understand your words, which were inspired by the Holy Ghost, purely and without error due to false speculation. For this is my supreme felicity. It is the goal of perfect contemplation, because even the purest soul will not discover anything beyond this – for there is nothing beyond it. (*Periphyseon* V 38)

Eriugena claimed that "No one can enter heaven except by philosophy" and that "philosophy or the pursuit of wisdom is not something other than religion," since "true philosophy is true religion, and conversely, true religion is true philosophy." He understood the pursuit of wisdom as the rational worship of God and the unique way to the happiness which lies in the search for truth and the grasp of it, and also as an anticipation of the delights of heaven. He did not differentiate between philosophy and theology, regarding the quest of the intellectual and the satisfaction deriving from it as being based on all the sources of truth available to him, including the Bible and early Christian literature.

Boethius of Denmark

Our second example of a medieval intellectual is a thirteenth-century Dane who, as a young Master of Arts, composed an essay entitled *On the Highest Good or the Life of the Philosopher*. The views of Boethius of Dacia were to occasion some upset to certain of the Paris theologians, who considered them controversial challenges to the Christian doctrine of happiness. The name of Boethius is linked with that of Siger of Brabant in the radical movement of arts masters which led to the Condemnation of 1277. His unreserved praise for the philosophical life has led some interpreters to regard him as a proponent of naturalism or rationalism. Yet Boethius was not opposed to Christianity or the church: there is some reason to believe that he joined the Dominican Order, presumably years after the composition of his booklet on the philosophical life (around 1270).

Boethius quoted an ancient philosopher (whom he wrongly took to be Aristotle, "the Philosopher") saying, "Woe to you men who are numbered among beasts and who do not attend to that which is divine within you!" Now, he argues, if there is anything divine in man it is the intellect. It follows that the supreme good should lie in the use of the mind, in both the speculative and practical orders (i.e., in knowledge of truth and enjoyment of it and in doing what is right and good). The greatest happiness of all belongs to God, according to Aristotle (*Metaphysics* XII 7, 1072b24), since highest intellectual capacity and supreme intelligibility are matched and united in the divine self-knowledge. The good of the human intellect is truth universally, which affords delight, while the good of the practical intellect lies in moral virtue. In short, "to know the true, to do the good, and to delight in both" is the highest good that is open to us. The cultivation of the moral and intellectual virtues, in other words, is the truest happiness we can have in this life. At this point Boethius refers to another state of happiness: on the authority of faith we believe in happiness in the life to come. What we enjoy in this life prepares us for that higher bliss by drawing us closer to it. He goes on to uncover the moral norm for judging intention and action universally. Just as one would expect, it turns out to be an intellectualist one of the kind that Plotinus or Eriugena might have proposed. Every thought and every action which conduces to the supreme good is right and proper and is in accordance with nature – the rational nature which is fulfilled precisely by the moral and intellectual virtues. In other words,

The happy man never does anything except works of happiness, or works by means of which he becomes stronger and better fitted for works of happiness. Therefore, whether the happy man sleeps or is awake or is eating, he lives in happiness so long as he does those things in order to be rendered stronger for the works of happiness. Therefore, all acts of man which are not directed to this supreme good of man which has been described, whether they are opposed to it or whether they are indifferent, all such acts constitute sin in man to a greater or lesser degree. ([265] 30)

Boethius accepts that the intellectualist ethic he proposes is elitist, since few give themselves to the pursuit of wisdom, whereas many are lazy, or pursue riches or pleasure, and thus miss the supreme human good. But the philosopher has tasted intellectual delight and cannot have too much of it (there being no excess in the order of supreme goods, Boethius reminds his reader, encouragingly). His desire to know will never be satisfied short of the absolute. Boethius invokes "the Commentator" (Ibn Rushd), who argues that knowledge and truth give rise to delight, but the movement of wonder and love which they inspire in us cannot be satisfied with anything less than the philosophical grasp of the first cause, who is the beginning, middle, and end of all finite things.

Boethius's essay could be described as a systematic, condensed presentation of the teaching concerning happiness, virtue, and contemplation developed by Aristotle in *Ethics* I and X and *Metaphysics* XII. The treatise ends with an acknowledgment that the first principle posited by the philosopher, and the glorious and most high God "who is blessed forever, Amen" are one and the same.

Siger of Brabant, Boethius's colleague in the arts faculty, also wrote a book on happiness, *Liber de felicitate*. It has been lost, but something of its contents is known through a report of it by Agostino Nifo (1472–1538).[5] Siger rejected the distinction between philosophical and theological conceptions of happiness. Like Boethius, he did not emphasize the practical aspect of happiness. *Felicitas* consists, he thought, in the contemplation of the essence of God. One of the propositions condemned in 1277 seems to have been directed against his book: "That we can understand God in his essence in this mortal life" (Proposition 38).

But could a Christian revert, intellectually speaking, to Aristotelianism and to living the philosophical ideal of the happy life, without challenging the church and putting his own faith at risk? This was the quite new question with which the radical party in the Parisian arts faculty confronted the theologians at the same university during approximately the ten years leading up to the fateful year 1277. The preceding decades had witnessed the rediscovery and Latinization of the *Physics, Metaphysics, Ethics,* and *Politics* of Aristotle. The university milieu found itself confronted by these books, which put forward answers to all the great questions in ethics and politics, natural philosophy, and even, in a way, religion (we have seen Boethius refer to the *Metaphysics* regarding the divine nature). The claim to totality of outlook and completeness of explanation attracted some, but it challenged many theologians by the radical terms in which it was put and by the converts it made in those two able young philosophy teachers, Siger and Boethius. The challenge was sharpened by the choice both men made of Ibn Rushd as the best interpreter of Aristotle, and his influence upon Siger and Boethius has led distinguished historians of the period to describe them as Latin Averroists.[6] It was, however, Aristotle who was their ideal, or even their idol; and they clung to him first and last, as being beyond comparison above all others. Their root-and-branch Aristotelianism gave them intellectual strength and a sense of the autonomy of their own faculty, even as it sapped their independence by making them in many ways the subjects of their own subject.

A sense of the autonomy of philosophy with regard to faith and theology can be gathered from the reading of Boethius's essay on the supreme good. His argument that the philosophical life both in action and in contemplation is the highest ideal we can have, and that the happiness it offers is without rival so far as this life is concerned, is not mitigated by reference to any religious concern or vocation, or to the Beatitudes of the Sermon on the Mount (Matthew 5:5–12). Is there a lay spirit at work here? Boethius seems to have been motivated more by methodology than by ideology. Perhaps he would have responded that he was speaking only as a philosopher, and only as a humble interpreter of the Philosopher, who had said it all (neither he nor Siger laid any claim to originality, indeed they repudiated any such notion even as an ideal); that comparison with faith was not his task as a professor of liberal arts and philosophy; that he himself sincerely believed in the afterlife and heaven; that truths of philosophy have a rational character, while faith is based on authority, miracles, and trust. But these considerations could not neutralize the shock waves sent out from the junior faculty to the senior one. The theological commission that was set up to inquire into the new, strange teachings, was particularly struck by Boethius's essay and took exception to his confident contention that the greatest happiness on earth is that of the philosopher and that the philosopher builds up his moral character and his speculative life purely out of his own resources.

Among the 219 propositions that the commission identified as unacceptable teachings in a Christian context, and which the bishop of Paris condemned on its recommendation (March 7, 1277), are the following, which mirror the teaching of Boethius's essay: "That there is no more excellent state than to study philosophy" (Proposition 40) and "That the only wise men in the world are the philosophers" (Proposition 154). The preamble to the condemnations pointed to the confused attitudes that came about through the claims of the radicals, who behaved "as though there were two contrary truths." While no one was officially named in the document, and neither Boethius nor Siger maintained a double-truth theory, the methodological issue they brought up was of fundamental importance: philosophy and theology differ in where they come from, reason in the former case, faith and tradition in the latter. But the intellectual difficulty experienced by the two men was compounded in a double way: by their being forbidden to teach any theology in the faculty of arts ("leave that to the theologians," they were instructed), and by their evident conviction that no one could surpass Aristotle as a philosopher but that one must instead rest content with finding out what he meant and teaching just that, without putting it into question or going beyond it. Boethius and Siger have been hailed as the first modern philosophers by historians who for various reasons (e.g., Marxist or liberal) regard mental autonomy (or freedom from religious authority and conviction) as the first condition of thought. In reality their institutional setting and their intellectual position precluded these radical Aristotelians from thinking out the relationship of reason and faith in any adequate way. The essay we have looked at here has an innocence about it that makes it seem like a reversion to the fourth century BCE. Its author simply jumps back over the centuries, bracketing Christianity, bypassing the rich Augustinian explorations of experience, and putting Aristotle's message into syllogistic shape and Latin words. Part of the shock and dismay that radical Aristotelianism occasioned was no doubt due to the naive, unhistorical and atemporal revival that was its centerpiece and its intention.

THEORIES OF FRIENDSHIP

Medieval ideas about friendship all exhibit some degree of continuity with the thought of the ancients. The schools of Pythagoras, Plato, Aristotle, the Stoa, and Epicurus all contributed something to a rich heritage of ideas upon which the Christian authors of medieval and Renaissance times drew liberally.[7] The most widespread of these ideas derived from Pythagoras: "Friends have all things in common." It may safely be said that no medieval author, whether monk, scholar, or master, wrote about friendship without evoking this notion of community. Augustine, for instance, recorded that a group of friends, of whom he was one, "hoped to make one common household for all of us, so that in the clear trust of friendship things should not belong to this or that individual, but one thing should be made of all our possessions, and belong wholly to each one of us, and everybody own everything" (*Confessions* VI 14). That project failed, but Augustine later rescued it by founding a monastery and by writing in a communitarian vein. He also presented the early Christian community of Jerusalem (Acts 2:42–47; 4:32–35) in a communalist light. Similarly, Aelred of Rievaulx developed the view that in the monastic community "what belongs to each one personally belongs to all, and all things belong to each one," adding that in heaven, where the supreme good will be held in common, the happiness of each will belong to all, and the entirety of happiness to each individual.[8]

Cicero and Seneca conveyed to their readers many Stoic ideas. The latter thought of personal friendship largely in terms of the spiritual direction given by a mature philosopher to an apprentice, as his *Moral Letters to Lucilius* amply illustrate. The theory and practice of spiritual friendship in the Christian age had a similar origin. Both were forms of educative love and therefore had a Socratic character, being based upon the development of self-knowledge. Cicero was by no means as true a Stoic as Seneca, but his works were the leading source of Stoic ideas in the Middle Ages. He insisted that the origin of friendship is to be sought not in need or desire but in nature itself; friendship derives from the natural sociability of humankind and from virtue, or "living in accordance with nature." Aquinas would maintain, in a similar vein, that "Every man is by nature a friend to every other man, by virtue of a sort of universal love," which is to be exercised as friendship even with regard to the stranger (*ST* IIaIIae,

q. 114, a. 1). Christianity, of course, brought with it its own specific kind of universality through its doctrine of love, even love of the enemy, and of forgiveness; nevertheless, the sentiments just quoted seem to be redolent of the ancient Stoa.

Aristotle formulated the most comprehensive ancient doctrine of friendship and related themes (such as civic trust and family affection). He argued that the self is an equivocal entity. Base self-love rules one out from friendship, which is generous. But if we love the better part of ourselves then we are capable of loving another in the same degree as we love ourselves, and the chosen friend will become "another self." We require friends if we are to progress in self-knowledge and in generosity, and this need is not a weakness in us – although it would be so in a god. Friendship with wisdom (*philosophia*) creates the highest intellectual communion that humans can experience.

Aristotle's message began to make an impact following the translation of the full text of the *Nicomachean Ethics* into Latin by Robert Grosseteste. Aquinas appears to have been forcibly struck by the verbal parallel between Aristotle's "the friend is another self" and the Gospel injunction to "love your neighbor as yourself" (Mark 12:31). He perceived in the notion of disinterested friendship (love characterized by benevolence; love of the other person for that person's own sake, i.e., as an end, not a means) the vital clue to the moral attitude of respect, not for friends alone but for every "other self" (*ST* IaIIae q. 26, a. 4; q. 28, a. 3). Henry of Ghent, also influenced by Aristotle, taught that due and proper *self*-love is required if we are to love someone else as much as we love ourselves.[9]

How might the specifically Christian dimension of medieval friendship theory be characterized? A few indications may be offered here on the basis of recent research.[10] The writers of patristic and medieval times consciously reflected upon the biblical references to friendship, notably the story of David and Jonathan, verses from the book of Proverbs, and the relevant New Testament passages, such as John 15:15. The basis of spiritual friendship was identified in the person of Jesus Christ.[11] Prayer for friends, the readiness to forgive and to accept forgiveness for offenses committed, the bearing of one another's burdens,[12] and the extension of pardon to the enemy, when taken together clearly reduced the classical emphasis on the equality of friends and the requirement regarding similarity in virtue. Two scholarly writers, Richard of St. Victor and Henry of Ghent, even sought to lay a Trinitarian foundation for friendship: the friendship of the three divine persons is the exemplar of all nonpossessive, self-giving *amicitia*, wherefore friendship is the natural virtue that draws closest to supernatural charity.[13]

The last of these novelties (by comparison with ancient theories) was also perhaps the most defining one. It lay in the inherent link forged between friendship and the happiness of the courts of heaven. The joys of friendship were widely regarded as an experiential mutual encouragement on the shared pilgrimage of life, the foretaste of heaven itself, "when this friendship, to which on earth we admit but few, will be extended to all, and by all will be extended to God, since God will be all in all" (Aelred, *Spiritual Friendship* III 134).

HAPPINESS AND PEACE AT THE END OF HISTORY: JOACHIM OF FIORE

All medieval thinkers who wrote on the subject conceived of happiness in both individual and social terms. The conviction that the human being is naturally sociable was unchallengeable: both religion and philosophy taught it. On the other hand, there was no serious medieval social (or socialist) utopian theory of happiness, nor any literary imitation of the Platonic *Republic*, nor any anticipation of the *Utopia* of Thomas More. There was, however, an interpretation of Christian eschatology, a form of apocalyptic thought, which (taking up Revelation 20:1–3) looked forward to a millennium of messianic peace and justice under the personal rule of Christ. Joachim of Fiore (c. 1135–1200), a Calabrian monastic reformer, developed these themes in his commentaries on Revelation, echoing in some respects the early Christian heresy of Montanism or chiliasm.[14] This amounted to the expectation of a temporal state of happiness at the end of history. Attempts were even made in the thirteenth century to predict (on the basis of symbolic numbers in the apocalyptic books of Daniel and Revelation) the moment when the expected end-time of peace would break into history, and what shape life might then take: the unification of the religions (Christian, Judaic, and Islamic) in one church; the waning of institutions and the spiritualization of humanity; the abolition of war; the presence of the Holy Spirit bringing a truly spiritual age (or third stage of humanity, in Trinitarian terms);

the advent of a world emperor, or an angelic pope. Although these currents of thought were influential, and even proved troublesome for the church at times, they did not manage to rally more than a minority. The interpretation of Revelation by St. Augustine, which ruled out millennialism and left the time of the Second Coming unknown to the church, proved too strong to be overturned. It has been argued, however, that secularized forms of the doctrine of inevitable historical progress toward unity, justice, peace, and happiness (in the Enlightenment, German Idealism, and Marxism) owe their shape, at least in a general way, to Joachimism.[15] Medieval philosophers believed in the underlying dignity and freedom of human nature and the goodness of the created order, but they also recognized the deeply flawed character of human action in history. As the following chapter will demonstrate, the political ideas elaborated in the light of these assumptions had a considerable measure of moral idealism and in some cases projected peace, justice, and communal well-being as genuine possibilities for this life. But regarding realization of the ultimate human good of beatitude, medieval thought could for the most part be described as realistically otherworldly and theocentric in character.

NOTES

1. Augustine argues for the connection between happiness, joy in the truth, and God in *On Free Choice of the Will* II. See especially II 13: "Man's Enjoyment of the Truth." Also see articles on Freedom, Happiness, and Truth, as well as those devoted to individual writings of Augustine in A. Fitzgerald [67].
2. D. Knowles [8] 55.
3. G. Wieland, *CHLMP* 679n.
4. Scotus discusses the position of Aquinas, without naming him, and opposes it at *Ordinatio* IV d. 49, q. 4. Ockham, too, argued that enjoyment (*fruitio*) is not a cognitive act but a volitional one. He maintained that the will itself is the immediate cause of the pleasure involved and that love of God, rather than love of the vision of God, is the essence of enjoyment. See Ockham *CT* II 349–417.
5. G. Wieland, *CHLMP* 682.
6. For example, E. Gilson [9] 387–402.
7. J. McEvoy [565].
8. Aelred of Rievaulx, *On Spiritual Friendship* III 79–80 [356] 111.

9. For Henry's ideas on friendship, see J. McEvoy [223]. The ways in which Aristotle's ethical thought was received by the university professors between *circa* 1300 and 1450 have not for the most part been studied consistently or in detail, since most of their commentaries are still in manuscript, and a number of them leave off at the close of Book V.

10. J. McEvoy [565] 34–36.

11. Cf Matthew 18:20.

12. Cf. Galatians 6:2.

13. Richard of St. Victor, *On the Trinity* III 12–15 [387]. For Henry see J. McEvoy [223].

14. M. Reeves [566].

15. Ibid. 166–75.

12 Political philosophy

The very existence of medieval political philosophy is sometimes questioned. The activities and problems that we think of as forming a distinctively political dimension of human life cannot, it is suggested, be isolated in the medieval period from other dimensions of human activity: centrally, that of religion. The *regnum*, the sphere of worldly administration, was only one half – and the lesser half at that – of the entire governance of humankind; the other being the *sacerdotium*, the priesthood, which is to direct us in our capacity to transcend this earthly existence. While worldly government was in the hands of the multifarious kingdoms, principalities, city-states, and feudal domains of medieval Europe, spiritual government was in the hands of the church and its head, the pope. In other words, what we call politics was then only a subordinate branch of religion: theology was the master-science of human life on earth, just as the church was its master-government – in theory at least.[1]

I disagree with this way of thinking about the medieval attitude to the political. As I shall seek to show, medieval thinkers were quite capable of (and, moreover, deeply interested in) addressing the activities and problems of human beings relating to each other within a common public space as a distinctive sphere of human life. This was in part because they were heirs to an Antique discourse of the political which did just that. Medieval theologians certainly did not consider the rationale of politics in this sense separately from questions of the overall rationale of human life, which involved them immediately in questions of religion and the church. But this does not depoliticize their discussions or reduce them to a localized historical phenomenon. On the contrary, it is the source of their abiding interest and relevance. For the important thing about medieval political philosophy is that the question of what *is* politics cannot be separated from the question of how to *value* it. In other words, establishing that there *is* such a distinctive area of human activity, which might aptly be termed *politics*, involves establishing what *good* it provides us.

The idea of a connection between politics and the human good was a keystone of the political discourse of Antiquity within which and upon which medieval philosophers worked. Ancient political philosophy meant no more than reasoning concerning the *polis*, the "city." Aristotle, perhaps its most famous ancient Greek exponent, opened his *Politics* as follows:

> Every city is a community of some kind, and every community is established with a view to some good... But, if all communities aim at some good, the city or political community, which is the highest of all, and which embraces all the rest, aims at good in a greater degree than any other, and at the highest good.[2]

By the term "*political* community" (emphasis mine), Aristotle meant to distinguish the city from any other form of community in which human beings – as naturally communicative animals – engage. He saw this form of engagement, beyond the limits of the household or even the extended kin group that makes up the village, as vital to human fulfillment: the life of moral and theoretical reason which is human excellence or virtue. This is the human good, without reference to which the city cannot be understood, just as we ourselves cannot be understood.[3] The city is therefore natural to us in the sense that it allows and completes our nature.

Aristotle's identification of and commitment to the city understood in this way, as vitally implicated in human teleology, was dependent on the political organization of ancient Greece, in which the *polis* was both the center of government and the center of cultured or educated life. This form of city-based culture was shared by the most famous city-state of all Antiquity, Rome. Rome expanded to a vast empire, but within its territories the same civic organization and civic culture, centered on the city or *civitas*, survived. Closely associated with the idea of *res publica* or "commonwealth," *civitas* meant not just the city but civilization, humanity as opposed to barbarity, virtue – human excellence – as opposed to the bestiality of animals. For the Roman philosopher Cicero, as much as for Aristotle, the city and its life represented the fulfillment of humanity's possibilities in the life of reason and reasoned speech, dominant over the more animal drives of appetite and sensuality.[4]

The idea that human beings by nature belong in a city did not imply, for either Aristotle or Cicero, that cities naturally coalesce in some organic, nonnegotiated way from their constituent individuals or lesser communities. Both philosophers understood that different individuals and groups have interests and appetites that may not always harmonize peaceably with those of others. As a result, they argued that no community can hold together without the virtue of justice, the virtue that gives to others what is rightfully their own.[5] Justice is that which enables human beings not just to look out for themselves but also to take into account the interests of others, and it is therefore that which enables them mutually to create a "public thing," a *res publica*. Justice is thus the foundation of any political society, and the justice of the ruler or the law is to respect and to foster the good of this public thing: the "common good," a key term of political philosophy both in Antiquity and throughout the Middle Ages and beyond.

If Aristotle and Cicero shared a broad ideal of politics and the political, of what it can do for humanity, they consequently also shared a sense of how much stands to be lost if something goes politically wrong: our very soul is at stake in the city. Political wrong or political vice is understood as injustice, the opposite of the virtue that holds the city together. If justice gives to each and all their own, injustice deprives them of their own – of ownership – and subordinates them to the ownership of another. This is domination, slavery, or tyranny: and the possibility of the corruption of the city into a form of domination was a central problem of ancient political philosophy, from Plato's *Republic* forward. But it was here that the first great philosopher of Latin Christianity, Augustine, offered a radical critique of the entire ancient political discourse.

THE ONE TRUE CITY

According to Augustine, *no* human city can avoid the corruption of domination, because by his own sin, man has made his own soul fundamentally corrupt.[6] This is a difference of the most profound nature. But while Augustine was the first philosopher of the medieval

Latin West, he was also one of the last ancient Roman philosophers, heir and in many ways committed to the ancient understanding of civility, the city, and all that it brought with it. The title of his great work on human life, *The City of God*, bears this out. It is sometimes said that this is a work of theology, not political theory, but this is a false dichotomy. Augustine shared with classical political theory the central understanding that our fulfillment will come only in a true city, in communication with others in freedom and in justice. The question was rather, what *is* that true city, and how does one gain citizenship in it? It is here that Augustine's Christian vision diverged so significantly from that of his predecessors. For his answer was that we can only be fully human in the city of God, not the earthly city, the city of man; and that citizenship of God's city comes through grace alone.

Augustine thus exploited the connected poles of classical political theory – the good, nature, reason, and justice – but he put them to very different use. For Augustine, God created human nature and created it good. Man was endowed with reason or understanding by which he lived in the knowledge of God. He was also created just. But here Augustine made a fundamental innovation in the ancient vocabulary of the political. Drawing on Plato but deploying the terminology of Roman law, he analyzed justice itself in terms of dominance: *rightful* dominance or *dominion* of the superior over the inferior. The superior who was rightfully dominant over all things was God, and therefore the justice of God's creature (and hence inferior), man, must begin with an acknowledgment of God as rightful master. Man was created in this justice but, at the Fall, turned away from his master, God, withdrawing from subordination and hence falling into injustice, a presumption of absolute autonomy or wrongful dominance (domination).

As a result, the sphere of relations between human beings apart from God – the ancient sphere of the political, the antithesis of domination – is for Augustine *necessarily* a sphere of domination, injustice, or corruption. The only state of true justice is the city of God: "true justice is found only in that commonwealth whose founder and ruler is Christ."[7] Consequently, the goal of *human* politics cannot be the establishment of a just city. Instead, it is a kind of peace. Through its coercive structure of laws, officers, and armies the earthly city can contain the worst effects of our human lust for domination (*libido dominandi*). This peace is not the peace of God, the only true peace, "a perfectly ordered and perfectly harmonious fellowship [*societas*] in the enjoyment of God, and of one another in God."[8] But even the peace of the earthly city preserves the integrity of nature in some way and therefore bears some relation to the goodness of God.[9] It may, and must, be used and upheld by those who are just, even though it is not ultimately valued by them. Augustine did not, then, devalue human politics entirely, but he saw the human good as lying outside the human city, in membership of the city of God on pilgrimage through this world (which Augustine tends to equate with the church, while recognizing that there are reprobate as well as elect within its ranks[10]), and in the households of just men. It is not in the human city that the good of our souls is at stake.

Augustine's medieval successors inherited his vision of the one true city as the dominant paradigm for thinking about the politics of this life. But they broke out of this paradigm in some ways while remodeling it in others. At the center of these developments was the reopening of the question of the value of the political within an expressly Christian religious framework.

REASON, NATURE, AND THE HUMAN GOOD

In what follows I shall be taking "medieval political *philosophy*" narrowly, primarily as a part of scholasticism, the formalized learning of the medieval universities. This is not to say that political discourse was limited to the universities in the Middle Ages. A flourishing literature existed, both courtly and popular, on the "art of ruling," the nature of good government, and the virtues of the ideal prince. There are sometimes direct connections between this discourse and the academic, as for example between the republican rhetoric of the northern Italian cities and the writings of Marsilius of Padua. Again, straddling the universities and the practical *fora* of government, lawyers – both civil and canon – were a critically important force in conceptualizing and defining political agents, bodies, powers, and relations. Nonetheless, I shall be concerned here chiefly with self-consciously theoretical and reflective treatments of the subject, mostly by university theologians. I shall use the work of several of the most important of these to illustrate some major themes of medieval meditation on the political.

The thirteenth-century recovery of Aristotle's moral and political thought in the Latin West is often considered the key moment in medieval reevaluation of the sphere of human government. It is by no means the case, however, that political arguments from human nature and the good were previously unknown.[11] Firstly, Cicero's understanding of the *civitas* and of our duties within the civic context had remained familiar after the demise of the classical world, mainly through his *On Duties*, but also through other treatises and in fragments of his writings handed on and discussed by the Latin fathers. Although Augustine had explicitly repudiated the Ciceronian understanding of the human commonwealth as a society held together by the bond of justice, he had allowed (as we have seen) that Christians have duties within this commonwealth, such as it is. The way was open, therefore, to a positive reassessment of civic life in terms of virtue and thus of the human good. John of Salisbury's *Policraticus* exemplifies this trend.[12] Through Cicero, too, the ancient argument that the city is natural to us was available. It has been suggested that, since Cicero's argument from nature does not assume a necessary and nonviolent development of the city, but rather recounts a passage from an original state of wildness by means of virtue and deliberate intervention, it could be accommodated to the Augustinian dimensions of history and human sinfulness.[13]

Thus, some of the ancient heritage that connected nature, the good, and the human city was available and being actively deployed prior to the recovery of Aristotle's texts.[14] Contributing to this way of thinking was that other huge intellectual heritage of Antiquity, the corpus of the Roman civil law, rediscovered in the libraries of the Italian peninsula and both studied and applied at the universities there from the early twelfth century.[15] Roman legal texts suggested the existence of a natural law governing human beings in their social relations – a moral law rather than a law backed by coercive sanctions.[16] The coercive legal framework of the city was seen as coming to exist subsequent to this original normative framework, again suggesting an evolving dynamic in human relations that could be connected with the historical perspective of Augustinian Christianity. Canon law, too, offered suggestions in this direction. Canonists used their texts to develop the idea of a natural *ius* in human beings – a natural right, rectitude, or law – by which they could discern right from wrong naturally.[17] Finally, the widespread organic analogy of the commonwealth, the "body politic," with the human body, the "body natural," was again a key locus for arguments from nature and the good.

In a series of ways, then, the argument from nature was being deployed within a specifically Christian framework prior to the recovery of Aristotelian moral and political texts in the mid-thirteenth century. It is fair to say, however, that these texts put the argument in a different and challenging form. The dominant position their recovery has enjoyed in the history of medieval political philosophy is to that extent justified, as is the parallel position of Thomas Aquinas, the theologian and philosopher who made their interpretation a central part of his intellectual endeavor.

In his treatise *On Kingship* addressed to the king of Cyprus, traditionally dated around 1266, Aquinas agreed with Aristotle that we are not just animals but rational animals, with an excellence to be achieved through living our lives in a reasoned manner.[18] Such a life is made possible for the individual through communication with other reasoning beings: "for it is for this that men gather together with each other, that they may live the good life together, which each of them could not achieve by living individually."[19] It was not immediately obvious, however, that this communication was the *political* community insisted upon by Aristotle. Its benefits seemed to spring simply from human society, apparently making us social but not necessarily political animals. Here, however, Aquinas filled out the Aristotelian text in his own way. We primarily need society. But society, being made up of individuals all pursuing their own good, will fall apart unless there is some common force directing that society to its common good. This force and its directives, and the communal order that it creates, properly constitute the political domain. Hence Aquinas made Aristotle his own by saying that "man is by nature a social and political animal"[20] – social in the first instance, political as a direct consequence.

Whether this is the first sketch of Aquinas's political theory or whether it in fact constitutes his final reflections on the subject,[21] we see that the political here is of critical importance to the distinctively human good but not constitutive of it. This ancillary role of the political domain was further underlined by a distinction Aquinas made within the human good. As we have seen, Aquinas accepted that part of this good could be realized within the human community.

This was the moral or ethical good, the life of natural human virtue. But as a Christian, Aquinas did not accept that that was the end of human life and human possibility. For Aquinas as for Augustine, the ultimate good is God, and all created good is referred to God. Therefore, although the life that we can achieve by our own natural abilities does have the *ratio* – the rational character – of an end and thus of a good, the life made possible through the supernatural gift of grace and the attendant theological virtues is the only one that has the character of an ultimate end and final good. Equally evidently, Aquinas argued, the political, which is a condition for achieving the natural end, must also serve the higher end; otherwise it is detached from the *ratio* – the overall rational structure – of the good. As a result, Aquinas did not hesitate to say that Christian kings must obey the spiritual governor, the pope, as they would the lord Jesus Christ himself.[22] Although Aquinas is often celebrated for reviving the idea of a natural moral life, of which politics is a part, it has to be realized that for him the moral autonomy of the human political domain is not unqualified.

In his magisterial *Summa theologiae*, Aquinas set the question of the political within the framework of one of his greatest achievements, a comprehensive elaboration of the concept of *law*. The *De regno* shows Aquinas using the notion of reason to bind together Aristotelian natural teleology with Christian eschatology. It is because we are rational creatures that we both live in the human community, achieving the good that it brings, and can also move beyond it toward the eternal contemplation of God. In the *Summa*, Aquinas argues that reason, directing a community to an end or good, has the rational character of law provided that the reason in question is sovereign over that community: law is defined as "an ordinance of reason for the common good, promulgated by him who has the care of the community" (*ST* IaIIae, q. 90, a. 4).[23] The primary law is the eternal law of God, the sovereign or lord of all things, and this law is nothing other than God's reason in its aspect as directing all things to their appointed end or good. Individual human beings, as made in the image of God, are naturally sovereign over themselves, in the sense that they are able to direct their own acts in virtue of having reason and choice (prologue to *ST* 2). This "participation" in God's rational direction of the universe is the law which is naturally in them, or natural law:

Among other animals the rational creature is subject to divine providence in a more excellent way, inasmuch as it too participates in providence, providing for itself and others. Whence it too shares in eternal reason, through which it has a natural inclination to its due act and end, and this participation of the eternal law in a rational creature is called "natural law."[24]

Everything individual human beings do should be in accordance with this law. But natural law itself directs us to move beyond individuality into community with others if we are to attain the good we seek: "Thirdly, there is in man an inclination to the good of his nature as rational, which is proper to him: as man has a natural inclination to know the truth about God and to live in society; and accordingly all those things which have respect to this inclination belong to natural law."[25]

The political community is thus a consequence of the precepts of natural law, and accordingly Aquinas argues that human law – the law promulgated by the political sovereign for the common good of the political community – must be in accordance with natural law or fail to have the true character of law. The law of the political sovereign covers all aspects of our life together, including issues of common morality. It is therefore no longer simply ancillary to society, as it is in *On Kingship*. But because it is not the final law, because it does not direct to the final good but only to the natural human good insofar as this is realized in common, it is not itself ultimately sovereign over us even in our common life. A fourth law, the redemptive law of Christ, is supreme. Hence, the common good at which the laws of the political community should aim is the "good regulated according to divine justice."[26] If the laws do this, then membership of a political community will itself contribute to the individual's good. If not, the laws may make one a good citizen but not a good human being.

It might be objected that Aquinas does not seem to have left much room for the political and its law, sandwiched as it is between the demands of natural law on the one hand and of divine law on the other. It is true that Aquinas will never allow political sovereigns to be a law unto themselves. But it is central to Aquinas's theology that sovereignty, dominance, or freedom is never something that is limited or frustrated by (true) law, whether we are talking of the sovereignty of God, of the individual under natural law, or of the

political sovereign. Directing oneself rationally and following rational directives are two sides of the same coin.

ELECTION AND CONSENT

Aquinas provided an account of how human law can be legitimate
and why we should obey it that is framed almost entirely in terms
of the authority of reason over rational human beings. He is not centrally concerned with the specific authority of this or that political
sovereign over this or that specific body of people, nor with the role of
the people in establishing the authority of their sovereign.[27] One author who tackled these questions directly was the English Franciscan
John Duns Scotus. In order to understand his position and his concerns, we need to know a little about the order to which he belonged.
The Franciscan Order professed a doctrine of meritorious poverty.[28]
Poverty meant the renunciation of any ability to command, that is,
the renunciation of any kind of right over or property in anything
(or anyone) else. In relinquishing these two kinds of dominion, the
Franciscans saw themselves as imitating the human life of Christ,
who, insofar as he was man, supposedly had nothing of his own.
This conception of the life of Christ carried with it an implicit commitment to an Augustinian understanding of the temporal sphere
as a world of domination: a product of the history of fallen man,
an adventitious order of human justice in which the one truly just
man, Christ, had no part, although he did not condemn or overturn it
either.

Scotus worked within this framework in his commentary on
Peter Lombard's *Sentences*, when he explained the nature of theft and
therefore of property through an account of the genesis of the human
city.[29] Scotus's explanation was historical: an account of human
relations before and after the Fall. In the beginning, in the state of
innocence, nothing belonged to one person rather than another. The
earth was possessed in common: "Let this be our first conclusion,
that by natural or divine law there are no distinct properties of things
for the period of the state of innocence."[30] After the Fall, however,
human viciousness meant that this community of property was impossible to maintain, and therefore, Scotus says, the precept of natural law concerning community of property was revoked, generating a
license for individuals to appropriate things for themselves. But this

by itself did not legitimate the new situation of private property: "Third conclusion: That when once this precept of the natural law concerning having all things in common had been revoked, and in consequence a license had been granted of appropriating and dividing all these common things, the actual division did not take place by means of natural law or divine law."[31] A new and specifically human law was needed to legitimate the new order. But the promulgation of a human law required in its turn the authority to do so. How could that authority be acquired?

> The fifth conclusion follows, which is that rulership or authority is twofold, that is, paternal and political; and political authority is itself twofold, that is, either in one person or in a community. The first authority, paternal, is just by the law of nature by which all children are bound to obey their parents ... Whereas political authority, which is over strangers, can be just (whether it resides in one person or the community) by common consent and the election of that community itself.[32]

Thus political authority, unlike the authority of a father over his children, does not spring up naturally but has to be ceded by a group of people to a particular individual or individuals.

Two things may be noted about Scotus's argument. Firstly, politics on his conception is about the creation of a new human order of justice and peace. It is not fundamentally about achieving the good of human beings but about securing their property and rights. In parallel, although Scotus does not deny the role of reason in the political sphere – indeed, he requires a law to be rational, the product of practical reasoning – it is not fundamentally reason that makes political sovereigns. Their authority does not come from themselves, however capable of ruling they may be, but from the people who originally gave it to them. As a consequence, Scotus can offer a very clear account not just of political authority in general, but of why one individual or group should have such authority over a particular community. The source of political power lies in human history as much as in human nature.

Locating the source of authority in an act of transmission was central in another, very different work of the late thirteenth century, *On Royal and Papal Power* by John of Paris. John was a Dominican, of the same order as Aquinas, and his political theory has sometimes been seen as specifically Dominican.[33] It is true that John began with the Thomist-Aristotelian account of the formation of the political community through nature, and in some passages he defended the natural human city as providing a life of natural moral virtue: "Its purpose is the common good of the citizens; not any good indeterminately, but that good which is to live according to virtue."[34] John's main concern, however, was not simply to understand the nature of the political community but to understand its relation to the spiritual community of the church – and particularly the relations of their respective powers. We have seen this as a tacit issue in Aquinas, who argued that the nature of the political community requires it to be subject to the directives of the church and its head, the pope. When John wrote, a generation after Aquinas, the increasingly strident claims of both kings and pope to overriding jurisdiction in the temporal realm demanded that this question of respective powers be handled more overtly.

John began this argument by distinguishing the nature of the community of the faithful from the nature of political communities. While there is "one church of all the faithful forming one Christian people," governed by the unitary headship of the pope as the successor of Peter, "it does not follow that the ordinary faithful are commanded by divine law to be subject in temporalities to any single supreme monarch."[35] This is said to be a *non sequitur* for a variety of reasons, the most important being, firstly, that human souls are universally alike whereas human bodies are diverse according to different localities; secondly, that the faithful share "one universal faith, without which there is no salvation," whereas what is politically salutary differs from place to place and therefore cannot unite all the faithful politically speaking. Spiritual and temporal are two very different communities, then, serving different ends, which John does not link in the way that Aquinas does. Indeed, defending the autonomy of the temporal community, he deployed the more Scotist notion of the ruler as an arbiter of property disputes, his jurisdiction being ceded by the people he rules: "For the reason that sometimes the peace of everybody is disturbed because of these possessions... a ruler has been established by the people to take charge of such situations."[36] This, John implies, is the source of authority in the temporal sphere, and for that reason the pope has no temporal authority except where the safety of the church is threatened. But what about papal authority within the spiritual community? On the one hand, John is clear that headship of the church does not come from any body of people but "from the very mouth of the Lord himself."[37] On the other hand, he will not allow that the body of the church therefore has no power whatever if the pope abuses his authority. In such a situation, the pope can be deposed or removed from authority, "because that is in a certain way natural."[38]

If we are speaking in terms of nature, therefore, authority is vested in the body of a community (whether it be the political or the spiritual community) and is ceded upward for the good of the community, which not only has an interest as a body but can also act as a body. In this critically important point, John was drawing on the heritage of Roman law and its theory of corporations, in which the individuals in a group can be understood not simply as a disconnected aggregate but rather as "incorporated" into one body.[39] This body is able to act as one through the appointment of a proctor or representative, who is answerable to the body as a whole on matters touching its interest. Using corporation theory to understand both the church (in the movement known as "conciliarism") and the political community allowed medieval political thinkers to attribute agency to the body of the community, and this ultimately opened the way to theories of a contractual relationship between the political community and its ruler.[40]

HIERARCHY AND GRACE

In articulating the human origins of jurisdiction over other human beings, Scotus and John of Paris were diametrically opposed to a thesis that was being deployed at around the same time to support papal claims to universal temporal jurisdiction. In his work *On Ecclesiastical Power* of around 1302, the Augustinian Giles of Rome used the twin principles of hierarchy and grace to argue that all rightful human relations of command – whether over other human beings (jurisdiction or government) or over things (property) – depend on their subordination to the command of the pope. Drawing on the writings of Dionysius the Pseudo-Areopagite,[41] Giles understood hierarchy as a plurality reduced to unity by the mediated subjection of the lowest to the highest. The ultimate unity or "one" was, of course, God, on whom the entire hierarchy of creation, from the highest angels down to the lowest inanimate beings, depended. Giles used the same principle to argue that the hierarchy of human beings over human beings and over property depended similarly on the "one" who was the fount of the justice of those relations: the pope as the vicar of Christ on earth:

Just as there is one fount in the government of the whole world – there is one God, in Whom there is every power, from Whom all other powers are derived, and to Whom all powers are reduced – so also, in the government of men and in the whole Church Militant, it must be that there is one fount, that there is one head in which is fullness of power: in which there is almost every power as over the Mystical Body or over the Church herself, and in which there are both swords [that is, the swords of governing both spiritual and temporal realms].[42]

Using as the key hierarchical relation the ordering of the material to the command of the spiritual, Giles argued that only in submission to the "spiritual man" could the legal institutions (jurisdiction and property) of the temporal or material domain have any legitimacy. This argument depended on a further position: that the temporal is not a source of rightfulness or legitimacy in itself. Against Aquinas's position, Giles held that "nature" after the Fall has no intrinsic goodness in terms of which human property and jurisdiction – dominion in general – could be understood as naturally or morally legitimate. Outside of grace, dominion is simply unjust domination, the sphere of *de facto* might as opposed to right.

The thesis that just dominion depends upon grace was revived toward the end of the fourteenth century by the Englishman John Wyclif, probably via the work of Richard FitzRalph. Wyclif's motives are not entirely clear, but the primacy of grace allowed him to criticize the current state of the English church and to expose as unfounded its claims to property and jurisdiction, thereby legitimating (among other things) royal taxation of the clergy.[43] Wyclif's teaching was vigorously combated by, among others, the Parisian theologian Jean Gerson, who developed his argument for a kind of natural right in every natural being partly in response to Wyclif's extreme Augustinianism.[44] Wyclif's teaching was condemned as heretical at the Council of Constance in 1414 and was opposed anew in the renaissance of Thomism in the sixteenth century. Francisco de Vitoria cited precisely the decrees of Constance in rejecting the argument that the American Indians did not have true dominion (and could therefore rightfully be dispossessed) because they were sinners and unbelievers.[45]

HISTORY, AUTONOMY, AND RIGHTS

In this final section I want to look at two thinkers who in very different ways used a combination of arguments from Aristotelianism and Augustinianism. The first is one of the most revolutionary political writers of the Middle Ages, Marsilius of Padua. A bit of context is necessary in order to understand the achievement of his astonishing major work, *The Defender of the Peace*.[46] Marsilius came from republican circles in Padua, a city-state of northern Italy, a region in which the former, communal system of government was increasingly being lost to the rule of *signori* or overlords. At the same time, the region was the major battleground between the papacy and the Holy Roman Empire, both trying to gain control or influence over the wealthy and strategically important cities. When Marsilius wrote *The Defender of the Peace*, the emperor, whose election was considered invalid by the pope, was setting about reestablishing his jurisdiction in cities that he claimed rightfully belonged to the empire. As a result, he had been excommunicated by the pope, and a bitter party war had broken out, with the emperor claiming in return that it was the pope who should be deposed for heretically denying the poverty of Christ. An uneasy alliance of Franciscans and imperialists had developed in consequence, and it was with this party that Marsilius aligned himself. His continuing allegiance to a distinctively republican understanding of the city, however, meant that he was able to transcend the limits of the dispute and to create a completely new understanding of the relationship between human nature, politics, and religion.

As a republican, Marsilius was committed to the idea of civic autonomy, that is, the idea that the city is sufficient to itself both for the necessities of life and in terms of law. He therefore had to repudiate Thomist political theory, in which the Aristotelian account of politics was sandwiched between natural law on one hand and divine law on the other, with the political legislator answerable both ways. Nonetheless, Marsilius wanted to use the Aristotelian argument from nature to argue for the life of the city as part of natural human activity. He therefore needed an understanding of nature that did not introduce natural law as an extracivic and precivic standard of the political. He found this understanding in a biological notion of nature as regularity: what all humans in fact *do*, when not impeded by disease or extraneous causes, is natural and good. With this, he was able to argue that all human beings naturally seek communication and community with others in order to become sufficient and to achieve the good life, that is, the cultivated life of excellence that is unavailable to solitary dwellers: "Let us therefore lay this down as the principle of all the things which are to be demonstrated here, a principle naturally held, believed, and freely granted by all: that all men not deformed or otherwise impeded naturally desire a sufficient life, and avoid and flee what is harmful thereto."[47] Self-sufficiency and cultivation reach their pinnacle in the city, and therefore the political community is natural to us. This does not mean, however, that a political community has to have existed in a "state of nature" or the original human condition. Marsilius is clear that if man had not fallen into sin, there would have been no political communities, because there would have been no need to *create* a sufficient life. It was already available.[48] Man deprived himself of that original good, and human history records his attempts to remedy his own deficiency. In this way, Augustinian ideas of sin, history, and the creation of a human order are fused with the Aristotelian concepts of nature and the good. The natural human good in our present state is to live the sufficient or good life together in a city, the condition of which is tranquillity or peace.[49] This life is threatened by strife and division, and Marsilius's book is in large part a prescription for avoiding these evils of "intranquillity."

As we have seen, for Marsilius there is no natural law in the Thomist sense. But law and justice – the definition and the rectification of injury – are required for the sufficient life, for otherwise the community will dissolve into quarrels and fighting. Humanity must therefore create law for itself and create a force to execute justice in accordance with that law. According to Marsilius, this human law is the law created by human beings insofar as they are collected into different communities for the sake of living well. The source of human legislation – the "human legislator" – is each human community itself or (as Marsilius adds) "the weightier part thereof": "the legislator, or the primary and proper efficient cause of the law, is the people or whole body of citizens, or the weightier part thereof, through its election or will expressed by words in the general assembly of the citizens."[50] Nothing and no one else can be a human legislator or claim to legislate for human beings in their communal life together, because nothing and no one else is competent to determine the common good of the human community. To execute its laws, that is, to exercise jurisdiction, the Marsilian community appoints a "ruling part." This part is like the heart of an animal, the part that keeps the whole animal going. Nonetheless, the ruling part is not a law unto itself but must follow the law of the community, which is also its law.

Marsilius's account therefore offers a definition of the political. It is the basic essential structure that a community must have in order to count as a political community, despite historical and geographical variations. The malfunctioning or corruption of the political domain comes when this organic structure develops a fault in some way and therefore starts to fall apart. The primary cause of such division comes when two entities each claim to be the ruling "part." In Marsilius's day in northern Italy, this meant the emperor and the pope. Marsilius's solution to the problem of conflicting temporal and spiritual authority was radical. He argued, appealing to the model of Christ himself, that there simply *is* no spiritual authority – in the sense of coercive jurisdiction – over human beings on earth. Therefore, papal claims to such authority, and its extension into the temporal domain, were not simply illegitimate but tyrannous; quite to the contrary of the claims of the papacy and of papalists such as Giles of Rome, Marsilius argued that the spiritual should be subject to the temporal:

Not only did Christ himself refuse rulership or coercive jurisdiction in this world, whereby he furnished an example for his apostles and disciples and successors to do likewise, but he also taught by words and showed by example that all men, both priests and non-priests, should be subject in property and in person to the coercive judgment of the rulers of this world.[51]

Marsilius held that a true spiritual jurisdiction *does* exist. It is that of Christ. But for the purposes of this life, the spiritual domain is one of teaching or doctrine and is thus a part of the city, not something set over and above it. To the extent that the church's doctrine is enforced, that enforcement belongs to the civil authority.

One way to read Marsilius is as offering a secular, republican theory of politics as a way of excluding the pope from any part in it. But
as I have already suggested, Marsilius does not discount the possibility that the ruling part of the human city may enforce religious
teaching, and he thinks it matters what religious teaching the citizens receive. Marsilius offered an account not simply of human politics but of Christian politics, and he accordingly gave the *faithful*
human legislator an active role in calling church councils and enforc-
ing their decisions.[52] For Marsilius, the correct functioning of both
the political and the spiritual sphere depended equally on the unim-
peded jurisdiction of the faithful human legislator, the Holy Roman
Emperor, over all Christians.[53] Marsilius's theory was thus not just a
theory of the human city but of the Christian city, that city in which
the demands both of humanity and of the Christian religion could
be satisfied.

We may contrast Marsilius's vision with that of the final thinker
I want to discuss, the English Franciscan William of Ockham.
Ockham too spent the last years of his life excommunicate in
Munich under imperial protection. He too defended the rights of
the Roman Empire and opposed the claims to temporal jurisdiction
of the current papacy (resident at the time in Avignon). But he did
not deny those papal claims on the ground that the pope had no independent jurisdiction whatever over human beings in this life. For
Ockham, it was clear that he did: but it was a *spiritual* jurisdiction
or principate, not a temporal one. The whole thrust of Ockham's enterprise, therefore, was to determine what *was* spiritual as opposed
to temporal jurisdiction.

In giving an account of temporal jurisdiction, Ockham appealed,
as had Aquinas and Marsilius before him, to human nature. And yet
his account of nature was different from both. Instead of interpreting
the requirements of nature in terms of natural law or of biological
regularity, Ockham built on a foundation of natural *rights*.[54] A right
he conceived in general as a juridical ability or licit power: thus,
the "right of using" is "a licit power of using some external object,
of which someone should not be deprived against his will without
fault on his part and without reasonable cause: and if he should be
deprived of it, he can call the person who deprives him into court."[55]
However, "the right of using is twofold. For there is a natural right
of using; and there is a positive right of using. The natural right of

using is common to all men, because it is held from nature and not from any subsequent establishment."[56] This conception of human beings as equipped with the natural right of using the things of the earth is distinct from the nonjuridical nature with which Marsilius began, but also distinct from Aquinas's framework of natural law. The natural rights with which Ockham credited individuals were not opposed to natural law as the dictate of right reason, sanctioned by God, but were nevertheless subjective in the sense that the individual acting by or with natural right had his actions justified in terms of himself and not (at least immediately) in terms of a higher order. For Ockham, rights serve and justify the dynamic aspect of human life on earth.

Ockham posited that we are naturally equipped with at least the basic right to self-sustenance. However, he followed Scotus in seeing two further steps necessary for a viable human life on earth after the Fall: the establishment of property and jurisdiction. But instead of the explanation that Scotus had offered in terms of license and fact, Ockham saw us as naturally possessed with the right to acquire property and the right to create jurisdictions. These rights are at once the explanation and the justification for the structures of the cities in which humans live. Although they are God-given, on Ockham's reading of the Bible, they are entirely independent of any religion, including the Christian religion: "This twofold power, to appropriate temporal things and to establish rulers with jurisdiction, God gave without intermediary not only to believers but also to unbelievers, in such a way that it falls under precept and is reckoned among purely moral matters. It therefore obliges everyone, believer and unbeliever alike."[57] Ockham appeals especially to Christ's tacit acknowledgment of Roman imperial jurisdiction to insist again and again that legitimate civic structures, especially that of the empire, predate Christianity and that their secular nature survives intact to the present.

The secular domain is thus natural to us in that we create it from our natural juridical abilities. This does not imply, however, that political relationships existed in the state of innocence. As I have already suggested, politics is for Ockham a sphere of human creativity within history after the Fall. It is legitimate and justified, but it is nonetheless marked by the urge to dominate which, in an Augustinian perspective, marks fallen humanity. Ockham is ambivalent as to whether any secular human city can avoid the corruption of domination or tyranny. One thing he is clear about. Whatever the case for the human city or temporal jurisdiction, the church or spiritual jurisdiction not only can but must avoid domination in order to count as a spiritual jurisdiction at all:

> For it can be clearly gathered from the words of Christ himself, that papal principate was instituted by him for the good of its subjects, not for its own honor or advantage, and should, therefore, be called not a "despotic" principate, or one "of lordship," but a principate "of service": in such a way that, insofar as it is ordained of Christ, it extends only to those things which are necessary to the salvation of souls and for the rule and government of the faithful, respecting always the rights and liberties of others.[58]

There is authority in the church, but since the gospel is a "law of liberty," that authority is exercised over free persons (free as Christians, even if in servitude temporally). Accordingly, authoritarian encroachment upon the rightful liberties of the faithful is tyranny. Paradoxically, the spiritual community is therefore – as Ockham explicitly points out – the only community that truly fulfills the demands of the classical city for freedom and justice. The sin of the present "Avignonese church" is, in an entirely transformed context, that fundamental fault identified by the ancients, that of turning a city into a domination.

CONCLUSION

Returning to our starting point, we can see that in one sense medieval political theory was dominated by the historically specific circumstances of medieval Europe and the medieval church, with its claims to temporal jurisdiction. Working out the correct relationship between temporal and spiritual domains preoccupied medieval theorists. And yet, as we have also seen, this was not simply because of the pressing issues of practical politics. The relationship was important because the basic question was not about the power of popes, emperors, and kings but about correct human governance as a whole: the justification or establishment of structures of rule which would both permit a sufficient life in this world and respond to the Christian assumption that human beings are more than natural creatures and have spiritual as well as temporal demands. In working through the problems of the political from this perspective, medieval thinkers created or developed a number of concepts that, with all due historical mutations and permutations, have shaped discussion of our common human life ever since: the idea of natural rights; of the human capacity for self-direction; of civic self-government; of the capacity of people to act as a body, not just as individuals; of freedom and tyranny. Above all, however, and with the most abiding relevance, they posed and pursued the most fundamental question about politics. What is it? What good is it?

NOTES

1. There are many good introductory treatments of medieval spiritual–temporal dualism and its political context: see the articles by J. P. Canning and J. A. Watt in J. H. Burns [13] or Canning's excellent introduction in J. P. Canning [14].

2. Aristotle, *Politics* I 1, ed. S. Everson (Cambridge, 1996) 11, translation altered. A helpful recent introduction to Aristotle's moral and political thought can be found in C. Rowe and M. Schofield, eds., *The Cambridge History of Greek and Roman Political Thought* (Cambridge, 2000), chs. 15–19.

3. Cf. *Politics* I 1, 1252b28–1253b1, Everson 13–14.

4. Cf. Cicero, *On Invention* I 2, trans. H. M. Hubbell (Cambridge, MA/London, 1949) 5–7.

5. Aristotle, *Nicomachean Ethics* V 1, trans. J. A. K. Thomson and H. Tredennick (London, 1976) 173–74; Cicero, *On Duties* I 20–23, ed. M. T. Griffin and E. M. Atkins (Cambridge, 1991) 9–10. For a good general analysis of Cicero's thought in its context, see E. M. Atkins in Rowe and Schofield (n. 2), 477–516.

6. Augustine of Hippo, *The City of God against the Pagans* XIII 12–14 [58] 522–23.

7. Ibid. II 21 [58] 75, criticizing the Ciceronian definition of the commonwealth as "the weal of the community," a community being "an association united by a common sense of justice and a community of interest."

8. Ibid. XIX 17 [58] 878.

9. Ibid. XIX 11–17 [58] 865–78.

10. Cf. ibid., e.g., at XX 11 [58] 920. The relationship between the city of God and the church is discussed in R. A. Markus [72] 117–25.

11. An outline of these arguments can be found in G. Post [585]; see also D. Luscombe [579].

12. John of Salisbury, *Policraticus* [158].

13. C. J. Nederman [582].
14. One should be aware, moreover, that before the recovery of Aristotle's actual texts – principally the *Nicomachean Ethics* and the *Politics* – certain key terms of Aristotle's framework were already available from various sources: see C. Flüeler [576] I 1–15 and G. R. Evans [574] 15–16.
15. For a general treatment of the application of law to questions of political thought in this period, see K. Pennington [584].
16. Especially the texts of the opening title of the *Digest*, "On justice and right" [577].
17. This language has been analyzed by B. Tierney [589] ch. 2.
18. This treatise (which used to be known as *On the Government of Princes* or *De regimine principum*) has been most recently edited and translated into English by J. M. Blythe as part of the larger work of Ptolemy of Lucca, *On the Government of Princes* [382], which represents a continuation of the treatise *On Kingship* generally attributed to Aquinas. Blythe's introduction provides a good overview of the problems of dating and authorship; see also C. Flüeler [576] I 27–29. The Latin text from which I have translated is edited as *De regno, ad regem Cypri* by H. F. Dondaine [224] XLII 449–71.
19. II 3, p. 466.
20. Ibid. I 1, p. 449.
21. As argued on grounds of citation by C. Flüeler [576]; see also the discussion in J. Miethke [581] 25–45, who accepts Flüeler's dating, making the *De regno* the mature statement of Aquinas's political philosophy.
22. II 3, p. 466.
23. Aquinas's treatment of law is given in the *Summa theologiae* IaIIae, qq. 90–97 [233] vol. 28; qq. 90, "the nature of law," and 91, "the varieties of law."
24. *ST* IaIIae, q. 91, a. 2.
25. *ST* IaIIae, q. 94, a. 2. There is an enormous amount written on Aquinas's idea of natural law. An introduction to the concept is provided by D. E. Luscombe in *CHLMP* 705–19; see also D. J. O'Connor [253]. More recently, J. Finnis includes a discussion of natural law in his *Aquinas* [240] 79–94; pp. 219–74 cover Aquinas's political thought.
26. *ST* IaIIae, q. 92, a. 1.
27. I am not convinced by the description of the "mixed constitution" at *ST* IaIIae, q. 105, a. 1. Aquinas makes it clear there that the role of the people is a second-best arrangement, owing to the defects of humanity; especially the supposed avarice of the Jews, whose law is in question here. For a different view, see J. M. Blythe [571] 47–56. This is not to deny that Aquinas sees human corruption as a very real problem and part of the proper domain of the political.

298   ANNABEL S. BRETT

28. For a general introduction to the idea of poverty and the juridical difficulties it immediately generated, see J. Coleman [573]; most recently and fully R. Lambertini [578].

29. Duns Scotus, IV *Sent.*, d. 15, q. 2, *Opera omnia*, 26 vols. (Paris, 1891–95) XVIII 256–71. I have discussed these themes in more detail in the introduction to [312] 14–17.

30. Scotus, 256.

31. Ibid. 265.

32. Ibid. 266.

33. J. Coleman [280]. In what follows I shall use the name "John of Paris," as is habitual, to refer to the author of the tract, although recognizing that the question of authorship is contested.

34. John of Paris, *On Royal and Papal Power*, ch. 1 throughout and ch. 17 [279] 182.

35. Ibid., ch. 3, 84–85.

36. Ibid., ch. 7, 103.

37. Ibid., ch. 3, 84.

38. Ibid., ch. 25, 252.

39. See B. Tierney [588], especially 132–78.

40. There is a large secondary literature on conciliarism and its relation to secular political theory. There are good treatments of conciliarism and its development in C. Fasolt [575] and two earlier studies by A. Black [568–69]. Its consequences for the understanding of secular politics are handled in the influential essays of F. Oakley collected in [583]. J. Quillet gives an outline of the more secular dimensions of this way of thinking in [586].

41. See above, p. 66.

42. Giles of Rome, *On Ecclesiastical Power* III 2 [270] 147. For the context, see W. Ullmann [590]; more recently, J. Miethke [581] 45–56.

43. See M. J. Wilks [354]; see also the remarks in A. Black [570] 79–82.

44. See B. Tierney [589] ch. 9 and A. S. Brett [572] ch. 2.

45. Francisco de Vitoria, "Relection On the American Indians" 1.2 [621] 240–43.

46. For a fuller account of this context, see Q. Skinner [587] I 12–22.

47. Marsilius of Padua, *The Defender of the Peace*, Discourse I 4.2 [303] 12.

48. Ibid., ch. 6.

49. As laid out in the first chapter of the first discourse ([303] 3).

50. Ibid., ch. 12.3 [303] 45. Marsilius spells out what he means by the "weightier part" in the same chapter, at §§4 and 5: it is determined either by "the honorable custom of polities" or in accordance with Aristotle's principles (a mixture of quantitative and qualitative considerations), and it is said to "represent" the citizens in their entirety so that the common

good should not be impeded by the "deformed nature" of some men. Critics have differed over what exactly is the meaning of this for popular sovereignty in the Marsilian city.

51. Ibid., Discourse II 4.9 [303] 119. See also, especially, Discourse II 9 and 25.

52. Ibid., ch. 21.

53. This equation of the emperor and the faithful human legislator is very clear in Discourse II 21, which discusses the authority to call a general council. Marsilius's definition of the legislator in Discourse I 12.3 explicitly allows for the "primary legislator" to entrust its function to a person or persons; a process of transference of legislative authority from Roman people to Roman emperor is clearly assumed in the *Defensor Minor*, ch. 12 [304]. Nonetheless, the end result is that the emperor appears to be both the supreme ruling part and the supreme legislator for the entire Christian people, which some scholars have seen as inconsistent with some of the more republican formulations of Discourse I. For an "imperial" interpretation of the *Defensor pacis*, see in particular J. Quillet [305]; for a "republican" interpretation, N. Rubinstein [306].

54. The conception of natural rights had a complex development even before Ockham came to use the notion: see B. Tierney [589] and A. S. Brett [572] ch. 1; most recently, V. P. Mäkinen [580]. For Ockham's development of his ideas in the context of the renewed debate over Franciscan poverty, see J. Miethke [321].

55. William of Ockham, *The Work of Ninety Days*, ch. 2 [310] 24.

56. Ibid., ch. 61 [309] II 559.

57. William of Ockham, *A Short Discourse on Tyrannical Government* III 8 [314]. The entire range of Ockham's political thought is discussed in detail in A. S. McGrade [320] and surveyed by J. Kilcullen in *CCOck* 302–35.

58. William of Ockham, *On the Power of Emperors and Popes*, ch. 7 [312] 90.

13 Medieval philosophy in later thought

Histories of medieval philosophy often conclude with chapters on the disintegration of the scholastic synthesis or the defeat and neglect of scholasticism. From the standpoint of the present volume, where scholasticism and medieval philosophy are not seen as identical and where synthesis is not regarded as incontestably the supreme philosophic ideal, the situation is more complicated. An adequate history of the presence of medieval philosophy in later thought would require a volume in itself. In what follows some major points are touched on, including those bearing on defeat and neglect, but the story concludes with an account of the revival of interest in medieval philosophy of which this Companion is itself an effect and which it hopes to augment.

THE RENAISSANCE AND SEVENTEENTH CENTURY (P. J. FITZPATRICK)

In Chaucer's *Canterbury Tales* the Oxford scholar would sooner have volumes of "Aristotle and his philosophy" than worldly attractions. For Bacon in 1597, philosophers of that tradition were *cymini sectores* – "hair-splitters," say – whose writings can help us to draw distinctions. And for Molière in 1673, they were people who explained how opium induces sleep by saying that it has a "dormitive virtue." Which gives us three topics: the place of Aristotle; the effect of distinctions; and medieval philosophy in the face of new discoveries.

The place of Aristotle

What made noteworthy the contribution of Thomas Aquinas to the scholastic assimilation of Aristotle was less his acceptance of so

300

much in Aristotle than his capacity to interpret apparently recalci-
trant texts there in a way that made them concordant with Christian
belief. In what we call the Renaissance, the sheer variety in the
literature and philosophy of the ancient world could now be seen,
and the sheer distance which separated that world from Christian
Europe. To effect a synthesis of ancient thought with Christian belief
was no longer what seemed urgent: first and foremost, the thought
of Greece and Rome had to be investigated for its own sake and on
its own terms. Philosophy in the ancient world had been largely in
Greek. The Middle Ages had had to use Latin translations – in some
cases, translations of translations. That would no longer do.

Tommaso de Vio Gaetano, commonly known as Cajetan, was a notable figure in his time. He wrote what became a standard commentary on the *Summa theologiae* of Aquinas; he became master-general
of the Dominicans and eventually a cardinal; he was consulted by
the Emperor Maximilian about a proposed crusade and by Clement
VII about Henry VIII's proposed divorce; and Leo X sent him as a
legate to meet Luther. It is not surprising, then, that at the time of
his death, in 1534, he was being talked about as a future pope. But
Cajetan did something else, which concerns us here. He was one
of only two members of the Fifth Lateran Council (1512–21) to vote
against a measure ordering teachers of philosophy to endeavor to vindicate Christian belief in the immortality of the soul. This dissent
embodies one of the changes that were coming over philosophy as
the Middle Ages came to an end.

In his commentary on *Summa theologiae* I in 1507, as in an Advent sermon preached at Rome in 1503, Cajetan had offered standard
arguments for the immortality of the soul: the independence of intellectual activity from the body, and the universal desire for a life that
is everlasting. In his sermon he mentions the difficulties felt by many
thinkers on the point but offers what he says as a solution to them
(Laurent [593] XXIII). Just so, in his commentary on the *Summa*, he
expresses no dissent from the arguments offered by Aquinas at *ST* I,
q. 75. But in 1510 he published a commentary on the *De anima*, the
work in which Aristotle considers, among other things, the status of
the soul and its relation to the body: the source of Cajetan's dissent
at the Lateran in 1513 appears in this commentary.[1]

The opening chapter of the *De anima* contains two texts to which
Cajetan repeatedly returns. Some activities, Aristotle writes, seem

to involve the body in their very notion – being angry is one example. He adds: "Understanding is most like something proper [to the soul]. But if this too is *phantasia* or not without *phantasia*, understanding itself will not exist without the body" (403a). *Phantasia* in Aristotle can have more than one meaning, but for Cajetan it amounts to sensory activity, and he employs the word *phantasma* (plural *phantasmata*) interchangeably with it. He takes Aristotle as seeing this indispensability of *phantasia* for thought as an obstacle to regarding intellectual activity as being "proper to the soul" – that is, as being an activity that does not essentially involve the body. It can indeed be distinguished from bodily activity, but the distinction does not amount to real separability. Rather, the distinction is like the distinction we draw about geometrical figures. As Aristotle wrote in the same chapter: "a straight line has, in virtue of its straightness, many attributes, such as touching a brazen sphere at one point only; but the straight line, if separated, would not so touch the sphere" (403a12).

Cajetan dwells on these texts (I Summary; 31; 40; 47) and states Aristotle's conclusion: that we have here no more than a "formal separation" – a distinction like that between a geometrical figure and its physical embodiment. The distinction does not allow us to infer that the figure could exist without any embodiment at all.

Cajetan keeps these texts before him when commenting on passages, in Book III of the *De anima*, which consider the possible separability of the soul from the body. It is only if understanding can be deemed an operation proper to the soul that the soul can be deemed separable. Cajetan then states that there are two kinds of independence from the body that such an operation can demand. One of them would exclude there being any organ of the intellect – and this position was adopted by Aquinas and other philosophers. But the other, stronger independence would exclude any kind of bodily dependence whatever, and for Cajetan this was the position adopted by Aristotle (III 106–08 [592]). Writers in the Middle Ages had developed Aristotle's distinction between the *potential* intellect (by which we think) and the *active* intellect (by which we bestow intelligibility on the *phantasmata* from the senses). Cajetan held that for Aristotle it was the active intellect alone that had the stronger independence. All the operations of the potential intellect are mixed with *phantasia*, mixed with the senses. It is the active intellect alone that thinks by its own substance and not intermittently; it is the active intellect alone that can be really separate (*separatus in essendo*); the potential intellect can be only "formally separate" (Cajetan cites again the analogy with the geometrical figure); it is the active intellect alone that is separable and immortal; the potential intellect is corruptible (III 93–95). And all this is said by Cajetan to be of a piece with other texts of Aristotle which claim that our capacity for happiness is limited and temporary, because our soul is intellectual only by sharing in the light of the active intellect (III 115; Cajetan refers to the *Nicomachean Ethics*).

More than once Cajetan insists that he is concerned only with expounding Aristotle: he is not to be taken as sharing in Aristotle's attacks or defenses (III 1). And, later in Book III, he denies that he has been trying to prove the potential intellect to be corruptible "according to philosophical principles." His text makes no appeal to the theory of two separate orders of truth. Faith shows the falsity of the proposition that the soul is corruptible, and a false proposition cannot be implied by what is true (i.e., by philosophical principles). He goes on: "I have been simply concerned to expound the view of that Greek [*istius graeci*], and I will try to demonstrate its falsity on philosophical grounds" (III 102) – which indeed he then goes on to attempt (III 103ff.). But before seeing something of what he does offer, we must see why his account of Aristotle's opinion raised the opposition it did.

Aquinas had proposed a view of the soul which offered a synthesis of what he deemed to be Aristotelian thought with inherited Christian belief. He accepted Aristotle's account of human knowledge as starting from the senses and from the *phantasmata* they provide. But this did not exclude for Aquinas the survival of the soul. Its dependence on *phantasmata* is a dependence on them only as *objects*. The intellect has no dependence on the body as an *organ* (in the way that sight depends upon the eye). When it is separated from the body, the absence of *phantasmata* as objects can be supplied by divine power (see, e.g., *ST* I, q. 89, art. 1). Aristotle was thus to be seen as providing a philosophical scheme which was compatible with, and supportive of, Christian belief.

But now an eminent theologian, a Dominican and a cardinal, was presenting an Aristotle who resisted such a synthesis. Cajetan's challenge was taken up by two other Dominicans, Spina and Catherinus.

Their attacks on Cajetan were angry and abusive: Aristotle has been
incorporated into the received wisdom of theologians and philosophers; in setting him apart from that tradition, Cajetan was misusing
his talents and causing alarm and despondency.[2]

The annoyance of Cajetan's adversaries was not lessened by his
undertaking to show, on philosophical grounds, that Aristotle was
wrong (III 102), or even by his claim that a proof of immortality can
be based on Aristotelian principles (III 103). He invokes the argument
used by Aquinas (*De Anima* III, n. 680), that the intellect has no bodily organ; so its dependence on the body, which for Aristotle was
unqualified, is in fact no more than accidental (*per accidens*). And
so is circumvented Aristotle's point that dependence on *phantasmata* prevented understanding from being an operation "proper to
the soul" (III 120). But to call the soul's dependence on the body
"accidental" does not go easily with the claim of Aquinas that the
intellectual soul is the form of the body (*ST* I, q. 76, a. 1). Again,
the distinction Aquinas draws between dependence as on an organ
and dependence as on an object is not considered – as it could hardly
be, given Cajetan's insistence that Aristotle claimed a radical dependence of intellectual activity upon the body. Most annoying of
all, perhaps, was the fact that he fills out the proof he has offered
with a further argument, found indeed in Aquinas (*ScG* II 68) but
Neoplatonic in origin, that the harmony of the universe calls for the
existence – above material forms but below the spiritual forms of
angels – of a form that in its way shares in both orders (III 122–23).
Thus alone, he adds, is the status of the soul preserved.[3] We have
come a long way from Aristotle.

We can now see more clearly the significance of Cajetan's dissent
at the Lateran Council. He was faced with a tradition of religious
speculation for which Aristotle was central, and with a centrality
given through the synthesis achieved by Aquinas. He was also faced
with attempts made in his own time to seize the thought of the
ancient world on its own terms. The two things simply did not go
together. Cajetan never considered denying the immortality of the
soul, but he was impressed by Aristotle's claim for a radical dependence of intellect upon the body, and his attempts to counter the
claim did not fit in easily with what Aquinas had written. The figure of Aristotle still exercised its power, though in a direction others
found unwelcome. In his later commentary on the Epistle to the

Romans, Cajetan classes the immortality of the soul with the riddles raised by predestination – they are matter for faith, not argument. Synthesis and harmonizing were for the Middle Ages; what Cajetan wrote showed that those ages were over.

The effect of distinctions

Cats learn to recognize cat doors; but it takes humans to reach the concept of a rectangle. According to Aquinas (see above, p. 218), conceptualizing is a process in which the active intellect raises the data provided by our senses, the individual phantasms existing in the sense organs, to a new and generalized mode of existence, producing in the potential intellect a representation of the common nature that is in the phantasm, but without the material and individuating conditions there. That is how we can see the cat door and also "see" its shape as sharing properties with the shape of the page of a book, and can call each of them a rectangle. This account tries to deal with a perennial problem, and a disagreement between two writers of the time can encourage thought about something else associated with medieval philosophy – its making of distinctions.

One of the two we have already met – Cajetan; here we shall be referring to his commentary on Aquinas's *Summa theologiae* (it is included in the Leonine edition of the *Summa*). The other, a century later, is the Spanish Jesuit Francisco Suárez (1548–1617). Both were concerned with texts in which Aquinas had discussed the matter; both were in sympathy with his reasons for holding the active intellect to be necessary; both went on to ask further questions about the nature of what it did.

Cajetan (commenting on *ST* I, q. 79, a. 3) states a medieval objection to any cooperation between the active intellect and the phantasm. If the phantasm is material, it cannot act upon the intellect, which belongs to a higher order; and this inability remains, even when the power of the active intellect is invoked – the phantasm is material, and what is material cannot affect what is spiritual. Cajetan replies that indeed we cannot treat the phantasm as if it contained the concept which the active intellect then educes from it; the phantasm is and remains of the material order. The effect of the active intellect is rather that the phantasm, previously existing independently, is now at the service of something else; it can now do more than it could; and the active intellect is able to educe the concept from the potential intellect itself (paragraphs 4 and 5).

He goes on to consider, among other things, the *abstraction* by which the phantasm is raised to the generalized intelligible order. For this, he makes a distinction to do with the effect of light. The *formal* effect is to illuminate the medium, the *diaphanum*, as the medievals called it; the *objective* effect is to illuminate bodies. The phantasm is illuminated *objectively* by the light of the active intellect, in such a way that there shines out, not everything in it, but the nature there without its singularity. The concept formed in the potential intellect is the *formal* effect of the active intellect's force, and is of its very nature abstract and spiritual. The objectively illuminated phantasm is abstract and spiritual only according to the illumination given it (paragraphs 9 and 10).

Suárez considers the same topic in Book IV of his *De anima*. He admits that both phantasm and active intellect are needed, but asks how we are to understand the illuminative function of the latter (IV 2.4 [616]). How can what Cajetan says be accepted? The whole action of the active intellect is spiritual; how can it affect the phantasm, which is material? But if the phantasm in itself is unchanged, in what sense can it be said to be illuminated (IV 2.5)? Some, he goes on, have suggested that the phantasm is an *instrument* of the active intellect, that there is a certain virtual contact between them. These are only words: how can an instrument of a lower order affect what is of a higher order? Do not theologians already have problems enough in explaining how God can use fire to punish demons (IV 2.7)? The closest union we can imagine between active intellect and phantasm is that both are rooted in the same soul. But that in itself is not enough to explain the instrumentality – you might as well argue that, since the phantasm is rooted in a spiritual soul, it needs no active intellect in the first place (IV 2.8).

It seems best to say, he concludes, that the phantasm's role is one of material, not efficient causality (IV 2.10). This does not mean that the concept, which is spiritual, is educed from the phantasm, which is material. But, because of the union of active intellect and phantasm in the same soul, the phantasm does offer the active intellect what is in a sense material for it to work on, as it were a sample (*exemplar*). Because of this union, they have a certain wondrous order and harmony (*consonantia*): by the very fact that the intellect operates, so does the phantasm – Suárez uses here the word *imaginatio* (IV 2.12).[4]

Cymini sectores – this disagreement can throw light on the medieval making of distinctions.

Distinctions are not dissections: distinguishing the color of an apple from its shape is not the same as peeling the apple. But dissection, taking apart, is the most vivid and most easily grasped way of showing that one thing is not another. To treat all words on the model of names has been a temptation that philosophers have not always resisted. Just so, I suggest, the elaboration of distinctions is liable to make them be taken as dissections – but dissections conducted in an order both elusive and intangible.

For note the difference between what Aquinas writes on this topic, and what we have seen in Cajetan and Suárez. At *Summa theologiae* I, q. 67, a. 1, Aquinas asks whether "light" can be used of spiritual things. He replies that we must distinguish the original application (*prima impositio*) of a name from the name's employment (*usus nominis*). Just as *see* is used originally of sight, but extended to other senses, so *light* is used originally of what makes things visibly manifest, but is then extended to what makes manifest in any kind of knowledge. We have already seen how words to do with light are extended to the role of the active intellect, but Aquinas states an objection to this usage at *ST* I, q. 79, a. 3, obj. 2: for vision, light is needed to illuminate the medium; but there is no medium for the intellect; so no illumination of the phantasm is needed. He replies that there are two opinions over the role of light: (1) it works directly on objects; (2) it works on the medium. For both of these, the active intellect resembles light, since the former is necessary for knowledge just as the latter is necessary for vision. But for (1), the resemblance goes further – as light makes colors visible, so the active intellect forms concepts. For (2), the resemblance is simply the general necessity that exists for light in one order and for the active intellect in the other: the medium plays no part in the comparison.

For Aquinas, in other words, the extension of visual imagery to the intellectual order does not commit us to claims about the mechanism of conceptualization. All that matters is that we can pass from the data provided by our senses to the concepts we employ. There is a "making manifest," and so we can apply to it the terminology of light.[5]

But applying the terminology in this way is in a sense an end in itself. We are simply saying that, just as colors of themselves do not amount to vision, so conceptualization is more than perception. We may find the analogy satisfying; or we may think it should be complemented by others; but the analogy as such gives us no information as to how conceptualization takes place. Or, indeed, whether it takes place at all or is only confusion – we cannot use the analogy with light to distinguish Euclid's rectangle from the phrenologist's "bump of benevolence." We may indeed think that "conceptualization" is too generic a notion to be useful. But whatever we think, we cannot go to the analogy with light for an answer, as if a closer scrutiny would reveal just what procedure is going on. Yet in my opinion that is just what Cajetan and Suárez are doing. For example, to ask how the spiritual operation of the active intellect can affect the material phantasm is to miss the point of the comparison with light. The comparison says in effect: as colors need light for there to be vision, so the phantasm needs to be raised to a higher and generalized order for there to be understanding. We cannot go on to treat this comparison as a suggested mechanism, and then disagree as to the exact nature of the mechanism.

We have thought about the disagreement between Cajetan and Suárez. We can end this section by thinking about what they have in common. For Aquinas, we call the power that enables us to generalize the "active intellect," and we extend to it the terminology of light. For Cajetan and Suárez, the image of light is itself the starting point of another problem: for Cajetan, the phantasm cannot act upon the intellect; for Suárez, the intellect cannot affect the phantasm. I have disagreed with their whole approach, but that approach shows something they have in common. In the context of conceptualizing, both separate the orders of "material" and "spiritual" in a way that Aquinas did not. We are moving toward a world in which extension and thought are to be put asunder. And to the world of the seventeenth century we now turn.

Tradition and innovation

"I shall detect [atoms] with the spectacles of my understanding, and with the microscope of my reason": so wrote in 1674 the author of a work on "Peripatetic atoms" – an attempt to combine atomism with the scholastic tradition.[6] The novelty of his language can introduce this section, because in the seventeenth century so many new things were happening: Gilbert and magnetism; Napier and logarithms; Kepler and the planetary orbits; Galileo and the telescope turned to the heavens; von Guericke and the vacuum pump; Boyle's awareness of the need for a new start in investigating the composition of bodies... So many new things, so many new questions. Those new things we should nowadays count as science, but philosophy was just as full of disconcerting novelties. Bacon in 1621, at the start of his *Novum organon*, had explicitly set himself apart from what had gone before; in 1651 Hobbes in his *Leviathan* (I 8) had given a passage from Suárez as a sample of "Insignificant speech"; and the language and style, let alone the content, of Descartes's *Discourse* (1637) seemed to proclaim a new beginning. Had the tradition inherited from the Middle Ages anything to set beside all this?

Some minor figures need to be considered in this section, because their writings can show the ordinary preoccupations of those who, trained in the scholastic way, either defended it against the innovators, or themselves found fault with it. And I hope that the investigation will show how distinctions drawn in medieval philosophy were touched by the new setting in which it was now having to be practiced.[7]

A standard charge against the Aristotelian tradition was that it was uninformative. We have already met Molière's jest that "a dormitive virtue" explains why opium induces sleep. That was in a comedy; but it was of a piece with what was said elsewhere. Le Grand, to whom is attributed the introduction of Descartes's philosophy into England, asks what would be the use of appealing to a scholastic "form" to explain the phases of the moon or of Venus ([610] Book I iv.7.6). So it is interesting to notice that the counterattack made against Cartesianism by Pardies was of more than one kind. He asks how much more informative Descartes is in explaining the nourishment of plants by "a certain shape (figure)" than the scholastics with their "intussusception" ([614] §§59–60) – so setting himself apart from the mathematical and quantitative approach that was to play such a part in explanation. He then makes a theoretical point that shows how far apart old and new were. Do not Cartesians stop at the surface of things, while the traditional philosophy, with its talk of forms, points onward to the reason for them? The new philosophers may well say they are preparing to investigate nature; we prefer to open the mind (*esprit*), and with an eye to theology ([614] §85). And to these objections he adds a social consideration. Is not the spirit of the Cartesians unsuitable for polite society (*les honnêtes gens*)? Thus, to say that a key can open a door because it has "an aperient virtue" is surely more suitable than to give a detailed account of its wards and mechanism – that would be turning philosophy into a locksmith's workshop ([614] §§76–81).[8]

Another countercharge made by Pardies – that Descartes's matter is too uniform to account for all the variety in the world – leads naturally to another theme that preoccupied both sides of the debate. The ultimately Aristotelian distinction between matter and form seemed (like some other things in that tradition) most persuasive when applied to what was living. There, the unity and the continuity over time of the object could be easily distinguished from its physical composition, which varied as time passed. But in the seventeenth century much attention was being paid to inanimate nature – the movement and collision of bodies, the laws of planetary motion, the compounding and separation of the stuffs that make up the world around us. What was to be made of the older distinction in such novel contexts?

For Goudin, mixtures were either imperfect (where the components retain their own nature) or perfect (where they do not). In perfect mixtures, he contends, the form of the mixture is more than a mingling (*contemperatio*) of the elements, it is something distinct and substantial ([606] Book II, ch. 2). Were the compound no more than a mingling, the result would be simply like a garment made of different materials ([606] II 2). But another defender of the older way, La Grange, complains that he has never encountered a traditional philosopher who has given a satisfactory proof of substantial forms, especially those of inanimate bodies ([600], preface 45). His own examples of accidental forms concern the human soul – knowledge and virtue are real and distinct from it (IV 1–3; III 2). There is no need to postulate any new entity to explain why a bent stick is bent one way rather than another: there is a need, if we are to say why the just man is inclined toward what is good (III 8). He does give one example from inanimate nature of where scholastics make change to be substantial – this is burning, where fire is converted into smoke and smoke into water. Here we have more than a change of shape, or a movement of parts (as there would be in carving a statue out of a column); rather, one entity is lost and another produced. The matter of the fire loses the form of the fire and acquires that of air (I 3).

Goudin writes in a similar way about burning. The influence of the fire produces an accidental change in the wood, and then eventually destroys it by inducing the form of fire into the wood's matter ([606] I 1). And in perfect mixtures there are properties more noble than the properties of what composes them. Of these, plants and their structure provide one example. Another is provided by the wondrous powers of minerals (*metalla*): the magnet, the mixing of gold and mercury (where the amalgam is denser than the mean of the two metals), and the capacities of jade to ease pain and of jasper to staunch blood (II 2.2). But, having said all that, he adds the qualification that the argument for forms works "at least for animals" (II 2.2). So a scholastic philosopher appeals to experience to vindicate Aristotle; but then seems to doubt whether the appeal is decisive or not. We might well wonder what could count here as decisive.

We have seen so far some differences of opinion about the terminology of medieval philosophy – its alleged lack of informativeness, the range of its applicability, and the adducing of experimental evidence to support Aristotelian distinctions. We now turn to a deeper dissent – the charge that both its terminology, and the distinctions embodied therein, are misleading and incomprehensible. Let us start with a simple example to see why. If I heat a vessel of cold water, the water becomes hot, but what is in the vessel all the time is water. If I end with the stuff with which I started, the change would be called one of quality or *accidental*. But if a vessel of wine turns into vinegar, I cannot ask what was in the vessel all the time, because I end with a different kind of stuff; the change is not accidental but *substantial*. But the distinction drawn in the former is now applied to the latter. Just as the water was first of all cold and then hot, so the *matter* of the wine is informed, first by the *form* of wine and then by that of vinegar. The water is *potentially* cold or hot; the matter is *potentially* wine or vinegar.

There are two observations to make about this: one concerns matter, the other concerns form. First for that concerning matter. If we have two different examples of substantial change (say, wine to vinegar and wood to ash), we cannot infer that we have the same matter in each case. That would be to pass from "in every substantial change, there is matter which is informed first one way and then another" to "there is matter which, in every substantial change, is informed first one way and then another." Apart from committing a logical fallacy, we should here be committing ourselves to holding that anything can change into anything, for we should be holding that the one matter underlies wine, vinegar, wood, and ash alike. And such a claim needs proof. But matter – *materia prima*, as it was called – was commonly seen in this way in the Middle Ages and also by those who came after. Valeriano Magni, when giving an exposition of the traditional view, says that all living things pass away into what is inanimate; inanimates in turn pass away into the elements; and the elements can be transformed into each other; prime matter is the ultimate subject of all these changes; it can become all things ([620] Book I, ch. 7). For Du Hamel, that is the trouble: what *is* this indeterminate matter that remains under all changes? All appeal to it, none explain it. Better to treat the elements as matter; they do not pass away into each other. They have each a definite character – how could anything as vague and indeterminate as *materia prima* exist ([602] *De consensu* II 11; Valeriano Magni makes the same point in [620] Book II, ch. 6)?

Now for the second observation, concerning form. We must not treat matter and form as if they were *things*. As Aristotle himself put it, if we do so we shall have to apply to *them* also the distinction between matter and form, and are thereby launched into an infinite regress (*Metaphysics* VII 8). The temptation to do so is strongest with substantial change because, when wine turns into vinegar, we cannot ask what was in the vessel the whole time. That is because the question makes no sense – but it is easy to give it an appearance of sense by making something indeterminate be in the vessel the whole time, which is determined first by the form of wine, then by the form of vinegar. And so we are faced with the further question, or rather conundrum of our own making – where do these forms come from and go to? Such complaints about forms are numerous in the authors we have seen objecting to the traditional distinctions. For Le Grand, scholastics must admit that there are many substantial changes each day – there will have to be just as many acts of creation and annihilation of forms. By what force? And what evidence is there for such acts (I iv.7.2–3 [610])? For Du Hamel, a form is a reality (*entitas*): if it did not previously exist, it must have been created; if it is "educed from the potentiality of the matter," as the scholastics say, how can matter provide so many forms without being depleted (II 2.7 [602])? Valeriano Magni also refers to the scholastic phrase, and also finds it unintelligible. What potentiality is this that matter has? Form is supposed to give matter its determination – how can it be "educed" from it (II 6 [620])?

Looking back on the controversy, we may feel that those who thus complained had only themselves to blame for misunderstanding the point of philosophical distinctions. Talk of substantial forms is meant to do justice to the unity, activity, and specific character of things. Leibniz praised the scholastic tradition for this, and for insisting on something he thought Descartes had neglected (*Discourse on Metaphysics* §§10–12). Indeed, in one work of 1670 he concludes with a letter devoted to the reconciliation of Aristotelianism with recent thought. But in the same letter he blames the scholastics for not accepting that specific explanations of phenomena must be given in terms of size, shape, and motion ([611]) and accuses some Aristotelians of his own day of tending to treat substantial forms as if they were "mini-gods" (*deunculi*).

The charge that philosophy was being confused with what we would call natural science can be illustrated by an example that was popular at the time: it can be found in Goudin (I 3.1 [606]), who defends its coherence, and in Valeriano Magni, who thinks it bewildering (II 6). Take a soldier, with his whiskers and his scars; suppose he is killed by a sword thrust and lies dead before us. What do we see? Not what we saw when he was alive: his soul, the form of his body, has gone, and so what we saw has been instantly corrupted to prime matter; but then just as instantly informed by the "cadaveric form." And if we think we are seeing what we previously saw, we are being deceived by similarity, as we might be over two eggs (Goudin I 3.1 [606]). In one sense, of course, Goudin is right: a corpse is not a living body. As Aquinas puts it, an eye in a corpse is an eye only equivocally (*ST* III 50.5; obj. 1 and 2 with responses). But the point here is one of philosophy – of logic, if we will. It is not a claim for some piece of physical legerdemain, in which instantaneous changes succeed each other. To say that – and Goudin's talk of eggs suggests that he was saying it – is to fall into just the confusion I have claimed to detect in Cajetan and in Suárez: it is to misread philosophy as talk of intangible mechanisms. There, we saw such talk about the work of the active intellect; here, we may say, we have it in an indeterminate matter with its complement of *deunculi*.

I suggest that one reason why scholastics were then tempted to talk in this way was the achievement of so many recent innovations. By such things, claims were being made about "how things worked" – and made with increasing success. The success was due to the pursuit of explanations in terms of, very generally, size, shape, and motion. Tradition, I suggest, was encouraged by what else was going on to treat its inherited distinctions as if they, too, were a kind of mechanism. Conversely, innovation saw itself as a rival to tradition: just as Du Hamel wanted to replace *materia prima* by elements, so he wanted an appropriate blending of elements to replace form. I said at the start of this section that we should count many innovations of the seventeenth century as science, and have gone on to complement them with examples of innovation in philosophy. The seventeenth century saw the distinction between the two disciplines being made, albeit not without pain and labor.

But the debate pointed to yet another disagreement between old and new. When Le Grand rejected as idle the scholastics' talk of forms, his attitude here was characteristic of the whole Cartesian tradition. It is instructive to see the response of the Jesuit Thomas Compton Carleton ("Comptonus"), who has been described as the first to defend substantial forms against such rejection (P. Di Vona [601]). Carleton's general tactic resembles what we have seen in Leibniz: the variety in things and the constancy of their behavior call for some principle of unity ([597] *Physica*, disputation 11). But he has far less to say about substantial forms than about the need for real *accidental* forms (disputation 12). And, as he makes clear, his reason is theological: such accidents are demanded by eucharistic theology. As he writes elsewhere in the same work: "To pursue philosophy as one should, it is important to be well versed in theology" (*De anima*, disputation 7).

The doctrine of transubstantiation called for the survival without their substance of the accidents of the bread and wine. It was not of course claimed that philosophy could prove the doctrine; but the Aristotelian distinction had at least to be deemed coherent, and speculations about the nature of qualities had to take account of this. The Council of Trent had declared in 1551 that "transubstantiation" was used "most fittingly" of the Eucharist. In other words, the language inherited from the Middle Ages had been, it was contended, in a certain measure consecrated by this theological use (La Grange, preface). Nor was it enough to say that Descartes was concerned only with natural topics – not enough, that is, unless we are to accept the doctrine of two unconnected orders of truth (Pardies [614] §§6–7). The older tradition was claiming to be divided from the newer theologically as well as philosophically.

But if substantial forms claimed less attention than accidental forms, still less attention – in fact none, as far as I can see – was bestowed on what we should now regard as the greatest novelty in Descartes: his methodic doubt, his setting his mind apart from all else, his invocation of God and self as what ultimately resists attempts to doubt. Such a starting point is, to put things mildly, alien to what is found in a thinker like Aquinas; yet it was neglected in the polemic of those defending the medieval tradition. A recent work by Stephen Menn [612] propounds an explanation – that Descartes can be seen as building on the tradition associated with St. Augustine, for whom God and the soul are the foundation for all else. His having long preceded the later medieval debates gave him the advantage of neutrality over what had followed; and the seventeenth century, which saw the tradition associated with Aristotle under such pressure, saw the prestige of Augustine ever greater, as both sides in the theological debates appealed to him. It would be wrong simply to identify the thought and interests of Descartes with those of Augustine, and the link between them did not preserve the Cartesians from attacks on eucharistic grounds; but Descartes's apparently new beginning was not as novel as it appears to us.

Better, the beginning itself was not so novel, but novel indeed was the range of ideas and systems as later philosophy went its own luxuriantly variegated way. Leibniz (and, derivatively, Wolff) explicitly preserved elements of the Aristotelian tradition, and any philosopher was liable to encounter problems that, unknown to him, medieval philosophers had already faced. But the medieval tradition itself contracted to settings that stood apart from development.[9] It lived on after a fashion in seminaries, where theological terminology called for some acquaintance with the older inheritance. Yet it is worth pointing out that, despite the attention paid by writers such as Carleton to the problems raised by the Eucharist for Descartes, Cartesian accounts of it were taught in seminaries until well into the nineteenth century.[10] Other survivals were picturesque rather than significant. The degree of Bachelor of Arts was still conferred in nineteenth-century unreformed Oxford by granting (quite vacuously) the license to lecture "upon any book of the logic of Aristotle." And there lingered on until my own day the custom at Ushaw College, Durham, of referring to a ration of extra sleep in the morning as "an Aristote." The language was French, but Aristotle himself was here accorded a dormitive virtue.

CURRENT ENGAGEMENTS (JOHN HALDANE)

Readers of this Companion will by now be able to detect the presence of medieval philosophy in a great deal of modern thought. Descartes was no Augustine (and Augustine had none of Descartes's interest in finding sure and certain foundations for the natural sciences), but the first-person starting point shared by the two thinkers determines other points of agreement, and Augustine's *Confessions* has never lacked for readers with theological or literary interests. Links to medieval philosophy have been noted earlier for the other two great continental rationalists, Spinoza and Leibniz. Renaissance scholars turned away from Aquinas's interpretation of Aristotle, and seventeenth-century scientists supposedly rejected the entire Aristotelian worldview, but scholastic Aristotelianism (Protestant as well as Catholic) underlay many of the positions taken by those who were most outspoken in rejecting it (including, again, Descartes, as we shall see). Even where direct acquaintance with medieval texts is difficult to establish, illuminating, if risky, comparisons can still be made (of Locke with Abelard on real and nominal essences, for example, or Hume with Ockham on impressions and ideas).

Though widely present, however, significant relationships of medieval to later philosophy were not generally acknowledged from the seventeenth through much of the nineteenth century.[11] The present lively interest in the subject of this volume is thus a comparatively recent phenomenon. In what follows I will trace briefly some of the roots of this renewal of historical awareness and philosophical engagement and indicate some of its major manifestations on the current scene.

Roots of renewal

By the middle of the nineteenth century a broad interest in medieval thought was occasioned by general cultural movements such as the Gothic revival in art, architecture, and literature and the development of medieval history. Even in countries such as Britain where the Protestant Reformation had been victorious, and in France where the tides of secularism had risen highest, the cultural rediscovery of the Middle Ages by the likes of the eclectic Victor Cousin (whose influence ranged as far as the American transcendentalists) and the multitalented historian Jean-Barthelemy Haureau favored the revival of medieval philosophy. The course of modern philosophy itself had run far enough in various directions to justify interest in medieval thinkers as providing fresh alternatives. Resources for the study of the large portion of medieval philosophy to be found in theological texts were increased dramatically by the publication of *Patrologia graeca* (162 volumes) and *Patrologia latina* (221 volumes) between 1844 and 1866 under the editorship of the abbé J. P. Migne. Other publications of medieval sources followed, generally with improved critical texts.

A powerful impetus to the study of Thomas Aquinas in particular was given by Pope Leo XIII's encyclical letter *Aeterni patris* (1878), which commends Aquinas as "the chief and master" of the scholastics, towering above all the others:

Philosophy has no part which he did not touch finely at once and thoroughly; on the laws of reasoning, on God and incorporeal substances, on man and other sensible things, on human actions and their principles, he reasoned in such a manner that in him there is wanting neither a full array of questions, nor an apt disposal of the various parts, nor the best method of proceeding, nor soundness of principles or strength of argument, nor clearness and elegance of style, nor a facility for explaining what is abstruse.[12]

Such high praise could not go unheeded in Catholic circles. Within two decades there had been established the Leonine Commission, charged with the task of producing scholarly editions of all of Aquinas's writings (a project still far from completion), and the Academy of St. Thomas in Rome and the Institute Supérieur de Philosophie at the University of Louvain, in both of which his thought might be studied.

Of these and other products of the nineteenth-century revival, by far the most important in shaping the course of European and, ultimately, North American study of medieval philosophy generally (not just of Aquinas and not just by Catholics) was the Louvain institute. The importance of Louvain lies in three areas. First, it engaged in serious and systematic scholarly research of a sort that raised the study of medieval figures to the best standards existing in other areas of history of philosophy. Second, it became increasingly self-conscious about its methodological and historiographical presuppositions, raising questions about the intellectual unity of medieval thought, the diversity of its sources, the range of its literary forms, the variety of its purposes, and suchlike. Third, it sought to engage medieval traditions in an intellectual exchange with contemporary philosophy and science, in the hope both of updating the older traditions in light of modern theories and concepts and of showing the continuing relevance of a system such as Aquinas's to the understanding of the metaphysical structure of reality.

The preeminence accorded to Aquinas in *Aeterni patris* as, in effect, "greatest of the great and truest of the true" produced a degree of pressure to harmonize interpretations of other figures with that of Aquinas in an assumed doctrinal unity among the church fathers and the original scholastics. The new scholarship had, however, revealed differences among medieval thinkers, the extent and depth of which has grown increasingly evident with subsequent study. Maurice de Wulf embarked on the task of producing a systematic and comprehensive history of philosophy in the medieval Christian West. De Wulf's *Histoire* was important in establishing, through successive editions, a series of possible bases upon which the proclaimed synthetic unity of medieval philosophy might be seen to be founded.[13] It would be fair to say that subsequent scholarship has tended to eliminate these as sole foundations, encouraging the present pluralistic assessment of those centuries as ones of quite considerable diversity, including at one end of a spectrum work that is essentially religious, at the other end that which is entirely independent of theological content, and in between the bulk which exhibits varying forms and degrees of connection with religious ideas.

Ironically, if one thinks of the recent relationship between the dominant French and Anglo-Saxon philosophical modes, it was in Paris that the most important developments for the study of medieval philosophy in the English-speaking world occurred. Jacques Maritain (1882–1973) and Etienne Gilson (1884–1978) were Thomists, each in his own way, but their approaches to Aquinas were also applicable to other medieval thinkers. For Maritain, a boldly restated Thomism provided a philosophy that spoke *of* the universe, *to* the world, and *about* the meaning of human life. More than any other author in the middle third of the twentieth century, Maritain threw a medieval system of thought into the general philosophical mix as a worthy intellectual alternative.[14] For Gilson the route to Aquinas was via his study of Descartes and an investigation of the intellectual background of Cartesianism, which, as he discovered to his surprise, was markedly scholastic. In tracing the threads of scholastic thought Gilson was led back to the ideas of Aquinas, which struck him as being better than those of the figure he had originally chosen to study. Stimulated by this discovery, he began a systematic exploration of the thought of the medievals, reading extensively through primary sources (Greek, Jewish, and Islamic, as well as western) and developing a broad metahistorical understanding of the period. As a result, although he remained a Thomist, Gilson was able to give generously positive accounts of figures quite different from Aquinas: Augustine, Bonaventure, Scotus, and even, at one stage, Ockham.[15]

War in Europe gave Maritain and Gilson reason and opportunity to visit North America, and they both became regular presences there. Gilson founded the Pontifical Institute of Medieval Studies (PIMS) at the University of Toronto, which soon became the leading center in North America for the study of medieval thought. PIMS produced several generations of scholars who spread the medieval revival throughout North America, its products generally holding to the Gilsonian contextualist historiography.

The study of medieval philosophy in the United States also owes a great deal to scholars such as Philotheus Boehner, an early associate of Gilson who inspired the serious study and editing of Ockham with the founding of the Franciscan Institute in St. Bonaventure, New York; Ernest Moody, whose own work on fourteenth-century logic and empiricism complemented Boehner's; Harry Wolfson, who provided a major impetus for the study of medieval Jewish,[16] and by extension Islamic,[17] philosophy in his many years at Harvard; and Norman Kretzmann. Apart from his own impressive scholarship, Kretzmann coedited with Anthony Kenny and Jan Pinborg the

influential *Cambridge History of Later Medieval Philosophy*
(*CHLMP*) and was one of the editors of the Yale Library of Medieval
Philosophy. At Cornell from 1966 he helped form several generations
of scholars and philosophers who engage with, and make theoretical
use of insights from, medieval philosophy, without themselves being
neoscholastics.

An encouraging result of the work of these and other scholars is
the extent to which the various strands of medieval philosophy –
Christian, Jewish, and Islamic; speculative and analytic; early and
late – have come to be considered together, both in publications and
at scholarly conferences, for example, in the sessions of the Society
for Medieval and Renaissance Philosophy in the United States and in
the international congresses and colloquia organized by the Société
Internationale pour l'Etude de la Philosophie Médiévale.

Another encouraging development is the entry of medieval
thought into the philosophical mainstream. For example, throughout
the twentieth century an interest in Aquinas's philosophical thought
has as often been associated with a concern for moral philosophy as
for philosophy of religion. Until the 1960s, Thomist ethics was pursued largely in isolation from the dominant Anglo-American tradition, but important work by the late Elizabeth Anscombe and by her
husband Peter Geach revealed to an analytical readership the interest and power of Aristotelian-Thomistic ideas. The same is true in
the field of logic. Both I. M. Bochenski in his *History of Formal Logic*
and William and Martha Kneale in *The Development of Logic* noted
the prejudice of earlier writers in assuming that little of interest was
produced after the Stoics prior to the modern period, and they began
to correct this by identifying areas of logic and semantics in which
the scholastics had been active. As these works and those of spe-
cialist medievalists like Moody came to be read, and as scholarly
editions and translations were produced, so logicians started to take
an interest, including some who were prominent in philosophical
logic, such as Arthur Prior and Peter Geach.[18]

The current scene

In its origins, the phenomenological-hermeneutic tradition in modern philosophy has significant relations with medieval philosophy.[19]
More recently, authors writing in this tradition or in one or another
of its postmodern transformations have explored points of analogy

between the thought of Aquinas and Heidegger, or Augustine and Derrida, and so on.[20] Related to these explorations, but more directly motivated by theological interests, is the work of the self-styled "radical orthodoxy" group.[21] Two points are worth noting in connection with the current engagements with premodern thought on the part of "continental" thinkers and the radically orthodox. First, in contrast with analytical philosophy, these movements show little interest in logic and the structural metaphysics of substances, properties and relations, identity, causality, supervenience, and so forth. Second, their attention tends to be directed toward either the pre- and early medieval era or the later medieval period, rather than upon such "golden age" figures as Aquinas, Scotus, and Ockham. These points are connected and related to the general and much discussed difference between contemporary continental and analytical thought as these are practiced independently of any historical interest.

The explanation, I believe, is that there is a parallel between the "scientific" character of analytical philosophy and the scholastic Aristotelianism of the likes of Aquinas; and another and quite different parallel between the "literary" nature of contemporary hermeneutical inquiry and the experiential, imaginative writings of Augustine, Eckhart, and Renaissance Neoplatonists. Moreover, the felt dissatisfaction of many with the domination of analytical philosophy by highly technical discussions closely parallels the complaints of Renaissance writers about the "logic-chopping" and "sophistical entanglements" of the scholastics. It will be interesting to observe, therefore, whether in coming decades analytical philosophy will be eclipsed as was its medieval counterpart by a quite different set of interests and modes of thought.

Beyond the development of post-phenomenological approaches, there are three other significant forms of contemporary engagement that are often combined to a greater or lesser degree. First, there is that motivated principally by a desire to understand the medieval thinkers, just as one might figures and ideas from other periods of the history of philosophy. Second, there is that which seeks to explore parallels between medieval and contemporary theories in the fields of logic, language, and the sciences ("natural philosophy" in medieval parlance) in the hope of illuminating both sides of the comparison. Third, there is that concerned to carry on philosophizing in the general tradition of the scholastics, but to do so aided by the techniques and insights of contemporary analytic thought. Let me term these three the "historical," the "comparative," and the "practicing" approaches, respectively, repeating the point that these are often combined, and adding that they are in any case broad tendencies rather than self-contained approaches.[22]

So far as the historical is concerned, this is practiced by scholars of quite different backgrounds and interests, some of whom focus on individuals, others on periods, others on broad areas such as metaphysics or ethics, and others on narrower fields exploring the ways these were treated by different writers or in different styles of work, such as commentaries, occasional questions, and extended systematic presentations. It is particularly important for this approach to have reliable critical editions of texts and precise yet informative translations supported by critical apparatus that complicates where complication is necessary but does not prevent a view of the woods as well as of the trees. Some of these texts are produced in the context of schemes involving publication of the entirety of a medieval figure's work – complete editions of Albert the Great, Aquinas, Henry of Ghent, Scotus, and Ockham are currently in process, as well as the first English translation of all of Augustine – but, increasingly, independent editions and translations are appearing reflecting the interests of individual scholars in such diverse figures as Abelard, Bradwardine, Grosseteste, Rufus of Cornwall, and Robert Holkot. A feature of this trend is that it is leading to a greater study of figures and periods both earlier and later than Aquinas, Scotus, and Ockham, whose work has long dominated the study of medieval philosophy.

Apart from its intrinsic value, this scholarship greatly assists pursuants of the second approach, for in order to explore parallels between medieval and contemporary thought one needs to have a good idea of what exactly the former involves. At times in the past, comparative work rested on superficial readings of medieval figures and sweeping generalizations about what "the medievals" thought or about the character of their work. As these readings have been corrected by historical and textual scholars, so the task of comparing and contrasting has become more precise with hitherto unnoted features becoming more prominent. Examples of this include the increased appreciation of the complexities in the understanding of mind, causality, and existence in someone such as Aquinas,[23] and the varieties and degrees of modality identified by scholastic writers.[24]

A rich area of comparative study is the broad field of logic and language. From the 1970s onwards there has been a steady flow of publications, some monographs but many single and multiauthored collections, covering such topics as truth, entailment, paradoxes, sophisms, reference, modality, and various applied and nonstandard logics such as deontic, epistemic, temporal, and relevance logic.[25] In tandem with this, authors such as E. J. Ashworth and Gabriel Nuchelmans have produced invaluable work on the philosophy of language in the medieval and later scholastic periods.[26]

Another fruitful field of comparative research, which also leads into the third category, the actual practice of philosophy in continuity with medieval thinkers, is philosophical theology. After a long period of trying to accommodate religious ideas to the dominant styles of English linguistic analysis before and after the Second World War, speculative thinkers interested in traditional Christian dogmas began to wonder whether the limitations lay less with theological thought *per se*, than with the empiricist assumptions of prevailing philosophical orthodoxies. Thus thinkers such as Alvin Plantinga and Richard Swinburne began to explore alternative possibilities at just the same time as other analytical philosophers such as Saul Kripke and Hilary Putnam were rediscovering traditional metaphysics, and yet others, such as Anthony Kenny and Norman Kretzmann, whose training equipped them to study the medievals but who were also well versed in analytical thought, saw the possibilities of drawing these sources together. So developed a broad movement, one expression of which was the Society of Christian Philosophers, whose journal *Faith and Philosophy* has provided a forum for inquiries that are as likely to draw on Aquinas or Scotus as upon William Alston or Swinburne.

As I indicated earlier, Norman Kretzmann's students at Cornell have typically engaged with medieval philosophy on its merits and thus qualify as practitioners in my sense of the term. I have in mind here especially Marilyn McCord Adams and Eleonore Stump. Kretzmann laid out a program of "faith seeking understanding" for modern philosophical theology in an essay using Augustine as the point of departure.[27] Toward the end of his life he pursued this program in critical dialogue with Aquinas,[28] a focus largely shared by Stump,[29] while Adams, now a professor of theology, finds insights in thinkers as diverse as Anselm and Ockham.[30]

Practitioners coming to engagement with medieval thought from other directions include Alasdair MacIntyre and John Finnis. MacIntyre's *After Virtue* was the first of a series of books in which he has developed a critique of modern ethical thought, and in providing an alternative he has drawn ever more deeply upon Aquinas (more precisely, on Augustine as corrected by Aquinas).[31] Finnis, first working in the context of English analytical jurisprudence, has come to present Aquinas as a source of important ideas about law and social morality, and this is beginning to find application in contemporary issues, both in his own work and in that of his former student Robert George.[32]

As in other areas, historical and comparative studies of medieval thinkers are set to enrich present philosophical practice. Quite how and how far this enrichment may occur depends in large part on the receptivity of philosophers who have no antecedent interest in medieval philosophy, as well as on those who practice in contemporary variants of medieval traditions, such as "analytical Thomists."[33]

A striking feature of current engagements with medieval philosophy is how they differ, not so much along the dimension marked out "historical," "comparative," and "practicing," as along that marked "analytical" and "radical hermeneutical." Certainly there are differences in what each chooses to focus upon in medieval philosophy, but it is hard to resist the thought that what is now called for is a phase of synthesis analogous to that achieved by the medievals themselves. I suggest that this might best be achieved by considering the ways in which they combined more effectively than later thinkers, our own generation included, the scientific and sapiential dimensions of philosophy. Be that as it may, what is certain is that medieval thought is now as much a part of the history of philosophy as is that of ancient Greece and Rome. This alone represents a major and welcome advance and one which is now set fair to be carried further forward.

NOTES

The first part of this chapter, on the Renaissance and Seventeenth Century, is by P. J. Fitzpatrick. The second part, on Current Engagements, is by John Haldane.

1. I cite Cajetan's commentary by book and paragraph in the edition of G. Picard and G. Pelland [592]. References to Laurent are to his introduction to I. Coquelle's earlier edition of the first two books [593]. In

[605] E. Gilson, developing and extending what Laurent wrote, gives a luminous survey of the controversies in Italy at that time concerning the immortality of the soul. I cite Aquinas's commentary on the *De anima* by *lectio* (lesson) and paragraph [225].

2. Spina's indignation can be seen from the passages given by E. Gilson [605].

3. Matters would not have been helped by remarks and interjections in Cajetan's text. Near the start of Book III, he reminds the reader that Aristotle has not justified the analogy he draws between intellect and sensation; adding that a proof will be offered later in the book – "and when you examine it you will see how great is our ignorance" ([592] 7). The circumvention of Aristotle's demand for dependence on *phantasmata* is followed by the insistence that Aristotle believed the dependence to be unqualified ([592] 111). The "Neoplatonic" proof is said to be the only way of safeguarding the status of the soul as a form and so spiritual and immortal – "although some obscurities may remain" ([592] 122–23). And objections to the position adopted are answered "for the comfort of novices, lest they be deceived" ([592] 124). People like Spina – and the Lateran Council, presumably – wanted something more than that.

4. Some have seen here an anticipation of Leibniz's "preestablished harmony" (E. Kessler [609] 516). Leibniz is said to have read Suárez's *Disputationes metaphysicae* like a novel (E. J. Aiton [591] 13). A survey of references by him to Suárez is in A. Robinet [615], but the references given there in the context of preestablished harmony all refer to prayer and grace, not to the intellect and *imaginatio*. The *Disputationes metaphysicae* had a long life as a textbook in many universities, and Schopenhauer – not the easiest person to please – commends it (*Parerga and Paralipomena* I, Sketch of a History of the Ideal and the Real, §6).

5. Cajetan at one place in his commentary on the *De anima* also seems to prescind from details in the analogy with light ([592] 78). But that does not inhibit his subsequent speculations ([592] 80–81).

6. Casimir of Toulouse, *Atomi peripateticae* [598] II 55.

7. I have chosen three authors to defend the scholastic tradition, and three to express difficulties raised by some inside that same tradition. Those favoring it are A. Goudin (d. 1695), a Dominican [606]; I. Pardies (d. 1683), a Jesuit [614]; and J. B. De la Grange, a member of the Oratory [600]. The reservations are expressed by J. B. Du Hamel (d. 1706), chancellor of the diocese of Bayeux, whose professed eclecticism is weighted against the scholastics [602]; A. Le Grand (d. c. 1700), a Franciscan missioner in England [610]; and Valeriano Magni (d. 1661), a picaresque Capuchin referred to in Pascal's *Provincial Letters* [620]. Editions of these authors vary, and pagination can be erratic. But their successive subdivisions

are clear, and I have given references by these. There is a useful list of authors in Casimir [598] preface. There is a very good recent treatment of the topic – more sympathetic than mine – in D. Des Chene [599].

8. The mathematical and mechanical skills of Pardies, the Cartesian tone of other writings of his (and, I should want to add, the elegant snobbery of what he writes about keys) have made some doubt the seriousness of his attack, which first appeared anonymously. But it seems (from the *Nouvelle bibliographie générale*) that he only prepared it for publication, and was not the author.

9. There were, of course, changes in some of the institutions claiming to continue the tradition of medieval philosophy, and the influence of Wolff showed itself. J. E. Gurr [607] has explored this topic and provides much information and guidance.

10. Brief details in P. J. FitzPatrick [603].

11. The neoscholasticism of the late eighteenth and early nineteenth centuries is a significant exception, on which see P. J. FitzPatrick in *CHLMP* 838–52. The major sources for current engagements with medieval philosophy do not lie in this movement, however.

12. For text of *Aeterni patris*, see V. B. Brezik [623] 173–97, quoted passage p. 187. See also J. Haldane, "Thomism," in *The Routledge Encyclopedia of Philosophy*.

13. The first edition of de Wulf's *Histoire* appeared in 1905. A translation of the sixth French edition was published in 1952.

14. See, for example, J. Maritain [633].

15. For E. Gilson, besides [9], [68], and [218], see [403] and note 27 below.

16. There has been a continuous awareness among Jewish philosophers of the importance of their medieval predecessors. See chapter 5 in this volume for the range of reactions, and see O. Leaman and D. Frank [12].

17. The modern study of medieval Islamic thought is a more recent and specialized field than the study of Latin medieval traditions. See T.-A. Druart [626] and chapter 4 in this volume, and S. H. Nasr and O. Leaman [11].

18. See, especially, P. T. Geach [627].

19. Several of the founders of this tradition were familiar with scholasticism and were or had been Catholics. Franz Brentano and Anton Marty had been priests. Martin Heidegger began at a Jesuit novitiate but quickly withdrew from it.

20. See J. Caputo [625] on Heidegger and Aquinas; G. Schufreider [144] in effect on Anselm and Heidegger; P. Rosemann [636] on Foucault; and, more generally, M. S. Brownlee *et al.* [624].

21. See J. Milbank and C. Pickstock [634].

22. For a different and finer-grained taxonomy see J. Marenbon [465].

23. See, for example, A. Kenny [631] and J. F. Wippel [262].
24. See S. Knuttilla [464].
25. See S. Read [47], P. V. Spade [475], and M. Yrjönsuuri [51].
26. See chapter 3 in this volume and G. Nuchelmans [468].
27. See N. Kretzmann [71]. For Gilson's earlier promotion of the idea of a Christian philosophy, see E. Gilson in A. Pegis [635] 177–91 and E. Gilson [628–29]. See F. van Steenberghen [637] for criticism of Gilson's project.
28. See N. Kretzmann [245–46].
29. See, for example, S. MacDonald and E. Stump [251] and E. Stump [259].
30. Besides M. M. Adams [318] see M. M. Adams [142] and her "Scotus and Ockham on the Connection of the Virtues" in L. Honnefelder et al., eds., *John Duns Scotus: Metaphysics and Ethics* (Leiden, 1996), pp. 499–522.
31. See A. MacIntyre [632].
32. See J. Finnis [240].
33. See J. Haldane [630].

14 Transmission and translation

As I write these words, I can see on my shelves an attractively bound set of sixteen volumes, each bearing on its spine the words "J. Duns Scotus Opera Omnia." One would be tempted to assume that these are *The Complete Works of John Duns Scotus*. Unfortunately, in medieval philosophy things are rarely so simple. Some of the works included in this set are not by Scotus at all, but were once attributed to him. Some of Scotus's genuine works, including his early *Lectura* on the *Sentences* of Peter Lombard, are not included. And what this set presents as Book I of Scotus's late (and very important) *Reportatio* is actually not the *Reportatio* at all, but another work whose authenticity and authority are vigorously disputed.

And there are further problems. The attractive modern binding belies the age of the edition itself. Open up any of the books, and what you will see is a photographic reprint of an edition first published in 1639. That edition (known as the Wadding edition, after its editor) is not a critical edition, made by weighing all the manuscript evidence according to established principles of textual scholarship in order to determine, with as much precision and certainty as possible, exactly what Scotus said or wrote. In many cases the editor simply looked at the one or two manuscripts he had handy and transcribed what he found there, sometimes without much attention to whether the resulting text even made good sense. Sadly, for much of Scotus's work this faulty edition is the best one we have. So one has to use it: but one has to use it with great care.

The pitfalls of the Wadding edition illustrate a general feature of the study of medieval philosophy: the gap that separates the authentic words of the medieval thinker one wishes to study from the Latin words one sees on the pages of a printed edition – and further still from the English words one sees in a translation. The aim of this chapter is to make clear both the nature and the size of that gap, not in order to dismay prospective students of medieval philosophy, but in order to explain the hazards in such a way that students can equip themselves properly to meet them. I will begin by discussing in a general way the channels of transmission by which medieval philosophy has made its way down to us. I then turn to three specific cases by which I illustrate some of those general points as they apply to texts of different sorts and from different periods. Along the way I draw attention to the kinds of errors that are liable to be introduced at the various stages of transmission between a medieval lecturer's spoken words and the text of a modern critical edition, and I outline the tools and techniques that the careful historian of medieval philosophy will use in order to minimize such errors, especially where no critical edition is available.

In the second half of the chapter I turn to problems of translation. I provide an example that shows how a reader can sometimes detect errors in a translation even without checking the Latin text, and another to illustrate how translations sometimes reflect controversial views about how a text is to be interpreted. I then conclude with a look at the translation of particular terms, discussing a number of standard translations that are apt to be misleading and giving some idea of the range of translation of certain key terms.

CHANNELS OF TRANSMISSION

In the ideal case we would have a carefully constructed and easily legible autograph (that is, a text in the author's own handwriting). Such ideal cases are exceedingly rare. Even in the few instances in which we do have autographs, the text can pose problems. An author can be careless about checking his work, or his handwriting can be dreadful. Aquinas, for example, is notorious for absent-mindedly setting down wrong words or phrases, and his handwriting is so difficult to read that only a handful of specialists can decipher it.[1]

In default of autographs (whether reliable and legible or not), we must rely on texts that are conveyed to us by some number of intermediaries. These range from (at one extreme) copies that were authenticated by the author himself to (at the other) distant descendants of lecture notes first recorded by a scribe who may not even have completely followed the discussion he was recording. Particularly in the days when philosophy was largely carried on orally, through lectures and formal public disputations,[2] the number of intermediaries between an author and our text, and hence the occasions on which errors and corruptions could be introduced, might be worrisomely great.[3]

For example, any given lecture (or series of lectures) might exist in two versions from the very beginning: one dictated by the master himself and another taken down by the students who attended. A statute of the University of Paris dated December 10, 1355 requires that masters of philosophy "utter their words rapidly so that the mind of the hearer can take them in but the hand cannot keep up with them," that they in fact speak "as if no one were taking notes before them."[4] Where this was the practice, student reports, called *reportationes*, were especially likely to contain omissions, mistranscriptions, and misunderstandings. Other students could make copies of such *reportationes*, thereby increasing the number of competing versions of one and the same lecture or disputation. Disputations were especially likely to generate discrepant *reportationes*, since not only were they more complex (and less orderly) than lectures, but they could also be reported either with or without the master's determination of the question.

A master who wished to establish a more definitive version of his text, an *ordinatio*, would revise and polish either his own notes or a student *reportatio* and present it to the university's official booksellers, or *stationarii*, for distribution. (When historians speak of "publishing" a work of scholastic philosophy, it is this official submission to the *stationarii* that they have in mind.) In making an *ordinatio* the master might reformulate certain arguments or add new material. Some errors in the original text might be corrected, but new ones could easily be introduced, especially if substantive revisions were not carried out consistently throughout the text. Often several years passed between the original lectures and the *ordinatio*; a master might choose to update his work to accommodate developments in his views in the meantime, but he might instead treat the earlier lectures as having a literary integrity of their own and refrain from substantial revisions.

The *ordinatio* would then circulate, not as a whole, but in units called *peciae*, unbound sets of (usually) sixteen pages each. As Jan Pinborg explains:

Since the *stationarius* normally has at least two sets of *peciae* of a given text, more or less identical, and since the *peciae* are hired one by one, any copyist may be combining *peciae* from two different sources into his copy, thus making different parts of his text of different critical value. Moreover, the *pecia* in itself is not a stable entity; it will suffer wear and tear, so that words or even whole sentences may have become difficult to read, corrections and marginal remarks (often totally irrelevant to the text) may have been added by less conscientious borrowers, etc. . . . We even have indications that some texts were changed so as to offer more acceptable doctrines.[5]

Further errors and changes could easily be introduced by copyists who were not philosophically sophisticated enough to understand the text well, others who were being paid piecework for their copying and had therefore a greater incentive for speed than for accuracy, and still others who were not interested in the text for its own sake but merely wanted to make copies of the bits they found useful. Some copyists simply became tired. And Anneliese Maier quotes a disgruntled copyist who refused to copy "a whole page of totally useless material" from Walter Burley.[6]

Error-prone though they undoubtedly are, these manuscripts are in some cases our only sources for a text, and in others they are an indispensable resource for correcting noncritical editions. A present-day user of manuscripts needs the specialized skills taught under three general headings: paleography, text editing, and codicology. Paleography is simply the study of writing. One needs some acquaintance with the variety of handwriting to be found in manuscripts, but what is especially important is familiarity with the complex system of abbreviations that scribes employed in order to save time and economize on writing materials (see figure 1). Fortunately, a modest competence in this field – enough to be of great help to a medievalist in philosophy who does not wish to be primarily a textualist – is surprisingly easy to acquire. One can get a good start by taking a one-semester course in medieval paleography or even by working through a paleographical manual on one's own.[7] Codicology, strictly speaking, is simply the study of *codices* (manuscript books). Its value for historians of medieval philosophy is that it can sometimes help

Figure 1 *Text of a passage from Scotus. Vienna, Österreichische National-bibliothek, cod. 1453, fol. 122 va, lines 22–29, used with permission. Transcription, translation, and commentary below.*

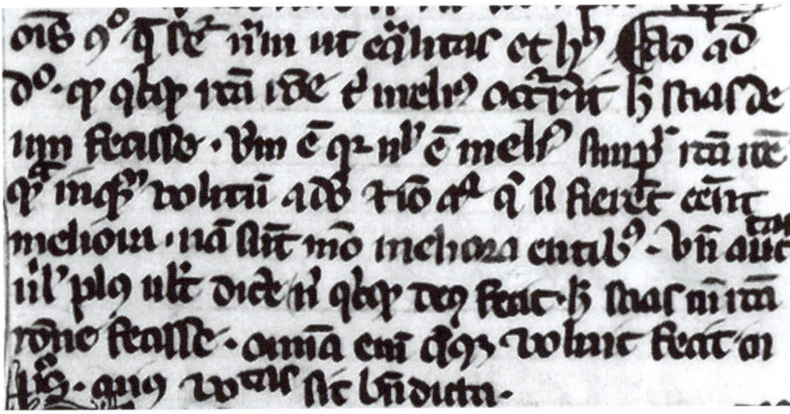

omnis con[diti]o quae se[quit]ur na[tura]m, ut [a]eq[u]alitas et huiusmodi. ¶ Ad a[liu]d | d[ic]o quod "q[u]icquid recta ratione t[ib]i melius occurrerit, hoc scias De | um fecisse": ver[u]m est quod nihil est melius simpl[icite]r recta ratione | quam inquantum volitum a D[e]o. Et ideo a[li]a quae, si fierent, essent | meliora, non sunt modo meliora entibus. Unde auc[tori]tas | nihil plus vult dicere nisi "q[u]icquid Deus fecit, hoc scias cum recta ratione fecisse; omnia enim quaecumque voluit fecit," in | Ps[alm]o – cuius vo[lun]tas sit benedicta.

[Translation] every feature that follows from the nature, for example, equality and suchlike. ¶ To the other [argument] I say that "whatever better thing occurs to you by right reason, know that God has made it": the truth is that nothing is unqualifiedly better according to right reason except insofar as it is willed by God. And so those other things that, if they were made, would be better, are not in fact better than existing things. Hence, the authoritative passage means nothing more than this: "Whatever God made, you must know that he made it with right reason; for all things whatever that he willed, he made," [as is written] in the Psalm – blessed be his will.

Manuscript dates from the fourteenth century and is written in an English semicursive hand. The heavily abbreviated style is characteristic of the period. Letters represented in the manuscript by standard symbols are underlined in the transcription; letters left out of words altogether are enclosed within square brackets. Thus, in the first line of the manuscript, "ois" with a line over it is transcribed as "omnis," since a horizontal line is a regular sign that an "m" or "n" has been omitted. The next combination is transcribed as "con[diti]o," since the first figure is a standard symbol for "con" or "cum," the final "o" is written out above the line, and the middle letters are simply dropped. Line breaks are indicated with a slash. Using these conventions, a patient reader will be able to piece together how one gets from the characters in the manuscript to the transcription. As can be seen, the punctuation in the transcription is largely editorial.

The text is from the replies to the objections at the end of John Duns Scotus's *Reportatio examinata* d. 44, q. 2. For a discussion of the significance of the second reply, see Williams [300] 195–98.

---

in retracing the process of transmission. Text editing is the study of the principles and techniques by which we determine the reliability and relative priority of particular manuscripts, identify families of related manuscripts, and (ideally) reverse the incremental changes introduced by successive copyists so as to produce a text as close as possible to the original.[8]

The next step in the process by which medieval philosophical texts have been transmitted to the present day is the early printed edition. As will become clear in the case studies below, these early editions are not especially scholarly. Nonetheless, they are our only printed source for some medieval texts, and in cases where the manuscripts from which they were derived are no longer extant, they provide an independent witness to the text that can be taken into account in a critical reconstruction. Modern critical editions are the final step. Modern editors take into account all the manuscript evidence (and that of early editions where these give an independent witness), form hypotheses about the development of the manuscript tradition and the relative critical weight of various manuscripts, and reconstruct the original text according to established principles of textual scholarship. But it is important to realize that even critical editions are not infallible. Some editorial decisions, for example, depend upon an editor's judgment about which reading gives the best philosophical sense in context; and that judgment may be disputable on philosophical grounds. Fortunately, critical editions provide an apparatus of variant readings, so that skeptical readers have at their disposal the information they need when a passage seems suspect. Moreover, the punctuation of a text – including sentence and paragraph divisions – is almost wholly editorial, since the manuscripts generally employ what might be called the random-dot method of punctuation, which is of almost no value as a guide to the sense of the text. Now it is not uncommon to find misleading or outright mistaken punctuation even in critical editions, and such mistakes can drastically alter the sense of a passage. The best advice is simply to ignore editorial punctuation altogether.

THREE CASE STUDIES

One can get a better sense of the varied fates of medieval philosophical texts by examining the works of specific thinkers. Here I offer three case studies, brief narratives of the channels by which the works of Anselm of Canterbury (1033–1109), John Duns Scotus (1265/6–1308), and Robert Holcot (d. 1349) have come down to us. The case studies have two aims. First, they are meant to give the reader a general idea about what to watch out for when studying medieval philosophy. The general lesson is that it is highly advisable, before undertaking serious work on a medieval philosopher, to acquaint oneself with the state of the manuscripts and editions of his work. More specific cautions will, I trust, become evident along the way. Second, the case studies are also meant to show how much textual and editorial work is yet to be done in medieval philosophy. Since it seems impossible to make any informative general statements about how much interesting work remains to be done along these lines, I have chosen three thinkers for whose works we have texts of quite different levels of reliability.

Anselm[9]

Many of the complexities in the process of transmission fortunately do not apply to Anselm's works, since they began life as written works and not as lectures. Moreover, we have at least one manuscript (Bodleian 271) whose scribe we can identify with reasonable certainty as a monk of Canterbury Cathedral known to have been in correspondence with Anselm himself about the correct reading of a passage in *De conceptu virginali*.[10] Anselm himself seems to have been especially conscientious about revising and perfecting his works before allowing them to be copied, although he does complain in one place that "certain over-hasty persons" have copied his dialogues in the wrong order,[11] and he does sometimes go back and make minor revisions and improvements. For example, the *Proslogion* originally had a different title and no chapter divisions. In this connection it is worth noting that chapter headings in medieval texts are often additions by later scribes, a point occasionally lost on interpreters who seek to make exegetical hay out of such inauthentic texts. The chapter titles in Anselm's works, however, originated with the author himself. It is their *placement* in modern editions and translations that is inauthentic: Anselm put the whole list of chapter titles at the beginning of a work and did not repeat them within the text itself.[12]

The early printed editions of Anselm are of almost no critical value. The first such edition, published in Nuremburg in 1491, was edited by an otherwise obscure scholar named Petrus Danhauser. F. S. Schmitt comments:

> It is not known which manuscript or manuscripts he used as the basis for the edition. To judge from the way the edition turned out, both on the whole and in details, they must have been exclusively late manuscripts that were easily accessible. Moreover, we cannot escape the impression that every now and then the young humanist laid an improving hand on the text that had come down to him.[13]

Since most later editions followed his text more or less uncritically, they are equally unreliable. Indeed, some editions actually made matters worse by adding to the number of inauthentic works Danhauser had included under Anselm's name. Not until the edition of Gabriel Gerberon in 1675 do we find an attempt to correct the received text on the basis of a large number of manuscripts, along with something approaching an apparatus of variant readings; but even then, the oldest and best manuscripts were not used. The critical edition of F. S. Schmitt, published in 1968, was therefore in essence a wholly new undertaking. Schmitt's edition is unusual in that it contains all the authentic completed works of a medieval philosopher as edited by a single hand and published in a single series,[14] making the present state of Anselm's texts enviably unproblematic. Only rarely have I found reason to question Schmitt's editorial decisions about which of a number of variant readings to accept; even the paragraphing shows great sensitivity to Anselm's text. So the student of Anselm's works can, to a remarkable degree, simply assume the reliability of the Latin text.

John Duns Scotus

As I have already suggested in my introduction, Scotus's works have come down to us in a particularly confusing state. Even the briefest attempt to tell the story of all his works would require far too much space,[15] so here I will illustrate the difficulties by discussing Scotus's *Ordinatio*, the revision of the lectures he gave as a bachelor at Oxford in the late 1290s. The basis for the revision was his original lecture notes, the *Lectura*. We can clearly discern at least two layers of revision. The initial revision was begun in the summer of 1300 and left incomplete when Scotus departed for Paris in 1302; it probably did not get much past Book II. Further revisions were made in Paris; we know that Scotus was still dictating questions for Book IV as late as 1304, as well as updating the parts he had already revised while still at Oxford. These updates were usually in the form of marginal additions or interpolated texts that reflected what Scotus taught in Paris. Our picture of the nature and extent of the second layer of revisions is, however, still murky, in part because the Vatican edition of the *Ordinatio* has reached only to the end of Book II, and no critical edition of the Paris *Reportatio* is available at all.[16] Much further study is needed in order to understand just how much the *Ordinatio* represents the views Scotus held at Oxford and how much he revised it to reflect developments in his views in Paris. At present, however, the most plausible view would seem to be that of Allan B. Wolter, who wrote that it is a

serious and inexcusable mistake for scholars writing on Scotus today to regard his *Ordinatio* as a seamless garment rather than a work begun in Oxford and left unfinished when he left Paris for Cologne. It is particularly unwise to consider the basic text of the eleven volumes of the Vatican edition so far printed as necessarily representative of his final views simply because parts were updated with a view to what he taught later in Paris.[17]

And Wolter argues persuasively that Book I of the *Ordinatio* "is simply a more mature expression of his early views, and needs to be supplemented by the later positions he held which can be found in the reports of his lectures at Cambridge and Paris"[18] – reports that for the most part have never been edited.[19] The paleographical skills needed to read the manuscripts of these *reportationes*, as well as those of the parts of the *Ordinatio* that have not yet been critically edited, are therefore highly desirable for a serious student of Scotus. The Vatican editors have already determined which manuscripts of the *Ordinatio* are most reliable, but modest skills in text editing are needed in order to weigh the merits of variant readings in those manuscripts and in the few available manuscripts of the *Reportationes*.[20]

Robert Holcot

The Oxford Dominican Robert Holcot is one of the many important medieval philosophers who have been seriously underappreciated and understudied. Although modern interest in Holcot has been somewhat sporadic, his influence in the late Middle Ages was great, as is evidenced by the great number of fourteenth- and fifteenth-century manuscripts of his work.[21] There are forty-eight manuscripts of his questions on the *Sentences* (compare this to the thirty-six manuscripts of Ockham's *Sentences* commentary) and an astonishing 175 manuscripts of his commentary on the book of Wisdom, a work that influenced Chaucer's "Nun's Priest's Tale."[22] He made important contributions to semantics, the debate over God's knowledge of future contingents, discussions of predestination, grace, and merit, and philosophical theology more generally. Here I will discuss only the fate of his questions on the *Sentences*.

Katherine Tachau comments that "for Holcot's *Sentences* questions... the evidence is strong that the *pecia* system was the basis for their dissemination."[23] Many manuscripts bear the traces of this system, as in a scribe's "crowding the margins with text for which he had not left sufficient room when copying *peciae* out of order, as they became available."[24] In some cases substantial portions of the text clearly dropped out in the course of transmission. Thus, in two early manuscripts, one counterargument to an earlier objection in Book II, q. 2, breaks off after just two sentences, and the counterarguments to the next three objections are missing altogether. Afterwards come the counterarguments to four more objections. In somewhat later manuscripts, those last four counterarguments have also dropped out, "almost certainly by the loss of a folio from an unbound quire."[25]

A text of Holcot's questions on the *Sentences* was printed at Lyon in 1497. In a cover letter to this edition Jodocus Badius notes that the scholar entrusted with reviewing the manuscripts had found the text in a disorderly state and that the manuscripts available did not allow him to establish a reliable text. Unfortunately, this edition is the only printed version of the *Sentences* available today.[26] No complete collation of the manuscripts of Holcot's *Sentences* questions has yet been made, and as far as I know, no critical edition is in preparation. Accordingly, Holcot is an outstanding example of a medieval thinker whose works offer a ripe field for both textual and philosophical study.

TRANSLATING MEDIEVAL PHILOSOPHY

We can think of English translations as the last, and inevitably the most problematic, step in the transmission of medieval philosophical texts. It is, of course, a very necessary step, not only for the wider dissemination of medieval philosophy to those who are interested in the subject but do not wish to become specialists, but also for the formation of specialists. For example, there is no telling how many people have been brought to a serious study of John Duns Scotus through the translations of Allan B. Wolter. More generally, it is surely no accident that the most widely translated medieval thinkers are also the most widely studied, for translations encourage study and studies encourage translation.

Given the aims of this chapter, I wish to concentrate here on matters that readers of English translations need to be aware of in order to make the most effective use possible of those translations. I should note first of all that even a modest amount of Latin can be very useful in working with an English translation and Latin text side by side, especially for thirteenth- and fourteenth-century texts, with their generally simple syntax and limited, largely technical vocabulary. (One rarely has the luxury, so common with classical texts, of working with multiple translations of the same text, which can be enormously helpful.) However good a translation is, certain passages will be open to misunderstandings that the translator could never have foreseen, and a reader with a bit of Latin can put herself back on the right track immediately.

Some faulty translations can be detected, if perhaps not also reme-
died, without any knowledge of Latin at all. Consider the following
passage from a widely used translation of Anselm's *Proslogion*:

Many words are used improperly, as, for example, when we use "to be" for
"not to be," and "to do" for "not to do" or for "to do nothing." Thus we
often say to someone who denies that some thing exists: "It *is* as you say it
is," although it would seem much more proper to say, "It *is not* as you say
it *is not*." Again, we say "This man is sitting," just as we say "That man is
doing [something]," or we say "This man is resting," just as we say "That
man is doing [something]." But "to sit" is *not* to do something, and "to rest"
is to do *nothing*.

The penultimate sentence has to be mistaken, since as this translator has rendered it, it does not offer the example that Anselm has
promised: that is, an example of "to do" being used for "not to do"
or "to do nothing." Moreover, the sentence is not properly parallel to the preceding one, as the "Again" leads us to expect it will
be. So simply by paying philosophical attention to the content of
the argument, we can know that there is something wrong with the
translation. A look at the Latin enables us to correct it to read as
follows:

Again, we say "This man is sitting just as that man is doing" or "This man is
resting just as that man is doing," even though "to sit" is not to do something
and "to rest" is to do nothing.

Now the passage gives the kind of example Anselm had led us
to expect. It should be noted that the translation I quoted first
is *grammatically* possible, given the Latin text; it just makes no
philosophical sense. Similar mistranslations occur when translators
attach modifiers, especially adverbial phrases, to the wrong element.
Once again, philosophical attention is all that is needed to recognize
the mistake, although recourse to the Latin text may be needed to
correct it.

In other cases, a translation might make enough sense in context
that one cannot recognize it as erroneous without comparing it to
the Latin original. Compare these two alternative translations of a
passage from Scotus,[27] both of which make perfectly good sense in
context:

A I say that God is no debtor in any unqualified sense save with respect to his own goodness, namely, that he love it. But where creatures are concerned he is debtor rather to his generosity, in the sense that he gives creatures what their nature demands, which exigency in them is set down as something just, a kind of secondary object of this justice, as it were. But in truth nothing outside of God can be said to be just without this added qualification. In an unqualified sense where a creature is concerned, God is just only in relation to his first justice, namely, because such a creature has been actually willed by the divine will.

B I say that God is a debtor, in an unqualified sense, only to his own goodness, that he love it. To creatures, however, he is a debtor in virtue of his generosity, that he communicate to them what their nature requires. This requirement is set down as something just in them, as a secondary object of God's justice. But in truth nothing external to God is just except in a certain respect, *viz.*, with the qualification "so far as it is on the part of a creature." The unqualifiedly just is only that which is related to the first justice, i.e., because it is actually willed by the divine will.

Note first that translator A says that God is a debtor *to* his generosity, whereas translator B says that God is a debtor *in virtue of* his generosity. This discrepancy is instructive because it reveals the extent to which translations are at the same time philosophically motivated (and therefore possibly tendentious) *interpretations* of the text being translated. In a number of influential articles and books, translator A has argued that according to Scotus, God owes it to himself to make his creatures good, so that God's generosity to creatures is itself a matter of justice: justice to himself, not (strictly speaking) justice to creatures. The expression "debtor to his generosity" would support that interpretation. Translator B, by contrast, has written a number of articles arguing that according to Scotus, God's justice to himself imposes no constraints on how he must treat individual creatures or the created universe as a whole. The words "a debtor in virtue of his generosity" are meant to suggest that it is solely a matter of generosity for God to give his creatures their characteristic perfections.[28]

The translations of the end of the passage also reveal an interpretive agenda at work. Scotus has identified God's "first justice" as his justice with respect to himself. When translator A says that "God is just only in relation to his first justice" when he "gives creatures what their nature demands," he conveys his view that in conferring perfections on creatures Scotus's God is being just, not really to his creatures, but to himself. By contrast, translator B's rendering of the sentence supports his reading of Scotus as an extreme voluntarist: what is unqualifiedly just is simply whatever God wills.

In cases like these, where faulty translations cannot be detected simply by philosophical vigilance, the user of translations needs to be able to form a judgment as to the general reliability of a translator. Consulting more senior medievalists about a translator's reputation can be helpful, but care is needed here, especially when the medievalists one consults are translators themselves, since translators seem to be temperamentally disposed to exaggerate the shortcomings of the works of others.[29] A better approach is to form one's own judgment about the translator's philosophical acuity by reading a representative selection of her articles. A sloppy philosopher will be a sloppy translator; an unreliable interpreter will be an unreliable translator. Indeed, to a limited extent, the translator's prose style is a good guide to the quality of her translations. A translator who habitually writes hazy English will produce hazy translations, but one who writes with precision will translate with precision. It is probably also true that someone who writes elegant English will produce elegant translations, but elegance, though gratifying to the reader, is seldom of philosophical significance, and the desire for elegance is a standing temptation to stray from strict fidelity to the text.

PAIRS AND SNARES

Strict fidelity to the text of course requires sound judgment in the choice of translations for individual words, and such judgment depends as much on philosophical sensitivity and an appreciation of English idiom as it does on one's command of Latin. In this section I wish to illustrate the difficulties that face translators by discussing words that are commonly mistranslated and words that defy exact translation. I also note the range of translation of some key philosophical terms.

Most common mistranslations result from a lazy preference for cognates. *Malitia* is often translated as "malice" and *officiosum* as "officious," to take just two examples. Now *malitia* can mean "malice" (a desire to inflict injury), but more often it means simply "badness." It is the opposite of "goodness," not of "benevolence." *Officiosum* is most commonly seen in the threefold classification of lies as *perniciosum, officiosum*, and *iocosum*. To translate these as "pernicious," "officious," and "jocose" is sheer laziness. "Officious" means "meddlesome" or "offensively forward in offering help or advice." A *mendacium officiosum*, however, is not a meddlesome lie but a serviceable and (as such) inoffensive one. (The meaning "obliging" for English "officious" has long been obsolete.) With both *malitia* and *officiosum* the correct translation is suggested not by the English cognate but by the Latin word formation: *malitia* is the abstract noun from "*malum*," meaning "bad" – hence "badness"; *officiosum* is the adjective from "*officium*," meaning "function" or "service" – hence "functional" or "serviceable." Attention to standard patterns of word formation when learning Latin is one of the best safeguards against this kind of mistake.

With *malitia* and *officiosum* perfectly good English equivalents are available but carelessly overlooked. For many other words there is no exact English equivalent, and one must make do with an approximation. There is, for example, no single English word that corresponds exactly to *appetitus* in its Aristotelian use: "tendency," "inclination," "desire," "directedness," and similar terms convey the right meaning in some contexts but not in others. The sensible convention is to use "appetite" as the invariable translation of *appetitus*, on the understanding that readers will recognize "appetite" as a term of art. Similar conventions justify the translation of *potentia* as "potency" or "potentiality," *actus* (in one of its senses) as "act" or "actuality," and *accidens* as "accident." However inexact such standard translations may be, they can hardly be called misleading, since any modestly well-trained reader of medieval texts will recognize them for the technical terms they are.[30] Indeed, there is some advantage to using words like "potentiality" that have no ordinary nontechnical use.

Sometimes, however, it is not clear whether a word is a technical term or not, or even whether it is being used with exactly the same meaning throughout a text. Does *honestum*, for example, describe items all of which exemplify some single property in a given thinker's moral ontology (say, intrinsic value), or is it a more general term of commendation whose exact meaning in its different occurrences depends on context? If the first alternative is the case, a consistent translation of *honestum* is probably advisable, although what that consistent translation should be is likely to be a contentious matter of interpretation; if the second alternative is the case, a consistent translation of *honestum* would be downright misleading. And of course these two alternatives do not exhaust the possibilities. Nor does the fact that a certain word is a technical term in one author imply that it is a technical term in any other author. For that matter, one and the same author may use the same term both as a technical term and as a nontechnical term even within a single work. Similar problems bedevil the translator faced with such protean terms as *principium* ("beginning," "origin," "premise," "principle," "starting point") and *ratio* ("argument," "basis," "concept," "definition," "essential nature," "feature," "ground," "intelligible nature," "meaning," "model," "reason," "theoretical account"). As is so often the case, it is not facility in Latin but exegetical and philosophical acuity that allows the translator to determine how a word is being used and, accordingly, how it ought to be translated.

A WORD OF ENCOURAGEMENT

I have focused here on the obstacles that confront the student of medieval philosophy. The reader should not suppose, however, that the work needed to overcome these obstacles is mere drudgery: far from it. As my colleague Katherine Tachau is fond of observing, doing paleographical work is like being paid to do crossword puzzles. Anyone who enjoys detective stories should enjoy codicological research and the editing of texts, which employ exactly the same skills of picking up clues and drawing inferences. And anyone who takes pleasure in finding just the right words to express a difficult philosophical thought should find deep satisfaction in the challenge of translation.

Above all else, however, the effort to recover the authentic words of medieval philosophers is worthwhile simply because those words are so philosophically interesting. Even after a few decades of renewed attention to medieval thought, there remains an astonishing amount of first-rate philosophy – technically proficient, inventive in argument, and attentive to questions of perennial interest – that has yet to be examined. The effort required to make these texts available for study is amply repaid by the opportunity to reclaim the treasures of a rich philosophical inheritance.

NOTES

1. For an example, see http://www.handwriting.org/images/samples/aquinas2.htm

2. See above, pp. 28 and 46–47.

3. The best summary account remains that of A. Kenny and J. Pinborg *CHLMP* 34–42, on which I rely heavily in what follows. More detailed treatments of the channels of transmission may be found in J. Destrez [642], A. Dondaine [643], and G. Fink-Errera [644–45].

4. *Chartularium universitatis Parisiensis* III 39–40, translated in L. Thorndike [650] 237–38. The practice of reading at such a pace is presented as already common; the decree simply forbids the alternative practice of dictating slowly. The decree is explicitly applied to both lectures and disputations. Student resentment was apparently expected, since the decree provides for stiff penalties for "listeners who oppose the execution of this our statute by clamor, hissing, noise, [or] throwing stones by themselves or by their servants and accomplices."

5. *CHLMP* 37–38. See also G. Pollard [648], and for detailed information on book production in the late medieval university, see L. J. Bataillon *et al.* [638].

6. Quoted in *CHLMP* 41.

7. For this purpose I recommend B. Bischoff [640]. The standard manuals of abbreviations are A. Capelli [641] and A. Pelzer [647]. The University of Bochum has produced an abbreviations CD-ROM [651]. Knowledge of abbreviations is useful not only for reading the manuscripts but also for detecting errors, since mistakes in copies are often attributable to misreading of abbreviations: see B. Bergh [639]. In volume VIII of the Vatican Scotus edition, the editors offer an instructive table of variant readings from the Scotus manuscripts that "arose from mistaken interpretation of abbreviations" ([281] VIII 69*). The results can range from the merely puzzling (as when "*satis patere*," "to be sufficiently evident," is copied as "*satisfacere*," "to satisfy") to the wholly misleading (as when "*diaboli*," "the Devil's," is copied as "*Domini*," "the Lord's").

8. Courses in paleography often include instruction in codicology and text editing, which are best learned through instruction and apprenticeship. Text editing in particular is difficult to encapsulate in a general handbook, since different kinds of texts call for different editorial techniques. An on-line paleography course has been produced by the University of Melbourne [652]. Other resources include the Notre Dame Summer Medieval Institute [646] and the Toronto Summer Latin Course [653].

9. A thorough discussion by F. S. Schmitt of the transmission of Anselm's works can be found in [138] I (I) 1*–239*, from which my remarks are derived.

10. Ibid. 226*–39*. R. W. Southern [145] 238n argues against Schmitt's attribution.

11. See the translator's preface to *On Truth*, *On Freedom of Choice*, and *On the Fall of the Devil* [141].

12. F. S. Schmitt [138] I (I) 37*.

13. Ibid. 10* (my translation).

14. Admittedly, it was originally published in separate volumes by different publishers, but it was reissued as a single set, with additions, corrections, and a long critical preface, by Friedrich Fromann Verlag in 1968.

15. See my summary account in *CCScot* 1–14.

16. Complicating matters even more is the fact that there are rival *Reportationes* of Scotus's Paris lectures: four on Book I (including a version examined by Scotus himself and therefore known as the *Reportatio examinata*), two on Book II, four on Book III, and two on Book IV.

17. A. B. Wolter [302] 39–40.

18. Ibid. 50.

19. The exception for Book I is the version identified by the Vatican editors as *Reportatio* 1B of the Paris lectures, which does exist in an edition published in Paris in 1517. But as we have seen, early printed editions must be used with caution, and in any event *Reportatio* 1B is of far less value than the hitherto unedited *Reportatio examinata* (*Reportatio* 1A).

20. T. B. Noone [297] contains an edition of *Reportatio* 1A, d. 36, with a discussion of the manuscripts on pp. 392–94. All the known manuscripts of Scotus's work are listed in the Prolegomena to the first volume of the Vatican edition [281] I 144*–54*.

21. See P. Streveler and K. Tachau [337] 2–3, 36–38. Katherine Tachau's introduction to this volume is a very informative source for details about Holcot's career and the transmission of his works; my discussion of the transmission of the *Sentences* questions is based on pp. 35–46.

22. R. A. Pratt [649].

23. P. Streveler and K. Tachau [337] 41.

24. Ibid.

25. Ibid. 45.

26. P. Streveler and K. Tachau [337] contains a partial edition of Book II, q. 2. Holcot's *Quodlibetal Questions* are similarly neglected: four questions are edited in Streveler and Tachau and three in H. G. Gelber [335], but otherwise the Lyon edition is the only printed source.

27. *Ordinatio* IV, d. 46, q. 1, n. 12: "dico quod non simpliciter est debitor nisi bonitati suae, ut diligat eam; creaturis autem est debitor ex liberalitate

sua, ut communicet eis quod natura sua exigit, quae exigentia in eis ponitur quoddam iustum, quasi secundarium obiectum illius iustitiae; tamen secundum veritatem nihil est determinate iustum et extra Deum nisi secundum quid, scilicet cum hac modificatione, quantum est ex parte creaturae, sed simpliciter iustum tantummodo est relatum ad primam iustitiam, quia scilicet actualiter volitum a divina voluntate."

28. As R. Cross puts it, "the claim is not that God is essentially generous, but that the term 'debtor' is being used metaphorically" ([293] 63).

29. I once heard a scholar dismiss an entire translation of the *Proslogion* because he disapproved of the rendering of one word in chapter 2, even though I could see no philosophical difference at all between the alternative translations, only a trifling disagreement about what was the more idiomatic English.

30. Analogously, the standard rendering of *eudaimonia* as "happiness" is as inaccurate as it is inevitable, but anyone who has heard even one lecture on Aristotle's *Ethics* knows exactly what is wrong with it and can effortlessly substitute the concept of *eudaimonia*, which no English word calls up, for the concept usually called up by the word "happiness."

CHRONOLOGY OF PHILOSOPHERS AND
MAJOR EVENTS IN MEDIEVAL HISTORY

In the tables of philosophers that follow, where the only information we have is date of death or date of activity, a lifespan of sixty years is indicated; date of activity is taken to be when the individual was 40 years old.

Fourth through sixth century

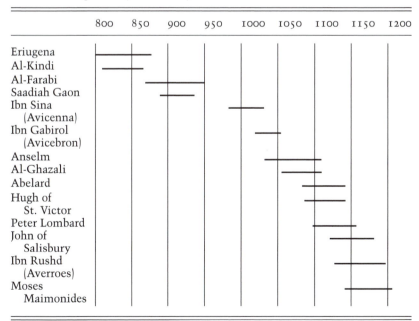

	300	350	400	450	500	550	600
Augustine							
Pseudo Dionysius							
Boethius							

Ninth through twelfth century

	800	850	900	950	1000	1050	1100	1150	1200
Eriugena									
Al-Kindi									
Al-Farabi									
Saadiah Gaon									
Ibn Sina (Avicenna)									
Ibn Gabirol (Avicebron)									
Anselm									
Al-Ghazali									
Abelard									
Hugh of St. Victor									
Peter Lombard									
John of Salisbury									
Ibn Rushd (Averroes)									
Moses Maimonides									

347

Thirteenth and fourteenth centuries

	1150	1200	1250	1300	1350	1400
Robert Grosseteste						
Albert the Great						
Peter of Spain						
Roger Bacon						
Bonaventure						
Henry of Ghent						
Thomas Aquinas						
Boethius of Dacia						
Siger of Brabant						
Giles of Rome						
Peter John Olivi						
Godfrey of Fontaines						
James of Viterbo						
John of Paris						
Duns Scotus						
Marsilius of Padua						
Peter Aureol						
William of Ockham						
Gersonides						
Robert Holcot						
Adam Wodeham						
Thomas Bradwardine						
John Buridan						
Nicholas of Autrecourt						
William Heytesbury						
Nicole Oresme						
John Wyclif						

MAJOR EVENTS IN MEDIEVAL HISTORY

315	Conversion of Emperor Constantine I to Christianity
325	Council of Nicaea, convened by Constantine, affirms the divinity of Christ
381	First Council of Constantinople formulates Nicene Creed
410	Sack of Rome by Visigoths; Augustine begins *The City of God*
451	Council of Chalcedon proclaims full humanity as well as divinity of Christ
529	Rule of St. Benedict, fundamental for western monasticism
529	? Closing of the schools of philosophy at Athens (see pp. 15–16 above)

622	*Hijrah*: Muhammad enters Medina; beginning of the Islamic era
732	Charles Martel defeats Muslims at Poitiers, halting their advance into western Europe
800	Charlemagne crowned emperor by Pope Leo III
1054	Schism between eastern and western churches
1077	Emperor Henry IV does penance at Canossa for resisting Pope Gregory VII's church reforms
1090–1153	Bernard of Clairvaux, Cistercian monastic critic of Abelard's theology
1096–99	First Crusade, sack of Jerusalem by the Crusaders
1187	Saladin recaptures Jerusalem without a sack
By 1200	Universities at Oxford and Paris
1202–04	Fourth Crusade. Crusaders sack Constantinople
1208–13	Albigensian Crusade against Cathars in southern France
1215	Fourth Lateran Council, first general council in western Europe
1220s	Founding of Franciscan and Dominican orders
1277	Condemnation of 219 propositions in theology and natural philosophy by the bishop of Paris
1265–1321	Dante
1309–76	Papacy at Avignon
1356	Golden Bull of Emperor Charles IV rejects need for papal approval of imperial elections
1338–1453	Hundred Years' War between England and France
1340–1400	Chaucer
Late 1340s	Beginning of Black Death
1378–1417	Great Schism in the papacy

BIOGRAPHIES OF MAJOR MEDIEVAL
PHILOSOPHERS

The biographies that follow are in chronological order, as in the chart on pp. 347–48. The bracketed number at the end of each life indicates the entry point for finding works by or about the individual in the bibliography. For short biographies of a larger number of medieval philosophers, see *CHLMP* 855–92.

AUGUSTINE (354–430) was born at Tagaste, in present-day Algeria. He studied at Carthage and taught rhetoric in Rome and Milan. His quest for wisdom, inspired by Cicero's lost *Hortensius*, led him through Manichaeism, skepticism, and Neoplatonism before his conversion to Christianity in 386/87. He returned to Tagaste in 388 and was bishop of the nearby coastal city of Hippo Regius from about 396, exercising great influence among the north African churches and beyond until his death during the siege of Hippo by Vandals. Augustine's immeasurable influence on later western thought depends especially on his many surviving commentaries and sermons on biblical texts and on three masterpieces: the *Confessions*, an autobiography addressed to God, with reflections on memory, creation, and time; *Trinity*, in which the triune nature of God (given its major official formulation in Augustine's lifetime) and the structures of mind and perception provide illumination for one another; and *On the City of God against the Pagans*, undertaken to refute the charge that abandonment of traditional gods in favor of Christianity was responsible for the sack of Rome by Visigoths in 410 but extended beyond this target to provide an account of human origins and destiny, from Paradise and the Fall, through the history of "earthly" and "heavenly" cities in this life, to a last judgment and everlasting punishment or bliss. His writings against the Donatist splinter church and against Pelagius were sources, respectively, for legislation against heresy and debates about grace and free will. Other works of particular interest for philosophy are *Against the Academicians* (with *Trinity* the chief source for Augustine's influence on Descartes), *On Free Choice of the Will*, and *The Teacher* (a more subtle account of language than the behaviorism of the *Confessions* criticized by Wittgenstein at the beginning of *Philosophical Investigations*). [55]

PSEUDO-DIONYSIUS (*fl. c.* 500) was a Christian Neoplatonist who presented himself as (and was regarded during the later Middle Ages and Renaissance as being) an Athenian convert of St. Paul (Acts 17:34), an identity which gave his writings great authority in the West, even during the period of Aristotle's greatest influence in the thirteenth and fourteenth centuries. [77]

Anicius Manlius Severinus **BOETHIUS** (*c.* 480–525/26), born into a patrician family in Rome, combined scholarship with public service at a time when Italy was ruled by Goths and knowledge of Greek was becoming rare in the West. He intended to translate all of Plato and Aristotle into Latin but got no further than Aristotle's logical treatises. He wrote the *Consolation of Philosophy* in prison, while awaiting execution on charges of treason. [84]

Johannes **SCOTTUS ERIUGENA** (*c.* 800–*c.* 877) combined Pseudo-Dionysius (whose writings he translated into Latin), other sources in Greek, and Augustine in a Christian Neoplatonism centered on a fourfold idea of nature as creating and not created, created and creating, created but not creating, and neither created nor creating. [90]

Abu Yusuf Ya'Qub Ibn Ishaq **al-KINDI** (d. *c.* 866–73), "the philosopher of the Arabs," active in Baghdad, encouraged translation into Arabic of Greek philosophers, especially Aristotle, and utilized these sources in his own thought. Another important early contribution to the integration of philosophy with qur'anic or biblical monotheism was the anonymous *Liber de causis*, a Neoplatonic treatise probably written in Baghdad in the ninth century. It was influential in the West from the twelfth century. [91]

Abu Nasr **al-FARABI** (*c.* 870–950), "the Second Master" (after Aristotle), has also been called "the Father of Islamic Neoplatonism," an indication of the breadth of his philosophic vision. He did important work in political philosophy, metaphysics, and logic. [93]

SAADIAH GAON (892–942), the first Jewish philosopher in the proper sense of the term, was born in Fayyum, Upper Egypt. In 928 he became head (Gaon) of the Sura Academy in present-day Iraq. His major philosophical work, the *Kitab al-mukhtar fi 'l-amanat wa-'l-'i'tiqadat* (Book of Doctrines and Beliefs), demonstrates his knowledge of Platonic, Aristotelian, and Stoic ideas, as well as the influence of the Islamic Mu'tazilites. Saadiah's defense of the harmony of reason and revelation, unequaled in medieval Jewish thought, was the *locus classicus* for Maimonides' critique. [106]

Abu 'Ali al-Husayn **IBN SINA (AVICENNA)** (980–1037) was born near Bukhara in present-day Uzbekistan. He was a highly systematic and creative thinker and greatly influenced later Latin as well as Islamic philosophy. His most seminal contribution to metaphysics was the distinction between essence and existence, universally applicable except to God, in whom they are identical. In philosophical psychology, he held that the soul was incorporeal, immortal, and an agent with choice between good and evil. [111]

Solomon **IBN GABIROL (AVICEBRON)** (1021/22–1057/58), a Jewish philosopher and poet, lived in Muslim Spain and wrote in both Hebrew and Arabic. His emphasis on the will of a creator God allowed him to propound a Neoplatonic vision of reality without the determinism commonly found in that tradition. His *Mekor Hayyim* (Fountain of Life, *Fons vitae*) had no influence on Jewish philosophy, but its highly original hylomorphism received serious attention from the Latin scholastics, especially Aquinas and Duns Scotus. [135]

ANSELM OF CANTERBURY (1033–1109) was born in Aosta in present-day Italy. As a monk at Bec in Normandy, he brought his extraordinarily acute analytical mind to bear on such topics as truth, freedom of the will, and the fall of the Devil. In his *Proslogion* Anselm formulated the most famous argument in the history of philosophy, the so-called ontological argument for the existence of God. In 1093 Anselm became the second Norman archbishop of Canterbury, where he contended vigorously for the autonomy of the church while producing significant further work in philosophical theology, including attempts to demonstrate the necessity of God's incarnation as a human being (*Cur Deus homo*) and the harmony of divine foreknowledge, predestination, and grace with human free choice. [138]

Abu Hamid **al-GHAZALI** (1058–1111), born in northern Iran, was one of the greatest Islamic jurists and the most acute critic of the Hellenizing philosophical tradition within Islam, a tradition that reached its peak in Ibn Sina. Convinced in the *Tahafut al-falasifa* (The Incoherence of the Philosophers) that philosophy could not provide a basis for accepting revealed truth, Ghazali turned to Sufi mysticism, in terms of which he reinterpreted traditional religious texts. [148]

Peter **ABELARD** (1079–1142) renounced his birthright as eldest son of a Breton knight for the arms of dialectic. He was a renowned teacher, a poet, and the tutor, lover, and (against her wishes) husband of Heloïse, the niece of a Parisian ecclesiastic in whose house Abelard lodged. In the course of such calamitous events as castration by order of Heloïse's uncle, threats of murder by the unruly monks of a monastery he had set out to reform, and repeated attacks on his orthodoxy by Bernard of Clairvaux, Abelard became a founding figure of medieval scholasticism. He has commonly been regarded as a brilliant but critical and unsystematic thinker. Recent research makes a strong case for the constructive and systematic character of his work in both logic and theology, especially moral theology. [152]

HUGH OF ST. VICTOR (d. 1141) inaugurated a course of study at the Parisian abbey of St. Victor that integrated philosophy into a monastic ethos centered on the Christian sacraments and meditative reading of the Bible. [155]

PETER LOMBARD (1095/1100–60) collected and discussed the judgments (*sententiae*) of a wide range of earlier authors in his *Sententiae in IV libris distinctae* (Four Books of Sentences), which became the major textbook in theology from the thirteenth through fifteenth centuries and hence the point of departure for philosophically significant thought by Aquinas, Duns Scotus, Ockham, and others. Lombard was critical of Neoplatonism and hospitable to Aristotelian ideas. [156]

JOHN OF SALISBURY (c. 1120–80) championed the union of wisdom with eloquence to combat vanity in royal courts and worldliness in the church. John's morally energetic Christian humanism drew on Roman models not only for the importance of grammar and rhetoric but also for a defense of tyrannicide. [157]

Abu'l Walid Muhammad **IBN RUSHD (AVERROES)** (1126–98) wrote in Islamic Spain. He came to be known as "the Commentator" for his massive explication of Aristotle's works. He defended philosophy against charges that it was contrary to Islam and held that the study of philosophy was obligatory for an intellectual elite, but should be forbidden to ordinary belivers. The Jewish and Latin Averroist traditions maintained his ideal of the philosophic life as the way to the highest possible happiness. [160]

Moses **MAIMONIDES** (c. 1138–1204) was the major Jewish philosopher of the Middle Ages, and his influence lasts to the present. He was born in Córdoba in Muslim Spain, whence his family was forced to flee in 1148, after the Almohads conquered Andalusia. He settled in Al-Fustat (Cairo) before 1168, where he also practiced and wrote as a physician. Maimonides was the leader of the Jewish community of his day and composed for it an authoritative code of rabbinic law. In his *Dalalat al-Ha'irin* (Guide for the Perplexed), written in Arabic, he confronted the apparent contradictions between biblical and philosophical (mainly Aristotelian) ideas. Maimonides' intellectualism in the *Guide* makes prophetic revelation an accommodation to the lower, material side of our nature, but a mutually fruitful (though challenging) relation between philosophy and religion is suggested by his insistence on the need for moral purity, his defense of the philosophical tenability of major articles of traditional belief, and his emphasis on the limits of philosophical knowledge of God (this last an important influence on Aquinas). [176]

Robert **GROSSETESTE** (*c.* 1170–1253) taught at Oxford, where he was an early supporter of the Franciscans, including Roger Bacon, who regarded him as the foremost thinker of the age. As bishop of Lincoln (hence the sobriquet "the Lincolnian"), Grosseteste continued an ambitious program of translation and commentary on Arabic and Greek texts not previously available or fully available in the Latin West, including especially Aristotle's *Ethics* and earlier commentaries thereon. Notwithstanding his major role in the reintroduction of Aristotle, Grosseteste himself was most deeply an Augustinian and Neoplatonist, affinities exhibited not only in his philosophy but also in his activity as a preacher and as pastor of one of the largest dioceses in England. [194]

ALBERT THE GREAT (ALBERTUS MAGNUS) (1200–80) was the first interpreter in the Latin West of Aristotle's work in its entirety. In distinguishing sharply between philosophy and theology and insisting that philosophical problems be solved philosophically, while at the same time integrating Neoplatonic themes into his interpretation, Albert presented an Aristotelianism that was more congenial to later defenders of a purely philosophical way of life than that of his pupil, Thomas Aquinas. Albert was the first German to become a master at the University of Paris. [201]

PETER OF SPAIN (*c.* 1205–77) was a Spanish Dominican who wrote the leading logic text of high scholasticism. He is no longer identified with the Portuguese author of medical works and a commentary on Aristotle's *De anima* who later became Pope John XXI. [206]

ROGER BACON (*c.* 1214–92/4), an irascible English Franciscan active at both Oxford and Paris, set forth in his *Opus maius* a detailed plan of curricular reform emphasizing mathematics, experimental science, moral philosophy, and the study of languages. Bacon disparaged reliance on the authority of past thinkers but was an unashamed admirer of non-Christian achievements in philosophy and science, which he attributed to divine illumination, the source of all knowledge. [208]

BONAVENTURE (John of Fidanza) (c. 1217–74) taught theology at Paris from 1243 until his election as minister-general of the Franciscans in 1257. He defended the importance of university studies for his order but aimed at a synthesis of the intellectual and the affective in such works as *The Mind's Journey to God*. Though antagonistic to the contemporary rage for Aristotle, he was expert in deploying "the Philosopher's" ideas to establish his own. As contemporaries at Paris, Bonaventure and Aquinas were opposed to one another in their attitudes toward Aristotle and on other issues in ways that were echoed in the subsequent teachings of their orders, the Franciscans and Dominicans. In the *Divine Comedy* Dante has each praise the founder of the other's order (*Paradise* XI–XII). [211]

HENRY OF GHENT (c. 1217–93), a master of theology at Paris by 1276, defended traditional Neoplatonic and Augustinian positions (he was a member of the commission which prepared 219 mainly Arab-Aristotelian propositions in philosophy and theology for condemnation by the bishop of Paris in 1277), but in the course of a long intellectual evolution integrated much of Aristotle into his own complex, markedly "essentialist" views. He was often cited by Franciscan thinkers, albeit often as a foil for their own views. [219]

THOMAS AQUINAS (c. 1225–74) was born at Roccasecca, between Naples and Rome, at a castle belonging to his family, a branch of the Aquino clan. After studying liberal arts and philosophy at the University of Naples, he joined the Dominican order, over strong objections from his family. He studied philosophy and theology under Albert the Great at Paris and Cologne and then began a career of teaching theology at the University of Paris (1251/52–59 and 1268–72), and in Naples, Orvieto, and Rome. Thomas wrote influential commentaries on biblical texts and on major works of Aristotle, including the *Posterior Analytics*, *Physics*, *De anima*, *Metaphysics* (through Book XII), *Nicomachean Ethics*, and *Politics* (to 1280a6). His own philosophy is primarily found embedded in his theological works. These include three systematic treatises: (1) his early Paris lectures on the *Sentences* of Peter Lombard; (2) the *Summa contra Gentiles* (A Summary against the Pagans), also known as *Liber de veritate de catholicae fidei* (Treatise on the Truth of the Catholic Faith) (1259–65); and (3) the *Summa theologiae* (A Summary of Theology) (1265–73, unfinished). Also important for philosophy are *On Being and Essence*, *On the Eternity of the World*, and treatises in question form on such topics as truth, evil, and the soul. Aquinas's thought is Aristotelian in framework but takes in much of Platonism as well as distinctively Christian sources. [224]

BOETHIUS OF DACIA (active *c.* 1275) taught in the arts faculty at Paris and defended the possibility of achieving happiness through philosophy. He treated theology and philosophy, including natural philosophy, as mutually independent systems of thought. [265]

SIGER OF BRABANT (*c.* 1240–*c.* 1284), like Boethius of Dacia, taught in the arts faculty at Paris. He expounded and at times defended Aristotelian positions included in the condemnation of 1277. Dante has Thomas Aquinas introduce him in Paradise (X.136–38) as one who "syllogized invidious verities." [266]

GILES OF ROME (Aegidius Romanus, Egidius Colonna) (*c.* 1243/47–1316) studied theology at Paris during Aquinas's second period of teaching there and took a provocatively Aristotelian line himself, furnishing in his *Sentences* commentary many of the propositions condemned in 1277. Giles withdrew from Paris and set to work commenting on Aristotle. He returned to Paris in 1285 as the first regent master of his order, the Augustinians. His writings were made the official teaching of the order in 1287, and he was elected general in 1292. He contributed influentially to the discussion of the distinction between essence and existence and wrote two significant political treatises: *De regimine principum* (On the Rule of Princes), a manual on rulership written for the future Philip IV (the Fair) of France; and *De ecclesiastica potestate* (On Ecclesiastical Power), a sweeping defense of papal authority in support of Philip's eventual adversary, Pope Boniface VIII. [269]

Peter John OLIVI (1247/48–98) was a Franciscan, controversial for his apocalypticism and advocacy of a "poor" lifestyle to maintain St. Francis's ideal of imitating Christ and the apostles. Olivi also participated in the main philosophical discussions of the day, showing little respect for Aristotle and taking original positions of his own. [271]

GODFREY OF FONTAINES (*c.* 1250–*c.* 1306/09) studied liberal arts at Paris under Siger of Brabant during Aquinas's second regency in theology, then theology under Henry of Ghent. Godfrey taught theology at Paris from 1285, stoutly criticized the 1277 condemnation, defended many of Aquinas's views, and carried on an often oppositional dialogue with Henry. He divided being into cognitive being and real being and held that even in creatures essence and existence were neither really nor "intentionally" distinct. [275]

JAMES OF VITERBO (*c.* 1255–1308) studied and taught theology at Paris, succeeding Giles of Rome in the Augustinian chair in 1293. He is best known for his defense of papal authority in *De regimine Christiano* (On Christian Government), but also wrote on metaphysical issues. [277]

JOHN OF PARIS (John Quidort) (*c.* 1260–1306) was an early Dominican defender of Aquinas's positions on the composition of essence and existence in creatures, on matter as principle of individuation, and on other issues. He argued for the mutual independence of ecclesiastical and lay authority. [278]

John **DUNS SCOTUS** (*c.* 1265/66–1308), a Franciscan, studied and taught at both Oxford and Paris. Known as "the Subtle Doctor," Scotus was one of the greatest medieval thinkers. His major works include at least three sets of lectures on the Lombard's *Sentences*, questions on Aristotle's *Metaphysics*, and a substantial body of quodlibetal questions. Major features of Scotus's thought include a univocal concept of being, a distinctive demonstration of the existence of God, the "formal" distinction among a thing's "really" identical characteristics (including its *haecceitas* or "thisness"), the grounding of knowledge in intuitive cognition rather than divine illumination, and a theory of the will as free at the very instant of choosing. [281]

MARSILIUS OF PADUA (1275/80–1342/43) was a student of medicine and natural philosophy, probably first at the University of Padua. He was rector of the University of Paris briefly in 1313. In 1324 he wrote the most revolutionary political treatise of the later Middle Ages, the *Defensor pacis* (Defender of Peace), which propounded a substantially complete theory of a community's competence to control its own affairs and attacked papal and priestly claims to political power as a major threat to civic tranquillity. [303]

PETER AUREOL (*c.* 1280–1322), a Franciscan, taught at Paris. His main contribution to contemporary debates about representationalism was the concept of "apparent being" (*esse apparens*), which provoked criticism from Ockham. [307]

WILLIAM OF OCKHAM (*c.* 1287–1347/48), an English Franciscan, studied at Oxford and taught there and at Franciscan houses of study while writing extensively on logic, Aristotelian physics, and theology. These works are the basis for Ockham's sometimes exaggerated reputation as the nominalist inaugurator of a *via moderna* in philosophy and theology. In the mid-1320s he was required to defend his teachings on grace, free will, and other topics at the papal court in Avignon. While there he came to believe that Pope John XXII was a heretic in denying the complete legal poverty of Christ and his apostles, a doctrine most Franciscans of the time considered essential to Christian belief. Ockham fled the curia in 1328 with the minister-general of his order and a few confreres, taking refuge with Ludwig of Bavaria, who was at odds with the papacy over the legitimacy of his title as Roman emperor. Ockham then wrote against John XXII's teachings, composed a massive dialogue on heresy, and discussed at some length the basis and functions of secular and religious governments. He died in Munich, possibly during an outbreak of plague. [308]

GERSONIDES (Levi ben Gershom) (1288–1344) was a Jewish philosopher, astronomer, and mathematician who lived in southern France. An abbreviated translation of his astronomical works was commissioned by Pope Clement VI and quoted by Kepler. In his *Milhamot ha-Shem* (The Wars of the Lord), Gersonides showed himself a more consistent Aristotelian than Maimonides, to the detriment of his reputation in later Jewish circles. He took original positions on such central points of medieval philosophical theology as creation *ex nihilo* (denied), divine omniscience (rejected regarding future contingents), and personal immortality (restricted to the rational part of the soul). [323]

ROBERT HOLCOT (c. 1290–1349) was an English Dominican who questioned the extent of theological and natural knowledge but has been considered semi-Pelagian in affirming the natural power of the will to achieve faith. [335]

ADAM WODEHAM (c. 1298–1358), an English Franciscan theologian, studied under Ockham and defended many of his views. Wodeham was also an original thinker, emphasizing the dependence of creation and salvation on God. In contrast with Ockham, he held that the objects of scientific knowledge were not propositions but states of affairs. [338]

Thomas **BRADWARDINE** (c. 1300–49) applied logic and mathematics in natural philosophy in a number of original and influential works. In theology, he defended a strong view of divine omniscience and the primacy of grace in every good human act. He was confirmed as archbishop of Canterbury shortly before his death. [339]

John **BURIDAN** (c. 1300–after 1358) was an arts master at Paris who wrote on logic, especially semantics, and commented on many texts of Aristotle. Human freedom, he argued, existed to allow us to live as reason dictates, and we can know enough of the world for reason to lead us toward the knowledge and love of God which constitutes our ultimate happiness. [341]

NICHOLAS OF AUTRECOURT (c. 1300–69) vigorously applied the principle of noncontradiction to Aristotelian knowledge claims, with highly skeptical results. [346]

William **HEYTESBURY** (before 1313–72), one of the "Oxford Calculators" (with Bradwardine, Richard Swineshead, Richard Kilvington, and John Dumbleton), developed the mathematics of uniform acceleration and the mathematical treatment of physical qualities such as heat. His influential treatise on sophismata dealt comprehensively with paradoxes of self-reference and the problems arising from intentional contexts. [348]

Nicole **ORESME** (c. 1325–82) followed the lead of the Oxford Calculators in applying mathematical techniques in natural philosophy, developing a sophisticated analysis of the intensities of speeds and qualities. He also wrote on economics and, under the patronage of Charles V of France, translated Aristotle's *Nicomachean Ethics* and *Politics*, with commentary bearing on current circumstances. [350]

John **WYCLIF** (c. 1330–84) was an Oxford secular master in arts and later in theology. Recent scholarship has increased respect for his metaphysics, especially with regard to the problem of universals, on which he opposed the nominalism fashionable in his day. He remains most well known for his radical opposition to church wealth and for his doctrine of predestination, both of which suggested a gulf between true Christianity and the institutional church of his day. [351]

BIBLIOGRAPHY

This bibliography gives full references to all the works cited in each chapter by a number in square brackets (e.g., P. Brown [66]). References are also provided for medieval texts cited by book and chapter or in similar fashion but not keyed to a specific edition (e.g., Augustine, *Confessions* X 3). A limited number of other resources are identified. References are not repeated for works cited by abbreviations given above, in the list preceding the introduction.

The bibliography is organized as follows:

Histories of medieval philosophy [1–14]
Collections of texts and translations [15–24]
Collections of studies [25–51]
Reference works and bibliographies [52–54]
Texts and studies of major medieval philosophers, in chronological order [55–354]
Texts and studies of other medieval thinkers [355–391]
Works on specific topics, in the order of the chapters in this volume [392–653]

The following journal abbreviations have been used:

ACPQ	*American Catholic Philosophical Quarterly*
AHDLMA	*Archives d'Histoire Doctrinale et Littéraire du Moyen Age*
ASP	*Arabic Sciences and Philosophy*
BEO	*Bulletin d'Etudes orientales*
CJP	*Canadian Journal of Philosophy*
DSTFM	*Documenti e Studi sulla Tradizione Filosofica Medievale*
ESM	*Early Science and Medicine*
FP	*Faith and Philosophy*
JHI	*Journal of the History of Ideas*

JHP	*Journal of the History of Philosophy*
JJS	*Journal of Jewish Studies*
JQR	*Jewish Quarterly Review*
JTS	*Journal of Theological Studies*
MPT	*Medieval Philosophy and Theology*
MRS	*Mediaeval and Renaissance Studies*
MS	*Mediaeval Studies*
NS	*The New Scholasticism*
PAAJR	*Proceedings of the American Academy for Jewish Research*
RM	*Review of Metaphysics*
RTAM	*Recherches de Théologie ancienne et médiévale*

Histories of medieval philosophy

[1] Armstrong, A. H., ed. *The Cambridge History of Later Greek and Early Medieval Philosophy* (Cambridge, 1967).
[2] Schmitt, C. B. and Q. Skinner, eds. *The Cambridge History of Renaissance Philosophy* (Cambridge, 1988).
[3] Marenbon, J. *Early Medieval Philosophy (480–1150). An Introduction*, revised edn (London/New York, 1988).
[4] Marenbon, J. *Later Medieval Philosophy (1150–1350)* (London/New York, 1987).
[5] Marenbon, J. *Medieval Philosophy* (London/New York, 1998).
[6] Spade, P. V. *A Survey of Medieval Philosophy*, version 2.0. http://www.pvspade.com/Logic/docs/Survey 2 Interim.pdf
[7] Copleston, F. *A History of Philosophy*, vol. III, *Late Medieval and Renaissance Philosophy* (New York, 1963).
[8] Knowles, D. *The Evolution of Medieval Thought* (London, 1962).
[9] Gilson, E. *History of Christian Philosophy in the Middle Ages* (London, 1955).
[10] Corbin, H. *History of Islamic Philosophy*, trans. L. and P. Sherrard (London, 1993).
[11] Nasr, S. H. and O. Leaman, eds. *History of Islamic Philosophy*, 2 vols. (London, 1996).
[12] Leaman, O. and D. Frank, eds. *History of Jewish Philosophy* (London, 1997).
[13] Burns, J. H., ed. *The Cambridge History of Medieval Political Thought c. 350–c. 1400* (Cambridge, 1988).
[14] Canning, J. P. *A History of Medieval Political Thought 300–1450* (London/New York, 1996).

Collections of texts and translations

[15] Macdonald, S., ed. *The Cambridge Translations of Medieval Philo-sophical Texts*, vol. IV, *Metaphysics* (Cambridge, forthcoming).

[16] Williams, T., ed. *The Cambridge Translations of Medieval Philosoph-ical Texts*, vol. V, *Philosophical Theology* (Cambridge, forthcoming).

[17] Hyman, A. and J. J. Walsh, eds. *Philosophy in the Middle Ages: The Christian, Islamic, and Jewish Traditions*, 2nd edn (Indianapolis, 1983).

[18] Kraye, J. *et al.*, eds. *Pseudo-Aristotle in the Middle Ages: The Theology and Other Texts* (London, 1986).

[19] Bosley, R. and M. Tweedale, eds. *Basic Issues in Medieval Philosophy. Selected Reading Presenting the Interactive Discourses Among the Major Figures* (Peterborough, Ontario, 1997).

[20] Spade, P. V., ed. *Five Texts on the Mediaeval Problem of Univer-sals: Porphyry, Boethius, Abelard, Duns Scotus, Ockham* (Indianapo-lis /Cambridge, MA, 1994).

[21] Lottin, O. *Psychologie et morale aux XIIe et XIIIe siècles*, 6 vols. (Louvain, 1942–60).

[22] Lerner, R. and M. Mahdi, eds. *Medieval Political Philosophy* (Ithaca, NY, 1963).

[23] Peters, E., ed. *Heresy and Authority in Medieval Europe. Documents in Translation* (Philadelphia, 1980).

[24] Denzinger, H., ed. *Enchiridion Symbolorum*, revised A. Schönmetzer, 33rd edn (Barcelona/Freiburg/Rome/New York, 1965). Latin texts of creeds and related documents.

Collections of studies

Since it was established in 1958, the Société Internationale pour l'Etude de la Philosophie Médiévale (SIEPM) has organized international congresses of medieval philosophy, every three years at the beginning, and then every five years, each congress with a single broad theme. Since 1989 the society has also organized symposia (*Rencontres*) concerned with specific research topics. The proceedings of both sorts of meetings have many papers in English. Proceedings of the congresses of the SIEPM include the following:

[25] Wenin, C., ed. *L'Homme et son univers au moyen âge* (Louvain-la-Neuve, 1986).

[26] Asztalos, M. *et al.*, eds. *Knowledge and the Sciences in Medieval Philosophy*, 3 vols. (Helsinki, 1990).

[27] Bazán, B. C. *et al.*, eds. *Les Philosophies morales et politiques au moyen âge/Moral and Political Philosophies in the Middle Ages*, 3 vols. (New York/Ottawa/Toronto, 1995).

[28] Aertsen, J. A. and A. Speer, eds. *Was ist Philosophie im Mittelalter?/ Qu'est-ce que la philosophie au moyen âge?/What is Philosophy in the Middle Ages?* (Berlin/New York, 1998).

Rencontres de philosophie médiévale (SIEPM) include the following:

[29] Santiago-Otero, H., ed. *Diálogo filosófico-religioso entre cristianismo, judaísmo e islamismo durante la Edad Media en la Península Ibérica* (Turnhout, 1994).

[30] Wlodek, S., ed. *Société et Eglise. Textes et discussions dans les universités d'Europe centrale pendant le moyen âge tardif* (Turnhout, 1994).

[31] Marenbon, J., ed. *Aristotle in Britain during the Middle Ages* (Turnhout, 1996).

[32] Benakis, L. G., ed. *Néoplatonisme et philosophie médiévale* (Turnhout, 1997).

[33] Brown, S. F., ed. *Meeting of the Minds. The Relations between Medieval and Classical Modern European Philosophy* (Turnhout, 1999).

[34] Hamesse, J. and C. Steel, eds. *L'Elaboration du vocabulaire philosophique au moyen âge* (Turnhout, 2000).

[35] Boiadjiev, T. *et al.*, eds. *Die Dionysius-Rezeption im Mittelalter* (Turnhout, 2000).

Other collections of articles:

[36] *Les Genres littéraires dans les sources théologiques et philosophiques médiévales. Définition, critique et exploitation* (Louvain-la-Neuve, 1982).

[37] Bazán, B. C. *et al.*, eds. *Les Questions disputées et les questions quodlibétiques dans les facultés de théologie, de droit et de médicine* (Turnhout, 1985).

[38] Burnyeat, M., ed. *The Skeptical Tradition* (Berkeley, CA, 1983).

[39] Flint, T. P., ed. *Christian Philosophy* (Notre Dame, IN, 1990).

[40] Gill, M. L. and J. G. Lennox, eds. *Self-Motion. From Aristotle to Newton* (Princeton, NJ, 1994).

[41] Kretzmann, N., ed. *Meaning and Inference in Medieval Philosophy: Studies in Memory of Jan Pinborg* (Dordrecht/Boston, MA/London, 1988).

[42] Leijenhorst, C. *et al.*, eds. *The Dynamics of Aristotelian Natural Philosophy from Antiquity to the Seventeenth Century* (Leiden, 2002).

[43] Long, R. J. *Philosophy and the God of Abraham. Essays in Memory of James A. Weisheipl* (Toronto, 1991).

[44] Morewedge, P., ed. *Islamic Philosophical Theology* (Albany, NY, 1979).

[45] Murdoch, J. and E. Sylla, eds. *The Cultural Context of Medieval Learning* (Dordrecht/Boston, MA, 1975).

[46] Nauta, L. and A. Vanderjagt, eds. *Between Demonstration and Imagination* (Leiden/Boston, MA/Cologne, 1999).

[47] Read, S., ed. *Sophisms in Medieval Logic and Grammar* (Dordrecht/ Boston, MA/London, 1993).
[48] Ridyard, S. and R. Benson, eds. *Man and Nature in the Middle Ages* (Sewanee, TN, 1995).
[49] Savory, R. M. and D. A. Agius, eds. *Logos Islamikos* (Toronto, 1984).
[50] Sylla, E., and M. McVaugh, eds. *Texts and Contexts in Ancient and Medieval Science* (Leiden/New York/Cologne, 1997).
[51] Yrjönsuuri, M., ed. *Medieval Formal Logic: Obligations, Insolubles and Consequences* (Dordrecht/Boston, MA/London, 2001).

Reference works and bibliographies

Craig, E., ed. *The Routledge Encyclopedia of Philosophy*, 10 vols. (London/ New York, 1998; also online with updates (http://www.rep.routledge.com/) and *Concise Routledge Encyclopedia of Philosophy* are generous and reliable in their coverage of medieval philosophy.

[52] *The Stanford Encyclopedia of Philosophy*, ed. E. Zalta. http://plato. stanford/edu/

Speculum (the journal of the Medieval Academy of America) and *JHP* devote much space to book reviews, and journal articles and reviews are covered in the *International Medieval Bibliography* published in print and on CD-ROM by the University of Leeds. Valuable information on work-in-progress on medieval philosophy and bibliographies on specific topics are to be found in the following:

[53] *Bulletin de Philosophie Médiévale*, ed. Société Internationale pour l'Etude de la Philosophie Médiévale.

For Islamic philosophy see:

[54] Daiber, H. *Bibliography of Islamic Philosophy*, 2 vols. (Leiden, 1999).

INDIVIDUAL PHILOSOPHERS AND TOPICS

Augustine

[55] Augustine. *The Advantage of Believing*, trans. L. Meagher (New York, 1947).
[56] Augustine. *Against The Academicians* and *The Teacher*, trans. P. King (Indianapolis, 1995).
[57] Augustine. *Answer to the Pelagians II*, trans. R. J. Teske (Hyde Park, NY, 1998). Includes *Answer to the Two Letters of the Pelagians* (97–219) and *Answer to Julian* (221–536).

[58] Augustine. *The City of God against the Pagans*, trans. H. Bettenson (London, 1972).

[59] Augustine. *Confessions*, trans. F. J. Sheed, revised edn (Indianapolis, 1993).

[60] Augustine. *De Dialectica*, trans. B. D. Jackson (Dordrecht/Boston, MA, 1975).

[61] Augustine. *De genesi ad litteram, The Literal Meaning of Genesis*, trans. J. H. Taylor, SJ, 2 vols. (New York/Ramsey, NJ, 1982).

[62] Augustine. *Of True Religion*, trans. J. H. S. Burleigh (Chicago, 1964).

[63] Augustine. *On Christian Doctrine*, trans. D. W. Robertson (Indianapolis, 1958).

[64] Augustine. *On Free Choice of the Will*, trans. T. Williams (Indianapolis/Cambridge, MA, 1993).

[65] Augustine. *The Trinity*, trans. E. Hill (Brooklyn, NY, 1991). New chapter divisions.

[66] Brown, P. *Augustine of Hippo* (Berkeley, CA, 1967; revised edn 2000).

[67] Fitzgerald, A. *St. Augustine Through the Ages: An Encyclopedia* (Grand Rapids, MI/Cambridge, 1999).

[68] Gilson, E. *The Christian Philosophy of St. Augustine* (New York, 1960).

[69] Kahn, C. H. "Discovering the Will. From Aristotle to Augustine," in J. M. Dillon and A. A. Long, eds., *The Question of Eclecticism. Studies in Later Greek Philosophy* (Berkeley, CA/Los Angeles, CA/London, 1985), 234–59.

[70] Kirwan, C. *Augustine* (London, 1989).

[71] Kretzmann, N. "Faith Seeks, Understanding Finds: Augustine's Charter for Christian Philosophy," in [39], 1–36.

[72] Markus, R. A. *Saeculum: History and Society in the Theology of St. Augustine* (Cambridge, 1970).

[73] Matthews, G. *Thought's Ego in Augustine and Descartes* (Ithaca, NY, 1992). Cf. [612].

[74] O'Connor, W. "The Uti/Frui Distinction in Augustine's Ethics," *Augustinian Studies* 14 (1983), 45–62.

[75] O'Daly, G. *Augustine's Philosophy of Mind* (Berkeley, CA, 1987).

[76] Rist, J. *Augustine: Ancient Thought Baptized* (Cambridge, 1994).

Pseudo-Dionysius

[77] Pseudo-Dionysius the Areopagite. *Dionysiaca*, ed. P. Chevallier, 2 vols. (Paris, 1937–50).

[78] Pseudo-Dionysius the Areopagite. *The Complete Works*, trans. C. Luibheid (New York, 1987).

[79] Pseudo-Dionysius the Areopagite. *Celestial Hierarchy. Denys l'Aréopagite, La Hiérarchie céleste*, ed. G. Heil, 2nd edn (Paris, 1970).

[80] Mahoney, E. P. "Pseudo-Dionysius's Conception of Metaphysical Hierarchy and its Influence on Medieval Philosophy," in [35], 429–75.

[81] Rorem, P. *Pseudo-Dionysius: A Commentary on the Texts and an Introduction to their Influence* (Oxford, 1993).

[82] Théry, G. *Etudes dionysiennes*, 2 vols. (Paris, 1932, 1937).

[83] Wenger, A. "Denys l'Aréopagite," *Dictionnaire de spiritualité* III (1957) cols. 307–09.

Boethius

[84] Boethius. *De consolatione philosophiae, Opuscula theologica*, ed. C. Moreschini (Munich/Leipzig, 2000).

[85] Boethius. *Consolation of Philosophy*, trans. J. C. Relihan (Indianapolis/Cambridge, 2001).

[86] Boethius. *The Theological Tractates*, trans. H. F. Stewart and E. K. Rand (Cambridge, MA, 1973).

[87] Marenbon, J. *Boethius* (New York, 2003).

[88] Marenbon, J. "Le Temps, la prescience et le déterminisme dans la *Consolation de Philosophie*," in A. Gallonier, ed., *Boèce ou la chaîne des savoirs* (Louvain/Paris, forthcoming), 159–74.

[89] Thierry of Chartres and his school. *Tractatus de sex dierum operibus*, in N. M. Häring, ed., *Commentaries on Boethius by Thierry of Chartres and His School* (Toronto, 1971).

Scottus Eriugena

[90] John Scottus Eriugena. *Periphyseon (The Division of Nature)*, trans. I. P. Sheldon-Williams, revised J. J. O'Meara (Montreal/Washington, DC, 1987).

Al-Kindi

[91] Al-Kindi. *Al-Kindi's Metaphysics: A Translation of Ya'qub ibn Ishaq al-Kindi's Treatise "On First Philosophy,"* ed. and trans. A. L. Ivry (Albany, NY, 1974).

[92] Druart, T.-A. "Al-Kindi's Ethics," *RM* 47 (1993), 329–57.

Al-Farabi (Alfarabi, Farabi)

[93] Al-Farabi. *On the Aims of the Metaphysics*, trans. in part in [124], 240–42.

[94] Al-Farabi. *Al-Farabi's Commentary and Short Treatise on Aristotle's* De interpretatione, trans. F. W. Zimmermann (London, 1981).

[95] Al-Farabi. *Al-Farabi on the Perfect State. Abu Nasr al-Farabi's Mabadi' Ara' Ahl al-Madina al-Fadila*, trans. R. Walzer (Oxford, 1985).

[96] Al-Farabi. *Alfarabi's Philosophy of Plato and Aristotle*, trans. M. Mahdi, revised edn (Ithaca, NY, 1969; reprinted 2001). (Includes *The Attainment of Happiness*.)

[97] Al-Farabi. *The Political Regime*, partial trans. F. M. Najjar, in [22], 31–57.

[98] Al-Farabi. *The Political Writings: Selected Aphorisms and Other Texts*, trans. C. E. Butterworth (Ithaca, NY/London, 2001). Includes the *Book of Religion* and *The Harmonization of the Opinions of the Two Sages: Plato the Divine and Aristotle*.

[99] Druart, T.-A. "Al-Farabi, Ethics, and First Intelligibles," *DSTFM* 8 (1997), 403–23.

[100] Druart, T.-A. "Le Sommaire du livre des 'Lois' de Platon (Gawami' Kitab al-Nawamis li-Aflatun) par Abu Nasr al-Farabi," *BEO* (Damascus) 50 (1998), 109–55.

[101] Galston, M. *Politics and Excellence: The Political Philosophy of Alfarabi* (Princeton, NJ, 1990).

[102] Gutas, D. "Galen's Synopsis of Plato's Laws and Farabi's Talkhis," in G. Endress and R. Kruk, eds., *The Ancient Tradition in Christian and Islamic Hellenism* (Leiden, 1997), 101–19.

[103] Lameer, J. *Al-Farabi and Aristotelian Syllogistics: Greek Theory and Islamic Practice* (Leiden, 1994).

[104] Mahdi, M. *Alfarabi and the Foundation of Islamic Political Philosophy* (Chicago /London, 2001).

[105] Parens, J. *Metaphysics as Rhetoric: Al-Farabi's* Summary of Plato's 'Laws' (Albany, NY, 1995).

Saadiah Gaon

[106] Saadiah Gaon. *The Book of Beliefs and Opinions*, trans. S. Rosenblatt (New Haven, CT, 1948).

[107] Saadiah Gaon. *Saadiah ben Joseph al-Fayyumi's Book of Theodicy, a Tenth Century Arabic Commentary and Translation of the Book of Job*, trans. L. E. Goodman (New Haven, CT, 1988).

[108] Finklestein, L., ed. *Rab Saadia Gaon – Studies in His Honor*, *JTS* (1944).

[109] Freimann, A., ed. *Saadia Anniversary Volume*, Proceedings of the American Academy for Jewish Research, 1943.

[110] Rosenthal, E. I. J., ed. *Saadya Studies*, *JQR* 33 (1942–43).

Ibn Sina (Avicenna)

[111] Avicenna wrote an extensive philosophical encyclopedia, the *Shifa'* (Healing), which he later abbreviated, mainly by excerpting, in the *Najat* (Salvation). An edition of the *Metaphysics of the Shifa'* with trans. by M. E. Marmura is forthcoming from Brigham Young University Press.

[112] Avicenna. *Healing: Metaphysics* I 5, trans. M. E. Marmura, in [49], 219–39.

[113] Avicenna. *Healing: Metaphysics* VI 1–2 [on causes], trans. A. Hyman, in [17], 247–55.

[114] Avicenna. *Healing: Metaphysics* X 2–5, trans. M. E. Marmura, in [22], 98–111.

[115] Avicenna. *Avicenna Latinus. Liber de anima seu sextus de naturalibus*, ed. S. Van Riet, 2 vols. (Louvain/Leiden, 1968–72).

[116] Avicenna. *Avicenna Latinus. Liber de philosophia prima sive scientia divina*, ed. S. Van Riet, 3 vols. (Louvain/Louvain-la-Neuve/Leiden, 1977–83).

[117] Avicenna. *The Life of Ibn Sina*, trans. W. E. Gohlman (Albany, NY, 1974).

[118] Avicenna. *On the Proof of Prophecies and the Interpretation of the Prophet's Symbols and Metaphors*, trans. M. E. Marmura, in [22], 112–21.

[119] Avicenna. *Avicenna's Psychology. An English Translation of Kitab al-Najat, Book II, Chapter VI*, F. Rahman (London, 1952).

[120] Avicenna. *On Theology*, trans. A. J. Arberry (London, 1951).

[121] Burrell, D. *Knowing the Unknowable God: Ibn Sina, Maimonides, Aquinas* (Notre Dame, IN, 1986).

[122] Corbin, H. *Avicenna and the Visionary Recital*, trans. W. R. Trask (London, 1960).

[123] Gutas, D. "Avicenna's Eastern ('Oriental') Philosophy: Nature, Contents, Transmission," *ASP* 10 (2000), 159–80.

[124] Gutas, D. *Avicenna and the Aristotelian Tradition. Introduction to Reading Avicenna's Philosophical Works* (Leiden, 1988).

[125] Gutas, D. "Intuition and Thinking: The Evolving Structure of Avicenna's Epistemology," in [133], 1–38.

[126] Hasse, D. N. "Avicenna on Abstraction," in [133], 39–72.

[127] Janssens, J. L. *An Annotated Bibliography on Ibn Sina (1970–1989)* (Louvain, 1991).

[128] Janssens, J. L. *An Annotated Bibliography on Ibn Sina. First Supplement (1990–1994)* (Louvain-la-Neuve, 1999).

[129] Marmura, M. E. "Avicenna's 'Flying Man' in Context," *Monist* 69 (1986), 383–95.

[130] Marmura, M. E. "Avicenna and the Kalam," *Zeitschrift für Geschichte der Arabisch-Islamischen Wissenschaften* 7 (1991–92), 172–206.

[131] Marmura, M. E. "Avicenna on Primary Concepts in the *Metaphysics* of his *al-Shifa'*," in [49], 219–39.

[132] Rahman, F. "Essence and Existence in Ibn Sina: The Myth and the Reality," *Hamdard Islamicus* 4, 1 (1981), 3–14.

[133] Wisnovsky, R., ed. *Aspects of Avicenna* (Princeton, NJ, 2002).

[134] Wisnovsky, R. "Notes on Avicenna's Concept of Thingness (say'iyya)," *ASP* 10 (2000), 181–221.

Ibn Gabirol (Avicebron)

[135] Ibn Gabirol. *Fountain of Life*, trans. A. B. Jacob (Philadelphia, 1954).

[136] Ibn Gabirol. *The Improvement of the Moral Qualities*, ed. and trans. S. S. Wise (New York, 1901; reprinted 1966).

[137] Löwe, R. *Ibn Gabirol* (New York, 1990).

Anselm of Canterbury

[138] Anselm of Canterbury. *Opera omnia*, ed. F. S. Schmitt, 6 vols. in 2 (Stuttgart-Bad Cannstatt, 1968).

[139] Anselm of Canterbury. *The Major Works*, ed. B. Davies and G. R. Evans, 2 vols. (Oxford, 1998) and *Anselm of Canterbury*, trans. J. Hopkins and H. Richardson, 4 vols. (Toronto/New York, 1976) both include *On the Trinity; The Harmony of the Foreknowledge, the Predestination, and the Grace of God with Free Choice*; and *Cur Deus homo* (Why God Became Man).

[140] Anselm of Canterbury. *Monologion and Proslogion with the Replies of Gaunilo and Anselm*, trans. T. Williams (Indianapolis, 1996).

[141] Anselm of Canterbury. *Three Philosophical Dialogues: On Truth, On Freedom of Choice, On the Fall of the Devil*, trans. T. Williams (Indianapolis, 2002).

[142] Adams, M. M. "Romancing the Good: God and the Self According to St. Anselm of Canterbury," in G. Matthews, ed., *The Augustinian Tradition* (Berkeley, CA/London, 1998), 91–109.

[143] Normore, C. "Anselm's Two 'Wills,'" in [27], 759–66.

[144] Schufreider, G. *Confessions of a Rational Mystic* (West Lafayette, IN, 1994). Text and trans. of *Proslogion*, 310–75.

[145] Southern, R. W. *St. Anselm and His Biographer* (Cambridge, 1963).

[146] Southern, R. W. *Saint Anselm: A Portrait in a Landscape* (Cambridge, 1990).

[147] Visser, S. and T. Williams "Anselm's Account of Freedom," *CJP* 31 (2001), 221–44.

Al-Ghazali

[148] Al-Ghazali. *The Incoherence of the Philosophers*, ed. and trans. M. E. Marmura (Provo, UT, 1997).
[149] Al-Ghazali. [autobiography] *Freedom and Fulfillment*, trans. R. J. McCarthy, S. J. (Boston, MA, 1980; reprinted as *Deliverance from Error*, Louisville, KY [1999?]).
[150] Marmura, M. E. "Ghazali and Ash'arism Revisited," *ASP* 12 (2002), 91–110.
[151] Marmura, M. E. "Ghazalian Causes and Intermediaries," *Journal of the American Oriental Society* 115 (1995), 89–100.

Peter Abelard

[152] Peter Abelard. Abelard to a Friend: *The Story of His Misfortunes*, in *The Letters of Abelard and Heloïse*, trans. B. Radice (New York, 1974), 57–106.
[153] Peter Abelard. *Peter Abelard's "Ethics,"* ed. and trans. D. Luscombe (Oxford, 1971).
[154] Marenbon, J. *The Philosophy of Peter Abelard* (Cambridge, 1997).

Hugh of St. Victor

[155] Luscombe, D. E. "The Commentary of Hugh of Saint Victor on the Celestial Hierarchy," in [35], 159–75.

Peter Lombard

[156] Colish, M. L. *Peter Lombard*, 2 vols. (Leiden, 1994).

John of Salisbury

[157] John of Salisbury. *The Metalogicon of John of Salisbury*, trans. D. D. McGarry (Berkeley, CA, 1955).
[158] John of Salisbury *Policraticus*, trans. C. J. Nederman (Cambridge, 1990).
[159] Wilks, M., ed. *The World of John of Salisbury* (Oxford, 1984).

Ibn Rushd (Averroes)

[160] Averroes. *The Epistle on the Possibility of Conjunction with the Active Intellect by Ibn Rushd with the Commentary of Moses Narboni*, ed. and trans. K. P. Bland (New York, 1982).

[161] Averroes. *On the Harmony of Religion and Philosophy*, trans. G. F. Hourani (London, 1976).

[162] Averroes. *Liber de medicina, qui dicitur Colliget*, in Aristotle, *Omnia quae extant opera* (Venice, 1552), X, fos. 4–80.

[163] Averroes. *Middle Commentary on Aristotle's* De anima, ed. and trans. A. L. Ivry (Provo, UT, 2002).

[164] Averroes. *Averroes on Plato's "Republic,"* trans. R. Lerner (Ithaca, NY/London, 1974).

[165] Averroes. *Tahafut al-Tahafut (The Incoherence of the Incoherence)*, trans. S. Van den Bergh, 2 vols. (London, 1954, reprinted 1969).

[166] Black, D. "Consciousness and Self-Knowledge in Aquinas's Critique of Averroes' Psychology," *JHP* 31 (1993), 349–85.

[167] Davidson, H. A. "The Relation between Averroes' Middle and Long Commentaries on the *De anima*," *ASP* 7 (1997), 139–51; A. Ivry's "Response," 153–55.

[168] Endress, G. and J. A. Aertsen, eds. *Averroes and the Aristotelian Tradition. Sources, Constitution and Reception of the Philosophy of Ibn Rushd (1126–1198)* (Leiden, 1999).

[169] Hyman, A. "Averroes' Theory of the Intellect and the Ancient Commentators," in [168], 188–98.

[170] Ivry, A. L. "Averroes' Middle and Long Commentaries on the *De anima*," *ASP* 5 (1995), 75–92.

[171] Ivry, A. L. "Averroes' Three Commentaries on *De anima*," in [168], 199–216.

[172] Renan, E. *Averroès et l'averroïsme* (Paris, 1852; 3rd revised edn 1866; reprinted with preface by A. de Libera, Paris, 1997).

[173] Rosemann, P. W. "Averroes: A Catalogue of Editions and Scholarly Writings from 1821 Onwards," [53] 30 (1988), 153–221.

[174] Sylla, E. "Averroism and the Assertiveness of the Separate Sciences," in [26], III, 171–80.

[175] Taylor, R. C. "Remarks on Cogitatio in Averroes' *Commentarium Magnum in Aristotelis De Anima Libros*," in [168], 217–55.

Moses Maimonides

[176] Moses Maimonides. *Crises and Leadership: Epistles of Maimonides*, trans. A. Halkin (Philadelphia, 1985).

[177] Moses Maimonides. *Ethical Writings of Maimonides*, trans. R. L. Weiss and C. E. Butterworth (New York, 1975).

[178] Moses Maimonides. *The Guide of the Perplexed*, trans. S. Pines, 2 vols. (Chicago, 1963).

[179] Moses Maimonides. *Mishneh Torah: The Book of Knowledge*, trans. M. Haymson (Jerusalem, 1965).

[180] Moses Maimonides. *Maimonides' Treatise on [the Art of] Logic*, trans. I. Efros (New York, 1938).

[181] Altmann, A. "Maimonides on the Intellect and the Scope of Metaphysics," in *Von der mittelalterlichen zur modernen Aufklärung* (Tubingen, 1987), 60–129.

[182] Buijs, J. A. ed. *Maimonides: A Collection of Critical Essays* (Notre Dame, IN, 1988).

[183] Dunphy, W. "Maimonides' Not So Secret Position on Creation," in [186], 151–72.

[184] Hyman, A., ed. *Maimonidean Studies*, 4 vols. (New York, 1991–96).

[185] Kraemer, J., ed. *Perspectives on Maimonides: Philosophical and Historical Studies* (London, 1996).

[186] Ormsby, E., ed. *Maimonides and His Times* (Washington, DC, 1989).

[187] Pines, S. and Y. Yovel, eds. *Maimonides and Philosophy* (Dordrecht, 1986).

[188] Strauss, L. "The Literary Character of the *Guide of the Perplexed*," in Strauss, *Persecution and the Art of Writing* (Westport, CT, 1952) 38–94.

Comparative studies include the following:

[189] Burrell, D. "Aquinas' Debt to Maimonides," in R. Link-Salinger *et al.*, eds., *A Straight Path* (Washington, DC, 1988), 37–48.

[190] Dienstag, J. I. *Studies in Maimonides and St. Thomas Aquinas* (New York, 1975).

[191] Dobbs-Weinstein, I. *Maimonides and St. Thomas on the Limits of Reason* (Albany, NY, 1995).

[192] Dunphy, W. "Maimonides and Aquinas on Creation: A Critique of Their Historians," in L. P. Person, ed., *Graceful Reason* (Toronto, 1983), 361–79.

[193] Kluxen, W. "Maimonides and Latin Scholasticism," in S. Pines and Y. Yovel, eds., *Maimonides and Philosophy* (Dordrecht, 1986), 224–32.

Robert Grosseteste

[194] Robert Grosseteste. *Epistolae*, ed. H. R. Luard (London, 1861).

[195] Robert Grosseteste. *On the Six Days of Creation*, trans C. F. J. Martin (Oxford, 1996).

[196] Callus, D., ed. *Robert Grosseteste: Scholar and Bishop* (Oxford, 1955).

[197] Crombie, A. C. *Robert Grosseteste and the Origins of Experimental Science 1100–1700* (Oxford, 1953).

[198] Friedman, L. M. *Robert Grosseteste and the Jews* (Cambridge, MA, 1934).

[199] McEvoy, J. *Robert Grosseteste* (Oxford, 2002).
[200] Marrone, S. P. *William of Auvergne and Robert Grosseteste* (Princeton, NJ, 1983).

Albert the Great

[201] Albert the Great. *Opera omnia*, ed. P. Jammy, 21 vols. (Lyon, 1651). *De homine* in vol. XIX.
[202] Albert the Great. *Speculum Astronomiae*, ed. and trans. S. Caroti *et al.*, in P. Zambelli, *The* Speculum Astronomiae *and its Enigma. Astrology, Theology, and Science in Albertus Magnus and his Contemporaries* (Dordrecht/Boston, MA/London, 1992).
[203] Albert the Great. *Summa theologiae*, ed. D. Siedler (Munster, 1978) (*Alberti Magni opera omnia*, XXXIV.1).
[204] Hackett, J. "Necessity, Fate, and a Science of Experience in Albertus Magnus, Thomas Aquinas, and Roger Bacon," in [48], 113–23.
[205] Weisheipl, J., ed. *Albertus Magnus and the Sciences* (Toronto, 1980).

Peter of Spain

[206] Peter of Spain. "Syllogisms," "Topics," "Fallacies (selections)," in *CT* I 216–61.
[207] De Libera, A. "The Oxford and Paris Traditions in Logic," in *CHLMP*, 174–87.

Roger Bacon

[208] Roger Bacon. *The Opus Majus of Roger Bacon*, trans. R. B. Burke, 2 vols. (Oxford, 1928).
[209] Lindberg, D. *Roger Bacon's Philosophy of Nature* (Oxford, 1983).
[210] The September 1997 issue of *Vivarium* is devoted to articles on Bacon.

Bonaventure

[211] Bonaventure. *Opera omnia*, 10 vols. (Ad Claras Aquas, 1882–1902).
[212] Bonaventure. *Collationes in Hexaemeron*, ed. F. Delorme, *S. Bonaventurae Collationes in Hexaemeron et Bonaventuriana quaedam selecta* (Ad Claras Aquas, 1934).
[213] Bonaventure. *Saint Bonaventure's Disputed Questions on the Mystery of the Trinity*, trans. Z. Hayes (St. Bonaventure, NY, 1979).
[214] Bonaventure. *Itinerarium mentis in Deum*, trans. P. Boehner, ed. S. Brown, *The Journey of the Mind to God* (Indianapolis, 1993).

[215] Bonaventure, *et al. De Humanae Cognitionis Ratione: anecdota quaedam Seraphici Doctoris Sancti Bonaventurae et nonnulorum eius discipulorum* (Ad Claras Aquas, 1883).
[216] Bougerol, J. G. "Saint Bonaventure et la hiérarchie dionysienne," *AHDLMA* 36 (1969), 131–67.
[217] Bougerol, J. G. "Saint Bonaventure et le Pseudo-Denys l'Aréopagite," *Actes du Colloque Saint Bonaventure, 9–12 sept. 1968. Orsay, Etudes franciscaines* 18 (1968), annual supplement, 33–123.
[218] Gilson, E. *The Philosophy of St. Bonaventure*, trans. I. Trethowan and F. Sheed (Paterson, NJ, 1965).

Henry of Ghent

[219] Henry of Ghent. *Opera*, ed. R. Macken (Leuven/Leiden, 1979–).
[220] Henry of Ghent. *Quodlibeta* (Paris, 1518; reprinted Louvain, 1961).
[221] Henry of Ghent. *Quodlibetal Questions on Free Will*, trans. R. J. Teske (Milwaukee, WI, 1993).
[222] Henry of Ghent. *Summae quaestionum ordinariarum theologi recepto praeconio solennis Henrici a Gandavo* (Paris, 1520; reprinted St. Bonaventure, NY, 1953).
[223] McEvoy, J. "The Sources and Significance of Henry of Ghent's Disputed Question, 'Is Friendship a Virtue?,' " in W. Vanhamel, ed., *Henry of Ghent* (Leuven, 1996), 121–38.

Thomas Aquinas

[224] Thomas Aquinas. *S. Thomae Aquinatis Doctoris Angelici Opera Omnia* (Rome, 1882–). *ST*, vols. IV–XII; *ScG*, vols. XIII–XV; *Quaestiones disputatae de veritate*, vol. XXII; *Quaestiones disputatae de malo*, vol. XXIII; *Quaestiones disputatae de anima*, vol. XXIV/1; *De regno*, vol. XLII; *De unitate intellectus*, vol. XLIII.
[225] Thomas Aquinas. *A Commentary on Aristotle's* De anima, trans. R. Pasnau (New Haven, CT/London, 1999).
[226] Thomas Aquinas. *Commentary on Aristotle's* Physics, trans. R. Blackwell *et al.* (Notre Dame, IN, 1999).
[227] Thomas Aquinas. *On Being and Essence*, ed. J. Bobik (Notre Dame, IN, 1965).
[228] Thomas Aquinas. *On the Eternity of the World*. Medieval Source Book. http://fordham.edu/halsall/basis/aquinas-eternity.html
[229] Thomas Aquinas. *Opuscula Theologica*, ed. R. A. Verardo *et al.*, 2 vols. (Turin, 1954).

[230] Thomas Aquinas. *Quaestiones disputatae*, ed. R. Spiazzi, 2 vols. (Turin/Rome, 1949). *De virtutibus in communi*, II, 703–51.

[231] Thomas Aquinas. *Selected Writings*, trans. T. McDermott (Oxford, 1993).

[232] Thomas Aquinas. *Summa contra Gentiles*, trans. A. C. Pegis *et al.*, 5 vols. (Notre Dame, IN/London, 1975; first published Garden City, NY, 1956 as *On the Truth of the Catholic Faith*).

[233] Thomas Aquinas. *Summa Theologiae*, ed. T. Gilby *et al.*, 61 vols. (London/New York, 1964–80). The Blackfriars edition: Latin and English, with extensive supporting material.

[234] Thomas Aquinas. *Truth*, trans. of *Quaestiones disputatae de veritate* by R. W. Mulligan *et al.*, 3 vols. (Chicago, 1952–54; reprinted Indianapolis, 1994).

[235] Ashworth, E. J. "Analogy and Equivocation in Thirteenth-Century Logic: Aquinas in Context," *MS* 54 (1992), 94–135.

[236] Ashworth, E. J. "Aquinas on Significant Utterance: Interjection, Blasphemy, Prayer," in [251] 207–34.

[237] Ashworth, E. J. "Signification and Modes of Signifying in Thirteenth-Century Logic: A Preface to Aquinas on Analogy," *MPT* 1 (1991), 39–67.

[238] Banez, D. *The Primacy of Existence in Thomas Aquinas*, trans. B. S. Llamzon (Chicago, 1966).

[239] Callus, D. A. *The Condemnation of St. Thomas at Oxford* (London, 1955).

[240] Finnis, J. *Aquinas* (Oxford, 2000).

[241] Gallagher, D. "Aquinas on Goodness and Moral Goodness," in D. Gallagher, ed., *Thomas Aquinas and his Legacy* (Washington, DC, 1994), 37–60.

[242] Hughes, C. *On a Complex Theory of a Simple God: An Investigation in Aquinas' Philosophical Theology* (Ithaca, NY/London, 1989).

[243] King, P. "Aquinas on the Passions," in [251], 101–32.

[244] Klima, G. "Aquinas on One and Many," *DSTFM* 11 (2000), 195–215.

[245] Kretzmann, N. *The Metaphysics of Creation: Aquinas's Natural Theology in* Summa contra Gentiles *II* (Oxford, 1999).

[246] Kretzmann, N. *The Metaphysics of Theism. Aquinas's Natural Theology in* Summa contra Gentiles *I* (Oxford, 1997).

[247] Kretzmann, N. "Warring against the Law of My Mind: Aquinas on Romans 7," in T. V. Morris, ed., *Philosophy and the Christian Faith* (Notre Dame, IN, 1988), 172–95.

[248] Luscombe, D. E. "Thomas Aquinas and Conceptions of Hierarchy in the Thirteenth Century," in [264], 261–77.

[249] MacDonald, S. "Aquinas's Libertarian Account of Free Choice," *Revue Internationale de Philosophie* 52 (1998), 309–28.

[250] MacDonald, S. "Egoistic Rationalism: Aquinas's Basis for Christian Morality," in M. Beaty, ed., *Christian Theism and the Problems of Philosophy* (Notre Dame, IN, 1990), 327–54.

[251] MacDonald, S. and E. Stump, eds. *Aquinas's Moral Theory* (Ithaca, NY, 1999).

[252] McInerny, R. *Ethica Thomistica*, revised edn (Washington, DC, 1997).

[253] O'Connor, D. J. *Aquinas and Natural Law* (London, 1967).

[254] Owens, J. "Aquinas on the Inseparability of Soul from Existence," *NS* 61 (1987), 249–70.

[255] Pasnau, R. *Thomas Aquinas on Human Nature: A Philosophical Study of ST Ia 75–89* (Cambridge, 2002).

[256] Pines, S. "Scholasticism after Thomas Aquinas and the Teachings of Hasdai Crescas and his Predecessors," *Proceedings of the Israel Academy of Sciences and Humanities* 1 (1967), 1–101.

[257] Pope, S., ed. *The Ethics of Aquinas* (Washington, DC, 2002).

[258] Rosier, I. "Signes et sacrements: Thomas d'Aquin et la grammaire spéculative." *Revue des sciences philosophiques et théologiques* 74 (1990), 392–436.

[259] Stump, E. "Aquinas's Account of Freedom: Intellect and Will," *Monist* 80 (1997), 576–97.

[260] Torrell, J.-P. *Saint Thomas Aquinas, volume I, The Person and His Work*, trans. R. Royal (Washington, DC, 1996).

[261] Wippel, J. F. "The Latin Avicenna as a Source for Thomas Aquinas' Metaphysics," *Freiburger Zeitschrift für Philosophie und Theologie* 37 (1990), 51–90.

[262] Wippel, J. F. *The Metaphysical Thought of Thomas Aquinas: From Finite Being to Uncreated Being* (Washington, DC, 2000).

[263] Wippel, J. F. "Thomas Aquinas and Participation," in [505], 117–58.

[264] Zimmerman, A., ed. *Thomas von Aquin* (Berlin, 1988).

Boethius of Dacia

[265] Boethius of Dacia. *On the Supreme Good. On the Eternity of the World. On Dreams*, trans. J. F. Wippel (Toronto, 1987).

Siger of Brabant

[266] Siger of Brabant. *Quaestiones in tertium de anima, de anima intellectiva, de aeternitate mundi*, ed. B. Bazán (Louvain, 1972).

[267] Van Steenberghen, F. *Maître Siger de Brabant* (Louvain/Paris, 1977).

[268] Wippel, J. F. *Medieval Reactions to the Encounter Between Faith and Reason* (Milwaukee, WI, 1995).

Giles of Rome (Aegidius Romanus, Egidius Colonna)

[269] Giles of Rome. *Apologia*, ed. R. Wielockx, volume III.1 of *Aegidii Romani Opera* (Florence, 1985–).
[270] Giles of Rome. *On Ecclesiastical Power*, ed. and trans. R. W. Dyson (Woodbridge, Suffolk, 1986).

Peter John Olivi

[271] Peter John Olivi. *Quaestiones in secundum librum Sententiarum*, ed. B. Jansen (Quaracchi, 1922–26).
[272] Boureau, A. and S. Piron, eds. *Pierre de Jean Olivi (1248–1298): Pensée Scolastique, Dissidence Spirituelle et Société* (Paris, 1999).
[273] Pasnau, R. "Olivi on Human Freedom," in [272], 15–25.
[274] Pasnau, R. "Olivi on the Metaphysics of Soul," *MPT* 6 (1997), 109–32.

Godfrey of Fontaines

[275] Godfrey of Fontaines. *Les Quodlibet Cinq, Six, et Sept*, in M. de Wulf and J. Hoffmans, eds., *Les Philosophes Belges* 3 (Louvain, 1914).
[276] Wippel, J. F. *The Metaphysical Thought of Godfrey of Fontaines*. (Washington, DC, 1981).

James of Viterbo

[277] James of Viterbo. *On Christian Government: De regimine christiano*, ed. and trans. R. W. Dyson (Woodbridge, Suffolk, 1995). Also see *CT* II 285–300, 321–25.

John of Paris

[278] John of Paris. F. Bleienstein, ed., *Johannes "Quidort von Paris." Über königliche und päpstliche Gewalt. De regia potestate et papali* (Stuttgart, 1969).
[279] John of Paris. *On Royal and Papal Power*, trans. J. A. Watt (Toronto, 1971).
[280] Coleman J. "The Dominican Political Theory of John of Paris in Its Context," in D. Wood, ed., *The Church and Sovereignty c. 590–1918* (Oxford, 1991), 187–223.

John Duns Scotus

[281] John Duns Scotus. *Opera omnia*, ed. C. Balić *et al.* (Vatican City, 1950–). *Ordinatio* I–II, vols. I–VIII; *Lectura* I–II, vols. XVI–XIX.

[282] John Duns Scotus. *Opera omnia*, ed. L. Wadding, 16 vols. (Lyon, 1639; reprinted Hildesheim, 1968). *Ordinatio* III–IV, vols. VII–X; *Reportatio*, vol. XI.

[283] John Duns Scotus. *God and Creatures: The Quodlibetal Questions*, trans. F. Alluntis and A. B. Wolter (Princeton, NJ, 1975).

[284] John Duns Scotus. *Questions on the Metaphysics of Aristotle*, trans. G. Etzkorn and A. B. Wolter (St. Bonaventure, NY, 1997).

[285] John Duns Scotus. *Quaestiones super libros Metaphysicorum Aristotelis*, ed. R. Andrews *et al.* in *Opera Philosophica*, vols. III–IV (St. Bonaventure, NY, 1997).

[286] John Duns Scotus. *Philosophical Writings*, trans. A. B. Wolter (Edinburgh, 1962; reprinted Indianapolis, 1987).

[287] John Duns Scotus. *John Duns Scotus: A Treatise on God as First Principle*, trans. A. B. Wolter (Chicago, 1966; revised edn 1983).

[288] John Duns Scotus. *Duns Scotus on the Will and Morality*, trans. A. B. Wolter (Washington, DC, 1986).

[289] Adams, M. M., ed. *The Philosophical Theology of John Duns Scotus* (Ithaca, NY, 1990).

[290] Boler, J. "Transcending the Natural: Duns Scotus on the Two Affections of the Will," *ACPQ* 67 (1993), 109–26.

[291] Cross, R. *Duns Scotus* (Oxford, 1999).

[292] Cross, R. "Duns Scotus on Eternity and Timelessness," *FP* 14 (1997), 3–25.

[293] Cross, R. "Duns Scotus on Goodness, Justice, and What God Can Do," *JTS* 48 (1997), 48–76.

[294] Cross, R. *The Physics of Duns Scotus* (Oxford, 1998).

[295] Ingham, M. "Duns Scotus, Morality and Happiness: A Reply to Thomas Williams," *ACPQ* 74 (2000), 173–95.

[296] King, P. "Duns Scotus on the Reality of Self-Change," in [40], 227–90.

[297] Noone, T. B. "Scotus on Divine Ideas: *Rep. Paris. I-A*, d. 36," *Medioevo: Rivista di storia della filosofia medievale* 24 (1998), 359–453.

[298] Pini, G. "Signification of Names in Duns Scotus and Some of His Contemporaries," *Vivarium* 39 (2001), 20–51.

[299] Williams, T. "The Libertarian Foundations of Scotus's Moral Philosophy," *Thomist* 62 (1998), 193–215.

[300] Williams, T. "A Most Methodical Lover? On Scotus's Arbitrary Creator," *JHP* 38 (2000), 169–202.

[301] Wolter, A. B. "Native Freedom of the Will as a Key to the Ethics of Scotus," in [289], 148–62.

[302] Wolter, A. B. "Reflections about Scotus's Early Works," in L. Honnefelder et al., eds., John Duns Scotus: Metaphysics and Ethics (Leiden, 1996), 37–57.

Marsilius of Padua

[303] Marsilius of Padua. The Defender of the Peace, trans. A. Gewirth (New York, 1956; reprinted Toronto, 1980).

[304] Marsilius of Padua. Marsiglio of Padua: Defensor minor and De translatione imperii, trans. C. J. Nederman (Cambridge, 1993).

[305] Quillet, J. La Philosophie politique de Marsile de Padoue (Paris, 1970).

[306] Rubinstein, N. "Marsilius of Padua and Italian Political Thought of his Time," in J. R. Hale and B. Smalley, eds., Europe in the Late Middle Ages (London, 1965), 44–75.

Peter Aureol

[307] Schabel, C. Theology at Paris, 1316–1345. Peter Auriol and the Problem of Divine Foreknowledge and Future Contingents (Aldershot, Hants., 2000).

William of Ockham

[308] William of Ockham. Opera philosophica et theologica [OPh and OTh], 17 vols., ed. G. Gál et al. (St. Bonaventure, NY, 1967–88). Ordinatio (I Sent.), OTh I–IV; Reportatio (II–IV Sent.), OTh V–VII.

[309] William of Ockham. Guilelmi de Ockham Opera Politica, ed. H. S. Offler et al. (Manchester [vols. I–III], Oxford [vol. IV], 1940–).

[310] William of Ockham. A Letter to the Friars Minor and Other Writings, ed. A. S. McGrade and J. Kilcullen (Cambridge, 1995).

[311] William of Ockham. Philosophical Writings and trans., ed. and trans. P. Boehner, revised S. F. Brown (Indianapolis, 1990).

[312] William of Ockham. On the Power of Emperors and Popes, ed. and trans. A. S. Brett (Bristol, 1998).

[313] William of Ockham. Quodlibetal Questions, trans. A. J. Freddoso and F. E. Kelly, 2 vols. (New Haven, CT/London, 1991).

[314] William of Ockham. A Short Discourse on Tyrannical Government, ed. A. S. McGrade, trans. J. Kilcullen (Cambridge, 1992).

[315] William of Ockham. Ockham's Theory of Propositions (Part 2 of the Summa Logicae), trans. A. J. Freddoso and H. Schuurman (South Bend, IN, 1998).

[316] William of Ockham. *Ockham's Theory of Terms (Part 1 of the Summa Logicae)*, trans. M. Loux (South Bend, IN, 1998).

[317] William of Ockham. *Ockham on the Virtues*, trans. R. Wood (West Lafayette, IN, 1997).

[318] Adams, M. M. *William Ockham*, 2 vols. (Notre Dame, IN, 1987).

[319] McGrade, A. S. "Ockham on Enjoyment," *RM* 34 (1981), 706–28.

[320] McGrade, A. S. *The Political Thought of William of Ockham* (Cambridge, 1974; pbk 2002).

[321] Miethke, J. *Ockhams Weg zur Sozialphilosophie* (Berlin, 1969).

[322] Panaccio, C. *Les Mots, les concepts et les choses: La sémantique de Guillaume d'Occam et le nominalisme d'aujourd'hui* (Montreal/Paris, 1991).

Gersonides

[323] Gersonides. *Levi ben Gershom (Gersonides): The Wars of the Lord*, 3 vols., trans. S. Feldman (Philadelphia, 1984–99).

[324] Dobbs-Weinstein, I. "Gersonides' Radically Modern Understanding of the Agent Intellect," in [33], 191–213.

[325] Eisen, R. *Gersonides on Providence, Covenant, and the Chosen People* (Albany, NY, 1995).

[326] Feldman, S. "Gersonides on the Possibility of Conjunction with the Agent Intellect," *Association for Jewish Studies Review* 3 (1978), 99–120.

[327] Freudenthal, G., ed. *Studies on Gersonides* (Leiden/New York, 1992).

[328] Harvey, S. "Did Gersonides Believe in the Absolute Generation of Prime Matter?," *Jerusalem Studies in Jewish Thought* 8 (1988), 307–18.

[329] Kellner, M. "Gersonides and his Cultured Despisers: Arama and Abravanel," *Journal of Medieval and Renaissance Studies* 6 (1976), 269–96.

[330] Kellner, M. "Maimonides and Gersonides on Mosaic Prophecy," *Speculum* 52 (1977), 62–79.

[331] Klein-Braslavy, S. "Gersonides on Determinism, Possibility, Choice and Foreknowledge," *Daat* 22 (1989), 5–53.

[332] Pines, S. "Scholasticism after Thomas Aquinas and the Teachings of Hasdai Crescas and his Predecessors," *Proceedings of the Israel Academy of Sciences and Humanities* 1 (1967), 1–101.

[333] Rudavsky, T. "Creation, Time, and Infinity in Gersonides," *JHP* 26 (January 1988), 25–44.

[334] Rudavsky, T. "Divine Omniscience and Future Contingents in Gersonides," *JHP* 21 (October 1983), 513–26.

Robert Holcot

[335] Gelber, H. G. *Exploring the Boundaries of Reason: Three Questions on the Nature of God by Robert Holcot, OP* (Toronto, 1983).
[336] Kennedy, L. *The Philosophy of Robert Holcot, Fourteenth-Century Skeptic* (Lewiston, NY, 1993).
[337] Streveler, P. and K. Tachau, eds. *Seeing the Future Clearly: Questions on Future Contingents by Robert Holcot* (Toronto, 1995).

Adam Wodeham

[338] Courtenay, W. J. *Adam Wodeham* (Leiden, 1978).

Thomas Bradwardine

[339] Thomas Bradwardine. *De causa Dei contra Pelagium et de virtute causarum* (London, 1618; reprinted Frankfurt, 1964).
[340] Sylla, E. "Thomas Bradwardine's *De continuo* and the Structure of Fourteenth-Century Learning," in [50], 148–56.

John Buridan

[341] John Buridan. *Summulae de Dialectica*, trans. G. Klima (New Haven, CT/London, 2001).
[342] Klima, G. "John Buridan on the Acquisition of Simple Substantial Concepts," in S. Ebbesen and R. L. Friedman, eds., *John Buridan and Beyond: The Language Sciences 1300–1700* (Copenhagen, forthcoming).
[343] Sylla, E. " 'Ideo quasi mendicare oportet intellectum humanum': The Role of Theology in John Buridan's Natural Philosophy," in [344], 221–45.
[344] Thijssen, J. M. M. H. and J. Zupko, eds. *The Metaphysics and Natural Philosophy of John Buridan* (Leiden/Boston, MA/Cologne, 2001).
[345] Zupko, J. "Freedom of Choice in Buridan's Moral Psychology," *MS* 57 (1995), 75–99.

Nicholas of Autrecourt

[346] Nicholas of Autrecourt. *Correspondence with Master Giles and Bernard of Arezzo*, trans. L. M. de Rijk (Leiden, 1994).
[347] Nicholas of Autrecourt. *The Universal Treatise of Nicholas of Autrecourt*, trans. L. Kennedy *et al.* (Milwaukee, WI, 1971).

William Heytesbury

[348] Longeway, J., ed. *William Heytesbury on Maxima and Minima* (Dordrecht/Boston, MA/Lancaster, 1984).
[349] Wilson, C. *William Heytesbury: Medieval Logic and the Rise of Mathematical Physics* (Madison, WI, 1960).

Nicole Oresme

[350] Hansen, B. *Nicole Oresme and the Marvels of Nature. The* De causis mirabilium (Toronto, 1985).

John Wyclif

[351] John Wyclif. *On Civil Lordship* (selections), in *CT* II 587–654.
[352] John Wyclif. *On Universals* (*Tractatus de Universalibus*), trans. A. Kenny, introduced by P. V. Spade (Oxford, 1985).
[353] Luscombe, D. E. "Wyclif and Hierarchy," in A. Hudson and M. Wilks, eds., *From Ockham to Wyclif* (Oxford, 1987), 233–44.
[354] Wilks, M. J. "Predestination, Property and Power: Wyclif's Theory of Dominion and Grace," in G. J. Cuming, ed., *The Church and Sovereignty c. 590–1918* (London/Edinburgh, 1965), 220–36.

Other medieval thinkers

[355] Adelard of Bath. *Conversations with his Nephew. On the Same and the different, Questions on Natural Science, and On Birds*, trans. C. Burnett (Cambridge, 1998). (Selections from Adelard's *Quaestiones naturales* in [401], 38–51.)
[356] Aelred of Rievaulx. *On Spiritual Friendship*, trans. M. E. Laker (Washington, DC, 1974).
[357] [Alan of Lille] D'Alverny, M.-T. *Alain de Lille. Textes inédits avec une introduction sur sa vie et ses œuvres* (Paris, 1965). Includes *Expositio prosae de angelis*, 206–10; *Hierarchia*, 223–35; and *Sermo in die sancti Michaelis*, 249–51.
[358] Alexander of Hales. *Summa Fratris Alexandri*, vol. I, ed. B. Klumper (Quaracchi, 1924).
[359] Alhazen. *The Optics of Ibn al-Haytham. Books I–III: On Direct Vision*, trans. A. I. Sabra (London, 1989).
[360] Avempace. *Ibn Bajjah's 'Ilm al-Nafs [On the Soul]*, trans. M. S. H. Ma'sumi (Karachi, 1961).
[361] Avempace. *The Governance of the Solitary*, partial trans. L. Berman in [22], 122–33.

[362] Benedict of Nursia. *The Rule of St. Benedict*, trans. A. C. Meisel and M. L. del Mastro (Garden City, NY, 1975).

[363] Meister Eckhart. *Parisian Questions and Prologues*, trans. A. Maurer (Toronto, 1974).

[364] McGinn, B., ed. *Meister Eckhart and the Beguine Mystics* (New York, 1994).

[365] Hermann of Carinthia. *De Essentiis*, trans. C. Burnett (Leiden/ Cologne, 1982).

[366] Ibn 'Adi, Yahya. *The Reformation of Morals*, Arabic text ed. S. Khalil, trans. S. H. Griffith (Provo, UT, 2002).

[367] Ibn Tufail. *The Improvement of Human Reason, Exhibited in the Life of Hai Ebn Yokdhan*, trans. S. Ockley (London, 1708; reprinted Hildesheim, 1983).

[368] Ibn Tufail. *Ibn Tufyal's Hayy Ibn Yaqzan: A Philosophical Tale*, trans. L. E. Goodman, 2nd edn (Los Angeles, CA, 1983).

[369] Conrad, L. I., ed. *The World of Ibn Tufayl: Interdisciplinary Perspectives on* Hayy ibn Yaqzan (Leiden, 1996).

[370] Al-Jami. "Al-Jami's Treatise on 'Existence,'" ed. N. Heer, in [44], 223–56.

[371] Richard Kilvington. *The Sophismata of Richard Kilvington*, trans., with introduction and commentary, N. Kretzmann and B. E. Kretzmann (Cambridge, 1990).

[372] Robert Kilwardby. *On Time and Imagination*, trans. A. Broadie (Oxford, 1993).

[373] *Liber de causis* (*Book of Causes*), trans. D. J. Brand (Milwaukee, WI, 1984).

[374] Miskawayh. *The Refinement of Character*, trans. C. K. Zurayk (Beirut, 1968).

[375] Nemesius of Emesa. *De natura hominis*, ed. G. Verbeke and J. R. Moncho (Leiden, 1975).

[376] Sylla, E. "Mathematical Physics and Imagination in the Work of the Oxford Calculators: Roger Swineshead's *On Natural Motions*," in E. Grant and J. Murdoch, eds., *Mathematics and Its Application to Science and Natural Philosophy in the Middle Ages* (Cambridge, 1987), 69–101.

[377] Sylla, E. "The Oxford Calculators in Context," *Science in Context* 1 (1987), 257–79.

[378] Sylla, E. "The Oxford Calculators and Mathematical Physics: John Dumbleton's *Summa Logicae et Philosophiae Naturalis*, Parts II and III," in S. Unguru, ed., *Physics, Cosmology and Astronomy, 1300–1700* (Dordrecht/Boston, MA/London, 1991), 129–61.

[379] Philip the Chancellor. *Summa de bono*, ed. N. Wicki (Berne, 1985).

[380] Poinsot, J. *Tractatus de Signis*, ed. J. Deely and R. Powell, *Tractatus de Signis: The Semiotic of John Poinsot* (Berkeley, CA, 1985).

[381] Proclus. *Elements of Theology*, ed. and trans. E. R. Dodds, 2nd edn (Oxford, 1963).

[382] Ptolemy of Lucca. *On the Government of Princes*, ed. and trans. J. M. Blythe (Philadelphia, 1997).

[383] Al-Razi. "The Book of the Philosophic Life," trans. C. E. Butterworth, *Interpretation* 20 (1993), 227–36.

[384] Al-Razi. *The Spiritual Physick of Rhazes*, trans. A. J. Arberry (London, 1950).

[385] Druart, T.-A. "Al-Razi's Conception of the Soul: Psychological Background to his Ethics," *MPT* 5 (1996), 245–63.

[386] Druart, T.-A. "The Ethics of al-Razi," *MPT* 6 (1997), 47–71.

[387] Richard of St. Victor. *On the Trinity*, in G. A. Zinn, ed., *Richard of St. Victor*, Classics of Western Spirituality (London, 1979).

[388] Suhrawardi. *The Philosophy of Illumination*, ed. and trans. J. Walbridge and H. Ziai (Provo, UT, 1999).

[389] Thomas of Sutton. *Quodlibeta*, ed. M. Schmaus (Munich, 1969).

[390] Al-Tusi. *The Nasirean Ethics*, trans. from Persian by G. M. Wickens (London, 1964).

[391] William of Auvergne. *De universo*, in William of Auvergne, *Opera omnia* (Venice, 1591), 561–1012.

TOPICS

Medieval philosophy in context

[392] Amory, P. *People and Identity in Ostrogothic Italy, 489–554* (Cambridge, 1997).

[393] Blumenthal, H. J. "529 and After: What Happened to the Academy?," *Byzantion* 48 (1978), 369–85.

[394] Brown, P. *The Cult of the Saints* (Chicago, 1981).

[395] Cameron, A. "The Last Days of the Academy at Athens," *Proceedings of the Cambridge Philological Society* 195 (1969), 7–29.

[396] Carruthers, M. *The Craft of Thought. Meditation, Rhetoric and the Making of Images, 400–1200* (Cambridge, 1998).

[397] Chadwick, O. *John Cassian. A Study in Primitive Monasticism*, 2nd edn (Cambridge, 1968).

[398] Cochrane, C. N. *Christianity and Classical Culture* (New York/Toronto, 1957).

[399] Coleman, J. *Ancient and Medieval Memories* (Cambridge, 1992).

[400] Courtenay, W. *Schools and Scholars in Fourteenth-Century England* (Princeton, NJ, 1987).

[401] Dales, R. C. *The Scientific Achievement of the Middle Ages* (Philadelphia, 1973).

[402] Dodds, E. R. *Pagan and Christian in an Age of Anxiety* (Cambridge, 1965).

[403] Gilson, E. *The Unity of Philosophical Experience* (New York, 1937).

[404] Goffart, W. A. *Barbarians and Romans, AD 418–584* (Princeton, NJ, 1980).

[405] Hadot, I. *Arts libéraux et philosophie dans la pensée antique* (Paris, 1984).

[406] Hadot, P. *Qu'est-ce que la philosophie antique?* (Paris, 1995).

[407] Hadot, P. *Philosophy as a Way of Life* (Oxford, 1995).

[408] Hissette, R. *Enquête sur les 219 articles condamnés à Paris le 7 mars 1277* (Leuven, 1977).

[409] Hodges, R. and D. Whitehouse. *Mohammed, Charlemagne and the Origins of Europe* (Ithaca, NY, 1983).

[410] Imbach, R. *Laien in der Philosophie des Mittelalters* (Amsterdam, 1989).

[411] Justin Martyr. *Dialogue with Trypho*, in M. Dods and G. Reith, eds., *The Apostolic Fathers with Justin Martyr and Irenaeus* (Buffalo, NY, 1887), 194–270.

[412] Lawn, B. *The Rise and Decline of the Scholastic Quaestio Disputata* (Leiden, 1993).

[413] Leclercq, J. *Love of Learning and the Desire for God* (New York, 1961).

[414] Levison, W. *England and the Continent in the Eighth Century* (Oxford, 1966; first published 1946).

[415] De Libera, A. *Penser au moyen âge* (Paris, 1991).

[416] De Libera, A. *Introduction à la mystique rhénane. D'Albert le Grand à Maître Eckhart* (Paris, 1984).

[417] De Lubac, H. *Medieval Exegesis*, vol. 1, *The Four Senses of Scripture*, trans. M. Sebanc (Edinburgh/Grand Rapids, MI, 1998).

[418] Markus, R. A. *The End of Ancient Christianity* (Cambridge, 1990).

[419] Moore, R. I. *The Formation of a Persecuting Society* (Oxford, 1987).

[420] Moore, R. I. *The Origins of European Dissent* (New York, 1977).

[421] Riché, P. *Education and Culture in the Barbarian West, Sixth through Eighth Centuries* (Columbia, SC, 1976).

[422] Rucquoi, A. "Gundisalvus ou Dominicus Gundisalvi?," [53] 41 (1999), 85–106.

[423] Ruh, K. *Kleine Schriften*, vol. II, *Scholastik und Mystik im Spätmittelalter* (Berlin, 1984).

[424] Smalley, B. *The Study of the Bible in the Middle Ages*, 3rd edn, revised (Oxford, 1983).

[425] Southern, R. W. *The Making of the Middle Ages* (New Haven, CT, 1953).

[426] Southern, R. W. *Medieval Humanism and Other Studies* (Oxford, 1970).

[427] Sulpicius Severus. *The Life of St. Martin*, in F. R. Hoare, ed. and trans., *The Western Fathers* (New York, 1954), 10–44.

[428] Tertullian. *On Prescription against Heretics*, in *The Writings of Tertullian*, vol. II, trans. P. Holmes (Edinburgh, 1870), 1–54.

[429] Trinkaus, C. *In Our Image and Likeness: Humanity and Divinity in Italian Humanist Thought* (London, 1970).

[430] Weijers, O. *La "disputatio" à la Faculté des arts de Paris (1200–1350 environ). Esquisse d'une typologie* (Turnhout, 1995).

[431] White, L. Jr. *Medieval Technology and Social Change* (Oxford, 1962).

Eternity

[432] Craig, W. L. *The Problem of Divine Foreknowledge and Future Contingents from Ockham to Suarez* (Leiden/New York/Copenhagen/Cologne, 1988).

[433] Dales, R. *Medieval Discussions of the Eternity of the World* (Leiden/New York/Copenhagen/Cologne, 1990).

[434] Fox, R. "The Concept of Time in Thirteenth-Century Western Theology" (Oxford D. Phil. thesis, 1998).

[435] Leftow, B. *Time and Eternity* (Ithaca, NY/London 1991).

[436] Newton-Smith, W. *The Structure of Time* (London/Boston, MA, 1980).

[437] MacBeath, M. "Time's Square," in M. MacBeath and R. Poidevin, eds., *The Philosophy of Time* (Oxford, 1993), 183–202.

[438] Sorabji, R. *Time, Creation and the Continuum* (London, 1983).

[439] Stump, E. and N. Kretzmann. "Eternity," *Journal of Philosophy* 79 (1981), 429–58.

[440] Stump, E. and N. Kretzmann. "Eternity, Awareness, and Action," *FP* 9 (1992), 463–82.

Hierarchy

[441] D'Alverny, M.-T. "Le Cosmos symbolique du XIIe siècle," *AHDLMA* 20 (1953), 31–81.

[442] Calvin, J. *Institutes of the Christian Religion*, 2 vols., ed. J. T. McNeill, trans. F. L. Battles (London, 1961).

[443] Congar, Y. M.-J. "Aspects ecclésiologiques de la querelle entre mendiants et séculiers dans la seconde moitié du XIIIe siècle et le début du XIVe," *AHDLMA* 28 (1961), 35–151.

[444] Daniélou, J. *Platonisme et théologie mystique. Doctrine spirituelle de Saint Grégoire de Nysse* (Paris, 1953).

[445] Endres, J. A. *Honorius Augustodunensis* (Kempton-Munich, 1906).

[446] Hadot, P. *Porphyre et Victorinus* (Paris, 1968).

[447] Lovejoy, A. O. *The Great Chain of Being. A Study of the History of an Idea* (Cambridge, MA, 1936).

[448] Luscombe, D. E. "Hierarchy in the Late Middle Ages: Criticism and Change," in J. Canning and O. G. Oexle, eds., *Political Thought and the Realities of Power in the Middle Ages* (Gottingen, 1998), 113–26.

[449] Luscombe, D. E. "The *Lex divinitatis* in the Bull *Unam Sanctam* of Pope Boniface VIII," in C. Brooke *et al.*, eds., *Church and Government in the Middle Ages* (Cambridge, 1976), 205–21.

[450] Luther, M. *Luther's Works*, vol. XXXVI, *Word and Sacrament* II, ed. A. R. Wentz (Philadelphia, 1959).

[451] Mahoney, E. P. "Lovejoy and the Hierarchy of Being," *JHI* 48 (1987), 211–30.

[452] Mahoney, E. P. "Metaphysical Foundations of the Hierarchy of Being According to Some Late-Medieval and Renaissance Philosophers," in P. Morewedge, ed., *Philosophies of Existence: Ancient and Medieval* (New York, 1982), 165–257.

[453] O'Meara, D. J. *Structures hiérarchiques dans la pensée de Plotin* (Leiden, 1975).

[454] Ullmann, W. *The Carolingian Renaissance and the Idea of Kingship* (London, 1969).

Language and logic

[455] Ashworth, E. J. *Studies in Post-Medieval Semantics* (London, 1985).

[456] Ashworth, E. J. *The Tradition of Medieval Logic and Speculative Grammar from Anselm to the End of the Seventeenth Century: A Bibliography from 1836 Onwards* (Toronto, 1978).

[457] Biard, J. *Logique et théorie du signe au xive siècle* (Paris, 1989).

[458] Covington, M. A. *Syntactic Theory in the High Middle Ages* (Cambridge, 1984).

[459] Dahan, G. "Nommer les êtres: Exégèse et théories du langage dans les commentaires médiévaux de *Genèse* 2, 19–20," in [460], 55–74.

[460] Ebbesen, S., ed. *Sprachtheorien in Spätantike und Mittelalter* (Tubingen, 1995).

[461] Green-Pedersen, N. J. *The Tradition of the Topics in the Middle Ages: The Commentaries on Aristotle's and Boethius' "Topics"* (Munich/Vienna, 1984).

[462] Jacobi, K., ed. *Argumentationstheorie: Scholastische Forschungen zu den logischen und semantischen Regeln korrekten Folgerns* (Leiden/New York/Cologne, 1993).

[463] Kneepkens, C. H. "The Priscianic Tradition," in [460], 239–64.

[464] Knuuttila, S. *Modalities in Medieval Philosophy* (London/ New York, 1993).

[465] Marenbon, J. *Aristotelian Logic, Platonism and the Context of Early Medieval Philosophy in the West* (Aldershot, Hants., 2000).

[466] Marmo, C. *Semiotica e linguaggio nella scolastica: Parigi, Bologna, Erfurt 1270–1330. La semiotica dei Modisti* (Rome, 1994).

[467] Montagnes, B. *La Doctrine de l'analogie de l'être d'après Saint Thomas d'Aquin.* Philosophes médiévaux 6 (Louvain/Paris, 1963).

[468] Nuchelmans, G. *Theories of the Proposition: Ancient and Medieval Conceptions of the Bearers of Truth and Falsity* (Amsterdam, 1973).

[469] Panaccio, C. *Le Discours intérieur. De Platon à Guillaume d'Ockham* (Paris, 1999).

[470] Pironet, F. *The Tradition of Medieval Logic and Speculative Grammar. A Bibliography (1977–1994)* (Turnhout, 1997).

[471] Rijk, L. M. de. *Logica Modernorum. A Contribution to the History of Early Terminist Logic,* 2 vols. in 3 parts (Assen, 1962–67).

[472] Rosier, I. *La Grammaire spéculative des Modistes* (Lille, 1983).

[473] Rosier, I. *La Parole comme acte. Sur la grammaire et la sémantique au XIIIe siècle* (Paris, 1994).

[474] Rosier, I. "*Res significata* et *modus significandi*: Les implications d'une distinction médiévale," in [460], 135–68.

[475] Spade, P. V. *Lies, Language and Logic in the Late Middle Ages* (London, 1988).

Philosophy in Islam

[476] D'Ancona Costa, C. *La Casa della sapienza. La transmissione della metafisica greca e la formazione della filosofia araba* (Milan, 1996).

[477] D'Ancona Costa, C. *Recherches sur le Liber de Causis* (Paris, 1995).

[478] Aydin, M. "Turkey," in [11], II, 1129–33.

[479] Black, D. L. "Imagination and Estimation: Arabic Paradigms and Western Transformations," *Topoi* 19 (2000), 59–75.

[480] Black, D. L. *Logic and Aristotle's Rhetoric and Poetics in Medieval Arabic Philosophy* (Leiden, 1990).

[481] Daiber, H. "The Reception of Islamic Philosophy at Oxford in the Seventeenth Century: The Pococks' (Father and Son) Contribution to the Understanding of Islamic Philosophy in Europe," in C. E. Butterworth and B. A. Kessel, eds., *The Introduction of Arabic Philosophy into Europe* (Leiden, 1994), 65–82.

[482] Davidson, H. A. *Alfarabi, Avicenna, and Averroes, on Intellect: Their Cosmologies, Theories of the Active Intellect and Theories of Human Intellect* (New York/Oxford, 1992).

[483] Davidson, H. A. *Proofs for Eternity, Creation and the Existence of God in Medieval Islamic and Jewish Philosophy* (New York/Oxford, 1987).

[484] Druart, T.-A. "Medieval Islamic Philosophy and Theology. Bibliographical Guide (1996–1998)," *MIDEO* (Cairo) 24 (2000), 381–414.

[485] Druart, T.-A. "Philosophical Consolation in Christianity and Islam: Boethius and al-Kindi," *Topoi* 19 (2000), 25–34.

[486] Fakhry, M. *Ethical Theories in Islam*, 2nd edn (Leiden, 1994).

[487] Frank, R. M. *Creation and the Cosmic System: Al-Ghazali and Avicenna* (Heidelberg, 1992).

[488] Frank, R. M. "Kalam and Philosophy: A Perspective from One Problem," in [44], 71–95.   .

[489] Frank, R. M. "Reason and Revealed Law: A Sample of Parallels and Divergences in Kalam and Falsafa," in *Recherches d'Islamologie. Recueil d'articles offerts à Georges C. Anawati et Louis Gardet* (Louvain, 1977), 123–38.

[490] Gutas, D. *Greek Thought, Arabic Culture. The Graeco-Arabic Translation Movement in Baghdad and Early 'Abbasid Society (2nd–4th/8th–10th Centuries)* (London, 1998).

[491] Hourani, G. F. *Reason and Tradition in Islamic Ethics* (Cambridge, 1985).

[492] Kraemer, J. L. *Humanism in the Renaissance of Islam. The Cultural Revival during the Buyid Age* (Leiden, 1986).

[493] Nasr, S. H. "Ibn Sina's 'Oriental Philosophy,' " in [11], 247–51.

[494] Nussbaum, M. C. *The Therapy of Desire: Theory and Practice in Hellenistic Ethics* (Princeton, NJ, 1994).

[495] Nussbaum, M. C., ed. "The Poetics of Therapy: Hellenistic Ethics in its Rhetorical and Literary Context," *Apeiron* 23, 4 (1990).

[496] Rosenthal, F. "On the Knowledge of Plato's Philosophy in the Islamic World," *Islamic Culture* 14 (1940), 387–422, and 15 (1941), 396–98.

[497] Russell, G. A., ed. *The "Arabick" Interest of the Natural Philosophers in Seventeenth-Century England* (Leiden, 1994).

Jewish philosophy

[498] Altmann, A. *Essays in Jewish Intellectual History* (Hanover, NH, 1981).

[499] Baron, S. W. *A Social and Religious History of the Jews*, vol. ix (New York/London, 1965).

[500] Burrell, D. "Maimonides, Aquinas, and Gersonides on Providence," *Religious Studies* 20, 3 (1984), 335–51.

[501] Pines, S. *Studies in the History of Jewish Thought: The Collected Works of Shlomo Pines*, vol. v, ed. W. Z. Harvey and M. Idel (Jerusalem, 1997).

[502] Twersky, I., ed. *Studies in Medieval Jewish History and Literature* (Cambridge, MA, 1979).

[503] Wolfson, H. *Studies in the History of Philosophy and Religion*, 2 vols. (Cambridge, MA, 1973–77).

Metaphysics: God and being

[504] Aertsen, J. A. "The Medieval Doctrine of the Transcendentals: New Literature," [53] 41, 107–21.

[505] Wippel, J. F., ed. *Studies in Medieval Philosophy* (Washington, DC, 1987).

Creation and nature

[506] Carvin, W. P. *Creation and Scientific Explanation* (Edinburgh, 1988).

[507] Chenu, M.-D. *Nature, Man and Society in the Twelfth Century*, trans. J. Taylor and L. K. Little (Toronto, 1997).

[508] Cunningham, A. "The Identity of Natural Philosophy. A Response to Edward Grant," *ESM* 5 (2000), 259–78; "A Last Word," 299–300.

[509] Duhem, P. *Etudes sur Léonard de Vinci*, 3 vols. (Paris, 1906–13).

[510] Duhem, P. *Le Système du monde*, 10 vols. (Paris, 1913–59).

[511] Eastwood, B. "Celestial Reason: The Development of Latin Planetary Astronomy to the Twelfth Century," in [48], 157–72.

[512] Grant, E. *The Foundations of Modern Science in the Middle Ages. Their Religious, Institutional, and Intellectual Contexts* (Cambridge, 1966).

[513] Grant, E. "God and Natural Philosophy: The Late Middle Ages and Sir Isaac Newton," *ESM* 5 (2000), 279–98.

[514] Grant, E. *God and Reason in the Middle Ages* (Cambridge, 2001).

[515] Grant, E. "God, Science, and Natural Philosophy in the Late Middle Ages," in [46], 243–67.

[516] Grant, E. *Planets, Stars, and Orbs: the Medieval Cosmos, 1200–1687* (Cambridge, 1994).

[517] Grant, E., ed. *A Source Book in Medieval Science* (Cambridge, MA, 1974).

[518] Kretzmann, N. "Incipit/Desinit," in P. Machamer and R. Turnbull, eds., *Motion and Time. Space and Matter* (Columbus, OH, 1976), 101–36.

[519] Lemay, R. *Abu Mashar and Latin Aristotelianism in the Twelfth Century* (Beirut, 1962).

[520] Maier, A. *Ausgehendes Mittelalter. Gesammelte Aufsätze zur Geistesgeschichte des 14. Jahrhunderts*, 3 vols. (Rome, 1964–67).

[521] Maier, A. *Studien zur Naturphilosophie der Spätmittelalter*, 5 vols. (Rome, 1952–68).

[522] Marrone, S. *The Light of Thy Countenance. Science and Knowledge of God in the Thirteenth Century*, 2 vols. (Leiden, 2001).

[523] Murdoch, J. "1277 and Late Medieval Natural Philosophy," in [28], 111–21.

[524] Murdoch, J. "From Social into Intellectual Factors: An Aspect of the Unitary Character of Late Medieval Learning," in [45], 271–339.

[525] Murdoch, J. "*Mathesis in philosophiam scholasticam introducta*. The Rise and Development of the Application of Mathematics in Fourteenth-Century Philosophy and Theology," in *Arts libéraux et philosophie au moyen âge* (Montreal/Paris, 1969), 215–54.

[526] Murdoch, J. "Philosophy and the Enterprise of Science in the Later Middle Ages," in Yehuda Elkana, ed., *The Interaction between Science and Philosophy* (Atlantic Highlands, NJ, 1974), 51–113.

[527] Murdoch, J. "Pierre Duhem (1861–1916)," in H. Damico, ed., *Medieval Scholarship. Biographical Studies on the Formation of a Discipline*, vol. III (New York/London, 2000), 23–42.

[528] Murdoch, J. "Pierre Duhem and the History of Late Medieval Science and Philosophy in the Latin West," in R. Imbach and A. Maierù, eds., *Gli studi di filosofia medievale fra Otto e Novecento: contributo a un bilancio storiografico* (Rome, 1991).

[529] Murdoch, J. "Propositional Analysis in Fourteenth-Century Natural Philosophy: A Case Study," *Synthèse* 40 (1979), 117–46.

[530] Oberman, H. "Reformation and Revolution: Copernicus's Discovery in an Era of Change," in [45], 397–429.

[531] Ragep, J. "Freeing Astronomy from Philosophy. An Aspect of Islamic Influence on Science," *Osiris* 16 (2001), 49–71.

[532] Sorabji, R. "Latitude of Forms in Ancient Philosophy," in [42], 57–63.

[533] Stock, B. *Myth and Science in the Twelfth Century. A Study of Bernard Sylvester* (Princeton, NJ, 1972).

[534] Sylla, E. "The A Posteriori Foundations of Natural Science; Some Medieval Commentaries on Aristotle's *Physics*, Book I, Chapters 1 and 2," *Synthèse* 40 (1979), 147–87.

[535] Sylla, E. "Autonomous and Handmaiden Science: St. Thomas Aquinas and William of Ockham on the Physics of the Eucharist," in [45], 349–96.

[536] Sylla, E. "Medieval Concepts of the Latitude of Forms: The Oxford Calculators," *AHDLMA* 40 (1973), 223–83.

[537] Thijssen, J. M. M. H. "Late Medieval Natural Philosophy: Some Recent Trends in Scholarship," *Recherches de Théologie et Philosophie Médiévales* 67 (2000), 158–90.

[538] Thijssen, J. M. M. H. "What Really Happened on 7 March 1277? Bishop Tempier's Condemnation and its Institutional Context," in [50], 84–114.

[539] Trifogli, C. Oxford Physics in the Thirteenth Century (ca. 1250–1270). Motion, Infinity, Place, and Time (Leiden/Cologne, 2000).

[540] Wallace, W. "Galileo and Reasoning Ex suppositione," in W. Wallace, Prelude to Galileo. Essays on Medieval and Sixteenth-Century Sources of Galileo's Thought (Dordrecht/Boston, MA/London, 1981), 129–59.

Natures: the problem of universals

[541] Gracia, J. Introduction to the Problem of Individuation in the Early Middle Ages (Munich/Washington, DC, 1984; 2nd edn 1988).

[542] Gracia, J. Individuation in Scholasticism: The Later Middle Ages and the Counter-Reformation (1150–1650) (Albany, NY, 1994).

[543] Klima, G. "The Medieval Problem of Universals," in [52], /archives/spr2001/entries/universals-medieval/

[544] Thijssen, J. M. M. H. "John Buridan and Nicholas of Autrecourt on Causality and Induction," Traditio 43 (1987), 237–55.

Human nature

[545] Dales, R. The Problem of the Rational Soul in the Thirteenth Century (Leiden, 1995).

[546] Des Chene, D. Life's Form: Late Aristotelian Conceptions of the Soul (Ithaca, NY, 2000).

[547] Dihle, A. The Theory of the Will in Classical Antiquity (Berkeley, CA, 1982).

[548] Irwin, T. "Who Discovered the Will?" Philosophical Perspectives 6 (1992), 453–73.

[549] King, P. "Scholasticism and the Philosophy of Mind: The Failure of Aristotelian Psychology," in T. Horowitz and A. Janis, eds., Scientific Failure (Lanham, MD, 1994), 109–38.

[550] Pasnau, R. "Divine Illumination," in [52], /entries/illumination/

[551] Pasnau, R. Theories of Cognition in the Later Middle Ages (Cambridge, 1997).

[552] Tachau, K. Vision and Certitude in the Age of Ockham. Optics, Epistemology and the Foundations of Semantics, 1250–1345 (Leiden, 1988).

[553] Wolfson, H. A. "The Internal Senses in Latin, Arabic, and Hebrew Philosophic Texts," Harvard Theological Review 28 (1935), 69–133.

The moral life

[554] Bloomfield, M. *The Seven Deadly Sins* (East Lansing, MI, 1952).

[555] Colish, M. "Habitus Revisited: A Reply to Cary Nederman," *Traditio* 48 (1993), 77–92.

[556] Janz, D. *Luther and Late Medieval Thomism* (Waterloo, Ontario, 1983).

[557] Kent, B. "Rethinking Moral Dispositions: Scotus on the Virtues," in *CCScot*, 352–76.

[558] Kent, B. *Virtues of the Will: The Transformation of Ethics in the Late Thirteenth Century* (Washington, DC, 1995).

[559] McGrath, A. *Iustitia Dei*, 2 vols. (Cambridge, 1986).

[560] Nederman, C. "Nature, Ethics, and the Doctrine of 'Habitus': Aristotelian Moral Psychology in the Twelfth Century," *Traditio* 45 (1989–90), 87–110.

[561] Oberman, H. *The Harvest of Medieval Theology: Gabriel Biel and Late Medieval Nominalism* (Cambridge, MA, 1963).

[562] Vignaux, P. "On Luther and Ockham," in S. Ozment, ed., *The Reformation in Medieval Perspective* (Chicago, 1971), 107–18.

[563] Wenzel, S. "The Seven Deadly Sins: Some Problems of Research," *Speculum* 43 (1968), 1–22.

[564] Wenzel, S. *The Sin of Sloth: Acedia* (Chapel Hill, NC, 1967).

Ultimate ends

[565] McEvoy, J. "The Theory of Friendship in the Latin Middle Ages: Hermeneutics, Contextualization and the Transmission and Reception of Ancient Texts and Ideas, from c. AD 350 to c. 1500," in J. Haseldine, ed., *Friendship in the Middle Ages* (Phoenix Mill, Stroud, 1999), 3–44.

[566] Reeves, M. *Joachim of Fiore and the Prophetic Future* (London, 1976).

[567] Wieland, G. "Happiness: The Perfection of Man," in *CHLMP*, 673–86.

Political thought

[568] Black, A. J. *Council and Commune. The Conciliar Movement and the Fifteenth Century Heritage* (London, 1979).

[569] Black, A. *Monarchy and Community. Political Ideas in the Later Conciliar Controversy 1430–1450* (Cambridge, 1970).

[570] Black, A. *Political Thought in Europe 1250–1450* (Cambridge, 1992).

[571] Blythe, J. M. *Ideal Government and the Mixed Constitution in the Middle Ages* (Princeton, NJ, 1992).

[572] Brett, A. S. *Liberty, Right and Nature: Individual Rights in Later Scholastic Thought* (Cambridge, 1997).

[573] Coleman, J. "Property and Poverty," in [13], 607–48.

[574] Evans, G. R. *Old Arts and New Theology. The Beginnings of Theology as an Academic Discipline* (Oxford, 1980).

[575] Fasolt, C. *Council and Hierarchy. The Political Thought of William Durant the Younger* (Cambridge, 1991).

[576] Flüeler, C. *Rezeption und Interpretation der Aristotelischen* Politica *im späten Mittelalter*, 2 vols. (Amsterdam, 1992).

[577] Justinian. *The Digest of Justinian*, ed. T. Mommsen and P. Krueger, trans. A. Watson (Philadelphia, 1985).

[578] Lambertini, R. *La poverta pensata* (Modena, 2000).

[579] Luscombe, D. "City and Politics Before the Coming of the *Politics: Some Illustrations*," in D. Abulafia, M. Franklin, and M. Rubin, eds., *Church and City in the Middle Ages* (Cambridge, 1992), 41–55.

[580] Mäkinen, V. P. *Property Rights in the Late Medieval Discussion on Franciscan Poverty* (Leuven, 2001).

[581] Miethke, J. *De potestate papae. Die päpstliche Amtskomptetenz im Widerstreit der politischen Theorie von Thomas von Aquin bis Wilhem von Ockham* (Tubingen, 2000).

[582] Nederman, C. J. "Nature, Sin and the Origins of Society: The Ciceronian Tradition in Medieval Political Thought," *JHI* 49 (1988), 3–26.

[583] Oakley, F. *Natural Law, Conciliarism and Consent in the Later Middle Ages* (London, 1984).

[584] Pennington, K. *The Prince and the Law 1200–1600* (Berkeley, CA, 1993).

[585] Post, G. "The Naturalness of Society and the State," in G. Post, *Studies in Medieval Thought, Public Law and the State 1100–1322* (Princeton, NJ, 1964), 494–561.

[586] Quillet, J. "Community, Counsel and Representation," in [13], 520–72.

[587] Skinner, Q. *The Foundations of Modern Political Thought*, 2 vols. (Cambridge, 1978).

[588] Tierney, B. *Foundations of the Conciliar Theory* (Cambridge, 1955).

[589] Tierney, B. *The Idea of Natural Rights* (Atlanta, GA, 1997).

[590] Ullmann, W. "Boniface VIII and his Contemporary Scholarship," *JTS* 27 (1976), 58–87.

Medieval philosophy in later thought: Renaissance and seventeenth century

[591] Aiton, E. J. *Leibniz: A Biography* (Bristol/Boston, MA, 1985).

[592] Cajetan, Tommaso de Vio. *Commentaria in Libros Aristotelis de Anima. Liber III*, ed. G. Picard, SJ and G. Pelland, SJ (Bruges, 1965).

[593] Cajetan, Tommaso de Vio. *Commentaria in De Anima Aristotelis*, ed. I. Coquelle, OP, intro. M. H. Laurent, 2 vols. (Rome, 1938–39).

[594] Cajetan, Tommaso de Vio. *Commentary on Being and Essence*, trans. L. J. Kendzierski and F. C. Wade (Milwaukee, WI, 1964).

[595] Cajetan, Tommaso de Vio. [*Prima pars*] *Summae Theologiae cum commentariis... Cajetani* (Antwerp, 1612).

[596] Cajetan, Tommaso de Vio. *The Analogy of Names and the Concept of Being*, trans. E. A. Bushinski and H. J. Koren (Pittsburgh, PA, 1959).

[597] Carleton, Thomas Compton. *Philosophia universa*, 2 vols. (Antwerp, 1684).

[598] Casimir of Toulouse. *Atomi peripateticae*, 6 vols. (Biterris, 1674).

[599] Des Chene, D. *Physiologia. Natural Philosophy in Late Aristotelian and Cartesian Thought* (Ithaca, NY, 1996).

[600] De La Grange, J. B. *Les Principes de la philosophie, contre les nouveaux philosophes* (Paris, 1675).

[601] Di Vona, P. *Studi sulla scolastica della contrariforma* (Florence, 1968).

[602] Du Hamel, J. B. *Operum philosophicorum Tomus I. Tractatus III: de consensu veteris et novae philosphiae* (Nuremberg, 1681).

[603] FitzPatrick, P. J. *In Breaking of Bread* (Cambridge, 1993).

[604] Gerhardt, C. J., ed. *Die philosophischen Schriften von Gottfried Wilhelm Leibniz*, 7 vols. (reprinted Hildesheim, 1960).

[605] Gilson, E. "Autour de Pomponazzi: problématique de l'immortalité de l'âme en Italie au début du XVIe siècle," *AHDLMA* 28 (1961), 164–279.

[606] Goudin, A. *Philosophia juxta inconcussa tutissimaque Divi Thomae dogmata... Tomus I: Logica; Tomus III: Tres posteriores partes physicae complectens* (Paris, 1685).

[607] Gurr, J. E. *The Principle of Sufficient Reason in Some Scholastic Systems, 1750–1900* (Milwaukee, WI, 1959).

[608] John of St. Thomas. *The Material Logic of John of St. Thomas: Basic Treatises*, trans. Y. R. Simon et al. (Chicago, 1955).

[609] Kessler, E. "The Intellective Soul," in [2], 485–534.

[610] Le Grand, A. *An Entire Body of Philosophy According to the Principles of the Famous Renate Des Cartes... Now faithfully translated... by Richard Blome* (London, 1694).

[611] Leibniz, G. W. F. *Epistola ad... [Jacobum Thomasium] de Aristotele recentioribus reconciliabili*, in [604], IV, 162–74.

[612] Menn, S. *Descartes and Augustine* (Cambridge, 1998).

[613] Nicholas of Cusa. P. E. Sigmund, ed., *Nicholas of Cusa. The Catholic Concordance* (Cambridge, 1991).

[614] [Pardies, I.] *Lettre d'un philosophe à un Cartésien de ses amis* (Paris, 1685).

[615] Robinet, A. "Suarez im Werk von Leibniz," *Studia Leibnitiana* 13 (1981), 76–96.

[616] Suárez, Francisco. *Tractatus de anima*, in D. M. André, ed., *Opera omnia*, vol. III (Paris, 1856).

[617] Suárez, Francisco. *Commentariorum...in primam partem Divi Thomae partis II de Deo creatore...Tractatus tertius De Anima* (Mainz, 1622).

[618] Suárez, Francisco. *On the Essence of Finite Being as Such, on the Existence of that Essence and their Distinction*, trans. N. J. Wells (Milwaukee, WI, 1983).

[619] Suárez, Francisco. *Disputationes Metaphysicae*, ed. C. Berton, 2 vols. (Paris, 1866; reprinted Hildesheim, 1965). Spanish trans. S. Rábade Romeo *et al.*, *Disputaciones Metafísicas*, 7 vols. (Madrid, 1960–66).

[620] Valeriano Magni. *Valeriani Magni fratris capuccini philosophiae pars prima* (Warsaw, 1648).

[621] Francisco de Vitoria. "Relection On the American Indians," in *Vitoria: Political Writings*, ed. and trans. A. R. D. Pagden and J. Lawrance (Cambridge, 1992), 233–92.

[622] Zabarella, Jacob. *De rebus naturalibus libri XXX* (Frankfurt, 1607; reprinted Frankfurt, 1966).

Medieval philosophy in later thought: current engagements

[623] Brezik, V. B., ed. *One Hundred Years of Thomism* (Houston, TX, 1981).

[624] Brownlee, M. S. and K. and S. Nichols, eds. *The New Medievalism* (Baltimore, MD, 1991).

[625] Caputo, J. *Heidegger and Aquinas* (New York, 1982).

[626] Druart, T.-A., ed. *Arabic Philosophy and the West* (Washington, DC, 1988).

[627] Geach, P. T. *Reference and Generality: An Examination of Some Medieval and Modern Theories* (Ithaca, NY, 1980).

[628] Gilson, E. *Elements of Christian Philosophy* (Garden City, NY, 1960).

[629] Gilson, E. *The Spirit of Medieval Philosophy*, trans. A. Downes (New York, 1940).

[630] Haldane, J., ed. *Mind, Metaphysics and Value in the Thomistic and Analytical Traditions* (Notre Dame, IN, 2002).

[631] Kenny, A. *Aquinas on Mind* (London, 1993).

[632] MacIntyre, A. *Three Rival Versions of Moral Enquiry* (London, 1990).

[633] Maritain, J. *The Degrees of Knowledge*, trans. R. McInerny (Notre Dame, IN, 1995).

[634] Milbank, J. and C. Pickstock. *Aquinas on Truth* (London, 2001).

[635] Pegis, A., ed. *A Gilson Reader* (Garden City, NY, 1957).

[636] Rosemann, P. *Understanding Scholastic Thought with Foucault: The New Middle Ages* (New York, 1999).

[637] Van Steenberghen, F. "Etienne Gilson, historien de la pensée médiévale," *Revue philosophique de Louvain* 77 (1979), 496–507.

Transmission and translation

[638] Bataillon, L. J. *et al.*, eds. *La Production du livre universitaire au moyen âge. Exemplar et pecia* (Paris, 1988).

[639] Bergh, B. *Palaeography and Textual Criticism* (Lund, 1978).

[640] Bischoff, B. *Latin Palaeography: Antiquity and the Middle Ages* (Cambridge, 1990).

[641] Capelli, A. *Lexicon abbreviaturarum*, 6th edn (Milan, 1961).

[642] Destrez, J. *La Pecia dans les manuscrits universitaires du XIIIe et du XIVe siècles* (Paris, 1935).

[643] Dondaine, A. *Les Secrétaires de Saint Thomas* (Rome, 1956).

[644] Fink-Errera, G. "De l'édition universitaire," in *L'Homme et son destin d'après les penseurs du moyen âge* (Louvain/Paris, 1960), 221–28.

[645] Fink-Errera, G. "Une Institution du monde médiéval: la pecia," *Revue Philosophique de Louvain* 60 (1962), 184–243.

[646] Notre Dame Summer Medieval Institute. http://www.nd.edu/ ~medinst/summer/summerprogram.html

[647] Pelzer, A. *Abréviations latines médiévales. Supplément au Dizionario di abbreviature latine ed italiane, de Adriano Cappelli*, 2nd edn (Louvain, 1966).

[648] Pollard, G. "The *Pecia* System in the Medieval Universities," in M. B. Parks and A. G. Watson, eds., *Medieval Scribes, Manuscripts and Libraries* (London, 1978), 145–61.

[649] Pratt, R. A. "Some Latin Sources of the Nonnes Preest on Dreams," *Speculum* 52 (1977), 538–70.

[650] Thorndike, L. *University Records and Life in the Middle Ages* (New York, 1944).

[651] University of Bochum. *Abbreviationes* CD-ROM. http://www.ruhr-uni-bochum.de/philosophy/projects/abbrev.htm

[652] University of Melbourne. paleography course. http://www.medieval. unimelb.edu.au/ductus/

[653] University of Toronto. Summer Latin course. http://www.chass. utoronto.ca/medieval/latexsum.html

INDEX

398